JEWISH AND CHRISTIAN APPROACHES
TO THE PSALMS

Jewish and Christian Approaches to the Psalms

Conflict and Convergence

Edited by
SUSAN GILLINGHAM

OXFORD
UNIVERSITY PRESS

OXFORD
UNIVERSITY PRESS

Great Clarendon Street, Oxford OX2 6DP,
United Kingdom

Oxford University Press is a department of the University of Oxford.
It furthers the University's objective of excellence in research, scholarship,
and education by publishing worldwide. Oxford is a registered trade mark of
Oxford University Press in the UK and in certain other countries.

British Library Cataloguing in Publication Data

Data available

ISBN 978–0–19–969954–4

Printed in Great Britain
on acid-free paper by
MPG Books Group, Bodmin and King's Lynn

This volume is respectfully dedicated to the memory of
Professor Erich Zenger (1939–2010)
and
Professor Klaus Seybold (1936–2011)
Ps. 116.15

Preface

This volume comprises twenty papers which were originally given at a conference, in association with the Theology Faculty at the University of Oxford, underwritten by the John Fell Fund of Oxford University Press, and hosted at Worcester College, Oxford in September 2010. All these essays have been revised and adapted for publication. An outline of their contents and an explanation of their particular order is given in the Introduction.

The conference was marred by the sudden death in April 2010 of Erich Zenger, who was due to give the final plenary paper at the conference. Frank-Lothar Hossfeld kindly agreed to present the plenary paper instead, and Klaus Seybold graciously accepted an invitation to speak on the theme originally allotted to Frank-Lothar. It was a double shock, therefore, to learn of Klaus Seybold's untimely death in May 2011, just one month after submitting his own paper revised for publication. It is fitting that this volume should be dedicated to the memory of these two great international Psalms scholars, for each has contributed so much to our understanding and appreciation of individual psalms and the Psalter as a whole.

I am most grateful for the warmth, goodwill, and support of all the contributors. Many travelled a long way to speak at the conference and all have produced very high-standard papers within the time constraints. A special note of thanks is due to three people not otherwise named in this book: to Esther Gillingham, the conference administrator, who at the time chose to be anonymous, for her efficiency in keeping the conference afloat; to Joanna Vitale, one of my doctoral students, for her help and enthusiasm in the final stages of the preparation of the manuscript; and above all, to Holly Morse, another of my doctoral students and long-time research assistant. Holly has seen this publication through from the early conference stage to the time of handing it on to Oxford University Press. Her consistent attention to detail has been exemplary: whatever errors remain are my responsibility alone.

Finally, it is particularly appropriate to thank John Barton for all his support in enabling this Oxford-based conference to find a final home with the Press. And so I am also most grateful to all the staff at OUP who have been involved with the publication; Tom Perridge, the Commissioning Editor in Religion and Theology, and Elizabeth Robottom, Senior Assistant Commissioning Editor, deserve especial thanks for their good humour, encouragement, and advice.

S.E.G.

Contents

viii   *Contents*

List of Contributors
(listed in order of their papers in this volume)

Peter W. Flint holds the Canada Research Chair in Dead Sea Scrolls Studies at Trinity Western University, British Columbia. He is the author of numerous studies on the Dead Sea Scrolls, including the critically acclaimed *The Dead Sea Psalms Scrolls and the Book of Psalms* (1997), and is co-author of the widely read *Dead Sea Scrolls Bible* (1999) and *The Meaning of the Dead Sea Scrolls* (2003). He is currently preparing the new edition of the Great Psalms Scroll for the series Dead Sea Scrolls Editions (Brill), and editions of the Book of Psalms for *The Oxford Hebrew Bible* and *Biblia Qumranica*.

Geza Vermes is Professor Emeritus of Jewish Studies at the University of Oxford and one of the world's leading Dead Sea Scrolls scholars, whose English translations brought these extraordinary documents to thousands, and whose life has been inextricably interwoven with the scrolls for over sixty years. His publication *The Complete Dead Sea Scrolls in English* (50th anniversary edition, 2011) is his best-known work. His most recent *Story of the Scrolls: The Miraculous Discovery and True Significance of the Dead Sea Scrolls* (2010) relates the controversial story of their discovery and publication around the world, revealing cover-ups, blunders, and academic infighting, but also the passion and dedication of many of those involved.

Adele Berlin is the Robert H. Smith Professor of Biblical Studies Emerita at the University of Maryland. She is Fellow of the American Academy for Jewish Research and a past President of the Society of Biblical Literature. She has held fellowships from the National Endowment for the Humanities, the John Simon Guggenheim Foundation, the American Council of Learned Societies, the Center for Advanced Judaic Studies at the University of Pennsylvania, and the Institute for Advanced Studies of the Hebrew University. She is best known for her work on biblical narrative and poetry—*Poetics and Interpretation of Biblical Narrative* (1983) and *The Dynamics of Biblical Parallelism* (1985)—and for her commentaries on Esther, Lamentations, and Zephaniah. She co-edited, with Marc Brettler, *The Jewish Study Bible* (2004), and is now at work on two Psalms Commentaries.

Corinna Körting is Professor for Old Testament Studies at the MF Norwegian School of Theology in Oslo, having previously been an Associate Professor at the University of Göttingen. She is member of the Wissenschaftliche Gesellschaft für Theologie, the Norsk Gammeltestamentlig Selskap, and the Global Network of Research Centers for Theology, Religious and Christian

Studies. Her main research interests are mirrored in two significant monographs: *Der Schall des Schofar. Israels Feste im Herbst* (1999), a study on the biblical calendars with focus on the three festivals in autumn; and *Zion in den Psalmen* (2006), on the Zion tradition in the Psalms, which argues that Zion is a fundamental topos for the theology of the Psalms, which, unlike Jerusalem, simultaneously fills and shatters the dimensions of space and time.

Susan Gillingham is Reader in Old Testament in the University of Oxford and Fellow and Tutor in Theology at Worcester College. She has published several books on the Psalms including a reception history analysis of the entire Psalter (*Psalms through the Centuries,* volume 1 [2008]). A monograph on the reception history of Psalms 1 and 2 is forthcoming (from Oxford University Press). She is also interested in the historical and literary aspects of psalmody, as seen in 'The Levitical Singers and the Editing of the Hebrew Psalter', which was published in *The Composition of the Book of Psalms* (ed. Erich Zenger, 2010).

Jonathan Magonet, having retired in 2005 as Principal of Leo Baeck College, is now Emeritus Professor of Bible. He has co-edited a series of prayer books for the UK Movement for Reform Judaism and edits the journal *European Judaism.* His book *A Rabbi Reads the Psalms* (1994, second edition 2004) explores the relationship between the structure and meaning of a variety of selected Psalms. For some forty years he has co-organized annual Jewish–Christian and Jewish–Christian–Muslim study conferences in Germany, which have included shared textual study now popularized under the term 'scriptural reasoning'.

Elizabeth Solopova is a Research Fellow in the English Faculty, University of Oxford. Her research interests include Old and Middle English language and literature, and medieval liturgical and biblical manuscripts. She is the author of a forthcoming catalogue of medieval liturgical psalters in the Bodleian Library, covering around 120 manuscripts from Western Europe ranging in date from the ninth to the sixteenth centuries. She is currently undertaking a study of the manuscripts of the Wycliffite Bible focusing on its production, ownership, and use between the 1380s and the 1520s.

Aaron Rosen is the Lecturer in Sacred Traditions and the Arts at King's College, University of London. He taught previously at Yale, Oxford, and Columbia Universities, after receiving his PhD from the University of Cambridge. He has written widely for popular and scholarly publications including *The Oxford Dictionary of National Biography, New Humanist, Jewish Quarterly, Art and Christianity, Religion and the Arts,* and *Literature and Theology.* His first book was entitled *Imagining Jewish Art: Encounters with the Masters in Chagall, Guston, and Kitaj* (2009). He is currently working on a book entitled *The Hospitality of Images: Modern Art and Interfaith Dialogue.*

David C. Mitchell is Precentor and Director of Music at the Anglican Pro-Cathedral in Brussels. His 1997 monograph *The Message of the Psalter: An Eschatological Programme in the Book of Psalms* proposes that the final form of the Book of Psalms was redacted around an eschatological programme similar to that of Zechariah 9–14. He has since published on the Psalms and other subjects, and is currently writing a volume on the Songs of Ascents with cantillational commentary and music score.

John F. A. Sawyer is Emeritus Professor of Biblical Studies at the Universities of Newcastle upon Tyne and Lancaster and was the 2011 President of the Society for Old Testament Study. Among his many publications are *The Fifth Gospel: Isaiah in the History of Christianity* (1996), the *Blackwell Companion to the Bible and Culture* (2006), and *A Concise Dictionary of the Bible and its Reception* (2009). In his recent collection of essays entitled *Sacred Texts and Sacred Meanings* (2011) he has included a chapter on the Psalm Headings, originally published in 1970, and in this volume brings to the study of Psalms a wealth of understanding about their reception history.

W. H. Bellinger, Jr., Craig Professor of Bible and Chair of the Department of Religion, Baylor University, currently chairs the Steering Committee for the Book of Psalms Section of the Society of Biblical Literature and is on the Editorial Board of the *Catholic Biblical Quarterly*. In 2008 he was named the John G. Gammie Distinguished Scholar by the Southwest Commission on Religious Studies. Seminal works on the Psalms include *Psalmody and Prophecy* (1984), *Psalms: Reading and Studying the Book of Praises* (1990), and *Diachronic and Synchronic: Reading the Book of Psalms in Real Time: Proceedings of the Baylor Symposium on the Book of Psalms* (ed. with Joel S. Burnett and W. Dennis Tucker, 2007). He is currently working on a commentary on the Psalms and a volume on Old Testament theology.

Dirk Human is Professor in Old Testament Studies at the University of Pretoria. He is Editor-in-Chief of *Verbum et Ecclesia* and chair of the South African Editors' Forum for Theology and Related Journals in South Africa. He studied in Munich (1991–2), Vienna (1999), and Marburg (2001–2) and is a member of the Old Testament Society of South Africa, Southern African Society for Biblical and Religious Studies, South African Society for Religious Studies, South African Society for Ancient Near Eastern Studies, and the Society for Biblical Literature. He is the editor and co-editor of books such as *Psalms and Liturgy* (2005; co-editor: C. J. A. Vos), *Psalms and Mythology* (2007), *Exile and Suffering* (2009), *Psalms and Hebrews: Studies in Reception* (2010), and *Psalmody and Poetry in Old Testament Ethics* (2012).

†**Klaus Seybold (1936–2011)** was Emeritus Professor in Old Testament
Theology in the Theology Faculty of the University of Basel. His
publications include his Habilitationsschrift, *Das Gebet des Kranken im Alten
Testament* (1973), which examines psalms of sickness and healing, *Die
Wallfahrtspsalmen* (1978), on the Psalms of Ascents (120–34), and *Die
Psalmen. Eine Einführung* (1986), a student guide to the psalms, translated as
Introducing the Psalms (1990). A seminal work is his commentary, *Die
Psalmen. Handbuch zum Alten Testament* (1996). His engagement with the
poetry of the Psalms is seen in his *Poetik der Psalmen* (2003), and with
different themes and styles of psalmody in *Studien zur Psalmenauslegung*
(1998) and *Studien zu Sprache und Stil der Psalmen* (2010). His chief concern
was the form, style, and structure of individual prayers and hymns, and their
placing within larger collections (for example, the Psalms of Ascents).

David M. Howard, Jr., is Professor of Old Testament at Bethel University,
St Paul, Minnesota. He studied Psalms and Hebrew Poetry with David Noel
Freedman at the University of Michigan, where his dissertation (since
published), *The Structure of Psalms 93–100* (1997), was one of the first dealing
with the composition of the Psalter as a whole. He has published several
articles on the editorial activity in the Psalter as well as on current trends in
studying the Psalms. Important works include *'My Words Are Lovely': Studies
in the Rhetoric of the Psalms* (2008). He is currently working on a commentary
on the Psalms in the New American Commentary series, as well *The Psalms in
Recent Research* in Eisenbrauns' Sources for Biblical and Theological Study
Series, co-edited with Patrick Miller.

Nancy L. deClaissé-Walford is Professor of Old Testament and Biblical
Languages at the McAfee School of Theology at Mercer University in Atlanta,
Georgia. She has spent most of her career studying issues in the shape and
shaping of the book of Psalms, resulting in numerous journal articles and
three books: *Reading from the Beginning: The Shape and Shaping of the Hebrew
Psalter* (1997); *An Introduction to the Psalms: A Song from Ancient Israel*
(2004); and *The Book of Psalms*, New International Commentary on the Old
Testament series (2012). She has served since 2006 as a biblical consultant for
'The Voice', a Bible translation project; is the managing editor of the journal
Review & Expositor; and is the Old Testament Editor for the Word Biblical
Commentary series. Her current research interest is the wisdom influence
on the shaping of the Psalter.

Philip S. Johnston is currently Senior Tutor at Hughes Hall, University of
Cambridge. He spent many years teaching and writing in the Theology
Faculty in the University of Oxford. His books include *Les Psaumes: Aide à
la lecture cursive du texte hébreu* (author of first half; 1995); *Shades of Sheol:
Death and Afterlife in the Old Testament* (2002); *Interpreting the Psalms: Issues*

and Approaches (lead editor; 2005). His articles include 'Ordeals in the Psalms?', in *Temple and Worship in Biblical Israel* (ed. J. Day, 2005); and 'The Psalms in their Setting', in *The Lion Handbook to the Bible* (2009). He has taught courses on Bible translations over several decades, has been a consultant for two modern versions (*NIRV* and *ESV*), and has been the leader of translation workshops in francophone Africa.

John Day is Professor of Old Testament Studies in the University of Oxford and Fellow and Tutor at Lady Margaret Hall. His books include *God's Conflict with the Dragon and the Sea* (1985), *Molech: A God of Human Sacrifice in the Old Testament* (1989), *Yahweh and the Gods and Goddesses of Canaan* (2000), and a comprehensive guide to *Psalms* (1990), which has been reprinted many times. He has edited four Oxford seminar volumes on *King and Messiah* (1998), *In Search of Pre-Exilic Israel* (2004), *Temple and Worship in Biblical Israel* (2005), and *Prophecy and the Prophets in Ancient Israel* (2010).

Erhard Gerstenberger is Emeritus Professor of Old Testament at the Philipps-Universität Marburg. Born and raised in the Ruhr area, he has published widely on the Psalms, including *Der bittende Mensch* (1980, reprinted 2010); *Psalms, Part I* (1988); *Psalms, Part II* (2001). His *Theologies in the Old Testament* (2002) also includes studies of the Psalms. Articles include 'The Psalms', in *Old Testament Form Criticism* (ed. J. H. Hayes, 1974); 'The Psalter' in *The Blackwell Companion to the Hebrew Bible* (ed. L. G. Perdue, 2001); 'Theologies in the Book of Psalms' in *The Book of Psalms* (ed. P. W. Flint et al., 2005); 'Praise in the Realm of Death' in *Lamentations in Ancient and Contemporary Contexts* (ed. N. C. Lee et al., 2008).

Frank-Lothar Hossfeld is a Roman Catholic priest and Emeritus Professor of the Old Testament at the University of Bonn. Together with Erich Zenger he has approached the Psalter as a redactional work, publishing many seminal books and articles in this area. His approach can be summarized as 'From Psalms Exegesis to Psalter Exegesis' and is best seen in his Commentary on the Psalms, co-edited with Erich Zenger, which is being published in German under HthKAT (2001, 2008) and in English in the Hermeneia Series (2005, 2011). He has been leading a Deutsche Forschungsgemeinschaft project in Bonn that will result in a commentary on the Theology of the Psalter, which can be summarized as 'From Psalms Theology to Psalter Theology'.

Till Magnus Steiner is a doctoral student and a research assistant of Professor Frank-Lothar Hossfeld at the Rheinische Friedrich-Wilhelms-Universität Bonn, and is also heavily involved in the Deutsche Forschungsgemeinschaft project whose research foundation is based in Bonn.

John Barton is Oriel and Laing Professor of the Interpretation of Holy Scripture, University of Oxford. He has written on many aspects of the Old Testament, including the biblical canon, Old Testament ethics, biblical prophecy, and hermeneutics. His best-known book is *Reading the Old Testament: Method in Biblical Study* (second edition 1996), which examines various methods, including form criticism, that have been used on Old Testament texts, including the Psalms. There is a further discussion of form criticism in his more recent *The Nature of Biblical Criticism* (2007). He is currently doing further work on ethics in the Old Testament, moving from an examination of legal and wisdom texts to narrative and poetic books.

List of Plates

Abbreviations

AMP	*Amplified Bible*, 1987
AV	Authorized Version, 1611
BHQ	*Biblia Hebraica Quinta*
BHS	*Biblia Hebraica Stuttgartensia*
CJB	*Complete Jewish Bible*, 1998
ECSL	*Electronic Corpus of Sumerian Literature*
ESV	*English Standard Version*, 2001; rev. 2005
ET	English translation
GWORD	*God's Word*, 1994
HCSB	*Holman Christian Standard Bible*, 2004
HUB	*Hebrew University Bible*
ICB	*International Children's Bible*
JPS	Tanakh, Jewish Publication Society, 1985
MT	Masoretic Text
NAB	*New American Bible*, 1991
NASB	*New American Standard Bible*, 1960; 1994 update
NEB	*New English Bible*, 1970
NET	*New English Translation*, 2005
NETS	*New English Translation of the Septuagint*, 2009
NIRV	*New International Revised Version*
NIV	*New International Version*, 1978; rev. 1984
NJB	*New Jerusalem Bible*, 1990
NKJV	*New King James Version*, 1982
NLT-SE	*New Living Translation*, 2nd edn, 2004
NRSV	*New Revised Standard Version*, 1989
OHB	*Oxford Hebrew Bible*, forthcoming
REB	*Revised English Bible*, 1989
RSV	*Revised Standard Version*, 1952
TNIV	*Today's New International Version*, 2002

ET in biblical references indicates chapter and verse numbers as used in English-language versions of the Bible, rather than Greek or Hebrew numeration.

Numbers of psalms and verses from psalms always accord with the *NRSV* unless otherwise stated.

Journal and Book Series Abbreviations in Bibliographies

AOAT	Alter Orient und Altes Testament
AS	Assyriological Studies
ATD	Das Alte Testament Deutsch
AthANT	Abhandlungen zur Theologie des Alten und Neuen Testaments
BARev	*Biblical Archaeology Review*
BASOR	*Bulletin of the American Schools of Oriental Research*
BBB	Bonner biblische Beiträge
BEThL	Bibliotheca Ephemeridum Theologicarum Lovaniensium
BJSUCSD	Biblical and Judaic Studies from the University of California, San Diego
BKAT	Biblischer Kommentar Altes Testament
BN	*Biblische Notizen*
BQ	Biblia Qumranica
BthS	Biblisch-theologische Studien
BWANT	Beiträge zur Wissenschaft vom Alten und Neuen Testament
BZ	*Biblische Zeitschrift*
BZAW	Beihefte zur ZAW
CANE	Civilisations of the Ancient Near East
CBQ	*Catholic Biblical Quarterly*
CChr	Corpus Christianorum
CTM	Calwer theologische Monographien
DJD	Discoveries in the Judaean Desert
FAT	Forschungen zum Alten Testament
FOTL	The Forms of the Old Testament Literature
FRLANT	Forschungen zur Religion und Literatur des Alten und Neuen Testaments
GHAT	Göttinger Handkommentar zum Alten Testament
HBS	Herders Biblische Studien
HThKAT	Herders Theologischer Kommentar zum Alten Testament
HThR	Handwörterbuch für Theologie und Religionswissenschaft
HTR	*Harvard Theological Review*
JNES	*Journal of Near Eastern Studies*
JSOT	*Journal for the Study of the Old Testament*
JSOTSup.	Journal for the Study of the Old Testament Supplement Series
JSS	*Journal of Semitic Studies*
LHBOTS	Library of Hebrew Bible/Old Testament Study
LThK	*Lexikon für Theologie und Kirche*
McCQ	*McCormick Quarterly*
MIO	*Mitteilungen des Instituts für Orientforschung*
NCB	New Century Bible
NEBAT	Neue Echter Bibel. Altes Testament
NICOT	New International Commentary on the Old Testament
OBO	Orbis Biblicus et Orientalis
OTL	Old Testament Library
PEQ	*Palestine Exploration Quarterly*
QD	Quaestiones disputatae

RB	*Revue Biblique*
RPP	*Religion Past and Present*
SBL	Society of Biblical Literature
SBLDS	SBL Dissertation Series
SBS	Stuttgarter Bibelstudien
SHCANE	Studies in the History of the Ancient Near East
SOTI	Studies in Old Testament Interpretation
SPCK	Society for Promoting Christian Knowledge
STDJ	Studies on the Texts of the Desert of Judah
SVT	Supplements to *Vetus Testamentum*
ThWAT	*Theologisches Wörterbuch zum Alten Testament*
TRE	*Theologische Revue*
TZ	*Theologische Zeitschrift*
UCOP	University of Cambridge Oriental Publications
VT	*Vetus Testamentum*
WMANT	Wissenschaftliche Monographien zum Alten und Neuen Testament
ZAW	*Zeitschrift für die alttestamentliche Wissenschaft*
ZThK	*Zeitschrift für Theologie und Kirche*

Introduction

Susan Gillingham

These papers are the result of a three-day conference held at Worcester College, Oxford, from 22 to 24 September 2010.[1] This published collection is the first of its kind from Oxford for over eighty years.[2]

The most distinctive feature of the conference was its collaborative forum, especially for Jewish and Christian scholarship. The Psalter, more than any biblical book, has resulted in inevitable controversies between Jews and Christians for two thousand years. It has only really been since the Second World War that the two traditions have worked side by side, often through a different academic enterprise: two obvious examples are Qumran and Septuagint studies of the Psalms. Part I of this publication provides the opportunity to look at Jewish and Christian Psalms scholarship from a position of convergence rather than conflict. A particularly collaborative emphasis is evident in the first six papers, where the format is a paper from one tradition followed by a response from the other.

In the first paper, Professor Peter Flint, the most prominent scholar on the Psalms Scrolls at Qumran, explains how the forty-one manuscripts containing Psalms have informed our understanding of the book of Psalms as a gradually evolving collection whilst also challenging earlier assumptions of translators that there was ever one original Hebrew *Urtext*. A project which highlights both these factors is a new edition of Psalms for the *Oxford Hebrew Bible*, to be published by OUP, for which Professor Flint is contributing a critical edition on the Psalms.

Responding, Professor Geza Vermes, one of the world's leading Dead Sea Scrolls scholars, broadly agrees with this suggestion, arguing that the concept of a 'canon' was undoubtedly fluid in early Judaism, a factor to which the Scrolls bear witness, and that the 'textual elasticity' of the Scrolls has indeed sounded the death knell of the myth of a biblical *Urtext*.

---

[1] Conflict and Convergence. Jewish and Christian Approaches to the Psalms, 22–24 September 2010.

[2] See D. C. Simpson (ed.), *The Psalmists* (Oxford: Clarendon Press, 1926).

The third paper, by Professor Adele Berlin, an international scholar with many publications on biblical poetry and Jewish medieval exegesis, also appeals to plurality in the Hebrew tradition, but this time within medieval psalm interpretation. Professor Berlin demonstrates the subtly different approaches of the four most famous Jewish scholars—Saadia, Rashi, Ibn Ezra, and David Qimhi. Each balanced differently a *peshat* interpretation with the rabbinic *midrash* they had inherited, each influenced to different degrees by their cultural settings (for example, Saadia and his opposition to the Karaites, Quimhi and his opposition to Christian exegetes).

Professor Corinna Körting responds by comparing the way these Jewish scholars react to their cultural situation and inherited tradition with the approaches of contemporary psalms scholars, Jewish and Christian, who have to undergo a similar process, as each wrestles with what they understand as 'divine instruction' and 'human teaching' in the language of the Psalms, and in what they seen as coming 'before' and 'after' the text.

Dr Susan Gillingham, who has recently written the first of two volumes on the reception history of the Psalter, brings together exegetical, artistic, and musical representations of psalmody in her paper on the reception history of Psalm 137. She argues that, unlike many psalms in the Psalter, Psalm 137 has not received the usual David-centred emphasis in Jewish tradition (it has no Davidic heading, and speaks anachronistically of the exile, for example), nor has it been used with any specific Christ-centred emphasis (the expressions of fierce loyalty to Jerusalem and the Temple and the final curses at the end make this difficult). Instead, this provides an excellent model of a more 'life-centred' reading of the psalms, in both Jewish and Christian traditions, interpreted frequently with a political as well as personal bias.

The response by Rabbi Jonathan Magonet takes further these observations. Reaffirming the particular Jewish emphasis which reads the psalm in its entirety, rather than selecting odd verses (as is more the case in Christian tradition), he discusses the inevitable theological consequences of incorporating the latter part of the psalm, with its passionate anger and curses on enemy nations, into our liturgy.

Conflicts are not only to be found within the different cerebral interpretations of texts by commentators: as reception history studies have shown, the Psalms (again more than any other biblical book) have been received in Jewish and Christian tradition not only as a text deserving intellectual enquiry but as a work received more imaginatively and aesthetically in art and music, often through liturgy. The next four papers stand side by side, the first looking at examples of artistic representations of the psalms by medieval Christians; the second, at artistic works by a modern Jewish artist; the third, at how the ancient Jewish music of psalmody might have been written and might sound today; and the fourth assessing the impact of the Psalms from a Reception History perspective. Each demonstrates how the reception of the

Psalms in Christian and Jewish art and music offers constructive contributions to interfaith dialogue.

Oxford's Collections of Western Manuscripts offer a rich resource of
illuminated Psalters.[3] So Dr Elizabeth Solopova, the author of a forthcoming
catalogue of medieval liturgical Psalters in the Bodleian Library, comments
on several illustrations from medieval Psalters. This introduces us to an
entirely different way of perceiving the Psalter, not as a Hebrew literary
compilation of five books in one, but as a Christian liturgical collection,
where the breaks in the Psalter (evident in psalms with specific, often typical
illuminations in different manuscripts) occur in up to eight different places.
For those with an interest in the Hebrew shape of the Psalter her observations
challenge traditional conclusions: looking at the Psalter from a Christian
liturgical perspective results in the Psalter having a very different structure.

Dr Aaron Rosen provides an engaging art-historical account to illustrate
how Marc Chagall's dictum—'When I Paint, I Pray'—was executed with
special reference to selected psalms. Examples include the stained-glass
window for Chichester Cathedral, for Psalm 150, and his windows for All
Saints' Church in Tudeley, Kent, some of which were inspired by Psalm 8.
The ecclesial setting of these works gives specific insights into what 'conflict
and convergence' means when Chagall works between the two religious
traditions.

Dr David C. Mitchell's paper argues that the ancient music of the
Psalms was never really lost. It was hidden in the cantillation marks of the
Masoretic text: what was lost was the ability to decipher it. However, recent
archaeomusicological advances—particularly the pioneering work of the
French archaeomusicologist Suzanne Haïk-Vantoura—have pointed the way
to decoding some of the Masoretic cantillation. Much work remains to be
done, but, Mitchell suggests, the ancient melodies of the Psalms have begun to
emerge from their ancient obscurity and their full deciphering is within our
grasp.

Professor John Sawyer looks at the Psalter as a whole in relation to Jewish
and Christian reception history, using Jewish and Christian images as well as
music to illustrate the potential for greater convergence when we approach
the Psalter using more than an exegetical and cerebral point of view alone.

The theme of Part II is the reading of the Psalter then and now. The eleventh
paper, by Professor Bill Bellinger, argues that the crisis of the exile and its
aftermath has left its effect on the shaping of the Psalter, especially in Books
Four and Five, and this is seen in two particular themes: the emphasis
on Yahweh's world dominion in the face of his apparent defeat by deities of
other nations (especially in Book Four), and the psalms of protest which

---

[3] Many can be now be accessed on LUNA, hosted by www.bodley.ox.ac.uk.

express that tension between faith and experience (especially in Book Five). The Psalter as a whole is not compiled *as* a theodicy; but its overall shape reveals that questions of theodicy were amongst the most prominent concerns of the editors.

The response by Professor Dirk Human takes these insights further, arguing that the mythical representation of Yahweh in Book Four offers a response to the crisis of the destroyed Temple, and the emphasis on Zion in the hymns as well as the laments in Book Five offers an answer to this crisis: far from being overwhelmed by the crisis of the exile, the overall tone of the Psalter—ending with hymnody more then lament—is one of celebrating God's purpose for his people rather than questioning it. Setting these papers side by side, Professor Bellinger's interests are more with entire Books in the Psalter, whilst Professor Human's are more with individual psalms and smaller collections of psalms.

Since the rise of literary interest in the Psalter as a book from the early 1980s (a reaction to the more piecemeal form-critical approach to individual psalms associated with Hermann Gunkel in the early twentieth century), it has become clear that what German scholarship means by 'literary criticism' is often quite different from what is being published and lectured on in American universities. In his paper, Professor Klaus Seybold offers some original suggestions as to how we are read the Psalter as a book; he asks how the many different individual psalms, composed by different authors and in different places, found their way into what we now know as the Hebrew Psalter. Contrary to Professors Flint and Vermes, he proposes the possibility of an actual *Urtext* of the Psalms, arguing that the first Book of the Psalms of David (comprising Psalms 3–41 and 51–72) formed a normative edition and was kept in the Temple. Using what we know of this collection of psalms from the Dead Sea Scrolls, which reveal different uses of an early collection both at Qumran and in Jerusalem, and adding to this evidence from the Old Greek Psalter, Professor Seybold argues for a single standard scroll, the 'proto-scroll', held at Jerusalem, whose emphasis was as much on Torah and Moses as on David (compared with the prominent emphasis on David the Prophet at Qumran). He concludes that from this 'proto-scroll' all other Qumran psalms scrolls, the Septuagint, and even the Masoretic Text derive.

His respondent, Professor David Howard, illustrates the point that the predominant American interests are less with the redactional concerns of 'how' and more with the theological issues of 'why'. Nevertheless, Professor Howard concedes that what has been argued by Professor Seybold has interesting implications for what a number of (particularly American) scholars are saying about the primary role of Moses, alongside David, in giving theological shape to the Psalter. It would not be too simplistic to conclude that Professor Seybold's interests are diachronic, and that of much American scholarship are synchronic: these two approaches to the Psalter undoubtedly lead to different emphases and different conclusions, but each can create an important dialogue with the other.

Professor Nancy deClaissé-Walford, having encountered various practical problems of translating the psalms when writing her New International Commentary on the Psalms and advising 'The Voice' Bible translation project, offers a more pragmatic paper on the relationship between Hebrew psalms and more contemporary English versions. In her paper she addresses several issues, including how one renders into English the powerful concrete imagery of the Hebrew language, how one represents the purposeful repetition of Hebrew sounds, verbal roots, words, and phrases, and how one maintains the word order of much of Hebrew poetry.

Philip Johnston offers a response which is both sympathetic and constructively critical, highlighting the difficulties of rendering the poetry of the psalms into any other language—and indeed, in different cultures using the same language—in a way which is both aesthetic and accurate.

Part III comprises four papers which look at the Psalms from both the perspective of their ancient past and their present contemporary setting. The two papers concerned with the historical context of psalmody focus on what we know of hymnody in the ancient Near East. They each demonstrate how the more contemporary academic interest of translators and commentators on the texts and versions of the Psalter have much to learn from these ancient Hebrew texts and their (in this case, Egyptian and Sumerian) counterparts.

The ongoing concern in ancient Near Eastern studies of the Psalms is taken up in the paper by Professor John Day, who gives an account of the similarities between Psalm 104.20–30 and six closely related parallels from Akhenaten's hymn to the Sun, found in the tomb of Ay at el-Amarna. Professor Day offers several intriguing suggestions as to how these correspondences might have come about—perhaps through some direct access to the original hymn in the tomb of Ay, possibly through some copying of later solar hymns to Amun-Re, but more probably through the reception of the hymn in Canaanite culture.

Professor Erhard Gerstenberger offers an account of the correspondences between Sumerian hymns and the hymnic forms in the Psalter, arguing that, although no direct association can be posited, there is clearly a general and pervasive tradition of ancient Near Eastern hymnology. This explains the common concerns expressed through common genres throughout the ancient world—'an intricate network of echoing voices and endless variations of basic liturgical themes', a network which Professor Gerstenberger then explicates and develops further.

The nineteenth paper, by Professor Frank-Lothar Hossfeld and Till Magnus Steiner, was the conference's final plenary paper. Professor Hossfeld, who has written prolifically on the theology of the Psalter as a whole, compares this book to a house with many rooms, and to an orchestra with many different instruments. Drawing together the diverse concerns of the conference, and expanding on a project which is a key concern at the University of Bonn, his plea is that what is now needed is a renewed emphasis on the theology of the entire Psalter—one which sees the Psalter as a microcosm of the theology of the Hebrew Bible/Old Testament as a whole. Such an approach must take into account complementary Jewish and Christian approaches; in this way, consonant with the project at Bonn, a multi-faceted 'Theology of the Psalter' can serve the purpose of convergence between the two traditions extremely well.

Professor John Barton, co-convenor of the conference with Dr Gillingham, reviews in an 'afterword' the cumulative influence of the previous nineteen papers on the Psalms. In noting the 'enormous theological, devotional, liturgical, and spiritual potential' of Psalms study, Professor Barton recognizes that this particular publication will help readers to appropriate the Psalms in their own time, which is akin to what the ancient authors and performers of the Psalms were also doing.

Professor Barton also asks why Psalms study has not taken a more strategic place at the centre of Old Testament/Hebrew Bible theology. He rightly recognizes a deficit which each of the papers published here sought to address. In several respects, this is a landmark publication. There have been two other academic conferences on psalmody in the United Kingdom over the last twenty years, one at Nantwich (2004), under the auspices of the Tyndale Fellowship Old Testament Group, and the other at St Andrews University (2009), in the annual series of the Bible in the Arts and Imagination Forum, but only the first of these has to date resulted in a publication.[4] There have also been two other publications from international conferences which have focused on the Jewish and Christian approaches to the psalms, one at Münster (1997) and the other at Yale (2002), but nothing of this nature has been done in Britain.[5] Furthermore, this volume serves as a memorial to the inspiration of three prominent (British) Psalms scholars who have all died in the past fifteen years (R. Norman Whybray [1923–1997]; John H. Eaton [1927–2007]; and Michael D. Goulder [1927–2010]), and so promotes Psalms studies here for another generation. Finally, this publication also counters the curious absence of a separate entry on the Psalms in the most recent edited

[4] See D.G. Firth and P. Johnston, *Interpreting the Psalms. Issues and Approaches,* Leicester: InterVarsity Press, 2006.

[5] The proceedings of this conference held at Münster, 1997, were published as *Der Psalter in Judentum und Christentum,* eds. E. Zenger and N. Lohfink (Freiburg: Herder, 1998); and that at Yale, 2002, as *Psalms in Community: Jewish and Christian Textual, Liturgical and Artistic Traditions,* eds H. W. Attridge and M. E. Fassler (New Haven: Yale University Press, 2002).

surveys published by the British Society for Old Testament Study (*The World of Ancient Israel* [1989] and *Text in Context* [2000]), demonstrating, conversely, that Psalms studies in the United Kingdom still has a future.[6]

'*Dominus Illuminatio Mea*': this is the motto of Oxford University, taken from Psalm 26 (27) verse 1. Psalmody continues to enlighten scholarship; and despite its earlier history of creating conflict between different theological persuasions it can also serve to break down the barriers between confessional and academic traditions, as this collection of papers has so clearly shown.

---

[6] See R. E. Clements (ed.) *The Social World of Ancient Israel: Sociological, Anthropological and Political Perspectives* (Society of Old Testament Study Monograph Series; Cambridge: Cambridge University Press, 1989); and A. D. H. Mayes (ed.), *Text in Context: Essays by Members of the Society of Old Testament Study* (Oxford: Oxford University Press, 2000).

Part I

Jewish and Christian Responses
to the Psalms

1

The Dead Sea Psalms Scrolls: Psalms Manuscripts, Editions, and the *Oxford Hebrew Bible*

Peter W. Flint

1. Introduction

Since 1987, one main focus of my research has been on the Psalms scrolls found at several locations in the Judaean Desert. The purpose of this paper is to:

1. briefly introduce the Psalms scrolls;
2. offer some observations on the Psalms manuscripts;
3. briefly survey scholarly interactions concerning the Psalms scrolls;
4. briefly introduce new publication projects featuring the Psalms scrolls;
5. comment on the new Psalms edition in preparation for the *Oxford Hebrew Bible* Project, with several pertinent examples;
6. provide a select bibliography.

2. A Brief Introduction to the Psalms Scrolls

Approximately 1,000 scrolls were found in the Judaean desert. Some 250—of which 230 were found at Qumran—are classified as 'biblical scrolls'. Forty-three of these manuscripts are Psalms scrolls or manuscripts that incorporate Psalms; forty were found in eight caves at Qumran, one in cave 5/6 at Nahal Hever, and two at Masada. Only Deuteronomy is represented by a higher number of copies (forty-six scrolls, of which forty-three at Qumran).

The prominence of the Psalms scrolls at Qumran highlights the importance of the Psalms among the *Yahad* or Essene movement, whose most prominent centre was at the site. As our earliest extant witnesses to the scriptural text of the Psalms, these scrolls also hold significant implications for understanding the Psalms in the later Second Temple period and their finalization as a collection.

3. Psalms Scrolls Discovered in the Judaean Desert

40 Scrolls found at Qumran

> **Three scrolls from Cave 1:**
> 1Q10 (1QPs^a)
> 1Q11 (1QPs^b)
> 1Q12 (1QPs^c)
>
> **One scroll from Cave 2:**
> 2Q14 (2QPs)
>
> **One scroll from Cave 3:**
> 3Q2 (3QPs)
>
> **Twenty-five scrolls from Cave 4:**
> 4Q83 (4QPs^a)
> 4Q84 (4QPs^b)
> 4Q85 (4QPs^c)
> 4Q86 (4QPs^d)
> 4Q87 (4QPs^e)
> 4Q88 (4QPs^f)
> 4Q89 (4QPs^g)
> 4Q90 (4QPs^h)
> 4Q91 (4QPs^j)
> 4Q92 (4QPs^k)
> 4Q93 (4QPs^l)
> 4Q94 (4QPs^m)
> 4Q95 (4QPs^n)
> 4Q96 (4QPs^o)
> 4Q97 (4QPs^p)
> 4Q98 (4QPs^q)
> 4Q98a (4QPs^r)
> 4Q98b (4QPs^s)

4Q98c (4QPs^t)
4Q98d (4QPs^u)
4Q98e (4QPs^v)
4Q98f (4QPs^w)
4Q98g (4QPs^x)
4Q98h (4QPs^y)
4Q522 (4QProphecy on Joshua)
4Q?Psalms (SW Baptist
 Collection)

One scroll from Cave 5:
5Q5 (5QPs)

One scroll from Cave 6:
pap6Q5 (pap6QPs)

One scroll from Cave 8:
8Q2 (8QPs)

Six scrolls from Cave 11:
11Q5 (11QPs^a)
11Q6 (11QPs^b)
11Q7 (11QPs^c)
11Q8 (11QPs^d)
11Q9 (11QPs^e)
11Q11 (11QPsAp^a)

Scrolls found at other locations

Two scrolls at Masada:
MasPs^a (M1039–160)
MasPs^b (M1103–1742)
One scroll at Nahal Hever:
5/6HevPs

4. Observations on the Psalms Manuscripts

A careful study of the Psalms scrolls reveals several features that contribute to our understanding of the book of Psalms and its completion as a collection or book of Scripture.

4.1. Datings of the Psalms Scrolls

The Psalms scrolls found in the Judaean Desert for which dates can be determined were copied from the second century BCE to the late first century CE.

At least fourteen are dated before the Common Era. The two oldest (4QPs^a, 4QPs^w) were copied *c.*150 BCE; another (4QPs^x) between 175 and 125 BCE; eleven in the first century BCE (1QPs^a, 4QPs^b, 4QPs^d, 4QPs^f, 4QPs^k, 4QPs^l, 4QPs^n, 4QPs^o, 4QPs^u, 4Q522, MasPs^b), and one (4QPs^v) is more loosely classified as 'Hasmonaean'. Six scrolls are generally classified as 'Herodian' (1QPs^c, 2QPs, 4QPs^h, 4QPs^m, 4QPs^p, 4QPs^r), and four are assigned to the first century CE (1QPs^v, 3QPs, 4QProphecy on Joshua, 5QPs, 8QPs). Ten others are dated more precisely to the early to mid-first century CE (4QPs^e, 4QPs^g, 4QPs^j, 4QPs^q, 4QPs^t, 11QPs^a, 11QPs^b, 11QPs^c, 11QPs^d, MasPs^a). The four latest Psalms scrolls (4QPs^c, 4QPs^s, 11QapocPs, 5/6HevPs) were copied in the mid-first century CE onwards.

4.2. Amount of Text Preserved in the Psalms Scrolls

In decreasing order, the Psalms manuscripts with the highest number of verses preserved (whether wholly or in part) are: 11QPs^a, 4QPs^a, 5/6HevPs, 4QPs^b, 4QPs^c, and 4QPs^e. Such scrolls most likely contained a form of the 'Book of Psalms' when they were fully extant. In their undamaged state, however, not all the Psalms scrolls were copies of the Psalter. Several originally contained only small sections (for example, 4QPs^{g-h}), or even individual psalms (5Q5, with only Psalm 119).

In the Hebrew Bible, and in the Protestant and Roman Catholic Old Testaments, the 'Book of Psalms' contains poems, songs, or hymns, many of which were likely performed in the Temple and religious services in Judaism from before the exile and into the Second Temple period. Of the 150 psalms in this Psalter, 126 are preserved in the Psalms scrolls from Qumran (including the Psalms Commentaries or *Pesharim*). In the Orthodox Bibles, there are 151 psalms, based on the collection preserved in the Septuagint. Psalm 151 is also found in the Great Psalms Scroll from Cave 11 at Qumran (11QPs^a), bringing the total to 127 represented Psalms from the Orthodox Psalter.

Most of the represented psalms are from the latter third of the book. Of Psalms 1–89, nineteen no longer survive (Pss 3–4, 20–21, 32, 41, 46, 55, 58, 61, 64–65, 70, 72–75, 80, 87), but of Psalms 90–150 only five are not represented (90, 108?, 110, 111, 117). The reason for this discrepancy is that the beginnings of scrolls are usually on the outside, and are thus far more prone to deterioration. All the remaining twenty-four psalms were most likely

represented, but are now lost because of the damaged state of the vast majority of the Psalms scrolls.

4.3. Formats of the Psalms Scrolls

Was poetic layout to be found in ancient Hebrew manuscripts, or was it a later
development? Several different arrangements of material are to be found in
the Psalms scrolls. At least ten are arranged stichometrically, or in poetic
format. Examples include 4QPs[b] and MasPs[a]. Twenty-one are arranged in
prose format (for example: 4QPs[a] and 11QPs[b]), and one (11QPs[a]) is a prose
collection with single piece written in stichometric format. These formats
reinforce the view of many scholars that in the later Second Temple period
more than one Psalter had varying liturgical functions.

4.4. Psalm Titles or Superscriptions

In comparison with the Hebrew Psalter in the Masoretic Text (MT), the
extant superscriptions in the Psalm scrolls show little variation, but there are
two interesting exceptions, both in 11QPs[a]. The first is an additional Davidic
title for Psalm 123 ('[A Song of] David. Of Ascents'), where the MT has no
superscription. The second is a different title for Psalm 145 ('A Prayer. Of
David'), where the MT reads 'A Song of Praise. Of David'.

4.5. Arrangement of Psalms in the Psalms Scrolls

Again, in comparison with the Hebrew Psalter (the 'MT-150 Psalter'), fourteen scrolls contain major disagreements that may be termed 'macro-
variants'. One such macro-variant is in the *arrangement* of psalms, which
occurs in seven manuscripts from Cave 4 (4QPs[a], 4QPs[b], 4QPs[d], 4QPs[e], 4QPs[k],
4QPs[n], 4QPs[q]), and two from Cave 11 (11QPs[a] and 11QPs[b]).

4.6. Contents of the Psalms Scrolls

Another striking feature of the Psalms scrolls is that four found at Qumran
(4QPs[f], 11QPs[a], 11QPs[b], 11QapocrPs) contain fifteen or sixteen psalms which
we would classify as apocryphal or extra-biblical. Seven of these were
previously familiar to scholars and some were found in early Bibles: Psalm
151A and 151B, for example, in the Septuagint, Psalms 154 and 155 in a Syriac
Psalter, David's Last Words in 2 Sam. 23.1–7, and the Catena (eight verses,
seven of them from Psalm 118, but in a different order) in Sir. 51.13–30.

The other eight or nine compositions (two may be parts of the same one) were unknown prior to the discovery of the scrolls. These include a prose epilogue (David's Compositions), hymns dedicated to themes such as the Last Days, Zion, Judah, and God the Creator (the Apostrophe to Judah, the Apostrophe to Zion, the Eschatological Hymn, the Hymn to the Creator, the Plea for Deliverance), and Three Songs (or Incantations) against Demons.

4.7. Four Noteworthy Psalms Scrolls

Four Psalms scrolls are especially important for understanding the development and shape of the Book of Psalms in the later Second Temple period: one is from Cave 4 (4QPs^a, copied *c.*150 BCE), two are from Cave 11 (11QPs^a (*c.*30–50 CE) and 11QPs^b (first half of the first century CE)), and one was found at Masada (MasPs^b, second half of the first century BCE).

5. Scholarly Interactions Concerning the Psalms Scrolls

The first Psalms manuscripts to be discovered were very fragmentary and seemed largely similar to the Masoretic Psalter,[1] so they did not arouse great excitement among scholars. But the situation changed decisively with James Sanders' publication of the Great Psalms Scroll (11QPs^a) in 1965,[2] and a more popular edition with additional text from the scroll and an English translation two years later.[3] This manuscript, as we have noted, diverges radically from the MT-150 Psalter, both in the ordering of contents and in the presence of eleven additional compositions. Fifty pieces are preserved—with at least one more (Psalm 120) now missing—in the following order (→ indicates that a composition follows directly, not by reconstruction):

Psalm 101→102→103; 109; 118→104→147→105→146→148 [+ 120] →121→122 →123→124→125→126→127→128→129→130→131→ 132→119→135→136→Catena→145(with postscript)→154→Plea for Deliverance→139→137→138→Sirach 51→Apostrophe to Zion→ Psalm 93→141→ 133→144→155→142→143→149→150→ Hymn to the Creator→David's Last Words→David's Compositions→Psalm 140 →134→151A→151B→blank column

---

[1] 1QPs^a, 1QPs^b, and 1QPs^c in Barthélemy and Milik (1955: 69–72 + plate xiii). Seven years later: 2QPs, 3QPs, 5QPs, pap6QPs, and 8QPs as recorded in Baillet, Milik, and de Vaux (1962: 1. Textes 69–71, 94, 112, 148–49, 174; 2. Plates xiii, xviii, xxiii, xxxi, xxxvii).

[2] Sanders 1965.

[3] Sanders 1967.

In a series of articles commencing in 1966,[4] Sanders developed several conclusions which challenged traditional views on the text and canonization of the Book of Psalms. Most notably, perhaps: that the Great Psalms Scroll contains the latter part of an authentic edition of the 'Book of Psalms', and was viewed by the community at Qumran as a true Davidic Psalter. A heated debate ensued between Sanders and scholars such as Shemaryahu Talmon, G. H. Goshen-Gottstein, and Patrick Skehan, who maintained that the MT-150 Psalter had already been finalized (or virtually so) several centuries before the Common Era, and that 11QPs[a] is a liturgical collection which is derived from, and secondary to, the MT. I have documented the details of this interchange elsewhere, so will not repeat them here.[5]

The resolution of this debate involves four questions, on which new evidence was to come forward in the Psalms scrolls from Cave 4,[6] one scroll from Cave 11 (11QPs[b]),[7] and the second Psalms scroll from Masada (MasPs[b]).[8]

1. Are there other Psalms scrolls that preserve the *distinctive arrangement* (sequence of Psalms) found in 11QPs[a]? At least eight Psalms scrolls diverge from the MT-150 Psalter in the ordering of contents (for example, 4QPs[b]), but only two follow the arrangement in 11QPs[a]: 4QPs[e] (most probably Psalms 104→147→105) and 11QPs[b] (Psalms 118→104→[147]→105→146).

2. Are there other Psalms scrolls that preserve the *distinctive arrangement* (sequence of Psalms) found in the MT-150 Psalter? While many Psalms scrolls from Qumran contain material that corresponds with the MT-150 sequence (for example, Psalms 125–130 in 4QPs[e]), these arrangements reflect the 11QPs[a]-Psalter as well. In fact, no Psalms scroll from Qumran *unambiguously* confirms the MT-150 order. For such confirmation we must turn to Masada, where in MasPs[b] Psalm 150 is directly followed by a blank column, thus denoting the end of that edition of the Book of Psalms.

3. Do any other Psalms scrolls contain the *distinctive contents* (compositions absent from the MT-150 Psalter) found in 11QPs[a]? Only three other Psalms scrolls contains such apocryphal compositions: 4QPs[f] (the Apostrophe to Zion, and the Eschatological Hymn and Apostrophe to Judah [which may be a single work]), 4QProphecy on Joshua (Psalm 122 following material on Jerusalem and the Davidic dynasty), and 11QPs[b] (the Catena, the Plea for Deliverance, and the Apostrophe to Zion).

---

[4] E.g. Sanders 1966: 83–94; 1968: 1–15; 1974: 79–99.

[5] E.g. Flint 1997: 135–49; 2006: 233–72.

[6] For the edition, see Skehan, Ulrich, and Flint 2000: 7–160, 163–68 + plates i–xx.

[7] For the edition of this and the other Cave 11 Psalms scrolls (excluding most of 11QPs[a], which was published in DJD 4), see Martínez, Tigchelaar, and van der Woude (1998: 29–78 + plates iii–viii).

[8] For the edition, see Talmon 1999: 76–97, including two plates.

4. If 11QPs[a] indeed contains the latter part of an authentic edition of the Book of Psalms, are there any Psalms scrolls that preserve *earlier sections* of this larger Psalter (that is, Psalms prior to 93, the earliest one preserved in 11QPs[a] in terms of the MT-150 numerical sequence)? 4QPs[e] preserves text from Psalms 76–89, and 11QPs[b] text from Psalms 77 and 78.

Taking into account the wider evidence from all the Psalms scrolls, and building on the research of Gerald H. Wilson,[9] it became increasingly clear to me that the many Psalms scrolls from Cave 4 attest to diversity concerning the shape of the Psalter, not to uniformity in accordance with the MT-150 Psalter. Another important contribution has been Eugene Ulrich's convincing findings that during the closing centuries of the Second Temple period, Judaism knew variant literary editions for half or more of the later *Tanakh*: at least eleven, and as many as fourteen books or sections of books, of the traditional twenty-four.[10] Professor Ulrich informs me he has further detailed and nuanced these results in an article forthcoming in *The New Cambridge History of the Bible*: that 'variant editions for half or more of the twenty-four books of the Hebrew Bible existed in Jewish circles at the birth of Christianity and Rabbinic Judaism.'[11]

We may conclude that three editions of the Psalms were in circulation in the late Second Temple period (at least among the among the *Yahad* or Essene movement whose most prominent centre was at Qumran):

Edition I. An early edition of the Psalter that was mostly stabilized, beginning with Psalms 1 or 2 and ending with Psalm 89 (the cutoff point is not certain). The earliest and most complete example is 4QPs[a], which preserves text from Psalms 5–71.

Edition IIa. The 11QPs[a]-Psalter, consisting of Edition I plus the Psalms 101–151 as found in the Great Psalms Scroll, and including at least Psalm 93. It is attested by at least three manuscripts (11QPs[a], 4QPs[e], and 11QPs[b]) with common arrangements of key compositions or blocks of material: the 'Catena,' 'Plea,' 'Apostrophe to Zion,' and the sequence Psalms 141→133→ 144 in 11QPs[a] and 11QPs[b]; and possibly the sequence Psalms 118→104→ [147]→105→146 in 4QPs[e].

Edition IIb. The MT-150 Psalter, comprising Edition I plus Psalms 73 or 90 to 150 as found in the MT and the Septuagint. It is surprising to find that this arrangement is not *unambiguously* confirmed by any Qumran scroll; the appeal to arrangements such as Psalms 125 to 130 in 4QPs[e] in support of the MT-150 Psalter is inconclusive, since this sequence is also found in 11QPs[a].

---

[9] Wilson 1983: 377–88; also 1985a: 624–42; 1985b.
[10] Ulrich 1999a: 17–33; 1999b: 99–120.
[11] By kind favour of Professor Ulrich via private correspondence; also Ulrich (forthcoming).

For clear confirmation, we have to turn to Masada, where MasPs[b] (dated to the second half of the first century BCE) ends in Psalm 150 (with blank leather following). The MT-150 Psalter, or parts of it, was most likely found in several Qumran scrolls before they were so damaged, but they are too fragmentary for any firm conclusion to be reached.

Additional Collections of Psalms. Further arrangements of psalms appear in several manuscripts from Qumran. The most prominent are: 4QPs[b] (which includes Psalms 103→112, with 104–111 lacking); 4QPs[d] (Psalms 106→147→104); 4QPs[f] (includes Psalms 107 [+ 108?] + 109 and several 'apocryphal' compositions); 4QPs[k] (preserves the bottoms of two adjoining columns, the first containing parts of Ps. 135.6–16 and the second portions of Ps. 99.1–5); 4QPs[n] (Ps. 135.11–12 followed directly by 136.22–23); and 11QapocPs (three 'apocryphal' compositions followed directly by Psalm 91). None of these can be viewed as editions of the 'Book of Psalms', but are rather arrangements of material from Edition IIa or Edition IIb and other poems.

The shape of the various Psalms scrolls brings about the following reassessment of the development of the Psalter in the Second Temple period. The 'Book of Psalms' was put together in a first stage: Edition I. This was followed by two parallel stages: Editions IIa and IIb (both containing Edition I plus Psalms 73 or 90 onwards, the precise cutoff point not being certain).

6. New Publication Projects Featuring the Psalms Scrolls

As detailed above, almost all the Psalms scrolls were published by Oxford University Press in the series 'Discoveries in the Judaean Desert' (DJD) from 1953 to 2000, and the two found at Masada were published in 1999 in the sixth volume (*Masada* VI) of the Yigael Yadin Excavations. What, then, lies in store for the Dead Sea Psalms scrolls? Three recent project series involve Psalms manuscripts from the Judaean Desert, thus attesting to the continued relevance of these scrolls for research on the biblical text and Second Temple Judaism.

6.1. A New Series: 'Dead Sea Scrolls Editions'

Several Dead Sea Scrolls have never been published in an official edition, for example: the *Genesis Apocryphon,* the *Habakkuk Pesher* (or *Commentary*), and the *War Scroll* (or *War Rule*) from Cave 1. In addition, an increasing number of 'new' scrolls have come to light in recent times. Since at least the 1980s, some scholars were aware of scrolls (mostly from Cave 4) in private hands that were being offered for sale. In the 'underground market' for these manu-scripts, dealings are often clandestine and complicated. Here are some scrolls that have been acquired since 2000:

2006: The Institute for Judaism and Christian Origins (Princeton, NJ) announced the acquisition of Dead Sea Scroll fragments of Deuteronomy, Nehemiah, and Jeremiah;

2009: Azusa Pacific University (Azusa, California) acquired five fragments with text from Leviticus and Daniel, two from Deuteronomy, and one possibly from Exodus. These featured in a successful exhibition, *Treasures of the Bible: The Dead Sea Scrolls and Beyond* (21–29 August 2010); and

2010: Southwestern Baptist Theological Seminary (Fort Worth, Texas) announced its acquisition of an ancient pen used at Qumran and frag-ments of Exodus, Leviticus, Deuteronomy, Psalm 22, and Daniel. These are featured in the exhibit, *Treasures of the Bible: The Dead Sea Scrolls and Beyond* (July 2, 2012–Jan. 13, 2013, 2010).

For the Psalms scholar, another Psalms scroll is to be welcomed. The fragment acquired by Southwestern Baptist Seminary is one of only three to contain text from Psalm 22 (the others being 4QPs[f] and the Nahal Hever Psalms scroll (5/6HevPs)). All these 'new' manuscripts will be published by respected scholars in journals, or in books associated with the institutions that have purchased them. In previous times, the official editions would appear later in the DJD series. While this series has ended, the need for official editions in an appropriate series has not.

Furthermore, some scrolls that have appeared in official DJD editions need to be thoroughly revised and expanded, using many other manuscripts that were not available to the original editors. One clear example is the Great Psalms Scroll (11QPs[a]), which was meticulously edited and published in a superb volume by James Sanders (DJD 4) in 1965. Most of the other Psalms scrolls were not available to Sanders at the time, so the abundance of data they provide could not be taken into account. Even a major portion of 11QPs[a] itself, Fragment E (with text from Psalms 118, 104, 147, and 105), only became available after DJD 4 had been published, and just as Sanders' more popular 'Cornell Edition' of 11QPs[a] was going to press. Fortunately, he managed to add it as the 'Postscriptum' (with a photograph, transcription, and com-mentary) at the end of the 1967 book.[12] Thirty-one years later, Fragment E and a further small one (Fragment F, with text possibly from Ps. 147.3) were published in the DJD series by Florentino García Martínez, Eibert J. C. Tigchelaar, and A. S. van der Woude.[13]

---

[12] Sanders 1967: 155–65.
[13] Martínez, Tigchelaar, and van der Woude 1998: 29–36 + plates iv–v.

It is thus necessary for the Great Psalms Scroll to be revised and published in a single and comprehensive edition. Together with several scrolls found early on that have not yet been edited for official editions, and with other 'new' scrolls coming to light, a series is called for in which the official editions of these manuscripts can appear. Further volumes in the DJD series are no longer possible, since it closed with the retirement of the Editor-in-Chief, Emanuel Tov, and with the appearance of the final volume in 2010. A total of forty DJD volumes was published over a span of thirty-eight years (1953–2011).

A new series has been established, 'Dead Sea Scrolls Editions', to be produced by Brill Academic Publishers. Eibert J. C. Tigchelaar is Editor-in-Chief, and will oversee the publication of new editions by various scholars. One of these will be the Great Psalms Scroll.[14]

6.2. A New Series Modelled on Origen's *Hexapla*: '*Biblia Qumranica*'

Biblia Qumranica presents a synoptic edition of all the biblical manuscripts from Qumran and other sites near the Dead Sea, together with the Masoretic text (the Leningrad Codex) and the Septuagint (from the Göttingen edition). The projected volumes will provide the first comparative edition of the biblical scrolls, and a unique tool for text-critical analysis and comparison of the textual witnesses of the Hebrew Bible that survive from the Second Temple period.

The first volume to be published was *The Minor Prophets* in 2004,[15] which provides a synopsis of the Minor Prophets scrolls, the Masoretic text, and the Septuagint. A sample of this edition is reproduced on pages 22–23, as a table, with Mic. 1.1–6 from five sources: the Septuagint (Göttingen edition), the Greek Minor Prophets Scroll from Nahal Hever (8HevXII gr), the *Pesher* on Micah from Cave 1 at Qumran (1QpMic), the Minor Prophets Scroll from Murabba'at (MurXII), and the Masoretic text (as in *BHS*).

Further books are in preparation, including *The Psalms*, which will have more columns than most other volumes in the series because of the great number of Psalms scrolls.[16]

---

[14] Flint et al., *The Great Psalms Scroll from Cave 11 (11QPsᵃ)* (Dead Sea Scrolls Discoveries series), Leiden: Brill, in preparation.

[15] Ego, Lange, Lichtenberger, and De Troyer 2004.

[16] Peter Flint et al. (eds.), forthcoming (b).

7. The Oxford Hebrew Bible Project

The most important contribution of the biblical scrolls from the Judaean Desert is to help in our understanding the development of the biblical text, and to assist scholars in arriving at the most accurate and preferred text of Scripture. These manuscripts will be a key resource for the *Oxford Hebrew Bible*, the first Critical Edition of the Hebrew Bible.

7.1. Manuscripts of the Masoretic Text

Editions of the Hebrew Bible used so far by scholars and laypersons contain the Masoretic text, which is by far the largest among all our textual witnesses of the Hebrew Bible. This text was developed over many centuries, and underwent three stages of transmission.[17]

Scrolls from the first period of transmission (up to 70 CE) include many of the Hebrew texts from Qumran (*c.*250 BCE to 68 CE), Masada (before 74 CE), and ancient translations such as *kaige-Theodotion* (mid-first century BCE).

Documents from the second period (70 CE to the eighth century) are several biblical scrolls from the Judaean Desert and some translations into other languages. The earliest scrolls—all written before 135—were found at Murabba'at (parts of the Torah, Isaiah, the Minor Prophets) and at Nahal Hever (Genesis, Numbers, Deuteronomy, Psalms). The 600-year period that followed (third to eighth centuries CE) is often called the 'silent era', since almost no Hebrew manuscripts from that time survived.

Manuscripts from the third period of transmission (from the seventh or eighth century onwards) are divided into two groups: those from the early Middle Ages (up to about 1100), and later ones. There are several prominent Masoretic manuscripts from this period, some of them with interesting origins and stories of preservation. The two most important are the Aleppo Codex and the Leningrad Codex.

Copied in about 925 CE, the Aleppo Codex forms the basis of the *Hebrew University Bible* (*HUB*) Project based in Jerusalem. A substantial portion, however, was lost, which means that for some books the *HUB* Project must rely on other manuscripts. The first volume to be published was *Isaiah* (1995), followed by *Jeremiah* (1997) and *Ezekiel* (2004). Many scholars consider the Aleppo Codex to be the most authoritative copy of the Masoretic text, in both its consonants and its vowels.

The Leningrad (or St Petersburg) Codex is used by most biblical scholars in its published editions, *Biblia Hebraica Stuttgartensia* (*BHS*), and now *Biblia Hebraica Quinta* (*BHQ*), on which almost all modern English translations of

[17] Tov 2012: 27–36.

Micah 1.1–6 in *Biblia Qumranica*, with parallel texts from five sources

	Septuagint (LXX)	8HevXIIgr
1:1	Καὶ ἐγένετο λόγος κυρίου πρὸς Μιχαίαν τόν Μωρασθι ἐν ἡμέραις Ιωαθαμ και Αχαζ καὶ Εξεκίου βασιλέων Ιουδα, ὑπὲρ ὧν εἶδε περὶ Σαμαρείας καὶ περὶ Ιερουσαλημ.	ΛΟΓΟΣ ⟨⟩[⟨⟩ ος εγενετο προς μιχαιαν τον] ΜΩΡΑΣΘΕΙ ΕΝ ΗΜ[εραις ιωαθαμ αχαζ εζεκιου] ΒΑΣΙΛΕΩΣ ΙΟΥΔΑ Ο[ν ειδεν περι σαμαροιας και ιερους]ΑΛΗΜ vac
1:2	Ἀκούσατε, λαοί, λόγους, καὶ προσεχέτω ἡ γῆ καὶ πάντες οἱ ἐν αὐτῇ, καὶ ἔσται κύριος ἐν ὑμῖν εἰς μαρτύριον, κύριος ἐξ οἴκου ἁγίου αὐτοῦ·	ΑΚΟ[υσατε προσεχετω γη] ΚΑΙ ΤΟ Π[λη]ΡΩΜΑ Α[υτης και εσται κυριος ⟨⟩ ΕΝ ΥΜΕΙΝ ΕΙΣ ΜΑΡΤΥ[ρα κυριος εκ ναου αγιου αυτου]
1:3	διότι ἰδοὺ κύριος ἐκπορεύεται ἐκ τοῦ τόπου αὐτοῦ καὶ καταβήσεται καὶ ἐπιβήσεται ἐπὶ τὰ ὕψη τῆς γῆς,	ΟΤΙ ΙΔΟΥ ⟨⟩ ΕΚΠ[ορευεται εκ του τοπου αυτου και] ΚΑΤΑΒΗΣΕΤΑΙ ΚΑ[ι επιβησεται επι υψη γης]
1:4	καὶ σαλευθήσεται τὰ ὄρη ὑποκάτωθεν αὐτοῦ, καὶ αἱ κοιλάδες τακήσονται ὡς κηρὸς ἀπὸ προσώπου πυρὸς καὶ ὡς ὕδωρ καταφερόμενον ἐν καταβάσει.	και τακη]ΣΟΝ[ται] ΤΑ ΟΡΗ Υ[ποκατωθεν αυτου και αι κοιλαδες ρα]ΓΗΣΟΝ[τα]Ι ΩΣ [κηρος] Ἀ[πο προσωπου του πυρος ως υδωρ] ΚΑΤΑΦ[ερ]ΟΜΕΝΟ[ν εν κα]ΤΑΒΑ[σει
1:5	διὰ ἀσέβειαν Ιακωβ πάντα ταῦτα καὶ διὰ ἁμαρτίαν οἴκου Ισραηλ. τίς ἡ ἀσέβεια τοῦ Ιακωβ; οὐ Σαμάρεια; καί τίς ἡ ἁμαρτία οἴκου Ιουδα; οὐχὶ Ιερουσαλημ;	δι ασεβιαν ιακωβ] ΠΑΝΤΑ Τ[α]ΥΤΑ ΚΑΙ [δι αμ]ΑΡΤΙΑΝ [οικου ισραηλ § τις] ΑΣΕΒΙΑ ΙΑΚΩΒ Ο[υ σα]ΜΑΡΟΙΑ ΚΑ[ι τις υψη ιουδα ου]ΧΙ ΙΕΡΟΥΣΑΛΗΜ
1:6	καὶ θήσομαι Σαμάρειαν εἰς ὀπωροφυλάκιον ἀγροῦ καὶ εἰς φυτείαν ἀμπελῶνος καὶ κατασπάσω εἰς χάος τοὺς λίθους αὐτῆς καὶ τὰ θεμέλια αὐτῆς ἀποκαλύψω·	ΚΑ[ι ϑ]ΗΣΟΜΑΙ ΣΑ[μαροιαν εις οπω]ΡΟΦΥΛΑΚΙΟΝ ΤΟΥ Α[γρ]ΟΥ ΚΑΙ ΕΙ[ς φυτειαν αμπελωνος] ΚΑΙ ΚΑΤΑΣΠΑΕΩ ΕΙΣ ΤΗΝ ΦΑΡΑΓΓΑ [τους λιθους αυτης] ΚΑΙ ΤΑ ΘΕΜΕΛΙΑ ΑΥΤΗΣ [αποκαλυψω

Source: after Ego, Lange, Lichtenberger, and De Troyer (eds.) 2004: 90–91.

the Old Testament are based. Copied in 1008 or 1009 CE, this is the earliest complete example of the traditional Hebrew Bible, or Masoretic Text, and is a primary source for the recovery of text in the missing parts of the Aleppo Codex.

All editions of the Hebrew Bible to be published so far—whether in the *HUB* based on the Aleppo Codex, or *BHS* and *BHQ* based on the Leningrad Codex—are 'diplomatic editions' (that is, based on a single manuscript).

7.2. The Need for a Critical Edition of the Hebrew Bible

Scholars whose work focuses on the biblical text—usually textual critics but sometimes Bible translators—know that every manuscript has errors. In many cases, the copyist was careless, or his eye skipped form one word to the

2pMic	MurXII	Masoretic Text (MT)	
	דֹ[ב]רֹ יהוה אשֹ[ר] הֹיֹה אל [מי]כֹה	דְּבַר־יְהוָה אֲשֶׁר הָיָה אֶל־מִיכָה	1:1
	המֹ[ורש]תֹיֹ [ב]ימי יותם אחז [י]חזקֹי[ה]	הַמֹּרַשְׁתִּי בִּימֵי יוֹתָם אָחָז יְחִזְקִיָּה
	מלכי יהודֹה אשר חזה [על] שֹמר[ו]ן	מַלְכֵי יְהוּדָה אֲשֶׁר־חָזָה עַל־שֹׁמְרוֹן
	וירושלם	וִירוּשָׁלָםִ׃
[7]א̇ רֹ̇אֹ̇]ארני יהיֹ	שֹמֹע[ו] עֹמים כלם וֹהֹקשֹי[ו]בֹי	שִׁמְעוּ עַמִּים כֻּלָּם הַקְשִׁיבִי	1:2
בכס]	אֹו̇ר[ץ] ומלֹאֹהֹ וֹיֹהֹי] אֹדֹני יֹהֹוֹה	אֶרֶץ וּמְלֹאָהּ וִיהִי אֲדֹנָי יְהוָה
	בֹכֹם לצֹוד אדנ[י] מֹהֹיֹכל קדשו	בָּכֶם לְעֵד אֲדֹנָי מֵהֵיכַל קָדְשׁוֹ׃
הֹג[ה 7]אֹ̇ר[7 מֹ[מקומו	כֹ̇י הנה יֹהֹ[וה] יֹֹצא מֹמֹקֹומו	כִּי־הִנֵּה יְהוָה יֹצֵא מִמְּקוֹמוֹ	1:3
במ[ותי הֹ̇אֹרֹ̇ץ	ויר[ד ויֹרֹך צֹֹל] ארץ	וְיָרַד וְדָרַךְ עַל־בָּמֳתֵי אָרֶץ׃
ההרי[ם תֹ̇חֹ]תיו	ונמסו ההרים תֹ[ח]תֹיו והֹעֹמֹ[ק]יֹֹם	וְנָמַסּוּ הֶהָרִים תַּחְתָּיו וְהָעֲמָקִים	1:4
ית[ב]קעֹו כדו[ו]נֹג מפֹנֹי הֹא[ש כ]וֹמ	[י]תבֹ[ק]עו כרוֹנֹג [מפ]וֹי הֹ[א]שֹ כמים	יִתְבַּקָּעוּ כַּדּוֹנַג מִפְּנֵי הָאֵשׁ כְּמַיִם
	מגרי[ם] במו[ר]ר	מֻגָּרִים בְּמוֹרָד׃
יעק[ב כול]וא[ת ובחטו]או	בֹפֹשֹע [יע]קֹב כל ואת ובחטא[ו]ֹת	בְּפֶשַׁע יַעֲקֹב כָּל־זֹאת וּבְחַטֹּאת	1:5
יע[קֹ]בֹ [ה]לֹ̇אֹ	בית ישראל מי פשע יעקב הלוא	בֵּית יִשְׂרָאֵל מִי־פֶשַׁע יַעֲקֹב הֲלוֹא
	שמרון ומי במות [י]הוֹדֹה הלוא	שֹׁמְרוֹן וּמִי בָּמוֹת יְהוּדָה הֲלוֹא
יר[ו]שֹלם	ירושלם	יְרוּשָׁלָםִ׃
[» ומה במות יהודה]		
לֹ[ע]י שדה]	ושמתי שמֹר[ו]ן לעי השדה למטעי	וְשַׂמְתִּי שֹׁמְרוֹן לְעִי הַשָּׂדֶה לְמַטָּעֵי	1:6
	[כר]ֹם והגרתֹי לגי אבניה וֹסֹדיה	כָרֶם וְהִגַּרְתִּי לַגַּי אֲבָנֶיהָ וִיסֹדֶיהָ
	אגלה	אֲגַלֶּה׃

same word in a passage (*homoiarkton* or *homoioteleuton*), thereby omitting a block of text. This is not the case with the Aleppo and Leningrad Codices, which were very carefully and meticulously copied.

There is, however, another type of error found in ancient manuscripts: problematic readings and errors in the text being copied. As is the case with Septuagint and New Testament manuscripts, most scholars agree that there are hundreds of problematic readings in the MT, and at least scores of these are errors. Many were already identified by early scribes as they transmitted the text. Since their reverence for the text prevented them from making changes or corrections, these copyists often wrote the correct or preferred form in the margin (the *Qere*).

In many such cases, the correct or preferred form is found in biblical scrolls from the Judaean Desert and/or in the Septuagint. Some of these are noted in the apparatus of *BHS*, and many more will be included in the apparatuses of *BHQ* and *HUB*.

For many scholars and for Bible readers, relegating correct or preferred readings to footnotes does not seem appropriate. Many modern English Bibles (such as the *RSV*, *NRSV*, *NAB*, *NEB*, and *NIV*) now include readings that are clearly better or correct in the translation itself, with the problematic or incorrect reading found in the MT as a footnote. Bearing in mind that the translation committees of most modern English Bibles are cautious about making changes and are composed of, or advised by, respected scholars in the field, we may conclude that these translations are from a presumed 'critical text' of Scripture. This text is very much like the MT, but includes an estimated two hundred readings that depart from it.

7.3. Description of the Oxford Hebrew Bible Project

The time has come for scholars to provide a critical edition of the Hebrew Bible. This will be the *Oxford Hebrew Bible* (*OHB*), featuring a critical text, apparatus, and text-critical introduction and commentary. Each book of the Hebrew Bible will be addressed in a separate volume, to be published by Oxford University Press, with a single volume each for the Minor Prophets, the *Megillot*, and Ezra–Nehemiah. Volumes are being prepared by an international team of experienced scholars well versed in textual criticism, with Ronald Hendel (University of California, Berkeley) as Editor-in-Chief.

This project represents a departure from the other major textual editions (*BHS*, *BHQ* and *HUB*), all of which are 'diplomatic editions'. Each volume will consist of an introductory chapter, the text-critical commentary, and the critical edition. The introductory chapter will address the text-critical character of the biblical book, including: the nature and affinities of the relevant Qumran manuscripts; the translation technique of the Septuagint translator and its value for textual criticism; the character and utility of the other major and minor versions; the textual history of the book; and special problems (such as multiple editions).

7.4. The Book of Psalms for the *Oxford Hebrew Bible*

Comparison of the Psalms texts found among the scrolls, Greek manuscripts, and the Masoretic text shows the text of individual psalms to be quite stable. There are, however, several problematic readings in the MT; for some of these, the preferred or correct text is to be found in key Psalms scrolls. If such is the case, these readings must be seriously considered on text-critical grounds for inclusion in the Critical Text, not the apparatus, of *Psalms* for the *Oxford Hebrew Bible*.

There follow five examples of readings in Psalms scrolls and other ancient manuscripts that are being considered for adoption in the critical Hebrew text of *OHB Psalms*. For each verse involved, the following elements will be provided: a synoptic view of the Psalms scroll, MT, Septuagint, and other versions; contrasting English translations;[18] and a note of which readings have been adopted by up to seventeen English Bible translations.[19] Each sample ends with a comment on the prospects of the reading in question being adopted in the Critical Text of *OHB Psalms*.

7.4.1. Critical Hebrew Text Supported by Context, Scroll(s), MT MS(S), Septuagint, Syriac, Psalms Scroll

Psalm 145.13—The *nun*-strophe in an acrostic poem

Here the MT contains a shorter text that lacks the *nun*-strophe that is found in 11QPs[a] (together with a refrain).

Ps. 145.13[fin] (col. 17, lines 2–3)   נאמן אלוהים בדבריו וחסיד בכול מעשיו
11QPs[a] M[ms] (Ken#142) G S

(God is faithful in his words, and gracious in all his deeds.)

The ‫נ‬-strophe; cf. v. 17] > M

MT:

מַלְכוּתְךָ מַלְכוּת כָּל־עֹלָמִים וּמֶמְשַׁלְתְּךָ בְּכָל־דּוֹר וָדוֹר:

11QPs[a]:

מלכותכה מלכות כול עולמים וממשלתכה בכול דור ודור
ברוך יהוה וברוך שמו לעולם ועדע נאמן אלוהים בדבריו
וחסיד בכול מעשיו

(Your kingdom is an everlasting kingdom, and your dominion endures
    throughout all generations.
Blessed be the LORD and blessed be his name forever and ever.
God is faithful in his words, and gracious in all his deeds.)

Septuagint:

ἡ βασιλεία σου βασιλεία πάντων τῶν αἰώνων καὶ ἡ δεσποτεία σου ἐν πάσῃ γενεᾷ καὶ γενεᾷ πιστὸς κύριος ἐν τοῖς λόγοις αὐτοῦ καὶ ὅσιος ἐν πᾶσι τοῖς ἔργοις αὐτοῦ

(Your kingdom is a kingdom of all the ages, and your dominion is in every generation and generation.)

[13a] (*Faithful is the Lord in his words, and devout in all his works* [NETS])

---

[18] Translations of Psalms scrolls are adapted from Abegg, Flint, and Ulrich (1999). Septuagint translations are from Pietersma and Wright 2009 (= *NETS*).

[19] See List of Abbreviations, p. xvii, for their names and dates of publication.

Option 1: 'God [or, 'the LORD'] is faithful in his words, and gracious in all his deeds'; supported by 11QPs[a], one medieval Hebrew manuscript, Septuagint, and the Syriac. This reading has been adopted by most English translations: *ESV, HCSB, NAB, NIV, NJB, NLT-SE, NRSV, REB, RSV,* and *TNIV.*

Option 2: The *nun*-verse absent; supported by the MT. Adopted by the following English translations: *AMP, CJB, GWORD, JPS, NASB, NET,* and *NKJV.* Several translations also refer to the Psalms scroll variant in a footnote: *ESV, HCSB, NET, NIV, NJB, NKJV, NRSV, REB,* and *TNIV.*

Comment: The *nun*-verse will be included in the *OHB* critical edition on the basis of: context, one Psalms scroll, one Masoretic manuscript, Septuagint, Syriac, and adoption by key translations (including *ESV, NAB, NIV, NJB, NRSV, RSV, TNIV*). It is still to be decided whether to adopt אלהים or יהוה. Proposed Critical Text (for translation, see above):

נאמן אלהים (? יהוה or) בדבריו וחסיד בכל מעשיו

Ps. 22.16 [Heb 22.17]—A significant variant reading

The reading in the MT (*like a lion*) is problematic in the context, and has been discussed by several commentators. The word in question is preserved in the Psalms scroll from Nahal Hever (5/6HevPs), but as a verbal form (*they have gouged* [or, *pierced*]).

Ps. 22.17 (frg. 11, line 4) כארו 5/6HevPs M[mss, edd] G($\mathring{\omega}\rho\nu\xi\alpha\nu$) s] כארי M; כרו M;
M[mss, edd]

MT:

כִּי סְבָבוּנִי כְּלָבִים עֲדַת מְרֵעִים הִקִּיפוּנִי כָּאֲרִי יָדַי וְרַגְלָי:

(For dogs have surrounded me; a gang of evildoers encircles me. *Like a lion are my hands and my feet.*)

5/6Hev:

[כי סבבוני כלבי]ִם עדת מרעים הקיפוני כארו ידי ורגלי

[For dog]s [have surrounded me; a gang of evil[doers] encircles me. *They have pierced* my hands and my feet.

Septuagint:

ὅτι ἐκύκλωσάν με κύνες πολλοί συναγωγὴ πονηρευομένων περιέσχον με ὤρυξαν χεῖράς μου καὶ πόδας

(because many dogs encircled me, a gathering of evildoers surrounded me. *They gouged* my hands and feet. [NETS])

---

* In the transcriptions of some Psalms scrolls, a circlet above a letter (for example, D̊) denotes a *possible* reading.

Option 1: 'They have dug (or pierced) my hands and feet,' supported by 5/6HevPs, several medieval Hebrew manuscripts and editions, Septuagint, and Syriac. This reading has been adopted by most English translations: *AMP, ESV, GWORD, HCSB, NASB, NIV, NJB, NKJV, NLT-SE, RSV,* and *TNIV.*

Option 2: 'Like a lion are my hands and feet,' supported by the MT. Adopted by the following English translations: *CJB* and *JPS.* Several translations also reference these witnesses in a footnote: *ESV, HCSB, NAB, NET, NIV, NJB, NKJV, RSV,* and *TNIV.*

Comment: 'They have dug (or pierced)' will most likely be included in the *OHB* critical edition on the basis of: context, one Psalms scroll, several Masoretic manuscripts and editions, Septuagint, Syriac, and adoption by key English translations (including *ESV, NIV, NJB, RSV*). Proposed Critical Text (for translation, see above):

כי סבבוני כלבים עדת מרעים הקיפוני כארו ידי ורגלי

7.4.2. *Critical Text Supported by Context, Scroll(s), MT MSS, Qere, Symmachus, Syriac, Targum*

Psalm 102.24

The *Ketib* reading in the MT (*his strength*) does not have significant manuscript support. In contrast, the *Qere* (*my strength*) is strongly supported by one Psalms scroll, several later Hebrew manuscripts, and most of the Versions.

Ps. 102.24 (col. 21:13) כֹחִי 4QPs^b M^q mss S T] כֹחו M G

MT:

עִנָּה בַדֶּרֶךְ כֹּחוֹ קִעַר יָמָי׃

(He weakened *his strength* on the way; he shortened my days.)

4QPs^b:

ענה בד־]רך [כֹחי קצר ימי

(He weakened *my strength* on the way; he shortened my days.)

Septuagint:

ἀπεκρίθη αὐτῷ ἐν ὁδῷ ἰσχύος αὐτοῦ τὴν ὀλιγότητα τῶν ἡμερῶν μου ἀνάγγειλόν μοι

(He answered him in the way of *his strength*, 'Tell me the paucity of my days.' [NETS])

Option 1: 'my strength,' supported by 4QPs^b, MT^qere ('what is read'), other medieval Hebrew manuscripts, Symmachus, Syriac, and the Targum. Adopted by most English translations: *AMP, CJB, ESV, GWORD, HCSB, JPS, NAB, NASB, NET, NIV, NJB, NKJV, NLT-SE, NRSV, REB, RSV,* and *TNIV.*

Option 2: 'his strength'; supported by MT[ketiv] ('what is written') and the Septuagint (which, however, gives a different sense to the wider verse). Apparently not adopted by any English translation, but the ancient witnesses are referenced in a footnote in *HCSB*.

Comment: 'my strength' will be included in the main text of *OHB* Psalms on the basis of: context, one Psalms scroll, MT[qere], several Masoretic manuscripts and editions, Septuagint, Syriac, Targum, and adoption by key English translations (including *ESV, NAB, RSV, NRSV*). Proposed Critical Text (for translation, see above):

ענה בדרך כחֹי קצר ימי

7.4.3. *Critical Text Supported by Context, Scroll, MT MSS, Sebir, Aquila, Syriac, Targum*

Ps. 144.2

The reading in the MT (*my people*) is also found in the Septuagint, as opposed to *peoples* in 11QPs[a], which is supported by several later witnesses.

Ps. 144.2 (col. 23:14) עמים 11QPs[a] M[mss, sebir](Ken, de Rossi); cf. Ps. 18.48//2 Sam. 22.48 s т] עמי м g (τὸν λαόν μου); –σου g[ms]; –αὐτοῦ g[ms]

MT:

... מָגִנִּי וּבוֹ חָסִיתִי הָרוֹדֵד עַמִּי תַחְתָּי:

(... my shield, and (the one) in whom I take refuge, who subdues *my people* under me.)

11QPs[a]:

... מגני ובו חסיתי הרודד עמים תחתי

(... my shield, and (the one) in whom I take refuge, who subdues *peoples* under me.)

Septuagint:

... ὑπερασπιστής μου καὶ ἐπ'αὐτῷ ἤλπισα ὁ ὑποτάσσων τὸν λαόν μου ὑπ' ἐμέ

(... my protector and in him I hoped, who subdues *my people* under me. [*NETS*])

Option 1: 'peoples'; supported by 11QPs[a], Hebrew manuscripts, *Sebir*, Syriac, and Targum (cf. Ps. 18.48 and parallel in 2 Sam. 22.48). Adopted by most English translations: *ESV, GWORD, JPS, NAB, NET, NIV, NJB, NLT-SE, NRSV, REB, RSV*, and *TNIV*.

Option 2: 'my people'; supported by the Masoretic text and Septuagint. Adopted by *AMP, CJB, HCSB, NASB*, and *NKJV*. Several translations also reference the Psalms scroll variant in a footnote: *ESV, HCSB, NIV, NJB*, and *TNIV*.

Comment: 'peoples' most likely will be adopted on the basis of: context, one Psalms scroll, MT[sebir], several Masoretic manuscripts, Septuagint, Syriac, Targum, and adoption by key English translations (including *ESV, NAB, NIV, RSV, NRSV*). Proposed Critical Text (for translation, see above):

. . . מגני ובו חסיתי הרודד עמים תחתי

7.4.4. Critical Hebrew Text Supported by Context, Scroll, BHS Note

Psalm 38.20 (cf. Ps. 35.19; 69.5)

This example illustrates the importance of one Psalms scroll, related Psalms passages, and scholarly research for determining the correct (or preferred) biblical text.

38:20 (frg. 7 ii, line 3)   חֱנם 4QPs[a] (cf. 35:19; 69:5; note 20[a] in *BHS*)] חיים M G

MT:

. . . וְאֹיְבֵי חַיִּים עָצֵמוּ

(But *my enemies are vigorous*, they are strong . . .)

4QPs[a]:

. . . ואיבי חֱנם עֹצמו

(But those who are *my enemies without cause* are strong, . . .)

Septuagint:

οἱ δὲ ἐχθροί μου ζῶσιν καὶ κεκραταίωνται ὑπὲρ ἐμέ . . .

(But *my enemies are alive* and are stronger than I. . . . [*NETS*])

Option 1: 'But those who are my enemies without cause.' Supported by 4QPs[a] (footnote in *BHS* proposes variant as a potential reading; cf. Ps. 35.19; 69.5). Adopted by several key English translations: *NAB, NET, NJB, NRSV, REB, RSV,* and *TNIV*.

Option 2: 'But my enemies are vigorous'; supported by the Masoretic text and Septuagint. Also adopted by several key translations: *AMP, CJB, ESV, GWORD, HCSB, JPS, NASB, NIV, NKJV,* and *NLT-SE*. Two translations also reference the variant form 4QPs[a] in a footnote (*NRSV* and *TNIV*).

Comment: 'without cause' will most likely be included in the *OHB* critical edition on the basis of: context and one Psalms scroll, and adoption by key English translations (including *NAB, NJB, RSV, NRSV*). This decision is difficult, however, since the support of the Septuagint for the MT reading is not easily dismissed, and is adopted by several English translations (including *ESV, JPS,* and *NIV*). Proposed Critical Text (for translation, see above):

. . . ואיבי חנם עצמו

7.4.5. *Critical Hebrew Text Supported by Context,*
Scroll Pesher, Septuagint:

Ps. 37.28—The *'ayin* strophe in an acrostic poem

This reading (*cannot understand*) in one Psalms scroll is supported by the
Septuagint and the Syriac, and appears to make better sense than the one in
the MT (*will not last*).

37.28 (col. 4:1)   עוֹֽלְהֶם לְעוּ[לָם נשמדו] 4QpPsᵃ (ע-strophe), cf. G (ἄνομοι
δὲ ἐκδιωχθήσονται); cf. *BHS* note and DJD 5.49] לעולם נשמרו M

MT:

כִּי יְהוָה אֹהֵב מִשְׁפָּט וְלֹא־יַעֲזֹב אֶת־חֲסִידָיו לְעוֹלָם נִשְׁמָרוּ
וְזֶרַע רְשָׁעִים נִכְרָת:

(For the LORD loves justice, and will not forsake his faithful ones. *They will be
kept safe* for ever, but the offspring of the wicked will be cut off.)

4QpPsᵃ:

[עולים לעו[לם נשמדו

(For the LORD loves justice, and he will not forsake his faithful ones. *Evildoers]
will be destroyed* for ev[er, and the offspring of the wi[cked will be cut off.)

Septuagint:

ὅτι κύριος ἀγαπᾷ κρίσιν καὶ οὐκ ἐγκαταλείψει τοὺς ὁσίους αὐτοῦ εἰς τὸν
αἰῶνα φυλαχθήσονται ἄνομοι δὲ ἐκδιωχθήσονται καὶ σπέρμα ἀσεβῶν
ἐξολεθρευθήσεται

(Because the Lord loves justice and will not forsake his devout, they shall be kept
safe forever. *But the lawless shall be chased away*, and the offspring of the impious
shall be destroyed. [*NETS*])

Option 1: '[Evildoers] will be destroyed.' Supported by 4QpPsᵃ (cf.
Septuagint). Adopted by several English translations: *NAB, NJB, REB*, and
TNIV.

Option 2: 'They (i.e., his faithful ones) will be kept safe'; supported by
the Masoretic Text. Adopted by most English translations: *AMP, CJB, ESV,
GWORD, HCSB, JPS, NASB, NET, NIV, NKJV, NLT-SE, NRSV*, and *RSV*.
Several translations (*NJB, TNIV, REB*) also reference the ancient witnesses in
a footnote.

Comment: '[Evildoers] will be destroyed' will very likely be included in the
OHB critical edition on the basis of: context (the *'ayin* strophe in an acrostic
Psalm), one Qumran scroll (4QpPsᵃ), the Septuagint, and its adoption by
some key English translations (for example, *NJB*). Although the Hebrew form
is reconstructed from the 4QpPsᵃ, which is a *pesher* and not a Psalms scroll,
the preservation of 'will be destroyed' in 4QpPsᵃ indicates that it very likely

also contained 'evildoers,' not 'they will be kept safe.' Proposed Critical Text (for translation, see above):

עוֹלִים לְעוֹלָם נשמדו

8. Concluding Observation

The biblical scrolls from the Judaean desert, including the Psalms scrolls, are important for understanding the development of the biblical text, and to assist scholars in arriving at the most accurate text of Scripture. The Psalms scrolls are a key resource for the *Psalms* volume in the *Oxford Hebrew Bible* series, which will be the first critical edition of the Book of Psalms in Hebrew. Since the *OHB* is a new project and series, the editors involved are fully aware that this is a new frontier in biblical scholarship, and that such a project may be controversial to some.

The reflections and sample texts offered in this paper are provisional, and can no doubt be further refined, expanded, or altered. Comments and feedback on the *OHB* project in general, and the *Psalms* volume in particular, are to be welcomed.

Bibliography

Editions and Translations of the Psalms Scrolls

Abegg, Martin, Flint, Peter W., and Ulrich, Eugene
    1999 *The Dead Sea Scrolls Bible* (San Francisco: HarperCollins); paperback edn: 2002.
Baillet, Maurice, Milik, Józef Tadeusz, and de Vaux, Roland
    1962 *Les 'Petites Grottes' de Qumrân. Exploration de la falaise. Les grottes 2Q, 3Q, 5Q, 6Q, 7Q, à 10Q. Le rouleau de cuivre* (DJD, 3; Oxford: Clarendon Press) 1. Texts; 2. Plates.
Barthélemy, Dominique, and Milik, Józef Tadeusz
    1955 *Qumran Cave I* (DJD, 1; Oxford: Clarendon Press).
Ego, Beate, Lange, Armin, Lichtenberger, Hermann, and De Troyer, Kristin
    2004 *Biblia Qumranica*, vol. 3: *Minor Prophets* (BQ, 3; Leiden: Brill).
Flint, Peter W.
    2000 'Biblical Scrolls from Nahal Hever and "Wadi Seiyal". 1b. 5/6HevPsalms', in James C. VanderKam and Monica Brady (consulting eds.), *Miscellaneous Texts from the Judaean Desert* (DJD, 38; Oxford: Clarendon Press): 141–66 + plates xxv–xxvii.
Flint, Peter W., et al.
    forthcoming (a) *The Great Psalms Scroll from Cave 11 (11QPs^a)* (Dead Sea Scrolls Discoveries series; Leiden: Brill).
    forthcoming (b) *Biblia Qumranica: The Psalms* (BQ series; Leiden: Brill).

Martínez, F. García, Tigchelaar, Eibert J. C., and van der Woude, A. S.
   1998 '11QPs^a, Fragments E, F, 11QPs^b, 11QPs^c, and 11QPs^e ?', in F. García
         Martínez, Eibert J. C. Tigchelaar and A. S. van der Woude, *Qumran Cave 11,
         vol. 2: 11Q2–11Q18, 11Q20–11Q30* (DJD, 23; Oxford: Clarendon Press),
         29–78 + plates iii–viii.
Pietersma, Albert, and Wright, Benjamin G. (eds.)
   2009 (updated edition) *The New English Translation of the Septuagint* [= NETS]
         (New York: Oxford University Press).
Sanders, James A.
   1965 *The Psalms Scroll of Qumrân Cave 11 [11QPs^a]* (DJD, 4; Oxford: Clarendon
         Press).
   1967 *The Dead Sea Psalms Scroll* (Ithaca, NY: Cornell University Press).
Skehan, Patrick W., Ulrich, Eugene, and Flint, Peter W.
   2000 'Psalms', in E. Ulrich et al., *Qumran Cave 4 vol. 11. Psalms to Chronicles* (DJD
         16; Oxford: Clarendon Press): 7–160, 163–68 + plates i–xx.
   2010 'Psalms: Fragments' in Eugene Ulrich (ed.), *The Biblical Qumran Scrolls:
         Transcriptions and Textual Variants* (VTSup, 134; Leiden: Brill), 627–93.
Talmon, Shemaryahu
   1999 'Hebrew Fragments from Masada: 1 (f) MasPs^a and (g) MasPs$^{b'}$', in
         Shemaryahu Talmon and Yigael Yadin, *Masada VI: The Yigael Yadin
         Excavations 1963–1965; Final Reports* (Jerusalem: Israel Exploration Society
         and the Hebrew University of Jerusalem): 76–97 + two plates.
Yadin, Yigael
   1966 'Another Fragment (E) of the Psalms Scroll from Qumran Cave 11
         (11QPs^a)', *Textus* 5: 1–10 + plates i–v.

The Oxford Hebrew Bible Project

Hendel, Ronald A.
   2008 'The Oxford Hebrew Bible: Prologue to a New Critical Edition', *VT* 58:
         324–51.
   forthcoming   'Reflections on a New Edition of the Hebrew Bible: A Reply to
         H. G. M. Williamson'.
Crawford, Sidnie W., Joosten, Jan, and Ulrich, Eugene
   2008 'Sample Editions of the Oxford Hebrew Bible: Deuteronomy 32:1–9, 1 Kings
         11:1–8, and Jeremiah 27:1–10 (34 G)', *VT* 58: 352–66.
Fox, Michael V.
   2006 'Editing Proverbs: The Challenge of the Oxford Hebrew Bible', *Journal of
         Northwest Semitic Languages* 32: 1–22.
Van Rooy, H. F.
   2004 'A New Critical Edition of the Hebrew Bible', *Journal of Northwest Semitic
         Languages* 30: 139–50.
Williamson, Hugh G. M.
   2009 'Do We Need a New Bible? Reflections on the Proposed Oxford Hebrew
         Bible', *Biblica* 90: 153–75.

Other Works (Most Cited)

Dahmen, Ulrich

    2003 *Psalmen- und Psalter-Rezeption im Frühjudentum. Rekonstruktion, Textbestand, Struktur und Pragmatik der Psalmenrolle 11QPs^a^ aus Qumran* (STDJ, 49; Leiden: Brill).

Flint, Peter W.

    1997 *The Dead Sea Psalms Scrolls and the Book of Psalms* (STDJ, 17; Leiden: Brill).

    2006 'Psalms and Psalters in the Dead Sea Scrolls', in James H. Charlesworth (ed.), *The Bible and the Dead Sea Scrolls*, vol. 1: *Scripture and the Scrolls* (Waco, TX: Baylor University Press): 233–72.

    2007 '11QPs^b^ and the11QPs^a^–Psalter', in Joel S. Burnett, William H. Bellinger, Jr., and W. Dennis Tucker (eds.), *Diachronic and Synchronic: Proceedings of the Baylor Symposium on the Book of Psalms, May 18–20, 2006* (London: T. & T. Clark): 157–66.

Sanders, James A.

    1966 'Variorum in the Psalms Scroll (11QPs^a^)', *HTR* 59: 83–94.

    1968 'Cave 11 Surprises and the Question of Canon', *McCQ* 21, 1–15. Reprinted in David N. Freedman and Jonas C. Greenfield (eds.), *New Directions in Biblical Archaeology* (Garden City, NY: Doubleday, 1969): 101–16; and in Shnayer Z. Leiman (ed.), *The Canon and Masorah of the Hebrew Bible: An Introductory Reader* (New York: KTAV, 1974): 37–51.

    1974 'The Qumran Psalms Scroll (11QPsa) Reviewed', in Matthew Black and William A. Smalley (eds.), *On Language, Culture, and Religion: In Honor of Eugene A. Nida* (The Hague: Mouton), 79–99.

Skehan, Patrick W.

    1978 'Qumran and Old Testament Criticism', in M. Delcor (ed.), *Qumrân. Sa piété, sa théologie et son milieu* (BETL, 46; Paris: Éditions Duculot; Leuven: Leuven University Press): 163–82.

Talmon, Shemaryahu

    1966 'Pisqah Be'emsaʿ Pasuq and 11QPs^a^', *Textus* 5: 11–21.

Tov, Emanuel

    1996 'Special Layout of Poetical Units in the Texts from the Judean Desert,' in J. Dyk (ed.), *Give Ear to My Words: Psalms and Other Poetry in and around the Hebrew Bible. Essays in Honour of Professor N. A. van Uchelen* (Amsterdam: Societas Hebraica Amstelodamensis): 105–28.

    2012 *Textual Criticism of the Hebrew Bible* (Minneapolis: Fortress, 3rd edn, rev. and expanded).

Ulrich, Eugene

    1999a 'The Bible in the Making: The Scriptures at Qumran', in Ulrich, *The Dead Sea Scrolls and the Origins of the Bible* (Studies in the Dead Sea Scrolls and Related Literature; Grand Rapids: Eerdmans; Leiden: Brill): 17–33.

    1999b 'Multiple Literary Editions: Reflections toward a Theory of the History of the Biblical Text', in Ulrich, *The Dead Sea Scrolls and the Origins of the Bible* (Studies in the Dead Sea Scrolls and Related Literature; Grand Rapids: Eerdmans; Leiden: Brill): 99–120.

    forthcoming 'The Old Testament Text and Its Transmission', in *The New Cambridge History of the Bible* (Cambridge: Cambridge University Press).

Wilson, Gerald H.

    1983 'The Qumran Psalms Manuscripts and the Consecutive Arrangement of Psalms in the Hebrew Psalter', *CBQ* 45: 377–88.

    1985a 'The Qumran Psalms Scroll Reconsidered: Analysis of the Debate,' *CBQ* 47: 624–42.

    1985b *The Editing of the Hebrew Psalter* (SBLDS, 76; Chico, CA: Scholars Press).

2

Reflections on the Canon and the Text of the Bible in Response to Peter Flint

Geza Vermes

To place this brilliant reconstruction of the text of the Psalms into a broader context, I would like to offer my own reflections on the contribution of the Dead Sea Scrolls to biblical studies. The outline will focus on two major topics: the canon and the text of the Scriptures.

1. The Biblical Canon

What constitutes the Bible is nowhere strictly defined in ancient Judaism. It was the privilege of the successive religious authorities to determine the list of books. Traditionally the canon is divided into two or three sections. We encounter in several of our sources the twofold designation referring to Scripture as the Law and the Prophets, but at the end the rabbis settled for the threefold *TaNaK*. About the end of the second century BCE, the grandson of Jesus ben Sira, translating into Greek his grandfather's work, speaks in his Prologue of 'the Law, the Prophets, and *the other books*', while Jesus is quoted in Luke as alluding to 'the Law, the Prophets, and the Psalms' (Lk. 24.44). One of the Dead Sea Scrolls, *Miqsat Ma'Aseh Ha-Torah*, also attests to 'the Law and the Prophets and David' (4QMMT lines 10–11). However, none of the surviving Qumran documents defines the content of the canon. Owing to this absence of a list and to the fact that even in the early second century CE questions were raised in rabbinic circles about the canonicity of the Song of Solomon and Ecclesiastes, more than one Qumran scholar maintain that no proper canon of the Old Testament existed until some time after the destruction of the Temple in 70 CE.

Such academic scepticism fails to pay sufficient attention to a statement of Josephus, who expressly declared that among the Jews only *twenty-two* books enjoyed confidence (*Against Apion* 1.8). Without citing individual titles, Josephus lists the five books of Moses, thirteen books of the Prophets, and four books of hymns and wisdom. According to St Jerome the figure of twenty-two was commonly accepted by Jews as representing the number of books in the biblical canon. So it can be assumed that the traditional Palestinian Hebrew canon of the Bible was already in existence in the first century CE, or maybe even in the first century BCE. There are Scrolls experts, for instance the compilers of *The Dead Sea Scrolls Bible* (Martin Abegg, Peter Flint, and Eugene Ulrich), who presume that at Qumran the Scriptures included works considered non-canonical in mainstream Judaism. They suggest that Ecclesiasticus and Tobit, from among the Apocrypha, and the Books of Jubilees and Enoch, from the Pseudepigrapha, as well as some apocryphal psalms included in the Psalms scroll from Cave 11, had attained canonical status among the Qumran people. The hypothesis is not unthinkable, but it is in no way compelling either. After all, the Letter of Jude quotes Enoch without necessarily implying that for universal Christianity the Book of Enoch counted as Holy Scripture (Jude 14–16).

2. The Biblical Text

The chief characteristic of the Masoretic Bible was textual uniformity. The strictly controlled medieval manuscripts displayed practically no meaningful variants. The Dead Sea scriptural scrolls present a more heterogeneous picture. The largest group is classified as proto-Masoretic. Another group attests the peculiar orthography and grammar of the Qumran scribes. There is a smaller group reminiscent of the Samaritan Bible and the Septuagint. Finally, a fair number of manuscripts are classified as non-aligned because they sometimes agree with the Masoretic text, sometimes with the Samaritan Torah or the Septuagint, and on other occasions depart from all of them. The distinctive mark of the biblical texts found at Qumran is their elasticity. Before the establishment of the authoritative wording of the Hebrew Scriptures, as a result of the Pharisaic-rabbinic effort to reorganize Judaism after the catastrophe of 70 CE, textual pluriformity reigned. The choice of the text and its interpretation were left in the hands of the representatives of doctrinal authority. We even have evidence that Qumran Bible commentators were aware of the existence of variants and were ready to employ them in their exposition of a biblical passage.

The causes of the textual elasticity of the Qumran Bible are manifold. On a superficial level they may be due to efforts of modernization of spelling and grammar, to search for stylistic variation and harmonization, but above all to 'insufficiently controlled copying'. Put positively, the Qumran scribes arrogated to themselves the right to creative freedom. Such relative liberty could go hand in hand with the conviction that all they were doing was to transmit faithfully the *true meaning* of Scripture. Flavius Josephus maintains that he reproduces the details of the biblical record without adding anything to it, or removing from it, when in fact he does the exact opposite. Allowing us to perceive the situation that preceded the enforced unification of the biblical text is one of the chief innovations of the Dead Sea Scrolls. Put bluntly, they have sounded the death knell of the myth of the biblical *Urtext*.

When in pre-Qumran, almost prehistoric, times I was first initiated in the textual study of the Hebrew Bible, the aim of the textual critic was to approximate as closely as possible, with the help of the Hebrew manuscripts and ancient translations, as well as scholarly ingenuity, the actual text of the original author of the Bible, which was implicitly believed by those who believed in such matters to be the inspired, if not the divinely dictated, word of God. Some among us, continuing in the footsteps of eighteenth- and nineteenth-century textual critics, will go on to build a *critical* text, which others reckon as artificial or invented. Others prefer to stick with diplomatic editions of the Bible. For others still, commentary should provide the framework for the establishment of the biblical text. We are living in a fluctuating and somewhat confused world.

St Jerome in his time considered the Hebrew text, *Hebraica veritas*, as his ultimate criterion of truth. He played on an easy pitch as none of his western contemporaries knew Hebrew. Today, however, Qumran has demonstrated that there is no single Hebrew truth, but multifarious *Hebraicae veritates*. Such a multiplicity echoes one's own experience.

When I first dealt with this issue in my Sacks Lecture, *The Dead Sea Scrolls Forty Years on* in Yarnton in 1987 (published by Oxford University Press in the same year), I noted that the text of my lecture was preceded by six earlier printouts. Each differed in some way from the rest, yet each was authentic, each was an *Urtext*, meant to be final. Usually the last version is taken as the ultimate truth. But sometimes an author changes his mind. I am told that after publishing *Ulysses* James Joyce revised it in a second edition, but in the third he reverted to the original wording. Now that is something for you to think about.

3

Medieval Answers to Modern Questions: Medieval Jewish Interpreters of Psalms

Adele Berlin

MODERATOR Welcome to 'Meet the Interpreters'.[1] Our guests today are four of the most famous medieval Jewish commentators on Psalms: Saadia, Rashi, Ibn Ezra, and David Qimhi. They lived from the ninth to the thirteenth centuries, and all four are practitioners of *peshat* interpretation, which flowered during that time. But before they introduce themselves, here's some background about medieval Jewish Bible interpretation.[2]

Medieval Jewish commentaries are heir to the rabbinic tradition of midrashic interpretation, but they employ primarily the newer, less homiletic or imaginative approach, designated by the term *peshat*, that is, contextual interpretations with a focus on linguistic analysis and rational thought. The balance between *peshat* and midrashic interpretation was negotiated differently by each of our exegetes. Moreover, even *peshat* exegesis was practised differently from one exegete to another, and therefore did not necessarily produce the same interpretation in every case. Additionally, the medieval exegetes were sensitive to their own social and religious contexts. Commentary-writing was not merely an intellectual pursuit; it had social and religious implications.

In France and Germany (Ashkenaz), the context was a Christian one, and a noticeable anti-Christian polemical edge, arguing against Christological interpretations of the Bible, is present in some Jewish Bible commentary. The book of Psalms, well-known to the medieval populace through its liturgical use in both Judaism and Christianity, and long a favourite locus of Christological interpretation, became an obvious site for

---

[1] The paper was originally presented with Professor Berlin as the interviewer with a panel of four Jewish interpreters. Here they are distinguished one from the other by different type faces.

[2] For an excellent and compact overview of Jewish biblical interpretation from the eighth to eighteenth centuries see Walfish 2004. See also Greenberg 1995; Greenstein 1984. For a recent discussion of some late medieval and early modern Jewish commentaries on psalms, see Cooper 2006.

medieval Jewish polemical interpretation. It exists, overtly or more subtly, most noticeably in the commentaries of Rashi and David Qimhi. Even in the Islamic East, Christian interpretation was known and argued against, if to a lesser degree; Saadia is one example.[3] Polemics directed against Islam were rarer and more muted, for Islam did not purvey an 'Islamological' interpretation of the Hebrew Bible in quite the same way that Christians did a Christological one (because the Hebrew Bible did not have the same status in Islam as in Christianity), although Muslims accused the Jews of falsifying their own Bible or failing to understand it correctly.[4] In Islamic lands, the study of Arabic language, poetry, and philosophy, and the methods for Quranic interpretation, influenced Jewish writers, who moulded them into useful tools for studying the Bible. Some of the Islamic attitudes also crept into the interpretation of the Bible, creating a gentler polemic, namely, that the Bible and its language were no less perfect than the Quran and its language. More vociferous Jewish polemics, especially in the tenth to twelfth centuries, are between Rabbanite Jews (followers of the rabbinic tradition of religious practice and biblical interpretation) and Karaite Jews (who rejected the rabbinic interpretative tradition and developed their own).

Some commonalities among the medieval exegetes distinguish them from modern scholars. The medievals hold traditional assumptions about the Davidic authorship of the book of Psalms and about the book's divine inspiration, and they operate within a traditional Jewish interpretative framework. Most significantly, they do not question the factuality of the text, as a modern interpreter is wont to do, although they do not take every word literally. While the *peshat* approach is closer to modern scholarship than *midrash* is, the medievals did not all limit their quest to the 'original meaning', the meaning for the first audience, as modern historical critics do. Although the medievals did have a sense of history, and asked what the psalms meant to David or to their other authors, many of them also understood prophetic and psalmic references to suffering and exile as referring to their own time, what they call 'the present exile' that began with the destruction of the Second Temple. And the messianic hopes expressed in some psalms were equated with the commentators' own hopes for the future, not merely taken as Persian-period hopes for the restoration of the Davidic monarchy. Thus, the medievals operated as both academic and confessional interpreters, blurring the distinction between what the

---

[3] See Schlossberg 2000.

[4] Ibn Ezra cites a tradition, apparently genuine, that Saadia made a translation of the Torah into Arabic characters (in addition to his Judaeo-Arabic version) that was directed to Muslims. Ibn Ezra wrongly deduced a polemical reason for the Arabic version, namely, that the Muslims would not think that there were words in the Torah unknown to the Jews (Blau 2001: 3–4). Brody (2000: 85) notes a veiled polemic against Islam in Saadia's commentary on Genesis 22.

Adele Berlin

text meant to an ancient Israelite and what it meant to their own generation.[5]

On the other hand, like modern approaches, a hallmark of medieval *peshat* is its application of reason and logic, and of the best available science and knowledge, especially linguistic knowledge, to arrive at interpretations (although, to be sure, the logic sometimes differed from ours, as did the science). The medievals share with modern scholars a sense of critical inquiry into the text and intellectual engagement with the interpretations of their predecessors and contemporaries. They pose a number of the same questions that we ask today regarding the Book of Psalms: who wrote the psalms, when were they written, is there a logic to the ordering of the psalms in the book, what genres does the book contain, and what are the best methods to interpret the psalms.

But now, let's meet our guests. We begin with the most senior, Saadia. Please tell us something about yourself and your approach to the book of Psalms.[6]

SAADIA   My name is Saadia ben Joseph al-Fayyumi, better known as Saadia Gaon (Hebrew acronym: רס״ג). I lived from 882 to 942, so I am now well over a thousand years old.[7] Born in Fayyum, in Egypt, I became the head of the academy (the 'Gaon') of Sura, the leading Babylonian Talmudic academy of my time. With all due modesty I will tell you that I had quite a high reputation, as a philosopher, a Bible translator and exegete, and a linguist. I am considered the most prominent exegete of my time, whose influence continued for many generations. I am proud to have been a leading spokesman for Rabbanite Judaism, especially as practised in Babylonia, and I did not hesitate to polemicize against the Karaites, and also against other heretics, even certain deviant Rabbanites.[8]

My greatest contribution to biblical studies is my *Tafsir*, the Judaeo-Arabic translation of the Bible. The translation is accompanied by a short commentary explaining the translation and highlighting important issues. As you modern biblical scholars know, it is mighty hard to restrain yourself from explaining why you translated something as you did. I like first to clarify points of vocalization and accentuation in the MT, grammatical forms, and lexical meanings.[9]

[5] See Cohen 2000: 412–13.

[6] The information in this essay is gleaned from the introductions and commentaries of the exegetes, as well as from the studies listed in the Bibliography. Introductions to Jewish biblical commentaries as a genre are discussed by Lawee (2003).

[7] On Saadia see Brody 2000; Simon 1991; and Ben-Shammai 2000, 2003a, 2003b.

[8] Brody 2000: 85. Saadia also polemicized against heretics who denied the authority of the Bible and against opposing Rabbanites, but he is best known for his anti-Karaite polemics.

[9] The comment at Psalm 1 itself is a shortened and poorer version of the material in Saadia's introduction.

Then I explain the meaning of specific verses, drawing on philology, philosophy, rabbinic sources, and current scientific knowledge.

I mostly aim to present the plain meaning of words, that is, the referential sense, or the commonly accepted apparent meaning, called in Arabic *zahir*.[10] (I did not use the term *peshat* to characterize my philological-contextual method.) However, there are situations when this 'literal' approach is not the best, and non-literal modes of interpretation are preferable. Those situations include: if sensory perception contradicts the plain meaning; if reason or intellect contradicts the plain meaning; if another biblical verse contradicts the plain meaning of the one in question; and if the plain meaning contradicts established rabbinic tradition.[11] For instance, for reasons that will become clear later, in my work on Psalms I never take literally anything that would cast aspersions on David.[12]

MODERATOR   Thank you, Saadia. We look forward to learning more about your work later, but let's now meet our next guest, Rashi.

RASHI   Hello, I'm Rashi. Actually, my name is Rabbi Solomon ben Isaac, but everyone calls me by my acronym, even in English. I lived from 1040 to 1105, mostly in northern France, so I am younger than Saadia by over a century, and quite removed from him geographically.[13] Now, while I did not have the prestigious position and title that Saadia had, I, too, was an eminent exegete, some say the most famous, widely read, and influential Jewish exegete of all, by virtue of my commentaries on the entire Bible and much of the Talmud. My Bible commentary was the first Hebrew printed book. I am considered the 'father' of *peshat* exegesis in northern France.[14] Like Saadia, whose *Tafsir* I probably didn't know

---

[10]   *Zahir* is a difficult term to translate. It refers to the literal or apparent meaning (and is not as fraught with difficulty as the term *peshat*). Ben-Shammai calls it 'the external meaning' (see his discussion in 2003b: 36–43).

[11]   Saadia's theory of interpretation is explained in his introduction to the Torah and in his *Book of Beliefs and Opinions*. See Brody (2000: 80), for a translation of the crucial excerpt; Ben-Shammai 2003b; Goodman 1990; Cohen 2003: 40–1. As Cohen notes, there is a discrepancy as to whether Saadia listed 'sensory perception' and 'reason' as one item or two. In any case the items listed are the sources of human knowledge and in Saadia's view there should be no contradiction among them.

[12]   Simon 1991: 28.   [13]   On Rashi see Grossman 2000: 334–45; Gruber, 2004: 1–164.

[14]   Although, to be sure, Rashi had a few less well-known predecessors. And his grandson and disciple Rashbam (Samuel ben Meir) was an even purer *pashtan* than Rashi. There has been considerable speculation on how and why *peshat* exegesis reached northern France (see Cohen 2008). Some scholars think it was a natural occurrence, a method whose time had come. Others have suggested that the literal exegesis practised by Christians, especially in the school of St Victor, in the same geographic area as Rashi, provided the impetus. Still others see it as a borrowing from Spanish-Jewish interpretation. Another possibility is that the *peshat* developed as an antidote to Christian allegorical interpretation, a way to undermine the Christian polemics against the Jews. Whether or not this last was the origin of *peshat* in France, it certainly was useful in Rashi's anti-Christian polemics.

Adele Berlin

because it was written in Arabic, I attached considerable importance to explaining linguistic and grammatical questions. For the meaning of words I drew on the Jewish linguists of tenth-century Spain, Menahem ibn Saruq, and Dunash ibn Labrat, who wrote in Hebrew. Unfortunately, I could not draw on the Arabic works of later and more accomplished Jewish linguists like Ibn Hayyuj and Ibn Janah. The *Targum* also served as a major source for my lexicography, as did Mishnaic Hebrew. To make sure that my audience understood my lexical interpretations, I often translated difficult terms into our vernacular, Old French. I liked to explain the realia of the Bible—geographic locations, historical background, everyday activities. I even drew maps and diagrams, but most of them were omitted in the printed editions of my commentaries.

MODERATOR   Very good, Rashi. Now let's hear from Abraham Ibn Ezra.

IBN EZRA   I'm Abraham Ibn Ezra (Hebrew acronym ראב"ע).[15] I lived from 1089 to 1164, which makes me a later contemporary of Rashi. I had an advantage over Rashi in that I knew Arabic and was familiar with the Jewish exegetical tradition that had blossomed in Muslim lands. I was born in Tudela, in Muslim Spain, but I found myself wandering, not by choice, through Italy, France, and England. Like Saadia, I had broad interests and was known as a poet, grammarian, translator, mathematician, astronomer, philosopher, and exegete. My biblical commentaries were not written until after I had left Spain in 1140 but they reflect the culmination of the Spanish-Jewish school of exegesis, with its emphasis on linguistic analysis and logical reasoning. I wrote commentaries on many biblical books, sometimes two on the same book, as I was constantly rewriting them.

Ever since Baruch Spinoza cited me in his *A Theologico-Political Treatise* (chapter 8), some centuries after my death, I have had the reputation as a radical or heterodox innovator. Now it's true that I *did* question the Mosaic authorship of parts of the Torah, and I also identified the author of Isaiah 40–66 as a prophet of the Babylonian exile. And it's also true that my tone is at times polemical and my criticisms of other exegetes might sound caustic (sorry for criticizing you, Rashi). But Uriel Simon makes a strong case that I, a man of strong religious sentiments, was actually an exegetical moderate and a judicious synthesizer of previous opinions, and that I was seeking to balance the diverse interpretations that preceded me.[16] When the meaning of a verse is equivocal and I cannot decide between alternatives, I present multiple interpretations. On occasion I even admit that the explanation of a verse eluded me.

---

[15] On Ibn Ezra see Simon (2000, 1992) (there is considerable overlap in these two essays); Sarna 1993. For more detail, see Simon 1991; Mordechai Cohen 2003.

[16] Simon 2000: 386–7; 1992: 135–6.

Like others among us, I offer explanations of philological and grammatical matters and I use rational judgement and scientific knowledge. I insist that biblical language should be analysed like any human language. It uses stylistic and rhetorical forms like repetition, parallelism, and ellipsis, that add no new meaning to the content; in this respect I differ from our ancient rabbis, who found new meaning in every synonym or repetition. Like Saadia, I try to avoid any contradiction between the meaning of a verse, sensory experience and logical reasoning, other verses in the Bible, and rabbinic halakhic conclusions. When confronted with such a contradiction, I employ figurative or other non-literal forms of interpretation. But one must not overuse this technique.

MODERATOR   Thank you Ibn Ezra. Now to our last guest, David Qimhi.

QIMHI   I am David Qimhi, also known as RaDaQ, of the famous Qimhi family of scholars and translators from Andalusia (Islamic Spain). I, however, was born in the Christian city of Narbonne, in Provence, around 1160, and I died in 1235.[17] A grammarian, exegete, and Talmud teacher, I was heir to the Spanish tradition of *peshat* interpretation, exemplified by Ibn Ezra. This mode of interpretation was conveyed to me by my father, Joseph, and after his death by my brother, Moses, both *peshat* exegetes in their own right. But I was also comfortable with the midrashic modes of interpretation that were prevalent in France, for which Rashi was my model.[18] While I am primarily a practitioner of *peshat* interpretation, I make extensive use of midrashic interpretation, as you will hear later.

Compared with our three other guests, whose commentaries tend to be terse, mine are expansive. I like to fill out the picture with illustrations from real life. I often paraphrase the text and intertwine it with my interpretation, so the explanations become less disjointed than those of other exegetes.

Let me also mention that I was concerned with the accurate transmission of the Masoretic Text and I noted discrepancies in comparing the biblical manuscripts available to me, the translations of the *Targums,* and the citations in rabbinic literature. In this I differ from my esteemed colleague Ibn Ezra, who did not engage in textual criticism.[19]

MODERATOR   Thank you, Rabbi Qimhi. Now that we have learned something about our guests, let's hear their answers to some specific questions about Psalms.

---

[17] On Qimhi see Mordechai Cohen 2000; 2003: 137–75, 272–322; and Perez 1995/2000.
[18] See Grunhaus 2003.
[19] See Cohen 2000: 408.

Question 1: You all favour the *peshat* method of interpretation, but are well-versed in rabbinic *midrash*. How do you deal with *midrash* in your commentaries? Do you incorporate it or avoid it?

SAADIA We all agree that rabbinic *aggadot* are authoritative but not binding, so we are free to pick and choose from them. They are, after all, not halakhic decisions. For me, it is not a question of whether or not to use *midrash*, but of getting at the best meaning, the meaning that lets me see the Bible as a coherent whole, and in harmony with rabbinic tradition and with current scientific knowledge. While I concentrate on the 'apparent meaning' (*zahir*) of the words, I frequently include midrashic material in my comments, more than some of the other Geonim did.[20] Invoking rabbinic sources helps to strengthen the rabbinic tradition among my readers; this is both an educational goal and part of my anti-Karaite programme.[21]

RASHI Despite my oft-quoted comment on Gen. 3.8, where I state that my goal is to present the *peshat* and that I include the *midrash* only when it supports my *peshat*, in practice I do not always stick to this rule. Sometimes I include a *midrash* that is far from the *peshat*, and on occasion my only comment is a midrashic one. My combination of *peshat* with the more homiletic *derash*, delivered clearly and concisely, made for a pleasing combination that appealed to generations of Jewish readers. My commentary was even known to some later Christians, who thought of it as the Jewish counterpart of the Glossa Ordinaria.[22]

However, while I am generally favourably disposed to the *midrash*, at least as a supplement to the *peshat*, let me give one example where I step back from it, because it may potentially mislead my readers. As you know, many of our commentaries contain polemics. In my commentary on Psalms, written after the First Crusade in 1096, when many Jews of Europe had been slaughtered, more than half the chapters contain anti-Christian polemics, mostly by allusion but occasionally by explicit mention. Typical is the identification of the unnamed enemies in Psalms with Esau, Edom, or Rome, all code-words for Christianity (e.g. Ps. 10.18; 39.9). An explicit polemic is my comment on Psalm 2, the psalm that talks about the nations assembling or conspiring against the Lord and his anointed (*meshiho*), and contains the phrase 'You are my son; today I have begotten you.' The Christians claim that this psalm refers to you-

---

[20] Brody 2000: 87.   [21] On Saadia's use of rabbinic material see Ben-Shammai 2000.

[22] Gruber 2004: 54–5. Gruber suggests that, just as the Glossa Ordinaria was a compilation based on the Church Fathers, so Rashi's commentaries were a compilation of rabbinic sources. He goes on to suggest, rather anachronistically (since the Glossa post-dates Rashi), that Rashi 'deliberately intended that his commentary would be the definitive Jewish counterpart to the Christian Glossa Ordinaria'.

know-who. This is nonsense and demoralizing for my community to hear, so I explain the correct meaning as follows:

> Our rabbis interpreted the subject of the chapter as a reference to the King Messiah (מלך המשיח, who will come after the war of Gog and Magog; *BT Berakhot* 7b). However, according to its basic meaning (משמעו) and for a refutation of the Christians (מינים) it is correct to interpret it as a reference to (David) himself in accord with what is stated in Scripture: 'When the Philistines heard that Israel had anointed (משחו; the same word as 'messiah') David as king over them' (2 Sam. 5.17), 'The Philistines gathered their troops' (1 Sam. 28.4), and they fell into his (David's) hands. It is about them (the Philistines in the cited verses) that he (David) asked here (in Ps. 2.1), 'Why do the nations assemble so that all of them are gathered together?'[23]

Now when our rabbis interpreted this psalm as referring to the messiah, they were speaking of the Davidic messiah yet to come in the eschatological age, but, lest my readers confuse the rabbinic interpretation with the Christological one, it is best to steer them away from any talk of a messiah.[24]

IBN EZRA   I generally distance myself from *midrash*, citing it much less often than Rashi and David Qimhi. Some of my comments are implicit arguments against the *midrash*, which tends to over-interpret literary and stylistic features. And I am also not so enamoured of its imaginative filling in of gaps. For the most part, I limited myself to the *peshat*, expressed tersely and directly, although occasionally I included philosophical comments.

By the way, Rashi, I agree that Psalm 2 is speaking of David. It was composed by one of the singers when David was anointed. This interpretation appeals to me because I make a point of dating the composition of all the psalms to the time of David. But I do not omit the idea that it may also refer to the (eschatological) messiah. Coming from the Andalusian school, I do not share your urgency for anti-Christian polemical interpretations.

QIMHI   Even though I am essentially a *peshat* exegete, I cite even more *midrashim* than Rashi does, generally in a separate comment following the *peshat*. At times I use them to support my *peshat* explanation; at other times I reject them; and at still other times I present them

---

[23] The translation is adapted from Gruber 2004: 177–80.

[24] Signer notes that 'King Messiah' is a neologism by Rashi and not used by the rabbis in this context. Rashi thereby emphasizes that the psalm is about David the anointed one. In his comments on v. 7, Rashi emphasizes the connections with Samuel and Kings, again emphasizing that the subject is David himself. But in v. 10, Rashi ties his own interpretation with the eschatological one held by the rabbis. Mordechai Cohen informs me that Maimonides used the term 'King Messiah' although he does not seem to have known of Rashi's use.

without comment, as if to say that both interpretations are sound. By setting *peshat* and *derash* alongside each other, I implicitly show the difference in their interpretative approaches. I also may have included some homiletical comments to please those in my French-Jewish audience who were 'lovers of *derash*' (as I put it in my introduction to the Former Prophets). Yet many *midrashim* contain valuable explanations and I wanted to draw on their literary and religious sensitivity. As a result, my commentary is much less cut and dried than Ibn Ezra's, which hones in on the *peshat* to the exclusion of the *midrash*. I balance linguistic analysis and historical thinking with respect for the rabbinic tradition and with midrashic attention to nuance and religious inspiration.[25] You can see this effort towards balance in my introduction to my commentary on Psalms, which opens and closes with rabbinic citations but which presents my rational explanation of the authorship of psalms and the terminology in the superscriptions, and matters relating to the genre and dating of the psalms. So, one may say that I am trying to bridge the *peshat* and *derash* methods of interpretation in a more integrated way than Rashi did, avoiding the extremes of both and bringing to the fore their most positive attributes. On occasion I may even create a new midrashic explanation.[26]

MODERATOR   Our next question is: who wrote the book of Psalms?

Question 2: All of you, to one degree or another, hold the traditional view that David wrote the book. But was he the only author? What about the men mentioned in the superscriptions? Did they write some of the psalms? And by the way, what do the superscriptions mean?

RASHI   That's easy. As the rabbis said, the book is composed of ten poetic genres, based on the terms in the superscriptions (leading, instrumental music, psalm, song, praise, prayer, blessing, thanksgiving, laudations, Hallelujah), and these ten genres correspond to the ten authors of the psalms: Adam, Melchizedek, Abraham, Moses, David, Solomon, Asaph, and the three sons of Korah.[27]

---

[25] So Mordechai Cohen, who makes a strong case that Qimhi was more innovative than he is usually given credit for. See n. 17 above.

[26] See Cohen 2000: 403.

[27] Gruber 2004: 165–69. Rashi adds that there is some disagreement about Jeduthun, another name that appears in psalm superscriptions. The formulaic number ten is obviously driving the rabbinic lists so that the terms for the genres and the names of the authors must somehow be made to add up to ten. The list of genres is based on *Midrash Tehillim* at Ps. 1 #6 (Braude 1959: II, 399 n. 27). The list of authors is also taken from *Midrash Tehillim* and differs slightly from the list in *b. Baba Batra* 14b. In rabbinic tradition, Ethan is Abraham.

Midrash Tehillim at Ps. 1 #6 also struggles with the question of authorship, balancing the idea

SAADIA Hold it there, Rashi. I have a rather different opinion on this question, as I explained at length in my first introduction to Psalms.[28] The entire book was revealed by God to David, who was a prophet. All the psalms were written by David, notwithstanding the super-scriptions naming other individuals. On that point I differ from our rabbis (as in *Baba Batra* 15a and elsewhere). The names in the super-scriptions belong to musicians or singers who performed the psalms, but they did not compose them.

Psalms is the book that the Levites recited in the Temple, and so I devoted considerable discussion to biblical music and musical instruments and to the Temple sacrifices and precincts. As for the ordering of the psalms within the book, it is not a chronological sequence in the life of David, but rather a ritual or liturgical ordering: perhaps it was the influence of the Temple precincts where the psalms were recited, or the liturgical occasion on which they were recited, or the Levitical family that recited them.

Moreover, and this may sound bizarre, the psalms were all the words of God directed to humans; they are divine instructions about how people should act, rather than human prayers directed to God. The ritual use of the psalms was limited to the Temple; that is the reason I discuss the Temple and its music as such length. The psalms are not prayers to be used today; their use nowadays is for didactic instruction.

My opinion on the nature of the book of Psalms is not merely an academic exercise but an important weapon in my battle against the Karaites.[29] The Karaites looked upon the book of Psalms as their one and only corpus of prayers, given to Israel as prayers for all time. They rejected the prayers that the rabbis had instituted, considering them valueless and lacking authority. By claiming that the psalms are not prayers, I undermine the Karaite position that the book is Israel's prayer book. Moreover, not only have the Karaites misunderstood the nature of psalms, but their use of them as prayers is counter to how God intended them to be used. To use the psalms liturgically outside

---

of Davidic authorship of the whole with the names of other individuals in the superscriptions. 'Though certain psalms bear the name of one of the ten authors, the book as a whole bears the name of David, king of Israel. As a parable tells us, there was a company of musicians that sought to sing a hymn to the king. The king said to them: To be sure, all of you are sweet singers, all of you are musicians, all of you have superior skill . . . yet let the hymn, in whose singing all of you will take part, bear the name of only one man among you because his voice is the sweetest of all your voices. . . . The singer who makes the Psalms of Israel sweet is David.'

[28] The text and Hebrew translation is found in Kafih (1966: 17–50). Sokolow translated it with a brief introduction (1984). Simon discusses it extensively (1991: 1–57).

[29] Simon (1991: 1–57) has explicated Saadia's position in detail.

the Temple is a religious transgression. Now, you may object that we Rabbanites also incorporate psalms into our liturgy. But I would distinguish between 'praying' the psalms, as the Karaites do, and 'reading' them, as we do as part of the Rabbanite liturgy. In my view, the Rabbanites do not perform psalms as ritual prayers, as had been done in the Temple.

IBN EZRA Now Saadia, you should know that no one accepts your idiosyncratic view about psalms not being prayers. It is forced and obviously motivated by your anti-Karaite agenda. I say that psalms are indeed prayers. Having been composed by divinely-inspired prophets, the psalms contain both prayer and prophecy, thus constituting a special genre of prophetic prayer.[30]

On the matter of Davidic authorship, I agree with you, with modifications.[31] I think that many of the psalms were composed by the prophet David and some were written by his contemporaries. The men named in the superscriptions are all contemporaries of David, and, unlike you, I credit them with having composed the psalms that bear their names. As for psalms lacking an authorial superscription, they may or may not have been written by David; we just don't know. My point is that all the psalms, whether or not composed by David himself, date from the time of David. On this matter I side with rabbinic tradition, differing from Rabbi Moses Ha-kohen Gikatilla (also spelled Chiqitilah), who opines that some of the psalms were written by poets living much later, at the end of the Judean monarchy or during the Babylonian exile, as in the case of Psalm 137, 'By the rivers of Babylon'. Rather, I insist that David, by virtue of his prophetic power, wrote this psalm as a prediction. He wrote it in the voice of the exiled Levite musicians.

As for the superscriptions, their words are difficult to understand. I explain some of the terms by examining their usage in other biblical passages and their etymologies. Some of the more obscure terms may have been the titles (incipits) of older songs to whose melodies the psalm was to be sung. Such was the practice in medieval liturgical poetry, where a 'superscription' containing the name of a known song was used to indicate that the new poem was to be sung to its tune.[32] An example is Ps. 56.1: עַל־יוֹנַת אֵלֶם רְחֹקִים. I know that Rashi and RaDaQ prefer to interpret this phrase as a term that David used to describe himself, but

---

[30] Kamin 1985: 253.

[31] Ibn Ezra discusses this topic at length in both his introductions to Psalms. The longer 'First Recension' was written in Italy between 1140 and 1143, and the 'Second Recension' was written in Rouen in 1156. Simon translated both recensions (1991: 308–33), and discussed them in detail (1991: 145–295).

[32] My student Michael Lesley informs me that medieval Masses did the same.

I am gratified that the New International Version translates the superscription as I would: 'To the tune of "A Dove on Distant Oaks"'.

QIMHI   I find myself in general agreement with Ibn Ezra, although my
discussion is fuller and more nuanced. Yes, the book was written
under divine inspiration (רוח הקודש), as the rabbis said, but, influenced by Maimonides, I would distinguish divine inspiration from
prophecy, rather than lumping them together, as Ibn Ezra seems to
do. This explains why the book is located in the Writings, not in the
Prophets. Nevertheless, divine inspiration permits a peep into the
future no less than prophecy. So David, writing Psalm 137 under
divine inspiration, could predict not only the Babylonian exile, but
also the destruction of the Second Temple by the Romans. This,
indeed, is the interpretation of 'Remember, O LORD, against the
Edomites' (Ps. 137.7), where 'Edom' refers to Rome.

As for whether David wrote all of the psalms, or whether the men
listed in the superscriptions wrote some of them, I don't see any
contradiction here. I explain as follows:

> David composed this book and he wrote along with his own words the
> words of the aforementioned singers [mentioned in the rabbinic sources
> that Qimhi had quoted]. Even the psalms that he composed himself he
> gave to the singers to sing . . . . And the psalms with the superscription
> לדוד – David composed, and the same for psalms that do not mention
> any author, David composed them [Qimhi is more definite than Ibn Ezra
> on this point]. In addition, there are occurrences of לדוד that mean 'for
> David' like Ps. 20.1 and 110.1 [Ibn Ezra made the same point]. There are
> psalms that were said on the occasion when David or Israel had enemies,
> and there are those that are praise and thanksgiving that do not refer to
> any specific event.
>
> He [David] also wrote in his book a prayer that he found already
> written, that was traditionally ascribed to Moses our Teacher, peace be
> upon him, as it says 'A prayer of Moses the man of God' (Ps. 90.1). He
> [David] also spoke there [in the book of Psalms] about future events after
> his time; he spoke in it about the Babylonian exile and this present exile,
> and of comfort, that the Davidic dynasty would be restored.[33]

MODERATOR   We come to our final question.

Question 3: What is your theory of lexical meaning? Does a word always
have the same meaning, or does it have different meanings in different
contexts? And how do you explain redundant words or phrases? Illustrate
your answers with reference to Ps. 1.2:

---

[33] My translation, based on the text in *Miqra'ot Gedolot Haketer*, לו-לז.

כִּי אִם בְּתוֹרַת ה' חֶפְצוֹ וּבְתוֹרָתוֹ יֶהְגֶּה יוֹמָם וָלָיְלָה (but their delight is in the law of the LORD, and on his law they meditate day and night).

SAADIA   I translated the first occurrence of *torah* by *shari'a* [religious law, the commandments] and the second occurrence by *Torah* [the Pentateuchal text] because the commandments are not 'meditated upon' and are not performed both by 'day and night.'[34] The verse means that the man desires to perform the commandments and that he occupies himself continually with Torah study.

RASHI   Torah is Torah. The word means the same thing in both occurrences. But in the second phrase, 'in his Torah he meditates', the possessive pronoun refers to the man, not to God. At the beginning (of one's study), it is called 'the LORD's Torah' but when a person has exerted himself over it, it is called 'his (the person's) Torah'.[35] As for the word יהגה, every occurrence of the root *h-g-h* means 'in the heart/mind (i.e., silently)'.

IBN EZRA   Rashi, you are adopting the rabbinic interpretation of 'his Torah' (B. *'Avodah Zara* 19a). The rabbis looked for new meaning in repetitions, so, while they think a word always has the same meaning, they want the second line of a parallelism to have a different meaning from the first. But I say that the repetition of 'torah' is elegant language; instead of saying 'on *it* he meditated' the text says 'on *his [God's] Torah* he meditated'. And as for the word יהגה, it can mean either 'in the heart, silently' (as in Ps. 49.4) or 'with the mouth, aloud' (as in Ps. 35.28).

QIMHI   The repetition of the word 'torah' is, as Ibn Ezra said, a case of elegant language, although I also note that the rabbis interpreted the phrase as Rashi mentioned. And I also agree with Rashi that יהגי means 'in the heart'.[36] The reason I think so is that the verse has already referred to study and practice (audible utterance) in the word חפצו and now, by the word יהגה, it is referring to the intention of his heart and mind—his mind is on the Torah day and night.[37]

---

[34] Kafih 1966: 39. As Kafih explains, Saadia means that a single commandment is not performed both during the day and at night.

[35] Gruber 2004: 173. See Cohen 2003: 238–9. Ibn Ezra makes the point that the psalm intentionally used the word *torah* twice, rather than replacing its second occurrence with the pronoun 'it', in order to produce the eloquent effect of the repetition. It is interesting to note that Revised English Bible has done what Ibn Ezra would object to; it renders the phrase 'it is his meditation . . .'. At the other extreme, the New American Bible has 'God's law' for תורתו, thereby resolving the ambiguity of the possessive pronoun that the *midrash* played upon.

[36] Here and elsewhere there is evidence that Qimhi knew Rashi's commentary and quoted from or alluded to it.

[37] Qimhi, who generally recognizes parallelism as a stylistic trope, 'repetition of the idea in different words', here seems to be saying, as he does occasionally, that the second line adds emphasis or clarity (see Cohen 2000: 402). In this instance he seems to come close to the definition of parallelism put forth by James Kugel and Robert Alter—that the two lines of the parallelism are not actually synonymous but that the second line modifies or goes beyond the first in some way.

But let me now turn to what the midrash says about הגה (which Rashi did not mention, perhaps because it contradicts his own interpretation). The *midrash* (Shoher Tov 1.13) offers the meaning 'to occupy himself in study' for הגה, which means 'to utter aloud'. (The meaning I rejected in my *peshat* explanation.) And it takes 'day and night' as 'all day and all night'. So it then asks: How could a person study Torah literally all day and night? When would he do his work to make a living? The *midrash* then decides that wearing *tefillin* (phylacteries), which contain the Shema prayer (composed of passages from the Torah), constitutes studying (Torah) day and night, since the Shema is to be recited in the morning prayers and in the evening prayers. But a better way for the *midrash* to look at it would be as follows. If we take הגה as 'study aloud (with the mouth)', as the *midrash* likes, then 'day and night' can mean any time during the day or night that he has a free moment from his work. In other words, the *midrash* need not take 'day and night' to a literal extreme.[38] This is one example of the way I engage with the *midrash*, improving upon its overly literal explanation even when I think my *peshat* explanation is better.

MODERATOR I see that our interpreters have different lexicological principles: some permit only one meaning per word and others accept multiple meanings. These conflicting principles go back to the earliest Bible translations. The Targum uses two different words for *torah* in Ps. 1.2: נימוסא [cf. Greek *nomos*] for the first and אורייתא (the usual rendering of *torah*) for the second, whereas the Septuagint renders both occurrences of *torah* by the same word, *nomos*.[39] The rabbis, unlike the Targum, tend to assign one meaning only to a word, as we saw from Rashi's comment on *torah*.

Richard Steiner, who has studied the lexicological explanations of Saadia and Rashi, calls Saadia a 'meaning-maximalist', since Saadia believed that a single word could have many meanings, and he often cites long lists of verses to prove this point.[40] Saadia tends to vary the translation of a word to fit its context. By assigning different meanings to the same word, Saadia could reconcile contradictions that might otherwise be perceived between one biblical verse and another, or between the Bible and rabbinic interpretation and/or reason, and it could also be useful in countering Karaite interpretation. Rashi, on the other hand, is a meaning-minimalist who thinks a term has only one core meaning, or at least one primary

---

[38] See Cohen (2000: 400), for another instance where Qimhi criticizes the *midrash* for being too rigid or exaggerated.

[39] Steiner 1998: 249. Steiner remarks that modern translators are constantly beset by the question of whether to vary the translation of a word according to context or to translate it uniformly in all occurrences.

[40] Saadia offers twelve permutations on the meaning of ידוע in Ps. 1.6.

meaning from which secondary meanings derive (the context may shade the meaning). Saadia's approach follows that of the Arab lexicographers of his time, although there was a gradual shift towards meaning-minimalism in the Spanish school at a later period. Ibn Ezra, for example, is often, but not always, a meaning-minimalist. Qimhi was, too.[41] Rashi, from France, seems to follow the principle found in rabbinic interpretation, which assigns just one meaning to a word.[42] So meaning-minimalism dominates among our four interpreters.

To conclude, I want to thank all four of you for giving us a taste of your theories and practice of Psalms interpretation. You confront other issues that interest modern scholars, such as the explanation of metaphors and of anthropomorphisms, but we do not have time for that today. You may take comfort in knowing that modern scholars of the psalms continue to wrestle with the same questions you addressed: the nature of the book, the authors and dates of the psalms, and the best modes of interpretation.[43]

Bibliography

Baker, Joshua, and Ernest W. Nicholson (eds. and trans.)
    1973 *The Commentary of Rabbi David Kimḥi on Psalms CXX–CL* (Cambridge: Cambridge University Press).

Ben-Shammai, Haggai
    2000 'הספרות המדרשית-הרבנית בפירושי רס"ג' ['The Rabbinic Literature in Se'adya's Exegesis'], in Joshua Blau and David Doron (eds.), *מסורת ושינוי בתרבות הערבית-היהודית של ימי-הביניים* [*Heritage and Innovation in Medieval Judaeo-Arabic Culture*] (Ramat Gan: Bar Ilan University Press): 32–68.
    2003a 'Extra-Textual Considerations in Medieval Judaeo-Arabic Bible Translations: The Case of Saadya Gaon', *Materia Giudaica* 8/1: 53–9.
    2003b 'The Tension between Literal Interpretation and Exegetical Freedom: Comparative Observations on Saadia's Method', in McAuliffe, Walfish, and Goering 2003: 33–50.

Bernstein, Moshe
    1997 'Torah and its Study in the Targum of Psalms', in Jeffrey S. Gurock and Yaakov Elman (eds.), *Hazon Nahum: Studies in Honor of Dr. Norman Lamm on the Occasion of his Seventieth Birthday* (Hoboken, NJ: Yeshiva University Press): 39–67.

---

[41] Steiner 1998: 252.

[42] Steiner (1998: 235) notes that Saadia must have been familiar with the rabbis' meaning-minimalism but avoided it because he may have associated it with midrashic interpretation, which was antithetical to his *peshat* approach.

[43] Many thanks to Mordechai Cohen for his gracious and very helpful comments on an earlier draft. This paper is to appear in *Methods for the Psalms*, edited by Esther Menn (Cambridge: Cambridge University Press, forthcoming).

Blau, Joshua

2001 'The Linguistic Character of Saadia Gaon's Translation of the Pentateuch', *Oriens* 36: 1–9.

Braude, William G. (trans.)

1959 *The Midrash on Psalms* (New Haven: Yale University Press)

Brody, Robert

2000 'The Geonim of Babylonia as Biblical Exegetes', in Sæbø 2000: 74–88.

Cohen, Menachem (ed.)

2003 *Miqra'ot Gedolot Haketer*. Psalms, Part 1 (Ramat Gan: Bar Ilan University Press).

Cohen, Mordechai Z.

2000 'The Qimhi Family', in Sæbø 2000: 388–415.

2003 *Three Approaches to Biblical Metaphor: From Abraham Ibn Ezra and Maimonides to David Kimhi* (Leiden: Brill).

2008 'Rashbam Scholarship in Perpetual Motion', *Jewish Quarterly Review* 98/3: 389–408.

Cooper, Alan

2006 'On the Typology of Jewish Psalms Interpretation', in Isaac Kalimi and Peter J. Haas (eds.), *Biblical Interpretation in Judaism and Christianity* (New York and London: T&T Clark): 79–90.

Gillingham, Susan.

2008 *Psalms through the Centuries*, vol. 1 (Oxford: Wiley-Blackwell).

Goodman, Lenn E.

1990 'Saadiah Gaon's Interpretive Technique in Translating the Book of Job', in *Translation of Scripture: Proceedings of a Conference at the Annenberg Research Institute, May 15–16, 1989* (Philadelphia: Annenberg Research Institute): 47–76.

Greenberg, Moshe

1995 'Exegesis', in Arthur A. Cohen and Paul Mendes-Flohr (eds.), *Studies in the Bible and Jewish Thought* (Philadelphia and Jerusalem: Jewish Publication Society): 361–8. (First published in *Contemporary Jewish Religious Thought* (New York: Charles Scribner's Sons, 1987): 211–18.)

Greenstein, Edward L.

1984 'Medieval Bible Commentaries', in Barry Holtz (ed.), *Back to the Sources* (New York: Summit): 213–59.

Grossman, Avraham

2000 'The School of Literal Exegesis in Northern France', in Sæbø 2000: 321–71.

Gruber, Mayer I.

2004 *Rashi's Commentary on Psalms* (Leiden: Brill).

Grunhaus, Naomi

2003 'The Dependence of Rabbi David Kimhi (RADAK) on RASHI in his Quotation of Midrashic Traditions', *Jewish Quarterly Review* 93: 415–30.

Hansberger, Therese

2002 'Mose segnete Israel mit "ashreha", und David segnete Israel mit "ashrai"' (*MTeh* 1,2). Psalm 1 und der Psalter im rabbinischen Midrash zu den Psalmen (*MTeh* 1)', *Biblische Zeitschrift* 46/1: 25–47.

Harris, Jay M.

1993 'Ibn Ezra in Modern Jewish Perspective', in Isadore Twersky and Jay M. Harris (eds.), *Rabbi Abraham Ibn Ezra: Studies in the Writings of a*

Twelfth-Century Jewish Polymath (Cambridge, MA: Harvard University, Center for Jewish Studies: distributed by Harvard University Press): 129–70.

Japhet, Sara

2004 'The Tension Between Rabbinic Legal Midrash and the "Plain Meaning" (*Peshat*) of the Biblical Text: An Unresolved Problem? In the Wake of Rashbam's Commentary on the Pentateuch', in Chaim Cohen, Avi Hurvitz, and Shalom M. Paul (eds.), *Sefer Moshe: The Moshe Weinfeld Jubilee Volume. Studies in the Bible and the Ancient Near East, Qumran, and Post-Biblical Judaism* (Winona Lake, IN: Eisenbrauns): 403–25.

Kafih [Qafih/Kapah], Yosef

1966 תהלים עם תרגום ופרוש הנגון רבינו סעדיה בן יוסף פיומי זצ״ל
[*Psalms with the Translation and Commentary of the Gaon Our Rabbi Saadiah ben Joseph Fyumi*] (Jerusalem).

Kamin, Sarah

1985 'Review of U. Simon, *Four Approaches to the Book of Psalms. . .*', *Journal of Jewish Studies* 36/2: 250–4.

Lawee, Eric

2003 'Introducing Scripture', in McAuliffe, Walfish, and Goering 2003: 157–79.

2007 'The Reception of Rashi's *Commentary on the Torah* in Spain: The Case of Adam's Mating with the Animals', *Jewish Quarterly Review* 97: 33–66.

Levenson, Alan

2006 'The Rise of Modern Biblical Studies: Preliminary Reflections', in Isaac Kalimi and Peter J. Haas (eds.), *Biblical Interpretation in Judaism and Christianity* (New York and London: T&T Clark): 163–78.

McAuliffe, Jane Dammen, Walfish, Barry, and Goering, Joseph Ward (eds.)

2003 *With Reverence for the Word: Medieval Exegesis in Judaism, Christianity, and Islam* (Oxford: Oxford University Press).

Maier, Johann

1987 'Psalm 1 im Licht antiker jüdischer Zeugnisse', in Manfred Oeming and Axel Graupner (eds.), *Altes Testament und christliche Verkündigung. Festschrift für Antonius A. H. Gunneweg zum 65. Geburtstag* (Stuttgart: Kohlhammer): 353–65.

Martínez Delgado, José

2003 'El comentario a Salmos de Mošeh ibn Chiquitilla', *Miscelánea de Estudios Árabes y Hebráicos*, 52, Sección de Hebreo: 201–41.

Ochs, Peter (ed.)

1993 *The Return to Scripture in Judaism and Christianity* (Mahwah, NJ: Paulist Press).

Perez, Ma'aravi

1995 'Il metodo esegetico di rabbi David Qimhi', in S. J. Sierra (ed.), *La lettura ebraica delle Scritture* (Bologna) 169–201. = לשיטתו הפרשנית של ר' דוד קמחי, *Beit Mikra* 45/163 (2000): 305–28.

Polliak, Meira

2000a 'תפיסת רב סעדיה גאון את תרגום התורה בהשוואה לתפיסת הקראים' ['Se'adya Gaon's Concept of Biblical Translation in the Light of the Karaite Concept'], in Joshua Blau and David Doron (eds.), *מסורת ושינוי בתרבות הערבית-היהודית של ימי-הביניים* [*Heritage and*

Innovation in Medieval Judaeo-Arabic Culture] (Ramat Gan: Bar Ilan University Press): 189–200.

2000b 'The Spanish Legacy in the Hebrew Bible Commentaries of Abraham ibn Ezra and Profayt Duran', in Carlos Carrete Parrondo et al. (eds.), *'Encuentros' and 'Desencuentros': Spanish Jewish Cultural Interaction throughout History* (Tel Aviv: University Publishing Projects): 83–103.

Sæbø, Magne (ed.)

2000 *Hebrew Bible/Old Testament: The History of its Interpretation*, Vol I/II. *From the Beginnings to the Middle Ages (until 1300); Part 2, The Middle Ages* (Göttingen: Vandenhoeck & Ruprecht).

Sarna, Nahum

1993 'Abraham Ibn Ezra as an Exegete', in Isadore Twersky and Jay M. Harris (eds.), *Rabbi Abraham Ibn Ezra: Studies in the Writings of a Twelfth-Century Jewish Polymath* (Cambridge, MA: Harvard University, Center for Jewish Studies: distributed by Harvard University Press): 1–27.

Schlossberg, Eliezer

2000 'פולמוסו של רב סעדיה גאון נגד הנצרות' ['The Polemic of R. Se'adya Gaon against Christianity'], in Joshua Blau and David Doron (eds.), *מסורת ושינוי בתרבות הערבית-היהודית של ימי-הביניים* [*Heritage and Innovation in Medieval Judaeo-Arabic Culture*] (Ramat Gan: Bar Ilan University Press): 241–62.

Signer, Michael A.

1983 'King/Messiah: Rashi's Exegesis of Psalm 2', *Prooftexts* 3: 273–84.

Simon, Uriel

1991 *Four Approaches to the Book of Psalms. From Saadiah Gaon to Abraham Ibn Ezra* (trans. by Lenn J. Schramm; Albany: State University of New York) [ארבע גישות לספר תהלים, Ramat Gan: Bar Ilan University Press, 1982].

1992 'The Spanish School of Biblical Interpretation', in Haim Beinart (ed.), *Moreshet Sepharad: The Sephardi Legacy* (Jerusalem: Magnes): 115–36.

2000 'Abraham Ibn Ezra', in Sæbø 2000: 377–87.

Sokolow, Moshe

1984 'Saadiah Gaon's Prolegomenon to Psalms', *Proceedings—American Academy for Jewish Research* 51: 131–74.

Stec, David M.

2004 *The Targum of Psalms* (The Aramaic Bible, 16; Collegeville, MN: Liturgical Press).

Steiner, Richard C.

1998 'Saadia vs. Rashi: On the Shift from Meaning-Maximalism to Meaning-Minimalism in Medieval Biblical Lexicology', *Jewish Quarterly Review* 88/3–4: 213–58.

Walfish, Barry D.

2003 'An Introduction to Medieval Jewish Biblical Interpretation', in McAuliffe, Walfish, and Goering 2003: 3–12.

2004 'Medieval Jewish Interpretation', in Adele Berlin and Marc Z. Brettler (eds.), *The Jewish Study Bible* (New York: Oxford University Press): 1876–1900.

4

Medieval Psalms Exegesis as a Challenge to Modern Exegesis: A Response to Adele Berlin

Corinna Körting

Professor Berlin's paper, which was learned, vivid, and substantial, has been a challenge to all of us to engage further with these four men and to reflect on their work. I would love to interview *her* now, but I will restrict myself to some observations and two questions.

My remarks will comprise three parts. First, I shall offer some comments on some aspects of hermeneutics which I found especially striking. Secondly, I shall reflect on how medieval Jewish exegesis might encounter the exegesis of the twenty-first century; and thirdly, I shall give attention to the implications of medieval exegesis for modern psalms research. In comparison with the vast amount of material which has been presented, I can only focus on some key themes; we enter such a broad field of research when we meet medieval exegetes and their work.

1. Aspects of the Hermeneutics of Medieval Jewish Psalms Exegesis

Professor Berlin started her interviews by referring to modern questions such as 'who was the author of the psalms?', 'when were they written?', and 'what are the best methods for interpreting the psalms?' In a fascinating way we received answers that are very close to what we know from today's commentaries; however, the way medieval exegetes approached the problem is somewhat different. The answers took us far beyond a simple reply to questions of 'who' or 'when'. They gave us a broader insight into the hermeneutics of medieval Jewish psalms exegesis. But it is especially the last question, about a choice of method, which dominates the discussion these four had to face. Theirs was a choice between tradition and truthfulness to the text, and they were challenged by the qualification of psalm language as human or divine.

One area I would like to reflect upon relates to the methods of *peshat* or *derash*. Rashi, for example, states that he is simply interested in the plain meaning of the Scriptures and in an *aggadah* that explains the biblical passages in a fitting manner;[1] this has to be in accordance with the rules of grammar and with the syntactical context.[2] His choice of method seems to be determined by didactic concerns.[3] Exegetes such as Rashi had to negotiate between tradition and their contemporary situation, and this influenced their choice of method as well. The most striking quotation referred to was from Rashi's commentary on Psalm 2: this expressed his hesitation about calling the king (who plays a central part in this text) the messianic king, in order to prevent Christians from identifying this messianic king with Jesus. Due to Rashi's determination to circumvent reading the text from a Christian perspective, he rejects rabbinic tradition as well and draws on the plain reading of מְשִׁיחַ. This tendency is even more obvious in his comment on Ps. 105.15, where such a 'defence' is not necessary. Here, the anointed ones are, according to the context, the patriarchs; to them the land was given, but they were few in number, wandering between nation and nation. On their behalf God said to the kings: do not touch my anointed ones. Nevertheless, Rashi states: '"My anointed ones", that is "my persons of high status". Every form of the verbal root represented by the gerund מְשִׁיחָה, "anointing", is a word referring to political power and high status.'[4] Thus, on the one hand, Rashi's choice of method depends on his avoiding a Christian reading, but, on the other hand, the method, in this case the attention to the literal meaning of the term מְשִׁיחַ, offers a reading which lies beyond the disputes of either a Jewish or Christian sovereign interpretation.[5]

In brief: all four Jewish exegetes in Professor Berlin's 'interview' answered the question about their use of method with a 'both/and': it was *peshat* as well as *midrash*. But they weighed each approach differently, and they came to a rational and reasonable decision;[6] this could result in using contradictory

[1] See Berliner 1905: 7–8; Grossmann 2000: 335; Japhet 2004: 406.
[2] Grossman 2000: 335.
[3] See Grossman 2000: 336. The intensive study of Arabic grammar and lexicography encouraged Jewish scholars to be more self-conscious about the nature of the Hebrew language: see Holladay 1996: 149. But often the decision had to be between the plain meaning, and unlimited freedom of interpretation such as the Karaites proposed (Walfish 2004: 1878).
[4] See Gruber 2004: 622.
[5] See Gruber (2004: 180), who notes that the search for the literal meaning by Rashi 'was motivated by the belief that the Bible understood on its own terms would demonstrate that Judaism rather than Christianity is the only legitimate heir to the legacy, which is commonly called the "Old Testament"'.
[6] See Walfish 2004: 1878; Simon 2000: 379.

biblical verses or using figurative speech for the one or the other.[7] They also had to take other aspects into account, such as the current religio-political situation: two examples are the disputes with the Karaites as well as the conflicts with the Christians.[8]

The oscillation between tradition and their contemporary religious and political setting shapes the approach to the Psalms by all four of these medieval exegetes. Another area of controversy is the understanding of the psalms as divine or human poetry.[9] For example, Ibn Ezra holds that biblical language should be analysed like any human language.[10] He states this on the basis of a distinction between form and content: while the form is human, its content is divine.[11] The assumption that the *biblical language is human language* opens several methodological issues about, for example, the status of the canon of Scripture, for if it uses human language it must conform to the rules of syntax, rhetoric, and poetry.[12] This accounts for the special interest in the study of poetry and grammar. Against the traditional background that no word in the Bible is superfluous and needs its own explanation,[13] the exegetes of the Spanish school, especially Qimhi, developed theories which were very close to what later became known as parallelism.[14] They felt free to consider repetition as an artistic device, adding elegance and beauty to the language of the texts; but they did not see this as creating any additional meaning.

These considerations of divine or human language have remarkable consequences. One question we have to ask is whether these four exegetes imposed any limitations on themselves because they were dealing either with *divine or human language*. For example, when faced with contradictions in the biblical text itself, or in the shaping of the Masoretic text, what is to be done? According to Saadia the text has to be interpreted so as not to have contradictions.[15] According to Ibn Ezra a metaphorical or allegorical reading

---

[7] Ibn Ezra argues that we can explain verses in Proverbs metaphorically, because the whole book is a parable; by contrast, the Torah must be interpreted according to its literal meaning (i.e. the plain meaning), provided this does not oppose common sense (Japhet 2004: 415; Brody 2000: 80–2).

[8] See Japhet 2004: 424; Grossmann states that more than half of the chapters of Rashi's Psalms commentary are linked in some way to the debate with Christianity (2000: 340).

[9] Saadia understands the psalms to be prophetically inspired: see Sokolow 1984: 154; Simon 2000: 383; 1991: 191. In this context, see also 11QPs[a] 27.2–11.

[10] See Walfish 2004: 1882.

[11] 'The words are like bodies and the meanings like spirits' (הדברים כגופות והדברים והטעם): so Simon 1991: 162; 308–9. This might explain why, when it comes to content, Ibn Ezra relies on the authority of the rabbinic tradition as a more dependable source than later generations (Japhet 2004: 416).

[12] Ibid.

[13] For a fuller discussion see ibid.: 1881.

[14] See Lowth 1753–1787; also Baker and Nicholson 1973: xxvi–xxviii; Cohen 2000: 401–406.

[15] See Walfish 2004: 1878.

might be possible,[16] alternatively, a historical explanation could be given.[17] According to Qimhi a critical look at the textual tradition was required.[18] To summarize: the inspired nature of the texts—their 'divine' content—prevents these exegetes from using unlimited exegetical freedom, but leads them rather to align their reading in accordance with tradition.

2. An Encounter with Modern Exegesis: The Nature of the Book of Psalms

To questions such as 'who wrote the Book of Psalms?' and 'what about those referred to in the superscriptions?' we saw that various answers were given, to the effect that 'David', 'the Levites', or the 'ten authors' were all seen as composers of the psalms.[19] However, the discussion revealed that this is not just a question of literary history. In the background is the problem of whether the psalms serve as prayer or education. So this leads us to ask: what is the nature of the Book of Psalms? Saadia offers us a most interesting answer, set in the context of his dispute with the Karaites on the use of the Psalms. According to Karaites, the Book of Psalms is the work of humans and has no divinely ordained moral instruction.[20] Saadia's response, by contrast, is that the biblical psalms were recited in the *Temple*, and because of this the Psalms conform to a liturgical order.[21] They are part of the temple service.[22] But what of religious practice without the temple? Here what Saadia says about the Torah is also true for the Psalms: 'it is a book which teaches the service of God, and the essence of the service of God is performance of the command-ments'.[23] So this means that the Psalms are divine instructions about how people should act, rather than human prayers: they are, in essence, didactic in their purpose.

Saadia's observations may be compared with two seminal Christian psalm exegetes who wrote much later, illustrating why his approach is in fact quite

---

[16] According to Walfish, in such cases Ibn Ezra makes a verse conform to reason by means of allegory or metaphor (2004: 1883).

[17] See Baker and Nicholson 1973: xvi; Cohen 2000: 407–10.

[18] Qimhi reads the MT critically, taking *ketib* as well as *qere* into account, and suggesting con-jectures that often agree almost verbatim with the Septuagint: cf. Baker and Nicholson 1973: xxiv.

[19] See Berlin, pp. 46–9 above.

[20] See Sokolow 1984: 131, 148–9; Simon 1991: 3–7; Brody 2000: 77. Saadia argues in fact that it was unacceptable to address God using the same words with which he had addressed humans.

[21] In this respect Saadia suggests the days of the year or twenty-four shifts (cf. Sokolow 1984: 174) but also refers to the practices in the temple precincts as well as the contributions of Levitical families.

[22] See Sokolow 1984: 165; Simon 1991: 22–7.

[23] See Simon 1991: 1–5; Brody 2000: 83.

modern. Moving on six hundred years to the time of Martin Luther, we see
how one key difference concerns *prayer*. Luther called the Book of Psalms a
prayer book: it is not so much a book of divine instruction as one depicting
human conversation with God. This conversation should be taken up by the
believer, who will thereby become part of the *communio sanctorum*.[24]

Moving on to the beginning of the twentieth century, we find the question
of *the book* discussed by Hermann Gunkel. While Saadia sees an internal
order and cohesion in the Psalms, Gunkel is convinced that he is reading a
loose collection of texts – hardly a book.[25] Gunkel's view had a strong impact
on psalm research during the twentieth century, which did not really change
until some thirty years ago: nowadays, many scholars conclude that the Book
of Psalms is a witness of Jewish piety that had its setting in teaching and
meditation;[26] this conclusion has vast consequences for contemporary
methods used to read the Book of Psalms. No longer is the ultimate perspective a history of its forms, but rather the history of its overall composition.[27]
Saadia came to the same conclusion for different reasons: he used important
keywords in his description of the character of the Book of Psalms, and these
have a resonance with the way we read the psalms today.

3. A Challenge for Modern Exegesis

What kind of resources do these medieval commentaries offer us in our
modern exegesis? One answer is to be found in reception history, which
shows how the study of the medieval sources has its place in modern
scholarship. Examples include Susan Gillingham's volume *Psalms through the
Centuries*, on the reception history of psalmody;[28] or the newly established
Encyclopedia for the Bible and its Reception;[29] or the comprehensive work of
Magne Sæbø, *Hebrew Bible/Old Testament: The History of its Interpretation*.[30]
All three works give weight to reception history, whether dealing with the
Psalms or with the whole Hebrew Bible. These challenge us to ask, first, what
influence this new approach has on our exegesis, and, secondly, how we
should treat these sources.

Saadia once said that exegetical freedom had to be limited by the dictates of
tradition.[31] In Professor Berlin's interview, Qimhi says: 'I balance linguistic
analysis and historical thinking with respect for the rabbinic tradition
and with midrashic attention to nuance and religious inspiration.'[32] In his

---

[24] See M. Luther, 'Zweite Vorrede auf den Psalter (1528)', in Bornkamm 2005: 68.
[25] See Gunkel 1985: 3.   [26] See Levin 1993: 358.   [27] McCann 1993.
[28] Gillingham 2008.   [29] Seow and Spieckermann 2009.
[30] Sæbø 1996, 2000, 2008.   [31] Walfish 2004: 1878.   [32] See Berlin, pp. 45–6.

introduction to the commentary on the Former Prophets, Qimhi describes this procedure as follows: 'I will also cite the words of our Rabbis, of blessed memory, in regard to passages where we require their interpretation, especially where they had a "*tradition*".'[33]

Qimhi offers us an intermediate standpoint between Rashi and Ibn Ezra when it comes to the question of authority of the rabbinic sources.[34] For example, in his commentary on Psalm 132 he considers that, for v. 5, the explanation of the rabbis ('our teachers, of blessed memory') is neither suitable nor fitting, and therefore he does not mention it. And when it comes to v. 6, Qimhi offers a long explanatory discussion, beginning with Rabbi Moses Ibn Gikatilla, moving on to Ibn Ezra and other teachers, but finally concludes: 'but to my mind the most plausible interpretation is . . .'[35]

Is this an example we can follow? The challenge for a modern exegete is how to integrate all these voices, and whether we are willing to give the same authority to 'tradition' as Qimhi and others do. Does 'tradition', with its sanction of antiquity, have any such authority for us?

If modern scholars were willing to understand the principles of medieval exegesis, they might be able to integrate these ideas better with their own research. The methodological plurality we adopt today opens up many different ways of approaching the text. There is still a tendency in modern research which gives special weight to everything, chronologically speaking, which comes 'before' the biblical text, particularly religio-historical sources, either as written documents or as archaeological or iconographical evidence; however, a most important question remains. In order to discover the full meaning of the biblical text, how do we give similar weight to what comes 'after'?

Bibliography

Baker, Joshua, and Nicholson, Ernest W., (eds. and trans.)
  1973 *The Commentary of Rabbi David Kimhi on Psalms CXX–CL* (Cambridge: Cambridge University Press).
Berliner, Abraham (ed.)
  1905 *Raschi. Der Kommentar des Salomo B. Isak über den Pentateuch* (Frankfurt a.M.: J. Kauffmann, 2nd edn).
Bornkamm, Heinrich
  2005 *Martin Luther. Vorreden zur Bibel* (Göttingen: Vandenhoeck & Ruprecht, 4th edn).
Brody, Robert
  2000 'The Geonim of Babylonia as Biblical Exegetes', in Sæbø 2000: 74–88.

---

[33] Baker and Nicholson 1973: xix: 'To Ibn Esra: "If the statement be based on tradition, we will accept it; if on reasoning, we hold a different opinion"' (Baker and Nicholson 1973: xix).

[34] See Baker and Nicholson 1973: xvii; Simon 2000: 381.

[35] Baker and Nicholson 1973: 48–9.

Cohen, Mordechai Z.
  2000 'Jewish Exegesis in Spain and Provence, and in the East, in the Twelfth and Thirteenth Centuries. The Qimhi Family', in Sæbø 2000: 388–415.
Gillingham, Susan
  2008 *Psalms through the Centuries*, vol. 1 (Blackwell Bible Commentaries; Oxford: Wiley-Blackwell).
Grossman, Avraham
  2000 'The School of Literal Jewish Exegesis in Northern France', in Sæbø 2000: 321–71.
Gruber, Mayer I.
  2004 *Rashi's Commentary on Psalms* (Leiden: Brill).
Gunkel, Hermann
  1985 *Einleitung in die Psalmen* (Göttingen: Vandenhoeck & Ruprecht; 4th edn).
Holladay, William L.
  1996 *The Psalms through Three Thousand Years* (Minneapolis: Fortress Press).
Japhet, Sara
  2004 'The Tension Between Rabbinic Legal Midrash and the "Plain Meaning" (*Peshat*) of the Biblical Text: An Unresolved Problem? In the Wake of Rashbam's Commentary on the Pentateuch', in Chaim Cohen, Avi Hurvitz, and Shalom M. Paul (eds), *Sefer Moshe: The Moshe Weinfeld Jubilee Volume* (Winona Lake, IN: Eisenbrauns): 403–25.
Levin, Cristoph
  1993 'Das Gebetbuch der Gerechten. Literargeschichtliche Beobachtungen am Psalter', *ZThK* 90: 355–81.
Lowth, Robert
  1753 *De sacra poesi hebraeorum praelectiones academicae Oxonii habitae*, published as: G. Gregory (ed.), *Lectures on the Sacred Poetry of the Hebrews* (London/ Hildesheim: Olms 1787).
McCann, J. Clinton (ed.)
  1993 *The Shape and Shaping of the Psalter* (JSOTSup, 159; Sheffield: JSOT Press).
Sæbø, Magne (ed.)
  1996 *Hebrew Bible/Old Testament: The History of its Interpretation*, vol. I/I *From the Beginnings to the Middle Ages (until 1300); Part 1, Antiquity* (Göttingen: Vandenhoeck & Ruprecht).
  2000 *Hebrew Bible/Old Testament: The History of its Interpretation*, vol I/II *From the Beginnings to the Middle Ages (until 1300); Part 2, The Middle Ages* (Göttingen: Vandenhoeck & Ruprecht).
  2008 *Hebrew Bible/Old Testament: The History of its Interpretation*, vol II/I *From the Renaissance to the Enlightenment* (Göttingen: Vandenhoeck & Ruprecht).
Seow, Choon-Leong, and Spieckermann, Hermann (eds.)
  2009 *Encyclopedia of the Bible and its Reception* (Berlin: de Gruyter 2009–   ).
Simon, Uriel
  1991 *Four Approaches to the Book of Psalms* (Albany, NY: State University Press).
  2000 'Jewish Exegesis in Spain and Provence, and in the East, in the Twelfth and Thirteenth Centuries. Abraham Ibn Ezra', in Sæbø 2000: 372–87.

Sokolow, Moshe

    1984 'Saadiah Gaon's Prolegomenon to Psalms', *American Academy for Jewish Research* 51: 131–74.

Walfish, Barry D.

    2004 'Medieval Jewish Interpretation', in A. Berlin and M. Z. Brettler (eds.), *The Jewish Study Bible* (Oxford: Oxford University Press): 1876–1900.

5

The Reception of Psalm 137 in Jewish and Christian Traditions

Susan Gillingham

Anyone who reads the biblical text with a commentary is undertaking one aspect of Reception History, albeit perhaps inadvertently, for they are 'receiving' the text through the medium of a third party. Of course, the significance of this relatively new discipline extends far beyond the use of a commentary. One notable contribution is the way it illustrates the different approaches of Jews and Christians to the same biblical text, offering a new context for theological dialogue. Psalm 137, which speaks of suffering and exile, is an excellent example of these multivalent readings. Jews have repeatedly used this psalm, in times of crisis, by creating a 'meta-narrative' from it: the psalm as a whole becomes a poetic story which initially addresses the material concerns of the entire community. By contrast, Christians have been more inclined to select individual verses or phrases and use them allegorically with a more spiritual application—not so much for the entire church, but for individuals within the church. Obviously there are exceptions and other permutations. Nevertheless, this paper will seek to show how these differences are borne out in the reception of Psalm 137—through commentaries, but not only through this medium—throughout its some two-and-a-half-thousand-year history.

1. Jewish Approaches to Suffering through the Creation of a 'Meta-narrative'

1.1. Psalm 137 in the Exilic and Post-Exilic Periods

Many Jews would read this psalm as originally from the Babylonian exile. More specifically, Jeremiah, as the 'weeping prophet', has been seen as the author: indeed, later Greek versions sometimes included the title τῷ Ἰερεμια. This results in reading the curse over the Edomites in v. 7 in the light of

Jer. 49.8–22, and the curse over the Babylonians in vv. 8–9 in the light of Jer. 51.1–64.[1] The fact that Jeremiah's exile was in Egypt, not Babylon, does not seem to be a problem: apparently the date could have been in the early part of the exile after Jeremiah had accompanied the first group of exiles as far as the Babylonian border, upon which he returned to Judah, or it could have been *after* his return from Egypt, once back in Judah.[2]

Other Jews see Psalm 137 as a composition *following* the exile, in Yehud, some time after 538 BCE: this reading was popular among the rabbis, who argued that the psalm was composed and sung by Levitical singers, but only when once again songs of Zion could be sung, in memory of the anguish and anger when such freedom of worship had been denied. So the use of 'there' (שָׁם) in vv. 1 and 3 is a time of looking back to Babylon from Yehud.[3] The fact that the psalmist never prays for the restoration of Jerusalem but only for the downfall of Babylon may well suggest a time after 538, when Jerusalem is in fact being rebuilt, but before Darius finally sacked the city of Babylon.

Nevertheless, in both readings Psalm 137 refers to the *first* exile; it is an earthly drama in three parts. First, it tells the story of the community's suffering (vv. 1–4: noting the use of the first person plural throughout); secondly, the self-imprecation (vv. 5–6: observing here the use of the first person singular) about never forgetting Jerusalem is for 'anyone' who cares passionately about Zion; and finally, the imprecation against the people's enemies (vv. 7–9 is mainly in the third person plural) applies literally to the Edomites and the Babylonians. The taunts of the Babylonians in v. 3 are matched by the derision of the Edomites in v. 7. The motif 'remember!' runs throughout each of the three parts (vv. 1, 6, 7); hence 'memory' holds together the psalm as a whole.

1.2. The Psalm in the Second Century BCE under Hellenistic Rule

After the time of Alexander the Great, and especially during the second century BCE at the time of persecution under Antiochus Epiphanes, with his austere programme of Hellenization, many Jews began to feel that the exile had never actually ended.[4] At this time Psalm 137 would be particularly

---

[1] √ נָפַץ ('shatter') which is in Ps. 137.9 occurs some nine times throughout Jeremiah, which may suggest further associations.

[2] The prophet's great age is problematic here. Another tradition was that after an enforced exile in Babylon, Nebuchadnezzar, in his thirty-third year, invaded Egypt and held the prophet hostage in Babylon. See Josephus in *Jewish Antiquities* 10.180–2, noted in Kugel (1990: 178–9). Other rabbinical sources, noting the associations between Psalm 137 and Lamentations, argue instead that Baruch was the author of the psalm: see *Megillah* 16b and *Shir ha-shirim Rabba* 5.4.

[3] שָׁם can denote present experience as well: see e.g. Pss. 48.6 (7) and 76.3 (4).

[4] See e.g. Dan. 9.24–7.

pertinent, with its focus on the disenfranchised community in vv. 1–4, on Jerusalem as one's 'highest joy' in vv. 5–6, and with its vitriol against pagan nations in vv. 8–9. The only real difference was that the 'Edomites' and 'Babylonians' would have now been read as those Hellenizers who had placed that 'abomination of desolation' within the Temple and so re-created that sense of being unable to worship in a 'foreign land'.

1.3. The Psalm after 70 CE under Roman Rule

The various versions of *Paraleipomena of Jeremiah* are usually dated between 70 and 135 CE. It is during this time that a different 'meta-narrative' emerges. Now, in the context of the *second* fall of Jerusalem and the Roman wars in 132–5, the psalm was understood as *from David*—prophesying the *future* suffering of the Jews—who not only foresaw the fall of Jerusalem between 597 and 587 BCE in the first part of the psalm (vv. 1–4, 5–6) but also the fall of Jerusalem in 70 CE until the final diaspora in 135 CE in the second part (vv. 7–9). Here both Babylon and Edom became synonyms for Rome—not least because the Roman Emperor Titus was believed to be of Edomite origin.[5]

1.4. The Psalm by the Sixth Century CE

By the time of the completion of Targum Psalms in about the sixth century CE, another layer of interpretation had begun to emerge. The expansion in v. 3 to some of the songs 'you used to utter' in Zion' (שירתא דהויתון אמרין בציון) again has a double point of reference, as after 70 CE the songs of Zion had again been silent. The reference to the gloating of the Babylonians at the people's distress, also in v. 3 ('because of their joy were saying. . .' [ובזוזנא על עיסק חדוא]), includes not only the Babylonian but also the Roman 'captivity'. In v. 4 the allusion to the psalmist as a *Levite* (i.e. not David, nor Jeremiah, nor Baruch) and the reference to the Levites maiming themselves to disqualify them from any enforced blasphemy in singing about Zion in alien land (מניד קטעו ליואי אליוניהון בככיהון ואמרין) serves as a didactic tool for a community oppressed by the Gentiles: it warns those (in their ongoing exile) not to capitulate to Gentile demands in any way.[6] The addition

---

[5] There is a clear reference to this in the Babylonian Talmud, *Gittin* 57b. See Kugel 1990: 174–5.

[6] The tradition of the self-mutilation of the Levites is also found in *Pesikta Rabbati* 136a, so is not unique to Targum Psalms. It also occurs in *Midrash Tehillim* 137:5. See Edwards 2007: 108–11.

in v. 5, 'the voice of the holy spirit replied and says' (מתיבא קל רוחא דקודשא), offers assurance directly from God to those who have been loyal in suffering. The expansion in v. 6, concerning 'the memory of Jerusalem' (דכרן ירושלם) is appropriate in the light of the fact that, since 70 CE, the Temple no longer stands. The additional reference to the Edomites in v. 7 ('who laid waste Jerusalem' [דאחריבו ירושלם דאמרין]) again suggests a double connotation—literally, the Edomites, but, later, the Romans. Most significantly, the speakers of the curses in vv. 7 and 8–9 are 'Michael prince of Jerusalem' (מיכאל רבה דירושלם) and 'Gabriel prince of Zion' (גבריאל רבה דציון): this raises this cry of vengeance to a supernatural level. The curse on the enemy comes not only from the people but from angelic beings as well.

The 'meta-narrative' of Targum transforms Psalm 137 into a drama of even more speakers. And this time the action does not take place solely in this world. At the beginning of the psalm it starts with the suffering community on earth, but by the middle of the psalm it has moved (by way of the reference to the *Holy Spirit*) to heaven, where it is God (not the psalmist) who vows loyalty to the memory of Jerusalem. This heavenly perspective continues in vv. 7–9 where it is no longer the people but the angelic protectors of the nation who cry out in vengeance against their enemies.[7]

1.5. The Psalm in the Middle Ages

The rabbis had always emphasized that Psalm 137 was about the physical sufferings of the people from the first exile of 587 onwards. This is clearly seen in the *Midrash Tehillim,* whose final date is approximately some seven hundred years after *Targum Psalms,* where the descriptions of suffering in the psalm are intensified. For example, the use of 'there' (שם) in vv. 1 and 3 is now used to heighten the fact that the Jews were allowed no rest-stop until they arrived in Babylon.[8] The reference to the weeping by (על) the Babylonian waters (v. 1) is on account of (על) the people and their children actually being poisoned by the waters of the river Euphrates.[9] The use of 'also' (גם) in v. 1 is an indication that the pain was so great that God Himself wept with them too.[10] The hanging up of the harps on trees, as an act of defiance in refusing to comply with the captors' demands, was in order to prevent them

---

[7] Several of these observations have been influenced by Bernstein (1994: 326–45, especially pp. 338–43). See also Stec 2005: 231.

[8] *Midrash Tehillim* 137.1 and *Pesiqta Rabbati* 130b also refer to this. See Kugel (1990: 180–2), showing how Lam. 4.19 and 5.5 were understood as *midrashim* on this verse.

[9] See *Midrash Tehillim* 137.1 and *Pesiqta Rabbati* 135a; referred to in Kugel 1990: 183.

[10] See *Midrash Tehillim* 137.1 and *Pesiqta Rabbati* 131b; referred to in Kugel 1990: 181 and 184.

being contaminated by foreign ground.[11] It seems that this interpretation, building further on the tradition that Jeremiah was the author of the psalm, has been influenced by 4 Baruch and especially by the *Paraleipomena of Jeremiah*, which explains how and why a letter from Jeremiah highlighted the people's grief, which in turn gave rise to his composition of Psalm 137 for them to use.[12]

This intensification of the physical suffering of the people has to be seen in the light of another crisis—the conflicts between Jews and Christians in the Middle Ages, fuelled by the Crusades, and resulting again in physical persecution. Whereas in *Targum* the emphasis was on the initiative of God who would soon vindicate those in exile, the emphasis in *Midrash Tehillim* is more on the accountability of the people and their need to repent. A further detail in this later Jewish meta-narrative concerns not only the self-mutilation of the Levitical singers in v. 5, but also the dreadful anger of Nebuchadnezzar, and the Levites' exemplary behaviour in response. *Midrash Tehillim* universalizes the vow concerning the memory of Jerusalem in v. 6; the vow made once by the Levites is now the vow of every Jew:

> If a man covers his house with plaster, he must leave uncovered a small space as a mourning reminder of Jerusalem. If a man prepares all that goes with a feast, he must leave out some small thing as a reminder of Jerusalem. If a woman is adorning herself, she must leave off some small thing as a reminder of Jerusalem, for it is said *If I forget thee, O Jerusalem, let my right hand forget her cunning.* (Ps. 137.5)[13]

So by identifying with the physical suffering of the first exiles the rabbis teach that those in the ongoing exile of the Diaspora must continue to preserve in practical ways the memory of Jerusalem expressed in this Psalm.

1.6. The Psalm in Thirteenth-Century Italy

One of the earliest Jewish illustrations of Psalm 137 is also from the thirteenth century (see Plate 1). This is the Parma Psalter (*c*.1280). Given the place of the Jews in Italian society at this time, living with the consequences of the Fourth Lateran Council in 1215, with forced conversions and burning of Jewish books, the production of such a lavish manuscript marked an act of defiance against the patron's Christian persecutors. Psalm 137 is thus a highly charged psalm: we see two figures, weeping, and compelled to draw the waters from the river which would eventually, according to the tradition, in *Midrash Tehillim*, poison them. Willow leaves frame the text, upon which are hung the lyres.

---

[11] See *Midrash Tehillim* 137:3 and *Pesiqta Rabbati* 144a and 144b; referred to in Kugel 1990: 185–9.

[12] See Bar. 6.4–6 and the discussion in Kugel 1990: 195–7.   [13] See Braude 1959: 81.

1.7. The Psalm in the Court of Mantua in Sixteenth-Century Italy

The earliest known musical representation of Psalm 137 in Jewish tradition is by Salomone Rossi, a court musician for Duke Vicenzo I in Mantua, some three hundred years after the production of the Italian Parma Psalter. Given the prohibition against singing this psalm, in memory of the fallen Temple, this is particularly fascinating. By the end of the sixteenth century Italy was becoming more tolerant of Jewish culture, for the Renaissance had revived many aspects of the classical world; so Rossi, still composing out of a profound concern for the future of the Jewish nation, used this new atmosphere to full advantage. He was the first Jewish musician to print Hebrew music for secular performances, taking popular tunes from the ghetto, and adapting them as polyphonic psalms, in Hebrew, for synagogue liturgy. In Psalm 137 the chorus is unaccompanied: Rossi still adhered to the ban on music in synagogue liturgy to observe the destruction of the second Temple: metaphorically speaking, the harps were still hung on the trees. Influenced by Monteverdi and the plainchant tradition of the church in Mantua, Rossi's psalms are melismatic chants, and the only elaborations are where the voices in the psalm suggest them. Psalm 137 is full of dissonant mournful chords, sung by low and heavy voices. They begin with a chromatic progression depicting the Hebrew word 'wept', and a flowing passage in unison for the Hebrew word 'river'. The hanging up of harps is achieved by lowering the key by a semitone, with an unexpected F sharp in the soprano part at the end of the phrase. The call for revenge at the end of the psalm ('Destroy it! Destroy it!') repeatedly uses harsh, grinding chords. This is another meta-narrative of Psalm 137: but it is in musical form.

1.8. The Psalm in the Twentieth and Twenty-First Centuries

Returning to reception through the written word, modern Jewish commentators, writing in the light of 1948, add their own 'meta-narrative' from a post-Holocaust perspective. Abraham Cohen, for example, first notes the tradition expressed in the Talmud (*Gittin* 57b) which cites the prophet David as envisioning the destruction of the first Temple in v. 1 and the second Temple in v. 7; he then reflects that 'if we think of him [the psalmist] as an exile recently back from Babylon, viewing with horror the havoc wrought in the city he dearly loved . . . Refugees from Europe, when they returned and saw how their native cities had been turned into masses of rubble by the Germans, surely shared this mood.'[14]

---

[14] See Cohen 1985: 447.

The commentary by Avrohom Chaim Feuer focuses on the way that the *continual* memory of Jerusalem's destruction needs preserving, even in family rituals. He quotes the importance of the recitation of v. 6 at weddings by the bridegroom, who, with symbolic ashes on his head to represent the devastated Jerusalem, remembers 'Jerusalem, my *highest* joy' as he awaits another joy— his bride. He also notes the importance of this verse as part of a grace after meals—symbolizing that when the body is full, the heart must still grieve. In these ways the tragedy of Jerusalem's destruction—whether in the sixth century BCE, the first century CE, or in the nineteenth and twentieth centuries—becomes a perpetual motivation towards repentance and prayer for protection.[15]

After 1948 some images of Psalm 137 take on more hopeful connotations. One example is by Marc Chagall and is found on the north side of the Chagall State Hall of the Knesset (Plate 2). It is the only reference to a psalm here and its imagery takes up the first verse ('By the waters of Babylon we sit down and weep') and the fifth ('If I forget you, O Jerusalem, let my right hand be crippled'). Set amidst four vibrant wall tapestries with the themes of diaspora and return, and complemented by the more mellow floor mosaics which represent the love of Jewish tradition past and present, is a vast wall mosaic, six metres high and five and a half metres wide. The mosaic uses Psalm 137 to depict the people's story of suffering, both past and present. The setting here is of prayers at the Western Wall (still under Jordanian control at the time of completion in 1966), with the Old City and Tower of David in the background. In the centre of the muted blues and greens a lighted Menorah hangs in space, a modern symbol of the harps which once hung unused on the trees, but the gold flames evoke light and hope. Above the golden light is an angel with a Shofar, calling the people below to return to Zion: this echoes the tradition about the angels who curse Edom and Babylon on behalf of Israel in the Targum and *Midrash Tehillim*. There are further hints of Messianic hope in the star of David, set in the heavens to bring the people home (see Num. 24.13–17). This is another 'meta-narrative', in visual form: but here there is more hope.[16]

A recent musical depiction of Psalm 137 interprets it as a poignant but ultimately cathartic lament. The composer Robert Saxton used this psalm in the first of an eight-scene opera, *The Wandering Jew*, broadcast on BBC Radio

---

[15] See Feuer (1980: 1624 and 1619 respectively) which is in part recapitulating the views expressed in *Targum,* and *Midrash Tehillim*.

[16] A year later of course the people did return to the Wailing Wall and the Shofar did actually sound out in Jerusalem. I am indebted to private correspondence with Ziva Amishai-Maisels for some these reflections and also for her advice on reproducing the image from the Knesset. See especially Amishai-Maiels 1973: 113–26.

4 in 2010.[17] The psalm is sung in Scene 1 by the chorus of Nazi death camp inmates whilst the 'wandering Jew' stands by, impotent to save them. It is the first music we hear: until then the only voice has been that of the 'narrator', the wandering Jew. The mixed chorus sings in low and sonorous tones, first in unison, then breaking into discord. A guard interrupts their singing, and two prisoners are removed, evoking the third verse of the drama of the psalm. The prisoners however resume the first verse of the psalm, which progresses into a more general words of lament, ending with Ps. 31.5: 'into thy hands I commend my spirit'. These haunting mourning sounds, descending in cadences in fifths from B flat down to the key of E minor, appear again in Scene 7, the penultimate scene, now sung by a 'ghost chorus', when the wandering Jew encounters Jesus a third time and both bear witness to their peoples' pain. This time we hear only the music, not the words of psalm; the setting is now the Feast of Tabernacles, and psalms appropriate to a more hopeful theme are intoned instead. Thus the psalm—or at least the music which reminds us of the psalm—acts as both an expression of the people's pain and in part a resolution to it.

So whether in commentary, music, or art, the Jewish reception of Psalm 137 has given it a pronounced physical and political emphasis. Even when it is given a more theological orientation, this is still in order to reinforce the material and physical hope for restoration of Jerusalem and of worship there.

2. Christian Approaches to Suffering through the Creation of Allegories

2.1. Psalm 137 through the Eyes of the Church Fathers

Jerome, followed by Bede, begins his commentary with a preface about understanding Psalm 137 in three ways—about the exile of the Jews to Babylon, about the expulsion of sinners from the church, 'and about the superior exile, by which a sometimes noble company is led forth into the vale of tears'.[18] It is the third of these readings which is the most common in Christian reception. Individual phrases and words from particular verses are allegorized to give the psalm a spiritual meaning: the 'superior exile' is about

---

[17] For Saxton's discussion of the performance, see http://www.youtube.com/watch?v=ifoWIqntl1E. The recording (*The Wandering Jew*, by BBC Symphonic Orchestra and BBC Singers with R. Williams, baritone) is on NMC Recordings Ltd, 2011 NMCD 170. It can be previewed on http://itunes.apple.com/us/album/robert-saxton-the-wandering/id441406269 (accessed March 2012).

[18] Translated by Holladay (1993: 172) from Morin (1959: 165–242). Bede's similar observations are found in Neale and Littledale (1879: 296).

the place of Christians in an evil world, as pilgrims awaiting their spiritual restoration in heaven.

The 'waters of Babylon', for example, are rarely understood literally, as a means of identifying with the pain of the Jewish people. These are no longer physically poisonous waters, but waters of passion in danger of drowning the soul. They represent everything which is alien to God, the place of confusion in this world, where 'the sinner who has fallen out of paradise . . . comes into the vale of tears.'[19]

The 'harps' have several connotations, although none of them is literal. They can be seen as a metaphor of worldly pleasures and bodily desires which have to be put aside; they are thus to be hung upon the tree, which is the cross.[20] A very different reading is from Origen: the 'hanging up of harps' suggests the ignorance of certain souls failing to use their God-given skills, and this is wrong because it prevents them being responsible in practical matters.[21] Jerome makes a similar point, followed too by Augustine—that if we hang our instruments on 'unfruitful trees' (the willow according to Jerome being a tree which always takes up moisture but bears no fruit) we leave ourselves open to 'vices, to lust, to wantonness' and cannot communicate the Gospel to unbelievers.[22]

The 'captors' and 'tormentors' are no longer the Babylonians, nor are they their successors, the Romans; they are, according to Augustine, 'the devil and all his minions, who have inflicted us with the wounds of sin'. But this is for a refining process, in preparation for life in the heavenly Jerusalem.[23]

Jerusalem is never the city itself: it is the Holy and Heavenly City, which forms a neat antithesis to Babylon, the worldly city and place of all confusion. 'Jerusalem is the height of joy where we enjoy God. . . there shall no tempter assail us. . . there nought will delight us but good: there all want will die, there perfect bliss will dawn on us.'[24] The vow never to forget Jerusalem, reinforced by references to the 'right hand', becomes another reference to eternal life, so that the sense runs 'if I forget the Church of God, let eternal life forget me'.[25]

Whereas references to the Babylonians evoke a more general inter-pretation—sin, passions, confusion, the devil and all his works—'Edom' has

---

[19] Taken from Jerome's Tractate on Psalm 137, translated by Holladay (1993: 173).

[20] See Methodius, *Symposium or the Banquet of the Ten Virgins* 4.3, cited in Wesselschmidt 2007: 379.

[21] 'Quaecunque animae sedent in umbra et ignorantia, sciendum est eas rationem habere sterilem, suspensis organis quae activae vitae inserviunt.' See Origen 1862: 1660.

[22] Translated from Jerome's Commentary on Psalm 137 by Holladay (1993: 172). See also Kirschner 1990: 253.

[23] See Kirschner 1990: 254.

[24] See http://www.ccel.org/ccel/schaff/npnf108.iiCXXXVII.html (on v. 6).

[25] See Neale and Littledale 1879: 300.

often a more precise and sinister reference. Edom is Esau, the 'false kinsman', set against Jacob, the true Israel, which is the Church. This is a particular theme in Augustine's sermons on the psalms—an odd theme, one might argue, given that the real enemies in the Church in Carthage were not so much Jews as imperial (pagan) rulers, with the Theodosian Code creating religious intolerance and persecution for the Church. Nevertheless, although Edom is more generally 'the carnal', and the expression of this is primarily in the Synagogue, 'the elder church which sought the life of the younger, and joined throughout . . . in the persecutions which the Pagan rulers stirred up against the Christians'.[26]

For Origen, however, the 'children of Babylon' are the confused thoughts that arise from the soul, and the one who subdues them does so by striking them against the firm and solid strength of reason and truth.[27] They are 'sins of the flesh born of a wretched mother (Babylon)' who have to be prevented from reaching adulthood where they will grow all the stronger and will attack us and even take us over; so in infancy they have to dashed either against the Rock which is the Word of God, or the Rock which is Christ himself.[28]

Even the crisis of the political vacuum left by the sack of Rome in 410 is used to read Psalm 137 in a spiritual way. Augustine, for example, preached on Psalm 137 on 31 December 412, in Carthage, to assure the North African churches of the eternal nature of the 'city of God' in a time of political turmoil. *De civitate Dei* was written shortly after this time.[29] Rome, a 'descendant' of Babylon, was, like Babel, transitory and destined for destruction; Jerusalem by contrast was always the 'heavenly city', transcending worldly cares. As Augustine said of vv. 8–9 in Psalm 137: 'sigh for the everlasting Jerusalem. . .Christ is now our Head; now he ruleth for us from above; in that city he will fold us to himself'.[30] The challenge to the church was to escape its own 'Babylonian captivity'.

---

[26] See Augustine in Neale and Littledale (1879: 301). Cassiodorus also implicitly identifies the Edomites as Jews, but speaks of them only as 'persecutors of God's people': see Neale and Littledale 1879: 364.

[27] Origen, *Against Celsus* 7.22, quoted in Wesselschmidt (2007: 379). Or again, Augustine: 'What are the little ones of Babylon? Evil desires at birth . . . When lust is born, before evil habit giveth it strength against thee, when lust is little, by no means let it gain the strength of evil habit; when it is little, dash it . . . "Dash it against the Rock, and that Rock is Christ" (1 Cor. 10.4).' See http://www.ccel.org/ccel/schaff/npnf108.iiCXXXVII.html (on v. 9).

[28] The text commonly quoted here is 1 Cor. 10.4. See e.g. Origen 1862: 1658–9. Cassiodorus, writing for his monastic community in Squillace, southern Italy, is keen to make the same point, concluding that the psalm as a whole is to enable us to escape the tyranny of sin: see Cassiodorus 1997: 363–4.

[29] See Kirschner 1990: 242–3.

[30] See www.ccel/org/ccel/schaff/npnf108.ii.CXXXVII.html.

2.2. The Psalm in Christian Illumination

Nearly four hundred years before the production of the Parma Psalter, illuminations of Psalm 137 in Christian manuscripts are beginning to create a different commentary tradition. One seminal example is the Utrecht Psalter (Plate 3), dating from the ninth century. It was once held at the Benedictine monastery of Hautvillers and used artists from the school at Rheims. The imagery is particularly complex: the Christian artists have selected six verses (1, 2, 3, 6, 7, and 8) and present these in an artistic sequence.

The 'rivers of Babylon' (as in v. 1) flow in a harsh line right across the bottom of the image, possibly symbolizing those 'waters of passion, drowning the soul'.[31] Verse 2 is represented in the right hand bottom corner, where a group of Babylonians demand a 'Song of Zion'. Verse 3 is represented in the middle of the bottom of the image, where a company of desolate Jews sits on the banks of the river, with their lyres hanging on the trees. In the top left corner, moving down through the middle of the illustration to the bottom left, is a particularly Christian illustration of vv. 6a and 6b. We see a small group of people looking up to heaven, from which emerges the hand of God, which is held up and blesses another group of people in front of what seems to be a tabernacle representing the Temple of Jerusalem. On a hill next to the tabernacle is a figure with a rayed nimbus, representing Jesus Christ. Next to him are three disciples; they and he are pointing to his lips. This probably refers to the prophecies of Christ concerning the destruction of Jerusalem, for example in Mt. 23.27; Lk. 13.34, 21.20–24; and Jn 2.19–22. Verses 7–8 are depicted in the left-hand corner: here we see Edom and Babylon being besieged and destroyed—but in the context of the earlier illustrations this is an omen of the fate to come to Jerusalem itself. This is an interesting example of an actual Christian meta-narrative in art, nevertheless using specific verses and reading them allegorically to make spiritual points. This is not so much about the suffering of the Jewish community as about a faith focused on Jesus Christ who, after the final destruction of Jerusalem and its Temple, embodies a new faith and hope which is not so much material and temporal as spiritual and eternal.

2.3. The Psalm through the Eyes of the Sixteenth-Century Reformers

By the time of the Reformation, Psalm 137 was still an allegory for the Christian life but it now has a physical application as well. This is clearly seen in the work of Martin Luther, once an Augustinian monk, who continued

---

[31] See n. 19 above.

to adapt the phrase 'the Babylonian Captivity of the Church' for his own generation, some eleven centuries after Augustine.[32] The Babylonian captivity had meant, for Augustine, the confusion and chaos of the world, exemplified by the Empire of Rome; for Luther, this meant, quite simply, the *Church of Rome*. Luther's second treatise of 1520 against the Church's teaching on the seven sacraments, which bears the influence of Augustine's *City of God*, refers to Psalm 137 on two occasions. He argues that the Roman Church is like Babylon, creating oppression and confusion. but the origin and destiny of the true Church was the heavenly city, Jerusalem. In the section on the 'Sacrament of Penance', Luther quotes the first two verses, adding: 'The Lord curse the barren willows of those streams!' as he highlighted the barren inefficacy of the sacraments of the Roman (Babylonian) Church. And on the 'Sacrament of Marriage', Luther concludes 'Herewith I hang up my harp, until another and a better man shall take up this matter with me' (Ps. 137.2).[33]

It is not difficult to see how this metaphor of the 'Babylonian Captivity of the Church' became a watchword in the later Reformation period, applied by all types of disenfranchised Christian groups, Catholic and Protestant. For Psalm 137, 'the quintessential psalm of the Renaissance and the Reformation', illustrated so well the pain of *physical* as well as *spiritual* exile.[34] Miles Coverdale and William Whittingham were Protestants when England was officially Catholic; and Richard Crashaw was a Catholic when England was officially Protestant. All three lived for some time in exile on the Continent, and all three made metrical paraphrases and commentaries on this psalm in which one senses that although the suffering is now more clearly physical there is spiritual suffering as well.[35] Coverdale, for example, writing

---

[32] Luther was by no means the first to use Psalm 137 in this way: in *Defence of the Holy Church,* a poetic attack on Lollardy addressed to the future Henry V, its author, John Lydgate, uses Psalm 137 at length to demonstrate how the Roman Church has created its own Babylonian capitivity, making the language of praise impossible; the curses are here directed at the Lollard heretics. See Kuczynski 1995: 153–63. The context is as much political as theological.

[33] Taken from Luther 1970: 209.

[34] See Hamlin 2002: 224–57; readapted in Hamlin 2004: 218–52. The quotation above is taken from Hamlin 2004: 219. In Hamlin 2002: 225 we also read: 'Of the Psalms, none was more widely read, quoted, translated, paraphrased and alluded to than Psalm 137'. Hamlin quotes extracts from poets such as Bacon, Sydney, Oldham, Sandys, and Spenser to make this point (2004: 220–7).

[35] Hamlin 2004: 241–3. Hamlin does not refer to John Calvin's commentary on this psalm, but Calvin's exposition of v. 4 is also quite telling: 'In our own day under the Papacy . . . whether Frenchmen, Englishmen, or Italians, who love and practice the true religion, even their native country is a foreign clime when they live under that tyranny. And yet there is a distinction between us and God's ancient people, for at that time the worship of God was confined to one place, but now he has his Temple wherever two or three are met together in Christ's name' (www.sacred-texts.com/chr/calvin/cc12/cc12020.htm).

a speedy production of an English Psalter which would suit both Archbishop and King did so with the knowledge that the threat of exile abroad was never far away: as he wrote, 'How shall we synge the Lordes songe in a straunge lande?'[36]

2.4. The Psalm in Eighteenth-Century America

The spiritual appropriation of Psalm 137, but with an additional political appeal, continued into the sixteenth and seventeenth centuries, for example in Isaac Watts' *Psalms of David Imitated in the Language of the New Testament* (1719). Replete with contemporary British comment, it was edited and given American colouring in the late eighteenth century in New England Congregationalist churches.[37] Timothy Dwight, grandson of the Jonathan Edwards of the 'Great Awakening', produced two settings of Psalm 137: one was a political version which speaks of the Church's *physical* captivity not amidst Babylon, or indeed in England, but in America:

> Lord, in these dark and dismal days,
> We mourn the hiding of thy face;
> Proud enemies our paths surround,
> To level Zion with the ground.
>
> Her songs, her worship, they deride,
> And hiss thy word with tongues of pride,
> And cry, t'insult our humble prayer,
> 'Where is your God, ye Christians, where?'

The political rhetoric of William Billings was more specific. The enemy 'Babel' again has a literal resonance: this time it is the British forces during the American Revolution in 1776. This metrical paraphrase was written during the British occupation of Boston:[38]

> By the waters of Watertown we sat down and wept
> When we remember thee, O Boston . . .
> For they that held them in bondage requir'd of them
> To take up arms against their brethren.

---

[36] As for Whittingham, his version of Psalm 137 was composed while actually in exile in Geneva during Queen Mary's reign. The reference to the 'king' in v. 4 scarcely disguises the political reference: the problem for Whittingham is no longer the impossibility of a 'Song of Zion' in a strange land, but rather under a strange queen: 'Alas (sayd we) who can once frame, | his sorrowfull hart to syng: | The prayers of our loving God, | Thus under a straunge kyng?' Quoted in Hamlin (2004: 244) from W. Whittingham, *Whole Booke of Psalms*, 1562.

[37] This and the following extract are from Stackhouse (1997: 43–70).

[38] Taken from Stackhouse (1997: 83–5).

Forbid it, Lord. God forbid!
Forbid it Lord, God forbid!
That those who have sucked Bostonian Breasts
Should thirst for American Blood! . . .[39]

2.5. The Psalm in the Twentieth and Twenty-First Centuries

A distinctive social and political reading is found in the Rastafarians' use
of Psalm 137. From their origins as a sect in Jamaica in the 1930s, the
Rastafarians have always combined their belief in black liberation with a
literal and Messianic use of the Hebrew Bible, especially the Psalms. 'Yah' of
the psalms is name of their God, Jah Rastafari, who spoke through their
Messianic leader, Emperor Haile Selassie I. By about the 1950s, Psalm 137
with its use of 'Babel' refers to those from western Europe who sold the
people of African ancestry into slavery in the Americas; the 'exiles' are the
harassed black Jamaican masses. When set to reggae rhythm, Psalm 137
becomes the agent of social change: its genre is reversed, so that the Hebrew
lament becomes a protest song, not wallowing in self-pity, but defiantly
'chanting down' in reggae rhythms 'Babylon's' might. The actual process of
singing is that which has the potential to effect social change. The 'jihad'
at the end of the psalm, against Babylonian domination, becomes the
revolutionary call for liberation and justice:

> By the rivers of Babylon,
> Where we sat down,
> There we wept
> When we remembered Zion.
>
> 'Cause, the wicked carried us away in captivity,
> Required from us a song.
> How can we sing King Alpha's song
> In a strange land?

Many musicians have adapted this version of Psalm 137. It was popularized
by the Melodians in 1969, and again in 1975 by the reggae star Bob Marley,
with Bonney Em. The Jewish protest singer Matisyahu, who combines Jewish
ideas with reggae, rock, and hip-hop, produced a version called 'Jerusalem' in

---

[39] Other political appropriations of this psalm may be found in nineteenth-century Italy. For
example, Giuseppe Verdi's *Nabucco*, which premiered in Milan in 1842, includes the famous
chorus of the Hebrew slaves, based upon Psalm 137; and Algernon Charles Swinburne's version
of 'Super Flumina Babylonis' compares Italy's sufferings at the time of the Franco–Prussian wars
with both the Babylonian captivity and with the sufferings (and resurrection) of Christ: 'By the
waters of Babylon we stood up and sang | Considering thee, | That a blast of deliverance in
the darkness rang, | to set thee free.'

2006. Sinead O'Connor did a more quiet and plaintive version on her album *Theology* in 2007.[40]

Another more recent musical version of Psalm 137, completed in 2010 and called 'Super Flumina', is a composition by Howard Goodall. The chorus ('Enchanted Voices'), most unusually, is female: the Tippett Quartet provides a 'string soundscape'.[41] So, instead of the more typical and often heavy male lament, the psalm starts with an exquisitely pure and haunting solo soprano voice; immediately we sense a grief which is more intensely personal. The strings—which we hear, *sotto voce*, immediately—remind us, paradoxically, of the harps and songs which were once denied, but they are now the means of expressing the memory of the pain and loss. The use of the high F sharp and G sharp and back to the low A—just a semitone less than the octave— emulate again and again the rise and fall of the distress. Gradually other female voices accompany the memory of the lament as well: 'As for our harps, as for our harps, we hanged them up'. The wistfulness (in singing what once could not be sung) continues to the end of the psalm, with its fading harmonies: 'How shall we sing? . . . How shall we sing?'

The physical appropriation of Psalm 137 is evident in art as well. Three examples each use the psalm to create some social comment. The first image is by Arthur Wragg (Plate 4), created during the time of the Depression in the 1930s. His raw and powerful black and white cartoon-like images are to show that the psalms can speak to our *physical* condition—at a time when poverty, unemployment, imprisonment, and the threat of war were frightening realities. His image of Psalm 137 is of two tenement block windows, the top one with a withered plant on the sill and a birdcage with a hazy image of a bird inside. It is unclear whether it is dead or alive. The bottom window is closest to us: we can see through the curtains into the blackened room. A second birdcage hangs there: this time the white upright silhouette of the bird is clear to see, but what is less clear is whether, being caged, it is unable to sing, or whether it is attempting some choked warbling. The overall impression seems to be silence. The caption under it is simply 'How shall we sing the Lord's song in a strange land?'

The second illustration is by a contemporary Oxford artist, Roger Wagner. *In a Strange Land* is a series of poems and engravings, many of which are of the then deserted docklands of East London. The colours of blue, black, and beige and the sense of utter barrenness with the empty cranes, piers, wharves, ladders, and warehouses criss-crossing our view echo the confusion and

---

[40] An entry of 'By the Waters' on YouTube will bring up these versions (accessed March 2012).

[41] 'Super Flumina' is from *Pelican in the Wilderness Classical FM Records* CFMD 13 (solo: Grace Davidson) and was performed live during the Psalms Conference. It can be previewed on http://itunes.apple.com/gb/album/pelican-in-wilderness-songs/id369907442.

bleak desolation which is as much spiritual as it is physical. Psalm 137 is interspersed through these scenes: a most moving one is of Canning Town (Plate 5).

A third illustration is by Michael Jessing, a Northumberland painter whose depiction of Psalm 137 relates to his experience of living in New York City as a child, when he felt detached from nature and his spiritual self (Plate 6). The Babylonian figures represent statues set up before the city; the river is the Hudson; the harp, the hope of playing again—and of painting again—dreams and hopes.

3. Conclusion: Jewish and Christian Reception of Psalm 137

This selective survey reveals that, whether in commentary, music, literary imitation, or art, the Christian reception of Psalm 137 moves in an opposite direction to the Jewish one. Whereas early Jewish readings had a more corporate and physical emphasis, as crisis after crisis threatened the identity of the Jews as a people, early Christian readings are more personal and spiritualized, heightened through the use of allegory. However, in later Christian reception, from the Reformation period onwards, we find an increasing emphasis on the literal and physical relevance of this psalm, while after the middle of the last century an individual and spiritualized emphasis is more apparent in Jewish readings of this psalm.

Many psalms inhibit Jewish–Christian dialogue because they lend themselves more to what might be called a 'David-centred' reading or a 'Christ-centred' reading. Psalm 137 is not such a psalm: it is as difficult to read it as either a psalm 'by' or 'of' or 'for' King David as it is as a psalm 'about' or 'to' or 'of' Jesus Christ. In the Hebrew version, Psalm 137 has no Davidic heading; the references to Babylon and Edom and to a shattered Jerusalem were usually deemed too late for a Psalm to have Davidic author-ship.[42] And Christian interpreters have been ill at ease about associating this psalm, with its passion for the physical place of Jerusalem, and its violent hatred of the people's enemies, as 'about' or 'to' or 'of' Christ. Psalm 137 is not cited at all in the New Testament.

The reception history of Psalm 137, whether Jewish or Christian, whether corporate or personal, physical or spiritual in its final appropriation,

---

[42] David as author of the psalm occasionally occurs in rabbinic tradition. Most Greek translators did assign it 'τῷ Δαυιδ ', but they were probably referring to the authority of David and not his authorship. The fact they gave Psalm 95 (Hebrew 96) a similar heading after stating 'when the house was being rebuilt after captivity' (ὅτε ὁ οἶκος ᾠκοδομεῖτο μετὰ τὴν αἰχμα-λωσίαν ᾠδή τῷ Δαυιδ) shows that the translators did not always think historically when they added their headings.

illustrates a *life-centred* approach to psalmody.[43] The 'I' of the middle of the
psalm is 'anyone' who maintains integrity of faith even when the going
is hard.[44] Ironically—given its negative conclusion—Psalm 137 therefore
encourages dialogue between the two faith traditions as it speaks to our
volatile human predicament in whatever century and in whatever context. For
Jews and Christians alike, Psalm 137 shows that we live in an insecure world,
both physically and spiritually, where God has to be pursued to demand that
justice is done—and *seen* to be done.

Bibliography

Amishai-Maisels, Ziva
    1973 *Tapestries and Mosaics of Marc Chagall at the Knesset* (New York: Tudor
          Publishing Company).
Baal-Teshuva, Jacob
    1998 *Marc Chagall 1887–1985* (Cologne: Taschen).
Bernstein, Moshe J.
    1994 'Translation Technique in the Targum to Psalms. Two Test Cases: Psalms 2
          and 137', *SBL Annual Meeting 1994:3 Seminar Papers* (Atlanta: Scholars
          Press): 326–45.
Braude, William G.
    1959 *The Midrash on Psalms*, vol. 2 (New Haven: Yale University Press).
Brueggemann, Walter
    1984 *The Message of the Psalms* (Minneapolis: Augsburg).
Cassiodorus
    1997 *Explanation of the Psalms*, vol. 3: Psalms 101–150 (trans. and annotated by
          P. G. Walsh; Ancient Christian Writers, 53; New York: Paulist Press).
Cohen, Abraham (ed.)
    1985 *The Psalms: Hebrew Text and English Translation, with an Introduction and
          Commentary* (London and New York: Soncino Press).
Crashaw, Richard
    1927 *The Poems English Latin and Greek of Richard Crashaw*, ed. I. C. Martin
          (Oxford: Clarendon Press).
Edwards, Timothy
    2007 *Exegesis in the Targum of Psalms: The Old, the New and the Rewritten*
          (Gorgias Dissertations, 28; BSI, Piscataway, NJ: Gorgias).
Feuer, Avrohom Chaim (trans. and commentary)
    1980 *Tehillim (Psalms 1–72)*, vol. 1, and *Tehillim (Psalms 73–150)*, vol. 2: *A New
          Translation with a Commentary Anthologized from Talmudic, Midrashic and
          Rabbinic Sources* (Artscroll Tanach Series; New York: Mesorah Publications).

---

[43] Several scholars have advocated the importance of this approach to the Psalms. They
include Westermann (1981), Brueggemann (1984), and Goldingay (1981: 5–90).

[44] Poignant musical examples include the sixteenth-century Giovanni Pierluigi da Palestrina,
who composed 'Super flumina Babylonis' upon the death of his wife in Rome in 1580; or the
British composer Herbert Howells, who over three hundred years later composed (but never
published) a version of Psalm 137 at the time of severe ill-health and the death of a close friend
in the First World War.

Goldingay, John
1981 'The Dynamic Cycle of Praise and Prayer in the Psalms', *JSOT* 20: 85–90.
Hamlin, Hannibal
2004 *Psalm Culture and Early Modern English Literature* (Cambridge University Press).
2002 'Psalm Culture in the English Renaissance: Readings of Psalm 137 by Shakespeare, Spenser, Milton and Others', *Renaissance Quarterly* 55: 224–57.
Holladay, William L.
1993 *The Psalms through Three Thousand Years* (Minneapolis: Fortress Press).
Kirschner, Robert
1990 'Two Responses to Epochal Change: Augustine and the Rabbis on Psalm 137 (136)', *Vigiliae Christianae* 44/3: 242–62.
Kuczynski, Michael P.
1995 *Prophetic Song: The Psalms as Moral Discourse in Late Medieval England* (Philadelphia: University of Pennsylvania Press).
Kugel, James
1990 'Psalm 137' in J. Kugel (ed.), *Potiphar's House: The Interpretive Life of Biblical Times* (Cambridge, MA: Harvard University Press): 173–213.
Luther, Martin
1970 'On the Babylonian Captivity' in *Three Treatises*, trans. A. T. W. Steinhauser, rev. F. C. Ahrens and A. R. Wentz (Philadelphia: Philadephia University Press).
Morin, Germain (ed.)
1959 *S. Hieronymi Presbyteri Commentarioli in Psalmos* (CChr Series Latina, 72; Turnhout: Brepolis).
Neale, John M., and Littledale, Richard F.
1879 *A Commentary on the Psalms from Primitive and Medieval Writers*, vol. 4 (London: J. Masters and Co.).
Origen
1862 'Psalmus CXXVI', in *Patrologiae Graecae Tomus XII: Origenis Opera Omnia: Exegetica in Psalmos:* 1658.
Schaefer, Konrad
2001 'Psalm 137' in *Psalms* (Berit Olam: Studies in Hebrew Narrative as Poetry; Collegeville, MN: Liturgical Press: 321–3.
Stackhouse, Rochelle A.
1997 *The Language of the Psalms in Worship: American Revisions of Watt's Psalter* (London: Scarecrow Press).
Stec, David
2005 *The Targum of Psalms* (The Aramaic Bible, 16; Collegeville, MN: Liturgical Press).
Wagner, Roger
1988 *Songs from a Strange Land* (Oxford: Besalel Press).
Wesselschmidt, Quentin F.
2007 *Psalms 51–150* (Ancient Commentary on Scripture, Old Testament, 8; Downers Grove, IL: InterVarsity Press).
Westermann, Claus
1981 *Praise and Lament in the Psalms*, trans. K. R. Crim and R. N. Soulen (Atlanta: John Knox Press).

Wragg, Arthur
   1933   *The Psalms in Modern Life* (London: Selwyn and Blount).

Websites (accessed March 2012)

www.facsimile-editions.com. (Parma Psalter)
http://www.youtube.com/watch?v=ifoWIqnt11E (Robert Saxton)
http://itunes.apple.com/us/album/robert-saxton-the-wandering/id441406269
   (Robert Saxton)
http://www.ccel.org/ccel/schaff/npnf108.iiCXXXVII.html (Augustine)
http://psalter.library.uu.nl (Utrecht Psalter)
www.sacred-texts.com/chr/calvin/cc12/cc12020.htm (Calvin)
http://itunes.apple.com/gb/album/pelican-in-wilderness-songs/id369907442
   (Howard Goodall)
www.rogerwagner.co.uk (Roger Wagner)
www.m-jessing.supanet.com (Michael Jessing)

6

Psalm 137: Unlikely Liturgy or Partisan Poem? A Response to Sue Gillingham

Jonathan Magonet

I find it quite a challenge to respond to Sue Gillingham's comprehensive, beautifully crafted and illustrated paper. She covers most effectively the relevant traditional Jewish materials, so I have little to add in that area.[1]

What is fascinating, in the light of current sensitivities, is how little the Jewish exegetical tradition seemed disturbed by the closing sentences of the psalm. The punishment exacted on the Babylonians was seen as an exact counterpart to the gruesome behaviour of the Babylonians during the conquest of Jerusalem and so fitted the expectations of a just, measure for measure requital at the hands of God (with the Persians acting as God's instruments).

However, as among our Christian counterparts, when the psalm is used creatively today in Jewish liturgy, usually in non-Orthodox circles, the closing verses are indeed omitted and the psalm ends 'comfortably' with v. 6. The underlying assumption is that the first part of the psalm is an expression of sadness at the fate of the exiles in Babylon, and that the oath is an understandable and appropriate response, a deeply felt commitment to remember Jerusalem as the symbol of a lost homeland. In effect the psalm becomes

---

[1] The traditional Jewish liturgical use of Psalm 137, at least in its entirety, is restricted to two occasions. The most obviously appropriate one is as a prelude to the evening service of *Tisha B'Av*, the fast which commemorates the destruction of both Temples. Whereas the reference to the 'rivers of Babylon' links it to the First Temple, the rabbis could identify 'Edom' with Rome and hence the destruction of the Second Temple. In a rabbinic opinion, this prophetic information was given to David at the time when he composed the psalm (*Gittin* 57b). The second usage is more puzzling as this psalm is to be read prior to reciting the Grace after Meals during weekdays. On Shabbat and Festivals it is replaced with Psalm 126, which is appropriately joyous and celebratory for such occasions. Therein lies seemingly the rationale for the contrasting use of Psalm 137, for even the pleasure of a meal should be diminished by recalling and mourning the destruction of Jerusalem and the Temple. This usage would fulfil the Psalmist's vow to hold Jerusalem above his 'highest joy'. Nevertheless, despite this rationale, and the fact that the passage is printed in traditional prayer books, it is an interesting question as to whether anyone actually reads it aloud or simply glosses over it, whereas Psalm 126 is joyfully sung as an integral part of the grace.

sentimentalized so that the closing section seems particularly shocking, a kind of betrayal of the acceptable emotions of the earlier sections. But it is questionable whether these earlier sections are any less problematic. The mocking demand by their captors for one of the 'songs of Zion' to people who, presumably, are part of the Temple choir, can only be a boastful reflection of their assumption of the defeat of Israel's God. As such, it must have seemed to be the final blow to the reality of conquest, destruction, and exile. The response 'How can we sing a song of the Lord on foreign soil?' cuts deep into the awareness of the totality of what has been lost. Here is despair and bitterness no less powerful than the anger expressed in the closing verses.

Moreover, the oath in vv. 5–6 is unique in the Bible in that it is explicit about what is to happen to the speaker if he fails to keep his vow, instead of using the customary euphemistic phraseology that accompanies biblical vows. The formulation 'may God do this and more to me if I do not do X',[2] in its several occurrences and variations, is deliberately not explicit about what punishment God might inflict if the speaker fails to fulfil the vow. However, I remember a suggestion by Raphael Loewe that the speaker would have made a gesture, like cutting his throat, to express the threat. As a variation, when David offers a curse upon himself if he does not react against the boorish Nabal (1 Sam. 25.22) the text substitutes for 'David' the phrase 'the enemies of David', though he continues to speak the oath in the first person.[3] Thus the destructive threat of the speaker in the psalm, to lose the musical and vocal skills that give him his identity and role, is as violent and destructive in its way as the threat in the closing section. Given the explicit violence in the first two sections, the third with its measure for measure conclusion, though shocking, should not be seen as inconsistent with what has gone before.

Sue Gillingham has already noted that the person changes in the three parts of the psalm—from the 'we' of the opening, to the 'I' of the oath to the second person expressions of the last part. Without questioning the essential unity of the psalm, I would like to suggest a way of reading these changes, by drawing on a rabbinic observation about a passage, from 1 Sam. 4.6–9:

> [6] When the Philistines heard the noise of the shouting, they said, 'What does this great shouting in the camp of the Hebrews mean?' When they learned that the ark of the LORD had come to the camp, [7] the Philistines were afraid; for they said, 'Gods have come into the camp.' They also said, 'Woe to us! For nothing like this

---

[2] 1 Sam. 3.17; 14.44; 20.13; 2 Sam. 3.9, 35; 19.14; 1 Kgs 2.23; 2 Kgs 6.31; Ruth 1.17.

[3] A similar insertion of אויבי ('enemies') protects David from the accusation of spurning God (2 Sam. 12.14). A different kind of substitution is noted by Rashi in the words of Dathan and Abiram during their rebellion against Moses when they accuse him of 'putting out the eyes of these men', as a substitute for themselves. Similarly in Exod. 1.10 Rashi quotes from *Sotah* 11a on the puzzling phrase 'and go up from the land': 'They spoke like a person who is pronouncing a curse against himself but attaches the curse to others (because he does not wish to use an ominous expression of himself), so that it is as though Scripture wrote "and we shall have to go up out of the land" and they will take possession of it.'

has happened before. [8] Woe to us! Who can deliver us from the power of these mighty gods? These are the gods who struck the Egyptians with every sort of plague in the wilderness. [9] Take courage, and be men, O Philistines, in order not to become slaves to the Hebrews as they have been to you; be men and fight.'

Rashi on v. 8 comments that in *Sifrei* (*Beha'alot'cha*) we learned that this passage is made up of statements by different people (literally: 'the one who said this did not say that').[4] The rest of Rashi's comments depend on a midrashic rereading of the text, but the principle of multiple voices would distinguish, for example, between those Philistines who despaired and those who encouraged the others to fight. On the same basis, it would be possible to see in the three parts of our Psalm 137 the juxtaposition of three different responses to the situation of defeat and exile: the despair and passive resistance of the Levitical singers; the personal commitment to remembrance and defiance of, presumably, one of the Levitical singers; and, in the third section, an appeal to God for a curse on the Edomites and Babylonians uttered by someone whose identity is not so clear. There is, however, a possible clue in the use of the word אַשְׁרֵי ('happy') in the closing verses. Of its thirty-eight appearances in the Hebrew Bible, twenty-five of them are in the book of Psalms.[5] Without exception they belong in hymnic evocations of the happiness of those who trust in God, whose sins are forgiven, and who are taught by God. Therefore the use of the word to describe the perpetrator of these violent acts is a deliberately shocking usage of this term, jarring and provocative in its exceptional nature. Again, it would suggest a voice out of the Levitical choir, this time turning the very language of the 'songs of Zion' against their captors. All three sections represent expressions of resistance but each is very different in its focus.

Regarding the vow in the second section, it could clearly exist independently of the rest of the Psalm and may well have done so at some stage. It feels intuitively like a song, in which case it is a kind of measure for measure response to the request of the captors for one of the songs of Zion. However, this is not a 'song of Zion' but a song of Jerusalem, a song of protest and resistance. This in turn raises questions about the difference between the use of the terms 'Zion' and 'Jerusalem', alluded to in Dr Gillingham's paper with reference to Adele Berlin's distinction between 'Zion-songs' and a 'Jerusalem-lament'.[6] Though the names are often synonymous, there is a suggestion that when they are used separately 'Zion' relates to the Temple as the religious centre of the nation, whereas the emphasis in the name 'Jerusalem' represents

---

[4] Citations from Rashi have been taken from *Mikraot Gedolot* 1959.
[5] Pss. 1.1; 2.12; 32.1,2; 33.12; 34.9; 40.5; 41.2; 65.5; 84.5,6,13; 89.16; 94.12; 106.3; 112.1; 119.1,2; 127.5; 128.1; 137.8,9; 144.15; 146.5.
[6] See pp. 66–7 above.

the capital city of the nation and its political centre.[7] The possibility of such a distinction is reinforced by the reference to Babylon as אדמת נכר ('foreign ground'), where one might expect instead a term denoting ritual 'unclean-ness', given the context of singing the 'songs of Zion'. The term 'foreign' defines the territory of Babylon in political terms rather than as a place that is ritually unclean. Such a distinction leads to the possibility that precisely here the experience of exile redefines the understanding of what has been lost: not only the religious centre but also land, people, and national autonomy. Hence the need for a political response; in place of a 'religious song' he offers a song of political defiance.[8] What further supports such a changed perspective is the use of the phrase 'above my highest joy', literally 'at the head of my joy' (v. 6). The word שמחה ('joy') has already appeared in v.3, where it is parallel to שיר ('song'), and the context there is the 'songs of Zion'. Thus, for the 'we' of the opening section, 'joy' is represented in terms of their task of praising God in the Temple. For the 'I' voice of the second section, the longing for and commitment to remembering Jerusalem, presumably as representing in its broadest sense his national home, is even greater than his desire to sing the songs of Zion. Since his oath is not directly addressed to God but to Jerusalem itself, this would support the political rather than religious nature of his words.[9]

In contrast to the absence of the name of God in this middle section, it is present in the other two sections by reference to the 'LORD's song' (v. 4, NRSV) and the imperative call to 'the LORD' to remember against the 'sons of Edom' the 'day of Jerusalem' (v. 7). If we continue with the hypothesis that this latter reflects a third 'attitude' to the events, it would be a 'religious' voice once again, effectively demanding divine retribution on the Edomites and Babylonians. Thus the overall effect is to enclose the oath section within two sections that emphasize the religious element, their loyalty to God in the first part and their expectation of God's intervention to effect justice in the second. The religious framework thus contains and controls, or at least, interprets, the political emphasis of the centre. Expressed in another way, the insult to God's honour by the mocking request to sing the 'songs of Zion'

---

[7] Though I recall hearing this suggestion some years ago, I understand that it has been explored more recently in Körting (2006). How far the 'religious' and the 'political' can be separated in the biblical world needs to be questioned. Nevertheless, though Psalm 122, for example, does begin and end with celebrating Jerusalem as the place of 'the house of the Eternal', the Temple, the centre of the psalm emphasizes that here were situated the thrones of judgment, thrones of the 'house of David'. The distinction and at the same time the unification of the two is also evident in Ps. 114.2, 'Judah became his sanctuary, Israel his dominion'. See Fokkelman 2001: 58–9.

[8] Cf. Fokkelman 2001: 61–2.

[9] The political nature of the use of 'Jerusalem' in this psalm is further emphasized in the term 'the day of Jerusalem', emphasizing the city itself rather than the Temple. That the name of the city is central to the thought of the author is further expressed in the wordplay denoting the 'joy' of the one who repays Babylon: אשרי שישלם ('*ashrei shey'shalem*').

evokes the expectation of God's intervention to restore the divine reputation, quite outside and beyond any oath that an individual may make.[10]

If I may move briefly from the role of exegete to that of liturgist, the absence of the closing section robs the reader of the psalm of the licence and opportunity to express anger within a liturgical context. Indeed we have to ask whether, and if so how, anger may be expressed as a legitimate emotion within a liturgical context. One rationale for using the psalm in its complete form is that the anger that arises in times of persecution or conflict also needs to find its expression before God, since for the religious mind everything must ultimately be offered to God. In that respect Psalm 137 is careful to leave the act of requital to God alone and not the Psalmist's own military activity.

The one traditional Jewish context for expressing such anger against violent treatment by the outside world is to be found in the *Seder* evening when the front door is opened and we recite a number of biblical verses beginning with Ps. 79.6: '*sh'foch chamat'cha . . .*', 'pour out your wrath upon the nations that do not know/acknowledge you'. The containment of such a sentiment within a liturgical context allows for the legitimate expression of heightened emotions but also provides a framework for displacing and releasing them. That at least is a possibility, though it can equally be argued that expressing that kind of anger may not release it but actually fuel it. Nevertheless, within the context of the *Seder* evening, the overall emphasis on the acts of salvation brought about by God, and the entire nature of this domestic ceremony, unite to distance the participants from the content of such sentiments and even to question them, or recognize how real they may be for others suffering persecution. It is the nature of a regularly repeated liturgy that there are times when it is merely neutral, and times when it exactly reflects contemporary events and challenges. Psalm 137 in its full version may not be the most appropriate text for a contemporary spirituality, but it does provide us with a reminder that there are dimensions of our personal and collective lives that do evoke anger and the desire for revenge, and that these cannot simply be wished away or ignored. How we address

---

[10] One further observation concerns the text itself. It is possible that the use of the term describing the 'daughter Babylon' as הַשְּׁדוּדָה ('*ha-sh'dudah*') is a conscious echo of another Biblical poem, the song of Deborah. In telling of the death of Sisera, the poem describes with repeated images how he bowed, fell and lay between the legs of his killer (Judg. 5.27): *Bein ragleha kara nafal shakhav | Bein ragleha kara nafal | Ba'asher kara sham nafal | Shadud!* ('He sank, he fell, he lay still at her feet; at her feet he sank, he fell; where he sank, there he fell dead.') The imagery can be read as sexual, though the preceding verse is more neutral about how he met his death. However, since it is immediately followed by the description of Sisera's mother eagerly awaiting his return, it could also hint at a miscarriage, the stillbirth falling to the ground between the mother's legs. The climactic '*shadud*' expresses the finality of the event of destruction. Perhaps the Psalmist had this passage in mind and applied it to the image of בַּת־בָּבֶל ('*bat bavel*', the 'daughter Babylon') likewise losing her children at birth—in anticipation of the climactic image of infants being smashed against the rocks.

them within a religious context still needs to be considered. We are not as nice as a sentimentalized version of religion would have us believe, nor does a bowdlerized spirituality, as by omitting the end of the psalm, give us the necessary resources to deal with such emotions when they arise. The very structure of the psalm would suggest that the task of religion is not to accept or promote violence, however much it may seem to be justified, but, paradoxically, by offering it to God, to contain and prevent it.

I would like to conclude with the words of Claude Montefiore who, as a leading figure in the creation of the Liberal Jewish movement in the UK, is surprisingly understanding in his treatment of the closing verses of the psalm. He writes about it in the separate volume on the Psalms extracted from his book *The Bible for Home Reading: With Comments and Reflections for the Use of Jewish Parents and Children.*[11]

> It would be tempting to omit the third stanza. But in a Psalm so famous as this it would be historically unfair. Doubtless the Psalmist had seen and heard of many deeds of heartless cruelty, which partly palliate the cruelty of his own heart's desire. For us, however, the close of the Psalm destroys the beauty of its opening. Realizing as we do that tit for tat is not the highest moral law, the vengeance cry of the Psalmist belongs for us to a lower and superseded religious plane. Yet it is not for us to forget that it is not *our* wisdom and piety which enable us to detect the religious deficiencies of our ancestors. Rather is it the sifted piety and purified wisdom of the past which enable the present to start at a higher moral and religious level. As the old saying goes, 'Dwarfs on giants' shoulders see further than giants'.

Bibliography

1959 *Mikraot Gedolot* (Tel Aviv: Schocken)
Fokkelman, Jan
    2001 *Reading Biblical Poetry: An Introductory Guide* (Louisville, KY: Westminster John Knox Press).
Körting, Corinna
    2006 *Zion in den Psalmen* (FAT, 48; Tübingen: Mohr Siebeck).
Montefiore, Claude G.
    1901 *The Book of Psalms* (London: Macmillan).

[11] Montefiore 1901: 478.

7

The Liturgical Psalter in Medieval Europe

Elizabeth Solopova

1. An Overview

The Psalter holds primacy among medieval Christian liturgical books in several important ways. From the early Middle Ages Psalters survive in larger numbers than any other liturgical books. They are also the most frequently and richly illuminated of medieval liturgical manuscripts, and probably of all medieval books. This reflects the exceptional importance of psalms in Christian liturgy. A group of psalms was sung each day at the canonical hours of the Divine Office and in the course of a week all 150 psalms were recited as part of the monastic liturgical cycle.[1] Psalms were used in the celebration of the Mass and played an important part in private lay devotion. The liturgical Psalter served as a prayer book for wealthy and literate lay people until the thirteenth century, when it was superseded in this role by the Book of Hours. The wide use and diverse audience of liturgical Psalters ensured that they were produced in relatively large numbers throughout the Middle Ages, and their textual contents, decoration, and physical make-up varied to satisfy the tastes and requirements of different patrons. Throughout the Middle Ages Psalters reflected a variety of local liturgical uses and practices of different religious orders.

The diversity of the contents and decoration of the liturgical Psalter may come as a surprise, considering that its basic structure was well-defined and fairly simple. It contained the psalms, but also other texts essential for its role as a liturgical book. The liturgical Psalter started with a calendar set before the 150 psalms, followed by the canticles for the daily offices and a litany of the saints.[2] This basic structure—calendar, psalms, canticles, and litany—is often found in early medieval Psalters. As with other liturgical books, Psalters were becoming more complex in the late Middle Ages, acquiring features of

---

[1] See Harper 1991: 67–72.
[2] The Vulgate numbering of psalms, with the Hebrew numbers given in brackets, is used throughout this paper. Quotations from the Bible are from the *NRSV* (1995).

liturgical compendia. Late medieval Psalters often contained a wide range of different texts, both original and added, including masses, offices, prayers, hymnals, antiphons and responses, sometimes with musical notation. Such complexity of content is, however, primarily characteristic of Psalters made for religious rather than lay patrons. Psalters made for the laity often had the traditional basic structure even in the late Middle Ages.

Luxury illuminated Psalters with simple textual contents, probably aimed primarily at wealthy lay patrons, were produced in Bruges and Ghent in the thirteenth century. These towns flourished economically and artistically, and seem to have housed workshops specializing in the production of illuminated liturgical manuscripts. Oxford, Bodleian Library, MS Liturg. 396 is a Psalter made in Bruges in the middle of the thirteenth century. Its calendar, decorated with the 'Labours of the Months', as was the custom in the Netherlands, England, and France, is fairly sparse and is not graded, suggesting that the manuscript was made for a lay patron. The Psalter was still in use in Flanders in the fourteenth and fifteenth centuries. The calendar page for February contains an added note with an explanation of bissext (see Plate 7), and the calendar page for March a note about the calculation of the date of Easter, both in Netherlandish, in a large, distinctive fourteenth-century hand.[3] MS. Liturg. 396 also has a fifteenth-century Netherlandish binding.[4]

Luxury Psalters often contained miniatures, most commonly placed after the calendar and/or at liturgical divisions within the book. MS Liturg. 396 is one of the oldest surviving Flemish Psalters with a Christological miniature cycle.[5] The cycle begins with seven full-page miniatures, following the calendar and depicting the Annunciation, Nativity, Annunciation to the Shepherds, Presentation in the Temple, Adoration of the Magi, Christ among

---

[3] *locus bissexti bissext es dat men heut tue daghe op de lettre van zente mathis daghe ende bissext gheualt alse men de iare van ons heren ghebornessen mach delen in viren eueneffene* ('bissext is that there are two days on the letter of St Matthew's day and bissext falls when the year of our Lord's birth can be divided equally into four parts') and *Wi selen nemen de niuwe mane nar de nonen van marte ende tellen tote . xiiii . ende derste zondach die comp nar die xiiii dat es pacshdach* ('We must take the new moon after the Nones of March and count to the 14th [day] and the first Sunday which comes after the 14th [day] that is Easter day').

[4] The provenance of MS Liturg. 396 after the fifteenth century is uncertain. Its calendar contains a post-medieval addition of the feast of the discovery of St Mark's relics during the construction of his basilica in Venice. The spelling '*euangieliste*' suggests that the addition was made by an Italian speaker. The manuscript must have been in the Bodleian Library before 1887. As is evident from its earlier shelfmark, 'Miscell. Liturg. 396', it was part of the Miscellaneous Liturgical collection, which was formed in 1860, but went on growing until 1887 (see Madan 1905: 844).

[5] See Carlvant 1978: 80–8, 276, 473, 480 and *passim*; Alexander and Temple 1985: no. 804; Haseloff 1938: 67, table 18. MS Liturg. 396 is close in style to several Psalters attributed to Bruges (cf. the 'Eerste Groep' of Carlvant 1978), particularly Brussels, Bibliothèque Royale, Ms. 5074; Saint-Omer, Bibliothèque de l'agglomération, Ms. 270; Baltimore, Walters Art Museum, W. 36; Edinburgh, University Library, MS 62; and Oxford, University College, MS 12.

the Doctors, Baptism of Christ, and the Last Judgement.[6] The cycle continues with eight further full-page miniatures at liturgical divisions within the text of the Psalter, and with nine historiated initials facing the miniatures and forming part of the cycle. The subjects include the Jesse Tree, the three Temptations, Christ and Mary Magdalene, the Entry into Jerusalem, Christ addressing the disciples, and a series of scenes from the narrative about the Passion and Resurrection.[7] The miniatures are on gold backgrounds, in rectangular frames, and are painted on the verso of each leaf, leaving the rectos blank, as is common in the thirteenth-century Psalters from Bruges.[8]

In a great majority of medieval liturgical Psalters psalms were written out in the biblical order, though there was also a limited tradition, best attested in fifteenth- and sixteenth-century Italy, of presenting psalms in the order in which they were recited during the week. Such Psalters are known as ferial. The ferial order was difficult to present in a book, because psalms and parts of psalms were used in more than one office during the week. As a result there was no single established way of constructing a ferial Psalter, and surviving manuscripts approach this task in different ways. In addition, psalms were recited in a different order in monastic and secular use,[9] and ferial Psalters, reflecting the weekly liturgical cycle of either use, were made in Italy in the fifteenth and sixteenth centuries.[10]

Psalms were rarely numbered in medieval manuscripts, because during the Middle Ages they were known and referred to by their opening words.[11] The numbering often found in the margins of liturgical Psalters is usually a later addition, supplied by early modern, sixteenth- and seventeenth-century owners. Medieval readers, trying to find their way around the book, were assisted by textual divisions, which marked psalms as particularly important in the weekly liturgical cycle. Textual divisions were signalled by larger

---

[6] The Last Judgement is in a different Franco-Flemish style and was probably added later in the thirteenth century; see Pächt and Alexander 1966–73: vol.1, no. 282.

[7] The subjects of the miniatures in the final part of the cycle include the Last Supper, Christ washing the disciples' feet, Christ in Gethsemane, the Betrayal, Judas receiving a bag of money from the Jews, Christ carrying the Cross, Flagellation, Crucifixion, the Harrowing of Hell, another version of the Crucifixion, and *Noli me tangere*. The Jesse Tree depicts Jesse sleeping and a large, full-length figure of an unidentified female saint holding a palm of martyrdom and probably a book.

[8] The only exception is the Betrayal, painted on fol. 88 verso. Such an approach testifies to a well-organized commercial book production: the miniatures were produced separately and inserted into books by stationers. See Carlvant 1985: 329 n. 14.

[9] See Harper 1991: 242–50.

[10] See e.g. Oxford, Bodleian Library, MS Canon. Liturg. 395, made in Dalmatia, possibly Trogir, early in the fifteenth century, as an example of a secular ferial Psalter; and Oxford, Bodleian Library, MS Add. D. 47 as an example of a Carthusian Psalter, made in Milan early in the sixteenth century.

[11] Original, rather than added, psalm numbers occur most commonly as part of psalm titles, found only in a small percentage of liturgical Psalters; see Salmon 1959.

and sometimes elaborately illuminated initials, and occasionally also by the inclusion of miniatures.

The textual divisions are found in all medieval liturgical Psalters, and were an absolutely standard feature of the presentation of psalms in such books. Their number and exact location, however, varied considerably. The common ways of subdividing the Psalter included the division into 'three fifties', with boundaries at Psalms 1, 51(52), and 101(102), and into eight sections according to the weekly liturgical cycle in the secular use.[12] The division into eight sections, starting at Psalms 1, 26(27), 38(39), 52(53), 68(69), 80(81), 97(98), and 109(110), was the best-known and the most common way of subdividing a liturgical Psalter in the late Middle Ages.[13] The first seven psalms were appointed to be recited first at Matins from Sunday to Saturday, whereas Psalm 109(110) was recited first at Vespers on Sunday. In England, the Netherlands, and northern France these eight liturgical divisions were often combined with the division into 'three fifties', resulting in a tenfold division of the text. This can be seen, for example, in MS Liturg. 369 which has large illuminated initials and miniatures at Psalms 1, 26(27), 38(39), 51(52), 52(53), 68(69), 80(81), 97(98), 101(102), and 109(110).

We have already seen that the eightfold division reflected how psalms were recited in the secular use, and there were significant differences between the weekly liturgical cycle in the monastic and secular church. In the late Middle Ages, however, the eightfold system became a traditional way of subdividing a liturgical Psalter, commonly found in manuscripts made for monastic as well as secular patrons. Some surviving manuscripts, however, emphasize psalms important in the monastic, rather than secular, liturgical cycle. Oxford, Bodleian Library, MS Canon. Liturg. 311, for example, is a Carthusian Psalter, made in Italy, probably Venice, in the third quarter of the fifteenth century. It has decorated initials at Psalms 20(21), 32(33), 45(46), 59(60), 73(74), 85(86), 101(102), 109(110), and 144(145):10. These psalms were recited first at Matins on Sunday and during the week, and at Vespers on Sunday and Saturday in the monastic use. Occasionally Psalters had larger initials marking important psalms according to both uses. Thus, Oxford, Bodleian Library, MS Gough Liturg. 2, written in the late twelfth or early thirteenth century in the north of England, has decorated initials at Psalms 1, 26(27), 38(39), 52(53), 68(69), 80(81), and 97(98), recited first at Matins

---

[12] The division into 'three fifties' is of uncertain early medieval origin and is found on its own in early medieval Psalters, and in combination with liturgical divisions in Psalters from the late Middle Ages. See an account of different ways of subdividing the Psalter in Leroquais (1940–1: vol. 1, lxxxvi–xcix).

[13] In spite of the wide use of the eightfold system in the late Middle Ages, it was certainly not the only way of subdividing the Psalter, and, as explained below, many Psalters had differently placed textual boundaries. Deviations from the eightfold system are potentially important as a source of information about the origin and patronage of Psalters.

during the week in the secular use; at Psalms 20(21), 32(33), 45(46), 59(60), 73(74), 85(86), 101(102), recited first at Matins during the week in the monastic use, at Psalm 109(110), recited first at Sunday Vespers in both uses as well as at Psalm 51(52), indicating the division into 'three fifties'. There were many other ways of subdividing the Psalter, which emphasized the penitential psalms, the beginning of the gradual psalms, and other devotionally important psalms in combination with liturgical subdivisions.

The eightfold division was often combined with the so-called 'literal' or 'Parisian' system of Psalter illumination.[14] This programme developed in France at the beginning of the thirteenth century, and became widely used in Europe in the second half of the thirteenth century, replacing local traditions. It remained popular until the end of the Middle Ages and was based on the literal illustration of the opening words of psalms, which occurred at the start of the eight sections. The iconography focused on King David as the 'author' of the Psalter. Thus, Psalm 26(27), beginning *Dominus illuminatio mea* ('The Lord is my light'), was illustrated with an image of King David, pointing to his eyes, whereas Psalm 52(53), beginning *Dixit insipiens* ('The fool says'), had a picture of a fool, occasionally on his own, but often in conversation with King David, a cleric, or Christ.[15] The fool was variously portrayed, sometimes as a beggar or a barely clothed madman, sometimes as a courtly jester, and some-times through a mixture of the two approaches. When depicted as a jester, he often wears a hood with bells and holds a bladder on a stick. When portrayed as a madman, he is frequently shown holding a club and either holding or eating bread, illustrating v. 4 of Psalm 52(53), which mentions the 'evildoers, who eat up my people as they eat bread'. Miniatures depicting these common subjects differed in detail, leaving plenty of scope for artistic creativity.

In England, the Parisian programme largely replaced an earlier programme of Psalter illumination which depicted events of Old and New Testament history. English Psalters of the eleventh to the thirteenth centuries were illustrated with narrative miniatures depicting Old Testament subjects and events from the life of Christ, including the Judgement of Solomon, which usually appeared in the initial of Psalm 38(39), and the Annunciation to the Shepherds, which appeared in the initial of Psalm 97(98).[16] In spite of its popularity in the late Middle Ages, however, the Parisian programme never completely eliminated other ways of illustrating the Psalter.[17] As pointed out by Nigel Morgan, there were local pockets of resistance to the Parisian system in all countries that came under its influence, and in the Netherlands Davidic cycles coexisted with Christological and hagiographical cycles.[18] As

---

[14] Leroquais 1940–1: vol. 1, lxxxvi–xcix; Sandler 1999: 21–6; Büttner 2004: 1–80.
[15] See Gifford 1974; Billington 1984; Neale 1985; Kolve 1997.
[16] Haseloff 1938: 8–18.   [17] Morgan 2008.   [18] Ibid. 69–71.

mentioned already, MS Liturg. 396 has a Christological cycle of full-page miniatures and historiated psalm initials, which include a depiction of the Second Temptation of Christ in the initial of Psalm 26(27) and of the Last Supper in the initial of Psalm 52(53).

The calendar and psalms in liturgical Psalters were followed by the canticles and litany. The canticles included two sets of texts: six Old Testament 'weekly' canticles, staring with *Confitebor*, which were sung at Lauds during the week in both the monastic and secular use; and a selection of the New Testament and non-biblical canticles and creeds.[19] Whereas the first set was very stable and always contained the same canticles in the same order, this second set varied greatly in its content and order. In MS Liturg. 396 the second set consists of three texts: the prose hymn *Te deum laudamus*, which was sung at the end of Matins on Sundays and at feasts of nine or twelve lessons; *Benedictus dominus deus* (Lk. 1.68–79), sung daily at Lauds; and the Athanasian Creed (*Quicumque vult . . .*).[20] This selection is smaller than what is found in the majority of Psalters. In spite of considerable variation, by far the most common set of the New Testament and non-biblical canticles, particularly in Psalters from England, consisted of *Te deum laudamus*, *Benedicite omnia opera*, *Benedictus dominus deus*, *Magnificat*, *Nunc dimittis*, and the Athanasian Creed.

The litany had a traditional order and layout, with apostles, followed by the martyrs, confessors, and virgins, but the choice of saints differed considerably, making litanies an important source of information about regional and institutional liturgical traditions, and an aid in the localization of liturgical books. The litany in MS Liturg. 396 contained saints particularly venerated in Bruges and Ghent.[21]

2. Non-Liturgical Use of Latin Psalters

Latin liturgical Psalters seem to have had a very long useful life. It is not at all uncommon to see evidence that medieval Psalters were still in use in the sixteenth and seventeenth centuries and in Italy even in the eighteenth century. Such evidence includes corrections, modifications, and annotations in Psalters in early modern hands. These additions comprise scholarly notes, such as those pointing out the differences between the Hebrew and Latin texts of psalms, but also liturgical notes and modifications, such as the changes made in order to update the calendar and litany by introducing new feasts

---

[19] See Mearns 1914; Pulsiano 1995; Harper 1991: 83, 91, 181, 256–7, 270–5.
[20] See Harper 1991: 83.
[21] The litany in MS Liturg. 369 is discussed and published by Carlvant (1978: 121, 509–30).

and the names of newly popular saints.[22] Many Psalters were extensively remodelled in the late Middle Ages. In some cases the calendar or litany, or both, were removed and replaced by a more modern calendar or litany, designed for the use by the community in which the Psalter was owned.[23] In other cases new texts were added, including hymnals, offices, masses and prayers, as well as antiphons, responses, and other texts, performed together with psalms. In fact it is difficult to find a Psalter without medieval and early modern additions and modifications.

The use of a medieval Psalter was not confined to liturgical and private devotional practice. As is well known, Psalters had a role in education and in what can be described as popular religion, medicine, prognostication, or even magic.[24] There is evidence that Psalters were used in trials by ordeal and were carried by their owners as amulets, but the connection of Psalters with popular ritual is most evident in their contents. Scholars have pointed out a certain overlap in the contents of medieval liturgical and medical manuscripts.[25] Medical collections could include liturgical material, such as instructions to recite particular prayers and psalms, whereas liturgical books could contain scientific and medical texts.

Discussing the contents of the British Library, Cotton MS Vitellius E xviii, Philip Pulsiano pointed out that the prefatory matter of this English mid-eleventh-century Psalter is a mixture of Latin and Old English material.[26] It includes computistical and calendarial texts, texts treating unlucky days for blood-letting and childbirth, charms to protect against theft, to discover theft, to protect cattle, to promote crops, medicine for cattle with different diseases, and finally a text with directions for secret writing. Pulsiano argued that this was not an arbitrary collection. Some of the charms included references to psalms and invitations to recite particular psalms. The psalms were often those that would seem relevant to the action the charm was trying to produce, if interpreted in a particular way. Pulsiano insisted that the prefatory matter

---

[22] Oxford, Bodleian Library, MS Laud Lat. 81, written in England in the second half of the eleventh century, contains Hebrew subtitles in Psalm 119, added by its sixteenth-century owner, Thomas Wood, rector of Stowting, Kent (see Maden and Craster 1922: no. 768); Oxford, Bodleian Library, MS Douce 49 contains running titles in the upper margin, added in a sixteenth-century hand, to indicate the subdivision of psalms into five books in Jewish usage. The same hand added short rubrics at the beginning of psalms, referring to their 'authorship' and use (e.g. '*david*', '*asaph*', '*canticum graduum*', '*aggei et zacharie*', '*oratio*', etc.), as well as the letters of the Hebrew alphabet, placed at the beginning of the sections of Psalm 118, some with their names in Latin transliteration, e.g. '*aleph*', '*beth*', etc. (see Madan 1897: no. 21623).

[23] Oxford, Bodleian Library, MS Auct. D. 4. 3, written in Flanders *c.*1265–75, has Sarum litanies added *c.*1400 in England; Oxford, Bodleian Library, MS Douce 18, written in England *c.*1433, has masses, office of the Virgin, calendar, astronomical tables, and diagrams, added *c.*1475; Oxford, Bodleian Library, MS Lat. liturg. e. 21, written in the second quarter of the fourteenth century in France, contains two added litanies.

[24] Heinzer 2008.

[25] Pulsiano 1998.

[26] Contents listed in Pulsiano 1998.

of the Cotton Vitellius Psalter should be studied with reference to its liturgical context, for this is essential for our understanding of how 'the psalms were regarded and understood by individual readers or within a larger literate community'.[27]

Psalters crossed the boundary between religious orthodoxy and popular ritual, between the public liturgical sphere and private devotional practice, and even extended their presence into secular areas of their owners' daily lives. There is evidence that Psalters were treated by their owners as deeply treasured personal objects. In many cases it was the only book that people owned, which accompanied them throughout their lives. There was a tendency among the late medieval owners to customize their books through the addition of texts, such as personal prayers or the records of family births and deaths, through the inclusion of devotional images, and sometimes even of objects, such as pilgrim badges which were occasionally sewn into the books.[28]

Much of this can be illustrated by Oxford, Bodleian Library, MS Lat. liturg. g. 1, a portable monastic Psalter, probably made in York at the beginning of the fifteenth century.[29] It is a very small book, only about 20 cm long and 8 cm wide. The first original item is the calendar for the use of the Benedictine Abbey of St Mary in York. The calendar contains three feasts of St Benedict, as well as the feasts of the archbishops of York and saints venerated in the north of England.[30] The calendar is followed by psalms, canticles, and litany, but in addition to these the manuscript also contains two prologues to the psalms, including an extract from Alcuin's *De psalmorum usu*. There is also a hymnal, containing, among others, hymns for St Benedict, as well as the Office of the Dead, and monastic canticles for Sundays and feasts during the year.[31]

Perhaps the most interesting aspect of this Psalter, however, is the texts and notes added by its owners. Though made for a monastic patron, it seems to have been in lay hands early in the sixteenth century. MS Lat. liturg. g. 1 contains an English poem added in an early sixteenth-century hand on an empty leaf facing the first page of the calendar (see Plate 8):

> Cryst that was in bedelem born
> & baptisyde was in flume iordane
> the flume was wood
> the chylde was good
> the chyld wyth the ryght hande blessyd the flode

---

[27] Ibid. 86.

[28] Similar 'devotional personalization' in the Books of Hours is discussed and extensively illustrated in Duffy 2006.

[29] See Madan 1905: no. 31379; Tolhurst 1932–42, vol. 6: 242; van Dijk 1957–60, vol. 2 (i): fol. 27.

[30] The calendar in MS Lat. liturg. g. 1 is similar to the calendar in another Bodleian manuscript, MS Rawl. C. 553, a Book of Hours from the Abbey of St Mary, York.

[31] The monastic canticles are discussed in Harper 1991: 91, 256–7.

the flode stylle stode
so do thys day or nyght thys mannys blode
In the name of goode
seynt J(o)hon and the baptysme
that Crist toke in flume Iordane.[32]

This poem is found in several Middle English medical collections and is a charm to stop bleeding. The earliest versions of a similar Latin formula date from the ninth and tenth centuries. It is based on a legend that the river Jordan stood still during the baptism of Christ.[33] The English poem appears with a variable number of lines, in several Middle English manuscripts containing medical recipes. In an early fifteenth-century manuscript, Trinity College, Cambridge, MS O. 9. 26, N, it has a title *Ad restringendum sanguinem* ('For the stopping of bleeding').[34] Blood-charms were used for women in childbirth, and MS Lat. liturg. g. 1 provides evidence for the connection of this charm with women. One of the empty leaves at the end of the book contains a faded name *elyzabeth* (fol. 202r), written in the same hand as the charm. In addition the calendar of MS Lat. liturg. g. 1 includes a note in Latin, in a fifteenth-century hand, different from the hand of the charm and from the main scribe of the manuscript, which records the birth in 1465/6 of princess Elizabeth of York (d. 1503), daughter of Edward IV and Elizabeth Woodville, and queen of England as wife of Henry VII:

Elisabeth prima genita Edwardi iiij[ti] Regis & Elisabeth' Regine Anglie . nata fuit inter horas terciam & quartam in Aurora diei Mercurij . viz xij[i] Februarii . Ann° Domini M°CCCClxv et Ann° regni dicti domini Regis v°. littera dominicali . E . (fol. 11v)

(Elisabeth, first-born of King Edward IV and Elisabeth the Queen of England, was born between the third and the fourth hour on the morning of Wednesday, 12th February, in the year of our Lord 1465 and in the 5th year of the reign of the said lord King, with the dominical letter E)

It would be tempting to think that there is a connection between MS Lat. liturg. g. 1, the blood charm, and Elizabeth of York, particularly considering that she died at the age of just 37, from a postnatal infection, eight days after giving birth to her daughter, Catherine Tudor. The connection, however, is almost certainly only indirect. The charm and the name 'elyzabeth' are not in the hand of Elizabeth of York or her mother Elizabeth Woodville, whose autographs survive.[35]

---

[32] Brown and Robbins 1943: no. 624; Cutler and Brown 1965: no. 624; Boffey and Edwards 2005: no. 624; Mooney and Solopova, *The Index of Middle English Verse*, no. 624.

[33] See Gray 1974: 62–3.

[34] See Mooney and Solopova, *The Index of Middle English Verse*, no. 624.

[35] See e.g. Duffy 2006: pl. 39.

Notes recording family births and deaths are common in the calendars of late medieval liturgical books, but this particular inscription suggests an interest in astrology, rather than simply a wish to record a family birth. The precise time and the day of the week, as well as the date of birth, were required for the casting of horoscopes. In addition the wording *prima genita* suggests that the record was made some time after the birth of Elizabeth of York, when she was no longer the only child. If the note were written at the time of her birth, the wording would have been different, perhaps something like *una genita*. All this takes us outside the royal circle, but there is little doubt that in the late fifteenth and early sixteenth centuries MS Lat. liturg. g. 1 was owned by a woman whose name was Elizabeth, who added a blood charm on an empty leaf, and who may have been interested in the horoscope of the queen, whose name also was Elizabeth. MS Lat. liturg. g. 1 contains further evidence of customization of an uncertain, possibly medieval date: two leaves contain an impression left by a heart-shaped object, possibly a pilgrim or a secular badge which was once inserted into the book by its owner.[36]

3. Vernacular Psalters

Even a very brief account of the medieval Psalter tradition would not be complete without mention of vernacular translations. In England word-for-word interlinear glosses in Latin Psalters are known from the ninth century onwards. Such glosses may have had an educational role and may have been used by younger or less learned clergy, or possibly by wealthy literate lay people. Of the forty Psalters and Psalter fragments surviving from Anglo-Saxon England, fourteen, an impressively large number, have an Old English gloss.[37]

A complete Old English translation of the Psalms, independent of the Latin text, is preserved in an eleventh-century manuscript, Paris, Bibliothèque Nationale, lat. 8824, known as the 'Paris Psalter'.[38] It contains a prose version of the first fifty psalms and a verse adaptation of the remaining hundred. It is unclear when or how the two translations were combined, but they were almost certainly originally independent. According to a medieval tradition

[36] Fol. 10r has glue marks and probably was a pastedown of a medieval binding. On the verso it has an imprint of a heart-shaped object, best visible with UV light. Fol. 9 appears to have been reversed, and probably originally followed fol. 10. It has incisions which may originally have held at the recto the heart-shaped object which left an impression on fol. 10v. A similar impression (but possibly a drawing) of a heart-shaped object, with a vertical bar inside and possibly pierced by an arrow on the upper left side, also appears on fol. 7r.

[37] See Pulsiano 1995; Gretsch 2001: 280–91.

[38] Colgrave 1958; Bately 1982; Frantzen 1986: ch. 6; O'Neill 2001.

the author of the prose translation is King Alfred.[39] His work on the translation of the Psalter, left unfinished at the time of his death, is mentioned by
William of Malmesbury.[40]

There are three independent Middle English translations of the Psalter,
produced before the middle of the fourteenth century.[41] In addition
vernacular psalms form a part of the Wycliffite Bible, the first full translation
of the Bible in English, which aimed to satisfy the need for a wide lay access to
the text of the Scriptures.[42] This translation was produced by the followers of
the Oxford theologian John Wyclif (1324–84), probably in the last third of the
fourteenth century, and survives in two versions: the Earlier Version, a more
literal translation of the Latin text, and the Later Version, a more idiomatic
revision. The manuscripts of the Wycliffite Bible comprise complete Bibles,
as well as selections of books and individual books of the Old and New
Testaments, including Psalters, which have similarities with Latin liturgical
Psalters.

Oxford, Bodleian Library, MS Bodl. 554 is a Wycliffite Psalter in the Later
Version of the Wycliffite Bible with extensive Middle English glosses. It was
written in the middle of the fifteenth century (see Plate 9) and, like Latin
liturgical Psalters, contains psalms followed by the canticles. Vernacular
versions of the six weekly canticles appear in their usual order, each preceded
by a Latin incipit, with references to their Old Testament sources in the
margins. The weekly canticles are followed by the translations of the New
Testament and non-biblical canticles, including *Benedicite omnia opera,
Benedictus dominus deus, Magnificat,* and *Nunc dimittis.* These end with a title
[t]e deum laudamus, apparently in the hand of the original rubricator, but
the initial is not filled in and the rest of the page is blank.[43]

The text of Psalms in MS Bodl. 554, similar to Latin liturgical Psalters, is
subdivided according to the eightfold system, with liturgical divisions
marked by larger penwork initials. The psalms have English titles, modelled
on Latin titles, which include psalm numbers. In addition each psalm has a
Latin incipit, such as *Dominus illuminatio* at Oxford, Bodleian Library, MS
Bodl. 554 Psalm 26(27), which in English begins *The lord is min ligtnyng.* This
feature helps the reader to identify psalms which, as mentioned already, were
known by their Latin incipits, but also encourages the use of the translation
alongside the Latin text. This is in fact characteristic of all Middle English
translations of the Psalter which show preoccupation with the liturgical use of

---

[39] The attribution of any texts to King Alfred is uncertain; see a recent discussion in Godden
2007 and Bately 2009.
[40] See Whitelock 1969.
[41] Sutherland 2008.
[42] See Hudson 1988: 228–77; Dove 2007.
[43] MS Bodl. 554 is probably unfinished and, according to Hudson, is among the very few
Wycliffite part-Bibles which may have been an amateur production (Hudson 1988: 203 n. 159).

psalms, rather than simply with their use as a book for reading and study. Almost all manuscripts of different Middle English translations of the Psalter provide English text together with a full or abbreviated Latin version.[44] As in MS Bodl. 554, the presentation of psalms in most manuscripts of different Middle English translations is influenced by their presentation in Latin liturgical Psalters, including the presence of liturgical divisions, the provision of texts, such as canticles and creeds, which were recited together with psalms and normally occur in liturgical Psalters, as well as the use of a layout characteristic of liturgical Psalters.[45]

MS Bodl. 554 is unique because it preserves the Wycliffite Psalter glosses better than any other known manuscript.[46] Most glosses derive from Nicholas of Lyra's *Postilles*, but some from Augustine's *Enarrationes in Psalmos*, Jerome, and Cassiodorus, often cited through Lyra, as well as the '*comun glos*' or *Glossa Ordinaria*.[47] The sources of most glosses are given at their end, such as '*lire here*', or '*austin here*'. The glosses are linked to their lemmata by special signs, such as a red circle with a stroke or similar, which appear at the beginning of the gloss and above the word on which it comments. The glosses explain difficult readings, give spiritual, moral and literal interpretation of the psalms, and comment on the differences between Jerome's translation and the Hebrew text.

The glosses appearing in the margins of Psalm 26(27) can illustrate the usual content of such commentary. The first gloss, attributed to Lyra, states that 'David made this psalm after Saul's death, before his anointing' (*Dauiþ made þis salm after sauls deþ bifor his anoyntyng*). It is not linked to any particular word and serves as an extension of the rubric 'the title of Psalm 26 of David' (*þe title of xxvi salm to dauiþ*). The second gloss, attributed to Augustine, comments on the phrase 'of whom shall I be afraid?' in the first verse of the psalm. It reads: 'A mortal man is surrounded [guarded] by the mortal men of arms, and he is not afraid, but is secure. A mortal man is defended by the living God. Shall he dread and tremble?' (*a dedli man is cumpassid wiþ dedli men of armes; & he drediþ not but is sikur | a dedli man is defendid of god vndedli; shal he drede & tremble*). Of a similar nature is another gloss attributed to Augustine, which comments on the phrase 'my heart shall not fear' in the third verse of the psalm, and explains that 'None but God can take away temporary things; God shall not take away spiritual gifts; not unless you forsake him' (*noon no but god mai take awei temperal þingis | god shal not take awei goostli giftis; no but þou forsake him*).

---

[44] See Sutherland 2008.

[45] See a discussion of the manuscripts of the Middle English *Metrical Psalter* in Sutherland 2008, and of the Wycliffite Psalters in de Hamel (2001: 182–3).

[46] Dove 2007: 161.

[47] Kuczynski 1994: 24; Kuczynski 1995: 21, 71–4, 173, 180, 214, 255 n. 16; Dove 2007: 161 n. 144.

The page also contains two glosses explaining the meaning of words which were believed by the glossator to be difficult for a reader, mostly because of a very literal nature of Middle English translation. The first gloss is linked to the word 'castles' in the verse 'Though castles stand together against me my heart shall not dread' (*Thoug castels stonden togidere agenes me; myn herte shal not drede*). The gloss reads 'that is hosts' (*þat is oostis*), explaining that 'castles' in this context means 'hosts' or 'armies'. The second gloss is linked to the word 'see' in the verse 'That I see the will of the lord' (*That I se þe wille of þe lord*). It reads 'that is know' (*þat is knowe*), explaining that in this context 'to see' means 'to know', and attributes this interpretation to Lyra.

The circulation of the Wycliffite translation of Psalms in the form of stand-alone books, sharing, like MS. Bodl. 554, many features with a Latin liturgical Psalter, is surprising considering the very ambiguous attitudes of the Wyc-liffites to conventional liturgical practice.[48] It attests to a wide dissemination of the Wycliffite Bible, many of whose fifteenth-century owners were probably perfectly orthodox.[49] It also demonstrates the resilience of the tradition of the liturgical Psalter; its ability to develop and cross the boundaries of ideology, education, and social class, in order to perform its many important roles in private and public lives of its lay and religious owners.

Bibliography

Alexander, Jonathan J. G., and Temple, Elzbieta
    1985 *Illuminated Manuscripts in Oxford College Libraries, the University Archives and the Taylor Institution* (Oxford: Clarendon Press).

Bately, Janet
    1982 'Lexical Evidence for the Authorship of the Prose Psalms in the Paris Psalter', *Anglo-Saxon England* 10: 69–95.
    2009 'Did King Alfred Actually Translate Anything? The Integrity of the Alfredian Canon Revisited', *Medium Ævum* 78: 189–215.

Billington, Sandra
    1984 *A Social History of the Fool* (Brighton: Harvester; New York: St Martin's Press).

Boffey, Julia, and Edwards, A. S. G.
    2005 *A New Index of Middle English Verse* (London: British Library).

Brown, Carleton, and Robbins, Rossell Hope
    1943 *The Index of Middle English Verse* (New York: printed for the Index Society by Columbia University Press).

Büttner, Frank O.
    2004 'Redaktionen der Psalter-Ikonographie', in Frank O. Büttner (ed.), *The Illuminated Psalter: Studies in the Content, Purpose and Placement of its Images* (Turnhout: Brepols): 1–80.

---

[48] See 'The Ideology of Reformation: (i) Theology' in Hudson 1988: 278–313.
[49] See 'Liturgical Use' in Dove 2007: 58–67.

Carlvant, Kerstin B. E.

1978 'Thirteenth-Century Illumination in Bruges and Ghent' (PhD thesis, Columbia University).

1985 'Trends in Bruges Illumination until 1260, apropos a Psalter Connected with Oostkerke', *Archives et bibliothèques de Belgique* 56: 321–63.

Colgrave, Bertram

1958 *The Paris Psalter: Ms. Bibliothèque nationale fonds latin 8824* (Early English Manuscripts in Facsimile, 8; Copenhagen: Rosenkilde and Bagger).

Cutler, John Levi, and Brown, Carleton

1965 *Supplement to the Index of Middle English Verse* (Lexington: University of Kentucky Press).

van Dijk, Stephen Joseph Peter

1957–60 *Handlist of the Latin Liturgical Manuscripts in the Bodleian Library, Oxford* (6 vols.; Oxford), vol. 2(i), *Office Books.*

Dove, Mary

2007 *The First English Bible: The Text and Context of the Wycliffite Versions* (Cambridge: Cambridge University Press).

Duffy, Eamon

2006 *Marking the Hours: English People and their Prayers, 1240–1570; the Riddell Lectures 2002* (New Haven: Yale University Press).

Frantzen, Allen J.

1986 *King Alfred* (Boston: Twayne Publishers).

Gifford, D. J.

1974 'Iconographic Notes towards a Definition of the Medieval Fool', *Journal of the Warburg and Courtauld Institutes* 37: 336–42.

Godden, Malcolm

2007 'Did King Alfred Write Anything?', *Medium Ævum* 76: 1–23.

Gray, Douglas

1974 'Notes on Some Middle English Charms', in Beryl Rowland (ed.), *Chaucer and Middle English Studies in Honour of Rossell Hope Robbins* (London: Allen & Unwin): 56–71.

Gretsch, Mechthild

2001 'The Junius Psalter Gloss: Tradition and Innovation', in N. J. Higham and D. H. Hill (eds.), *Edward the Elder: 899–924* (London: Routledge).

de Hamel, Christopher

2001 *The Book: A History of the Bible* (London: Phaidon Press).

Harper, John

1991 *The Forms and Orders of Western Liturgy from the Tenth to the Eighteenth Century: A Historical Introduction and Guide for Students and Musicians* (Oxford: Oxford University Press)

Haseloff, Gunther

1938 *Die Psalterillustration im 13. Jahrhundert: Studien zur Geschichte der Buchmalerei in England, Frankreich und den Niederlanden* (Kiel: n.pub.).

Heinzer, Felix

2008 'Holy Text or Object of Display? Functions and Guises of the Psalter in the Middle Ages', *Bodleian Library Record* 21: 37–47.

Hudson, Anne
  1988 *The Premature Reformation: Wycliffite Texts and Lollard History* (Oxford: Oxford University Press).
Kolve, V. A.
  1997 'God-Denying Fools and the Medieval "Religion of Love" ', *Studies in the Age of Chaucer* 19: 3–59.
Kuczynski, Michael
  1994 'A Fragment of Richard Rolle's *Form of Living* in MS Bodley 554', *Bodleian Library Record* 15: 20–32.
  1995 *Prophetic Song: The Psalms as Moral Discourse in late Medieval England* (Philadelphia: University of Pennsylvania Press).
Leroquais, Victor
  1940–1 *Les psautiers: Manuscrits latins des bibliothèques publiques de France* (3 vols.; Mâcon: Protat Frères).
Madan, Falconer
  1897 *A Summary Catalogue of Western Manuscripts in the Bodleian Library at Oxford*, vol. 4 (Oxford: Clarendon Press).
  1905 *A Summary Catalogue of Western Manuscripts in the Bodleian Library at Oxford*, vol. 5 (Oxford: Clarendon Press).
Madan, F., and Craster, H. H. E.
  1922 *A Summary Catalogue of Western Manuscripts in the Bodleian Library at Oxford*, vol. 2 (Oxford: Clarendon Press).
Mearns, James
  1914 *The Canticles of the Christian Church, Eastern and Western, in Early and Medieval Times* (Cambridge: Cambridge University Press).
Mooney, Linne R., and Solopova, Elizabeth
  No date *The Index of Middle English Verse, Based on the Index of Middle English Verse (1943), its Supplement (1965), and Archival Research* (http://www.cddc.vt.edu/host/imev/Index.html, accessed March 2012).
Morgan, Nigel
  2008 'Resistance to Paris in the Iconography of 13th-century English, Netherlandish, North and East French Psalters in the Bodleian Library', *Bodleian Library Record* 21: 62–74.
Neale, R. A.
  1985 'The Fool and his Loaf', *Medium Ævum* 54: 104–9.
O'Neill, Patrick P.
  2001 *King Alfred's Old English Prose Translation of the First Fifty Psalms* (Cambridge, MA: Medieval Academy of America Books).
Pächt, Otto, and Alexander, Jonathan J. G.
  1966–73 *Illuminated Manuscripts in the Bodleian Library, Oxford* (3 vols.; Oxford: Clarendon Press).
Pulsiano, Philip
  1995 'Psalters', in R. W. Pfaff (ed.), *The Liturgical Books of Anglo-Saxon England* (Old English Newsletter Subsidia, 23; Kalamazoo, MI: The Medieval Institute, Western Michigan University): 61–85.
  1998 'The Prefatory Matter of London, British Library, Cotton Vitellius E. xviii', in Philip Pulsiano and Elaine Treharne (eds.), *Anglo-Saxon Manuscripts and their Heritage* (Aldershot: Ashgate): 85–116.

Salmon, Pierre

1959 *Les 'Tituli psalmorum' des manuscrits latins* (Rome: Abbaye Saint-Jérôme; Vatican City: Libreria Vaticana).

Sandler, Lucy Freeman

1999 *Der Ramsey-Psalter: vollständige Faksimile-Ausgabe im Originalformat von Codex 58/1 der Stiftsbibliothek St. Paul im Lavanttal (fols. 2–5, 11–174) und Ms M.302 der Pierpont Morgan Library in New York (fols. 1–5 = fols. 6–10 der Originalhandschrift).* Commentary/Kommentar (Graz: Akademische Druck- u. Verlagsanstalt).

Sutherland, Annie

2008 'English Psalms in the Middle Ages', *Bodleian Library Record* 21: 75–92.

Tolhurst, John Basil Lowder

1932–42 *The Monastic Breviary of Hyde Abbey, Winchester: mss. Rawlinson liturg. e. 1*, and Gough liturg. 8, in the Bodleian Library, Oxford* (Henry Bradshaw Society, 69–71, 76, 78, 80; 6 vols.; London: Harrison and Sons).

Whitelock, D.

1969 'William of Malmesbury on the Works of King Alfred', in Derek Albert Pearsall and R. A. Waldron (eds.), *Medieval Literature and Civilization: Studies in Memory of G. N. Garmonsway* (London: Athlone Press): 78–93.

8

True Lights: Seeing the Psalms through
Chagall's Church Windows

Aaron Rosen

In 1962, upon completing his celebrated stained-glass windows at the Hadassah Medical Center synagogue in Jerusalem, Marc Chagall spoke about the challenges which this commission imposed. The medium of stained glass, he suggested, not only made certain formal demands, it also posed a more conceptual problem as he attempted to craft images of the twelve tribes of Israel. 'To read the Bible', commented Chagall, 'is to perceive a certain light, and the window has to make this obvious through its simplicity and grace.'[1] In interpreting the properties of stained glass metaphorically—as a source of spiritual illumination—Chagall was, of course, following a long-standing tradition in the history of art. In the twelfth century, the great patron of gothic architecture Abbé Suger famously inscribed the following lines on the doors of Saint-Denis in Paris: 'the work I Should brighten the minds, so that they may travel, through the true lights, I To the True Light where Christ is the true door'.[2]

While the Hadassah synagogue windows steer clear of such Christological associations, relying strictly on imagery from the Hebrew Bible—and even scrupulously avoiding the human figure so as to avoid offending Orthodox Jewish sensibilities—the case is much more ambiguous when it comes to Chagall's other windows. Chagall executed the vast majority of his works in stained glass for churches,[3] blending imagery from the Hebrew Bible with Christian symbolism. In this way, Chagall's windows usefully dramatize a problem which runs throughout his oeuvre: to what extent do the works of this Jewish artist invite Christian interpretation? Or, put another way, to what extent does the 'certain light' which shines through Chagall's windows convey to Christian worshippers the 'True Light' of Abbé Suger?

---

[1] Chagall 2003b: 145.   [2] Frisch 1987: 7.
[3] Chagall's other stained-glass works included his memorial window for Dag Hammarskjöld at the United Nations Building in New York, an installation for the Art Institute in Chicago, and windows for his Musée National Message Biblique in Nice.

I want to examine this question by looking closely at the stained-glass windows in four churches for which Chagall executed works: Notre-Dame de Toute Grâce in Assy, France, All Saints Church in Tudeley and Chichester Cathedral, in England, and Sankt Stephan Kirche in Mainz, Germany. In the first instance, this selection of churches provides us with a geographical as well as chronological spectrum, running from Chagall's windows at Assy in the 1950s to the Mainz windows left incomplete at the artist's death in 1985. Most importantly, the windows in these four churches each draw upon the Psalms, allowing us not only to compare their different ecclesial contexts and iconographical strategies with one another, but to wrestle with the theme of this book—the conflict and convergence of Jewish and Christian interpretations of the Psalms—in a very focused way.

For everything else that they are, the Psalms are, at their root, texts of worship and prayer. As much as Chagall insisted that 'when I paint, I pray',[4] this does not mean that it was *only* in painting that he prayed, or that he was unaware of or insensitive to the very particular practices of Jewish prayer. The Psalms are redolent with liturgical associations for Jews, which Chagall knew well from his Jewish upbringing in Vitebsk, and his continued study of the Hebrew Bible. Throughout his career, Chagall repeatedly engaged with the Psalter, most explicitly in his *Psaumes de David*, a series of thirty etchings from 1979, completed when the artist was 92. That Chagall often chose to illustrate texts which resonated with Jewish moments of anguish or celebration—as he did in his choice of Psalm 137 as the inspiration for a mosaic in the Knesset—reveals a personal, and I think quite Jewish, attachment to these texts. If the act of art-making in general constituted an act of prayer for Chagall, setting the Psalms to paper, canvas, or stained glass seemed to excite a particular devotion in Chagall.

Given this Jewish interest which the Psalms seemed to have held for Chagall, and his awareness of their traditional importance for Jewish observance, his decision to draw frequently upon the imagery of Tehillim in his commissions for churches is intriguing. Sharpening the questions I posed at the outset, we might ask: how do contemporary Jewish and Christian viewers experience such works *in situ*? To what extent does Chagall's pictorial Psalter succeed in speaking the language of the Hebrew Bible to Jewish viewers, and the language of the 'Old Testament' to Christian viewers? And, finally, what might Jews and Christians learn from listening to both voices?

In order to answer these questions, I want to take a few moments to contextualize Chagall's relation to the Bible during his long, almost Methuselan career. It is useful to begin by distinguishing between how Chagall deals with the imagery of the New Testament, and how he approaches

[4] Bella Meyer, 'An Evening with Bella Meyer', lecture at the Museum of Biblical Art, New York City, 23 October 2008.

the Hebrew Bible. Roughly speaking, the New Testament operates for Chagall, we might say, not so much as a scriptural or religious canon, as an art-historical canon, dominated by the image of the crucified Jesus. Throughout his career, the figure of Jesus oscillates in Chagall's imagination between, in his words, 'the true type of the Jewish martyr'[5] and, as he asserts elsewhere, the 'great poet whose poetical teaching had been forgotten by the modern world'.[6] In the 1930s and 1940s, as the events of the *Shoah* unfolded, it was the agony of the Crucifixion which compelled Chagall above all else. It is from this period that we get what is probably Chagall's most iconic image, the *White Crucifixion* from 1938 (Plate 10), in which he desperately attempts to awaken Christians to the suffering of European Jews. After the Second World War, this balance began to shift in favour of the poetic, with Jesus' identity as a Jewish victim fading into the background as Chagall explored how Jesus might serve as a symbol for the modern Jewish artist, or even the rebirth of Jewish culture. As I argue at length elsewhere,[7] the crucifixion offers Chagall an opportunity to grapple with his place within the Western canon, painting himself into dialogue with all the great artists who have treated the theme in the past, from Grünewald to Picasso.

When he turns his attention to the Hebrew Bible, not only does Chagall tend to avoid the kind of direct, polemical address which issues from the *White Crucifixion*, the art-historical allusions inscribed into his images of Jesus also tend to fade into the background. When tackling the Hebrew Bible, Chagall often explicitly opts for subjects with few artistic precedents, or—when he does take on familiar narratives—makes a decided effort to reverse or eschew famed examples. Overall, Chagall displays an extraordinary intimacy with the text of the Hebrew Bible, often displaying a sensitivity to Jewish tradition, as in his refusal to depict anything more than the hands of God reaching down from heaven.[8] We might say that where Chagall *sees* the New Testament, echoed in the masterpieces of Western art, he *reads* the Hebrew Bible.

Chagall's finest and most sustained treatment of the Hebrew Bible occurs in the biblical illustrations commissioned by the Paris art dealer Ambroise Vollard in 1931, for which Chagall made a trip to Palestine the same year in order to observe the native flora and fauna. This suite of 105 etchings, which was finally completed in 1956, would serve as a sourcebook for much of Chagall's post-war works, especially his stained-glass windows. For all his fame as a colourist, the process of etching—with its hunched, almost scribal exertions—seemed to draw Chagall particularly close to the biblical text,

---

[5] Amishai-Maisels 1993: 185.   [6] Chagall 2003a: 67.   [7] Rosen 2009: 19–47.

[8] In his *Bible* series described in detail below, Chagall consistently notes God's presence in the scriptural narrative either by depicting angels or by inscribing the Tetragrammaton in Hebrew in a simple circle in the heavens.

and this first series of biblical etchings reveals Chagall's sensitivity, and imagination, as a biblical exegete. As Meyer Schapiro notes, it is remarkable how seldom Chagall's biblical etchings make reference to any established iconography.[9] One of the more concrete instances occurs in his depiction of *Jacob's Ladder* (1956), which recalls Jusepe de Ribera's *Jacob's Dream* (1639) in the Prado, which Chagall would have seen during his 1934 trip to Madrid.[10] Yet even in this instance, Chagall deliberately reverses Ribera's composition, leaning Jacob in the opposite direction and propping him up on the opposite hand. Furthermore, while Ribera never illuminates the content of Jacob's dream, Chagall explicitly takes the viewer into the biblical narrative, including two angels ascending a ladder marked by the Hebrew name of God. Chagall also adds a floating, topsy-turvy Hasidic Jew who points down at Jacob's head. This curious figure not only further distinguishes Chagall's vision from that of any artistic precursor, it also underscores for Chagall the importance of Jacob's dream as a specifically Jewish story, bearing a distinctly Jewish promise. The Lord promises Jacob that his 'offspring shall be like the dust of the earth', and assures him of his enduring presence: 'Know that I am with you and will keep you wherever you go, and will bring you back to this land; for I will not leave you until I have done what I have promised you' (Gen. 28.13–15). These words would have addressed Chagall at both a communal and personal level after the Second World War, when he returned to France after the devastation of European Jewry, and the death of his beloved wife Bella in 1944. Unlike the 'poetical teaching' which he recognized in the New Testament, it was this message of spiritual reassurance which Chagall seemed to seek, above all else, in the Hebrew Bible.

When we turn to Chagall's commissions for churches, this situation becomes more complicated. In his depictions of scenes from the Hebrew Bible within Christian spaces, Chagall continues to speak—first and foremost—in a voice inflected by Jewish associations; whether personal, historical, or liturgical. Yet, in a way which he does not do in his biblical etchings—from his first works for Vollard to his late *Psaumes de David*— Chagall creates consciously porous works: images which, while they do not declare a Christian message outright, present opportunities for the Christian viewer to interpolate such meanings for himself or herself. Put another way, we could say that there is a fundamental hospitality at the heart of these works, which Chagall extends to his viewer. Chagall entrusts the Hebrew Bible to the Christian worshipper, allowing it to become—under his or her gaze— the 'Old Testament'. There is a daring in this artistic act which has too often been ignored. On the one hand, Chagall risks the opprobrium of Jews, many of whom have been, and continue to be, unsettled by his use of Christian imagery and his acceptance of Christian commissions. On the other hand,

---

[9] Schapiro 1978: 126.   [10] Rosensaft 1987: 132.

Chagall displays a deep faith in his Christian viewer, trusting—with no assurance—that the viewer will not read his images as an acceptance of Christianity's greater truth, and a warrant for theological supersessionism.

Chagall found his ideal patron in the Dominican priest Father Marie-Alain Couturier, who instigated a series of visionary commissions for French churches from the 1930s until his death in 1954. For the Church of Notre-Dame de Toute Grâce, Couturier enlisted, in addition to Chagall, such modern titans as Pierre Bonnard, Georges Braque, Fernand Léger, Jacques Lipchitz, Henri Matisse, and Georges Rouault. While some, like Rouault, were devout Catholics, Couturier also sought out artists with no religious commitment, and—in the case of Chagall and Lipchitz—artists who came from other faiths. Far from being an inconvenient fact, however, the Jewish identities of Chagall and Lipchitz were central to Couturier's aesthetic and theological wager that the best modern art, regardless of the artist's religious persuasion, could successfully function in a Christian sacred space. As he wrote in 1947, 'We knew very well that some of the artists were not strictly Christians; that some were separated from us by serious divergences of a political as well as of an intellectual order. Trusting in Providence, we told ourselves that a great artist is always a great spiritual being, each in his own manner.'[11] If the great artist was an inherently 'spiritual being', and the Catholic Church drew from the same spiritual wellspring, so Couturier's syllogism went, then the artist could not help expressing realities in consonance with Christian truths. In other words, Chagall's acknowledged 'poetical' response to Christianity could provide ample grounds for a *religious* response from his viewers.

This multivalence comes across clearly in Chagall's ceramics, sculptures, and stained-glass works at Assy, finally installed together in 1957. In the tiled mural for the church's baptistery wall, Chagall depicts the exodus from Egypt in ways which critically anticipate his engagement with the Psalms. To the left, a gleaming Moses conducts the proceedings with his uplifted staff (or is it a paintbrush?).[12] As he so often does, Chagall depicts Moses with the rays of light which, according to the biblical narrative, he will only properly attain

---

[11] Couturier 1947: 122.

[12] If we pursue this reading, it is surprisingly Moses, and not his wayward brother Aaron, fashioner of the golden calf (Ex. 32.2–4), who becomes an artist. We might recall Heinrich Heine's reflection along similar lines: 'Moses, in spite of his enmity toward art, was yet himself a great artist, and possessed the true artistic genius. But this artistic genius was with him, as with his countrymen the Egyptians, directed only toward the colossal and the indestructible. He did not however, like the Egyptians, fashion his works of art of bricks and granite. He erected human pyramids, he carved out human obelisks, he took a poor shepherd tribe and created therefrom a people fit to defy the centuries, a great, a holy, an eternal people, a People of God, that should serve all other peoples as an example, yea, that should be the prototype of all humanity : he created Israel! More justly than the Roman poet, might this artist, the son of Amram and of Jochebed, boast that he had erected a monument that should outlive all the creations of brass' (Heine 1888: 257).

when he descends from Sinai for the second time (Ex. 34.29). There is a respectful nod here to Michelangelo's famous horned Moses—based on the Vulgate translation—but there is also a gentle insistence on the original Hebrew, on rays which only resemble horns. In a large painting entitled *Exodus*, from 1952–66, Chagall casts the same subject in a much darker light. There, Moses himself appears to be lost in the commotion, fearfully cradling the tablets of the law just as the terrified mothers around him grip their infants to their breasts. Against the charcoal sky, the crucified Christ stands starkly illuminated; embodying the torment of the masses, but unable to stop it. In Assy, the roles—and even the proportions—of Jesus and Moses are reversed. The crucified Christ is present here, too, but he is displaced to the upper right of the composition, a passive witness to the salvific events choreographed by the heroic figure of Moses. Where Chagall is willing to make the crucified Jesus a symbol of the decimation of the Jewish people, he shies away from depicting a risen Christ, a Jesus who could be construed as the Saviour. And yet, by weaving the reduced figure of Jesus into his image, Chagall displays a sensitivity to the ecclesial context of his work. In a way which Couturier would have appreciated, Chagall permits the parting seas of the image to evoke the saving waters of the baptismal font which stands before it. If to Jewish eyes the figure of Jesus is a minor and curious addition to the scene of exodus, to Christian eyes it can be the key which unpuzzles the theology of the entire scene: a reminder, in the words of St Paul, that their 'ancestors were all under the cloud, and all passed through the sea, and all were baptized into Moses in the cloud and in the sea. . . . For they drank from the spiritual rock that followed them, and the rock was Christ'(1 Cor. 10.1–4).[13]

Chagall picks up on this symbolism in two stained-glass windows, which flank the mural on the west and east walls. Rendered in grisaille in order to provide the tile with maximal illumination, the windows also serve to reinforce the connection between the iconography of the mural and the baptismal rite. In the western window, an angel holds a vessel of holy water, while to the east another angel descends with a candelabra and flowers, as if to congratulate the celebrant. The final touch to this room, which forms a *Gesamtkunstwerk* within the church as a whole, is provided by two plaster bas-relief sculptures, which Chagall places next to the windows. Together, the sculptures develop the imagery of angelic flight and spiritual thirst through specific reference to the Psalms. In both works, Chagall conjures Jewish associations from the imagery of the Psalms while simultaneously allowing Christian meanings to ripple outward from this engagement. In the sculpture

---

[13] William Rubin obscures this point, insisting that presence of the Crucifixion in the work is 'unrelated to the Christian sacraments', and merely the product of the artist's personal 'symbolic vocabulary'. See Rubin 1961: 141.

on the western wall, Chagall illustrates v. 7 of Psalm 124, which he inscribes in French along the perimeter of the image: 'We have escaped like a bird from the snare of the fowlers; the snare is broken, and we have escaped'. Like the story of Exodus, Psalm 124—a song of communal or national thanksgiving for a narrow escape—emphasizes the sense of bittersweet deliverance which dominated Chagall's imagination in the wake of the *Shoah*. Perhaps Chagall was even aware of the link which the Talmud draws between Psalm 124 and the story of the Jewish people's deliverance from Haman in the book of Esther;[14] a connection which would have only sharpened the psalm's evocation of the deadly net which Hitler cast over Europe. These reverberations of the Holocaust need not speak solely to the Jewish viewer, and perhaps one of the aims of Chagall's image is not only to remind Christians of their own reprieve from the 'snare of the fowlers'—whether personal or communal—but to remind them of the fate of European Jewry, and French Jews in particular.

A similar undercurrent of trauma runs through the other psalm which Chagall illustrates for Assy: Psalm 42. For the Psalmist, water often bears with it the threat of inundation (cf. Psalm 18.4), and in the 'deep calls to deep' of v. 7 we might hear an intimation—as Rashi does—of the way one misfortune calls out to the next.[15] And yet, Chagall does not dwell on these associations, nor the elegiac voice of the Psalmist as he laments his separation from the 'house of God', where he once led the multitude in 'songs of thanksgiving' (Psalm 42.4). Chagall takes his imagery instead from the first line of the psalm, which he jots along the edge of the work: 'As a deer longs for flowing streams, so my soul longs for you, O God'. While we might recall rabbinic meditations on the special piety of the hart, who supplicates the heavens for water on behalf of other animals,[16] Chagall's image owes less to any specific textual sources than to his strong personal identification with animals, evident throughout his work. At a more general level, Chagall's attachment to this psalm—one of Rabbi Nachman's ten 'Psalms for General Healing'[17]—may owe something to the Hasidic milieu of his early life. Christian viewers, meanwhile, may find that the image of the hart lapping at the stream again draws them back to the vivifying waters of baptism, a connection which has been made in images ranging from the twelfth-century St Albans Psalter to the paintings of the contemporary Oxford-based artist Roger Wagner.[18]

While the church at Assy is justly celebrated as a pantheon of modern religious art, All Saints' Church in Tudeley, the only church in the world to

---

[14] *BT Megillah* 11a.
[15] Feuer 1980: 531.   [16] Feuer 1980: 524.   [17] Gillingham 2008: 237.
[18] Ibid. 99, 297; Wagner 1994. As Susan Gillingham notes, the image of the hart in Psalm 42 also chimes with compositions by Felix Mendelssohn and Herbert Howells (Gillingham 2008: 222, 299).

have all of its windows executed by Chagall, remains an under-appreciated masterpiece. The church's windows were commissioned from Chagall by Lady d'Avigdor Goldsmid and her husband Sir Henry in 1967, in memory of their daughter Sarah, who had died four years earlier in a boating accident.[19] On the east window of the church (Plate 11), Chagall depicts Sarah caught in the churning waters of the ocean, her splayed arms linking her to Christ, who serenely surveys the scene from the cross.[20] The two halves of the window, the tumult below and the crucifixion above, are connected by a ladder, which a risen Sarah ascends towards Christ. On the one hand, the ladder harks back to a long iconographical tradition, evinced in such canonical works as Rogier van der Weyden's *Deposition* (*c*.1435–40) and Rembrandt's *Descent from the Cross* (1634). At the same time as Chagall evokes this Christian artistic heritage, he also etches potential Jewish associations into the work. In Chagall's richly intertextual imagination, the ladder—a near constant presence in his crucifixion images—is never simply the implement of the Deposition, it is also Jacob's ladder. Playing with the familiar flow of Christian typology, in Chagall's hands the New Testament can in fact predict and anticipate the Old. Like the ladder in Jacob's dream, this ladder can be travelled in either direction. Neither the promise signalled by the Crucifixion, nor the promise made to Jacob—'I am with you and will keep you wherever you go' (Gen. 28.15)—need eclipse the other.

Chagall's selection of Psalm 8 (Plate 12) for the windows along the north aisle of the church preserves this delicate balance between Jewish readings of the Hebrew Bible and what C. S. Lewis would call its 'second meanings' for Christians.[21] For Jews, the psalm has been read traditionally as a hymn to creation, and Chagall's windows revel in all that the Lord has set under human dominion: 'all sheep and oxen, and also the beasts of the field, the birds of the air, and the fish of the sea, whatever passes along the paths of the seas' (Ps. 8.7–8). Chagall's depiction of Adam and Eve, on an opposite window, reminds us of the strong parallel between the Psalmist's language and that of Gen. 1.26–30, further emphasizing the theme of God's majesty *qua* Creator. The twilit blues and indigos which prevail in Chagall's east window are carried over into the north windows, suggesting that Chagall, like traditional Jewish sources, seems to have imagined David composing this psalm at night.[22] Omitting the sun in his citation of celestial bodies, the Psalmist cries out in astonishment at God's munificence: 'I look at your heavens, the work of your fingers, the moon and the stars that you have

---

[19] Blakesley 2010: 74.

[20] This essay is dedicated to my beautiful sister Whitney Hammond (1986–2008), who also died at far too young an age.

[21] Lewis 1958: 99.

[22] Feuer 1980: 125.

established' (Ps. 8.3). For Chagall, the Psalmist's attention to 'the work of [God's] fingers' may have awakened analogies to his own practice as an artist, in this case one who literally illuminates God's handiwork through his own creativity.

While Chagall's emphasis on creation bears the imprint of Jewish tradition, he was probably aware that the language of Psalm 8 has, through its long reception history, spoken very differently to Christian ears. Matthew, for instance, places the second verse of the psalm in the voice of Jesus, who— upon hearing his name praised by children in the Temple—asks the assembled officials: 'have you never read, "Out of the mouths of infants and nursing babies you have prepared praise for yourself?"' (Mt. 21.16). Just as important for Christian interpreters is the fourth verse of Psalm 8, which the NRSV renders 'what are human beings that you are mindful of them, mortals that you care for them?' but which the KJV translates: 'What is man, that thou art mindful of him? And the son of man, that thou visitest him?' While recent translations have thus generalized the Hebrew *ben adam*, literally 'son of man', to 'mortals', preserving the connotations of the term in ancient Hebrew, the KJV bears witness to a long-standing tendency to read the term typologically. In his Letter to the Hebrews, Paul cites vv. 4–6 of the psalm, in which humans are said to have been made 'little lower than God', and to have 'all things under their feet' (Ps. 8.5–6). Paul explains: 'As it is, we do not yet see everything in subjection to them, but we do see Jesus, who for a little while was made lower than the angels, now crowned with glory and honour because of the suffering of death, so that by the grace of God he might taste death for everyone' (Heb. 2.8–9; cf. 1 Cor. 15.27). On the basis of this exegesis, Psalm 8 has traditionally been read on Ascension Day. Perhaps, seen in this light, Chagall's north windows may speak subtly to the crucified Christ of the east window, reminding Christians of his assured return to the heavens, to be seated at the right hand of the Father.

At the age of 90 Chagall took up one final commission in England, at the behest of the then Dean of Chichester Cathedral, Walter Hussey, a modernizing patron in the mould of Couturier. After initially assigning Chagall the broad theme of 'worship', in discussions with the artist he suggested that Chagall might take particular inspiration from the penultimate line of Psalm 150, 'Let everything that hath breath, praise the Lord!'[23] For an artist in his dotage, tackling the final hymn in the Psalter may have held special meaning. Beyond that, the musicality of this psalm—beginning with its call to employ everything from the trumpet to the cymbals in celebration of the Divine—must have appealed to Chagall, whose tastes ranged from

---

[23] Gillingham 2008: 292.

Yiddish folk tunes to the productions of the Paris Opera House. The psalm's internal melodies are only enhanced by its reception history, ranging from its use in the liturgy of the Jewish morning service to arrangements by Bach, Schumann, Elgar, Stravinsky, and Bernstein, many of which Chagall would have known. Both the Menorah at the centre of the composition, and the tablets of the Ten Commandments wedged into the apex of the window (Plate 13)—a sort of thematic keystone for the composition—recall the Psalmist's injunction to 'Praise God in his sanctuary', in the Temple in Jerusalem (Ps. 150.1). The very structure of the window, divided by saddle bars into ten sectors, draws attention to the structure of the psalm itself, with its ten calls to praise. Rabbinic authorities have tied this number of praises to the Decalogue, as Chagall himself seems to do by depicting the tablets of the Ten Commandments.[24]

Altogether, the imagery of Chagall's Chichester window seems to convey a fervent hope that Jews and Christians—in fact 'everything that breathes'— might in some way learn to worship alongside one another. We might read the Psalmist's shout, 'Praise God in his sanctuary', as a subtle challenge to Jews and Christians alike. For Christians, Chagall's window—with its joyous figures clasping the instruments of Temple worship—is an invitation to *imagine* worshipping God in the Temple, as Jews have done for nearly two millennia. Meanwhile, by embedding this scene of Temple worship in the walls of a cathedral, Chagall challenges Jews not only to feel God's transcendence within 'his mighty firmament' (Ps. 150.1), but to praise his immanence in unlikely sanctuaries, perhaps even within a church. If Jews and Christians can thus attune themselves to the spaces and practices of the other's faith, perhaps it is possible, Chagall hints, for Jews and Christians not only to speak to one another but—just as importantly—to *sing* with one another.

While Chagall's Chichester window thus bathes us in an optimistic image of communal worship, Chagall was also poignantly aware of the challenges of consummating such a vision, especially after the traumas of the recent past. Where Chagall created stained-glass windows for multiple public buildings in England, France, and America, he designed windows for only one building in Germany, Sankt Stephan Kirche in Mainz, and this only after persistent

---

[24] *BT Rosh Hashanah* 32a. We might find another numerical wrinkle in the number of *Sefirot*, the ten aspects of the Godhead according to Kabbalah; surely a factor in Rabbi Nachman's inclusion of the psalm—along with Psalm 42—in his ten 'Psalms for General Healing'. Intriguingly, the criss-crossing motion of the figures in the window resembles the movement in traditional Kabbalistic diagrams of the *Sefirot*. Following this interpretation, the tablets of the Ten Commandments in Chagall's window fittingly take the uppermost position in the picture, the position allotted in Kabbalistic diagrams to the *Ein Sof*, the unknowable essence of God. (Rabbi Professor Jonathan Magonet, personal communication, 23 September 2010.)

urging by the church's priest, Monsignor Klaus Mayer. Chagall's first window for Sankt Stephan was fitted in 1978, and nine were complete by the artist's death, with the rest of the twenty-eight portals completed in a similar style by the master glazier Charles Marq, Chagall's long-time assistant in his stained-glass commissions. But if Chagall's eventual acceptance of this commission in Germany signals his belief in the importance of reconciliation—a message reinforced by the tranquil blue light exuded by the windows—there is also a certain subtext of reservation in the work, encoded in the windows' allusions to Psalm 119.

King David appears again and again in the Mainz windows, emphasizing the nationhood of the Jewish people. At times, an angelic figure hovers above him as he strums his harp, reminding us of rabbinic legends that the presence of the Lord, the Shekhinah, alighted on David as he composed the Psalms.[25] In one image, a hunched-over figure—probably David once more—reads intently from a book. Above him, the words of Psalm 119—'Your word is a lamp to my feet and a light to my path' (v. 105)—spring to life in the form of a massive candelabrum, lighting the way of an angel holding an open book. This reminder of the enlightening power of Scripture symbolizes the concerns of the entire Psalm, an acrostic which spells out the Psalmist's devotion to the law in twenty-two stanzas, each headed by consecutive letters of the Hebrew alphabet. On the one hand, Chagall's reference to Psalm 119 underscores the steadfastness of Jewish faith, even in the midst of the *Shoah*. 'They have almost made an end of me on earth,' declares the Psalmist in v. 87, 'but I have not forsaken your precepts'. This insistence on faithful observance affirms Jewish innocence and survival; however, it is also a reminder to the German people of the fundamental commandments violently trangressed during the Holocaust. Psalm 119, 'the language of a man ravished by a moral beauty',[26] is an appropriate text to celebrate shared values and aspirations between Jews and Christians, but its promise of peace and prosperity is—from the start—conditional upon upright actions: 'Happy are those whose way is blameless, who walk in the law of the Lord' (Ps 119.1). A common destiny is yearned for, fervently, but not guaranteed.

Ultimately, if Chagall succeeds in Assy, Tudeley, Chichester, and Mainz—both religiously and aesthetically—he does so not just because his depictions of the psalms completely harmonize with Christian worship but also because they introduce subtle dissonances, revealing alternative meanings and histories. On the one hand, such Jewish notes in Chagall's windows serve to stimulate and enrich Christian self-reflection. Just as importantly, however, they reverberate outwards, gently insisting on the importance of

[25] Magonet 1994: 2.   [26] Lewis 1958: 60.

Jewish–Christian dialogue.[27] In this inscription of difference within a communal space, we might locate a revealing parallel with the language of the Psalms themselves. In the *Star of Redemption*, the Jewish philosopher Franz Rosenzweig suggests that the Psalms reflect a critical point in the religious experience of the individual, as he or she enters into a deeper sense of community. Rosenzweig explains: '[In the Psalms] [t]he community is not, is not yet, everyone; its We is still limited, it remains simultaneously bound to a You; but—yet—it claims to be everybody. This "yet" is the world of the Psalms.'[28]

Only in Psalm 115, for Rosenzweig, do we experience, for a brief moment, a form of address which begins as a 'They', transforms into a 'You', and becomes—finally—an authentic 'We'; a community who 'will bless the Lord from this time on and for evermore' in the Psalmist's words. Despite his concern in the *Star* for the intersecting destinies of Jews and Christians, Rosenzweig was speaking principally to Jews when he offered these reflections on the Psalms. Our examination of Chagall, however, suggests a way in which we might profitably tinker with Rosenzweig's analysis. By creating images which remain steadfastly multivocal—neither definitively Jewish nor Christian—Chagall captures the 'not yet' of Jewish–Christian dialogue, which asserts a 'we' which is, in the truest sense, yet to come. In doing so, Chagall dares us to imagine a more encompassing 'We' than the Psalmist could ever have imagined; a grammar so challenging, perhaps, that we need to learn it first through pictures.

---

[27] It would be fascinating to compare Chagall's ecclesial works with those of other modern Jewish artists who have created works for Christian spaces. One recent example is the work of the New York-based textile artist Laurie Wohl, who has created several major installations for American churches. Where Chagall sees the New Testament refracted through the lens of Western art, Wohl presents an intriguing counterpoint: a Jewish artist who engages sensitively with the *texts* of the New Testament, often quoting them in her work in the original Greek. In what she calls 'unweavings', Wohl unpicks canvases and binds them back together, a process which evokes the rifts dividing Jews and Christians, as well as their intertwining destinies, capable of being knit together in new ways. In the *Psalms Project* (2003) for the Fourth Presbyterian Church in Chicago, Wohl draws special inspiration from Psalm 133, in which the Psalmist marvels, 'How very good and pleasant it is when kindred live together in unity' (Ps. 133.1)! Perhaps even more daringly, in *There is a River* (2010) for the Central Presbyterian Church in Atlanta, Wohl integrates Ps. 46.4—'There is a river whose streams make glad the city of God'—with Rev. 22.1: 'Then the angel showed me the river of the water of life'. In a move evocative of Chagall, Wohl's work insists that just as Christians might read the 'Old Testament' in light of the New Testament, so too Jews might immerse themselves in the study of Christian Scripture, allowing their knowledge of the Hebrew Bible to inflect it with Jewish resonances. Among other things, then, Jewish–Christian dialogue becomes a process of identifying and seizing upon such scriptural threads, tugging them together to see where they might lead.

[28] Rosenzweig 2005: 268.

Bibliography

Amishai-Maisels, Ziva
1993 *Depiction and Interpretation: The Influence of the Holocaust on the Visual Arts* (Oxford: Pergamon Press).

Blakesley, Rosalind
2010 'A Modernist Monument in Rural Kent', in Nathaniel Hepburn (ed.), *Cross Purposes* (Paddock Wood, Kent / London: Mascalls & Ben Uri Galleries): 74.

Chagall, Marc
2003a 'Some Impressions Regarding French Painting — Address at Mount Holyoke College, March, 1946', in Harshav 2003: 65–79.
2003b 'The Stained Glass Windows in Jerusalem: At the Opening of the Synagogue with Chagall's Stained Glass Windows in the Hadassah Medical Center, Jerusalem 1962' in Harshav 2003: 145–46.

Couturier, Marie-Alain
1947 'A Modern French Church in the Alps', *Harper's Bazaar*, 81 (Dec.): 122.

Feuer, Avrohom Chaim (trans. and commentary)
1980 *Tehillim (Psalms 1–72)*, vol. 1, and *Tehillim (Psalms 73–150)*, vol. 2: *A New Translation with a Commentary Anthologized from Talmudic, Midrashic and Rabbinic Sources* (Artscroll Tanach Series; New York: Mesorah Publications).

Frisch, Teresa (ed.)
1987 *Gothic Art 1140–c.1450: Sources and Documents* (Toronto: University of Toronto Press).

Gillingham, Susan
2008 *Psalms through the Centuries*, vol.1 (Oxford: Wiley-Blackwell 2008; paperback edition 2011).

Harshav, Benjamin (ed.)
2003 *Marc Chagall on Art and Culture* (Stanford, CA: Stanford University Press).

Heine, Heinrich
1888 *Wit, Wisdom, and Pathos from the Prose of Heine, with a Few Pieces from the Book of Songs*, trans. John Snodgrass (London: Trübner).

Lewis, C. S.
1958 *Reflections on the Psalms* (London: Geoffrey Bles).

Magonet, Jonathan.
1994 *A Rabbi Reads the Psalms* (London: SCM Press).

Rosen, Aaron
2009 *Imagining Jewish Art: Encounters with the Masters in Chagall, Guston, and Kitaj* (London: Legenda).

Rosensaft, Jean
1987 *Chagall and the Bible* (New York: Universe Books, distributed by St Martin's Press).

Rosenzweig, Franz
2005 *The Star of Redemption*, trans. Barbara Galli (Madison: University of Wisconsin Press).

Rubin, William
1961 *Modern Sacred Art and the Church of Assy* (New York: Columbia University Press).

Schapiro, Meyer
  1978 *Modern Art, 19th and 20th Centuries (Selected Papers)* (London: Chatto & Windus).
Wagner, Roger
  1994 *Book of Praises*, vol. 2 (Oxford: Besalel Press).

9

How Can We Sing the Lord's Song?
Deciphering the Masoretic Cantillation

David C. Mitchell

Some years ago, I began travelling more by Metro. Forty-five minutes each way adds up and, since memorizing the Hebrew Psalms was something I had done over the years, I resolved to make progress. But the more I did so, the more the absence of music pressed upon me. These, I said, are songs for singing, but where is the tune? I began to investigate the matter. After some research, I happened upon the work of Suzanne Haïk-Vantoura, who proposed not only that the Masoretic cantillation marks (or *te'amim*) preserve the Temple song, but that she had decoded the *te'amim*.[1] I was sceptical. But, aware of the Temple origins of the *tonus peregrinus*, I turned to its ancient text, Psalm 114. Surprisingly, the melody that emerged from applying Haïk-Vantoura's system to its *te'amim* was recognizably similar to the *tonus*. My respect for her system grew.[2]

1. Haïk-Vantoura's System

Haïk-Vantoura's fundamental idea—and her point of divergence from synagogue cantillation—is that the sublinear *te'amim* represent the steps of a diatonic scale.[3] The seven sublinear signs of the poetic books with their equivalent notes are shown in Ex. 1.

---

[1] Haïk-Vantoura 1978; with a recording by Harmonia Mundi France (1976); also Haïk-Vantoura 1985. All are now out of print. However, the English translation of the second edition of the book is available as *The Music of the Bible Revealed* (Haïk-Vantoura 1991).

[2] For more on Haïk-Vantoura's hypothesis and its application to Psalm 114, see Mitchell 2012: 355–78.

[3] There are seven sublinear signs in the poetic books (Psalms, Proverbs, and Job 3.1–42.6) and eight in the other 'prosodic' books. Her view that they represent the steps of a scale is supported by recent archaeomusicological discoveries pertaining to the music of Sumeria and Egypt (Mitchell 2012).

Ex. 1. Sublinear signs

The supralinear *te'amim*, on the other hand, she interprets more in the fashion of the synagogue cantoral system, that is, as ornamental motifs on the underlying theme.

2. Psalms Transcribed According to Haïk-Vantoura's System

2.1. Psalm 23

For Haïk-Vantoura, the sublinear *te'amim* indicate steps of the scale. Yet knowing which step of the scale (that is, which harp-string) a *ta'am* represents does not reveal how the harp was tuned. If the tonic is E, the third string up can be tuned to G or G♯. One will give a minor tonality, the other a major, each with a different effect. In modern notation, such matters are conveyed by key signature. But biblical cantillation has no key signature. Its ancient masters recorded the mode of each song in phrases such as *Ayyelet ha-shaḥar* or *Shoshanim*. But, the meanings of these headings being lost, the likely mode must be surmised from the melodic movement and the text.

Haïk-Vantoura suggests several scales were used in biblical cantillation, including our major scale, the scales known to the Greeks as Dorian and Phrygian, and those known in the synagogue as Ahavah Rabbah and Adonai Malakh.[4] However, she suggests that the most prevalent mode of the Psalms is our harmonic minor scale. This is the mode in which she sets Psalm 23.[5] With E as the tonic, it is: E F♯ G A B C D♯.

---

[4] Idelsohn too notes the ancient use of the Dorian, Phrygian, Lydian (major), and Ahavah Rabbah in Israelite music (1948: 25–6). Likewise, Sachs, citing Clement of Alexandria, notes that the modes of ancient Jewish melodies were determined by the character of the songs. Epic melodies (narrations of the Pentateuch) are generally Dorian, lyric chants (lamentations) are Phrygian, and jubilant songs of praise are Lydian (1943: 81–95). This nomenclature follows Aristoxenos (fourth century BCE) and not Glareanus' *Dodecachordon* (1547), which confused the ancient terminology, reversing the Phrygian and Dorian modes and muddling the others. While Glareanus' terms are used by musicians today, archaeomusicologists prefer the ancient ones, often with a less-ambiguous description such as 'white-note scale from D to D' or 'D-mode'.

[5] The *Keter Yerushalayim* (Aleppo Codex text) and *BHS* disagree with Ginsburg and Letteris on the cantillation of *ta'arokh* in v. 5. I have followed Ginsburg since the *Keter* is a reconstruction (Psalm 23 is among the missing pages of Aleppo), while Ginsburg's note claims to be Ben Asher's reading. The *Keter* reads B on -*rokh*, whereafter all notes are a sixth lower to the end of *shulḥan*.

Ex. 2. Psalm 23

2.2. Characteristics of the music emerging

When the Psalms are reconstituted according to Haïk-Vantoura's system, they can initially sound predictable. If we were expecting *Va, pensiero* we might be disappointed by these arpeggiated tonic triads and cadences on the subdominant and tonic. Yet such impressions attend the approach to any new musical language, which takes on its authentic colours with familiarity. So with this music. Its initial sameness masks a surprising variety of word-paintings, phrase-shapes, cadences, and structures. Nor should its arpeggiated melodic lines surprise us; it was made for singing with harps. In fact, in comparison with Gregorian or traditional synagogue psalmody, it comes off rather well.

Let us begin with word-painting, that is, the musical illustration of the words of the text. This is absent from Gregorian and synagogue psalmody whose melodies simply repeat every verse.[6] But now turn to v. 4 of Psalm 23. After the strong *gam*, calling attention to the new thought of deadly peril about to arise, the voice drops to the lowest note (D♯) for the 'valley'. It rises briefly to emphasize 'death' with the *pazer* ornament, resting again on D♯ to unite the morbidity of valley and death. Then, to declare the psalmist's fearlessness of this evil, the voice pauses on the high C of 'evil'. The words 'for you are with me' approach the *atnaḥ* pause by the rising sequence E-F♯-A, the most open-ended and questioning of all the *atnaḥ* phrases, resolved by the explanation that the shepherd's rod and staff will guide even through death. There is a fitness of the melody to each word of the verse.

We turn from word-painting to cadential structure, which is, in many ways, the defining element of this psalmody. In Gregorian or synagogue psalmody every verse of text is forced into the repeated chant. Every Gregorian melody, for instance, is bipartite, with the first cadence off the tonic and the second on. When faced with a tripartite or quadripartite verse, it resorts to various ruses to shoehorn the extra stichs into the same two musical phrases. However, the psalmody of the *te'amim* is characterized by a melody sculpted to fit the text. Look again at v. 4, which is quadripartite. The first stich cadences with *pazer* over *galgal*, giving the low D♯ pause on *mawet*. The second stich cadences with *revia* over *mehuppakh*, making a rise to a high C on *ra'*. The third stich signals a return to more familiar territory with the *atnaḥ* cadence (A) on the last syllable of *'immadi*. Then the fourth and longest stich brings the verse from *atnaḥ* through *revia mugrash* to the final close on *silluq* (E). The melody has exactly the number of cadences required for the verse, neither

---

[6] The Gregorian system has eight tones (chant-melodies) to one of which every psalm is intoned, except Psalm 114 (Vulgate 113) which has its own tone, the *tonus peregrinus*. Likewise, in synagogue psalmody, one melody is repeated for every verse of the Book of Psalms, without regard for the *te'amim*. However, some ancient cantoral traditions possess vocal melismas associated with each *ta'am*.

more nor less. Each is in the right place. And the verse differs from every other verse in the book of Psalms.

In fact, the possible combinations of cadences available to the psalmists provide a kaleidoscopic variety of cadence-structures. Here are a few examples.

2.2.1. Unipartite verse

Some short psalm verses (including many psalm-titles) have only a single cadence on *silluq*. (Haïk-Vantoura's assumption that *silluq* represents the tonic or key-note seems watertight: closure on the tonic is universal in Gregorian and synagogue psalmody.)

Ex. 3. Psalm 126.5

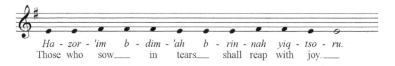

2.2.2. Bipartite

The vanilla of the Temple ice-cream parlour was the bipartite *atnaḥ* → *silluq* sequence. It occurs in Ps. 23.1–3 and in a majority of all psalm-verses. In Haïk-Vantoura's system, *atnaḥ* is the fourth or subdominant step of the scale.

Ex. 4. Psalm 93.2

However, other bipartite cadential structures are found. For instance, there is *ʿoleh we-yored* → *silluq*. As its name requires, *ʿoleh we-yored* consisted of a rising and falling. In Haïk-Vantoura's system it is a rise of a fourth from the subtonic, tonic, supertonic, or sixth, which falls again to the starting note, then rests on the supertonic *merkha*. Here it is in Ps. 1.2:

Ex. 5. Psalm 1.2

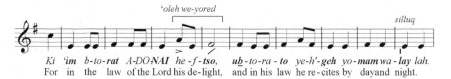

124   *David C. Mitchell*

Other bipartite structures include *revia* → *silluq* (*e.g.* 4.1) and *revia-mugrash* → *silluq*, as in Ps. 99.3, which, with Haïk-Vantoura's system, would read as in Ex. 6.

Ex. 6. Psalm 99.3

Yo - *du* shi-m - *kha* ga - *dol* w - no - *ra'*   qa - *dosh* *hu'*.
They praise your name, so great and_ feared,   for holy it is.

2.2.3. Tripartite

Tripartite structures abound, such as *'oleh we-yored* → *atnaḥ* → *silluq* in Ex. 7.

Ex. 7. Psalm 42.12

Mah tish - to - ha - ḥi naf - shi___ u - mah te - he - mi 'a - lay
Why are you down - cast my soul,_ and why dis - turbed on me?

ho - ḥi - li l'e - lo - him ki 'od o - den-nu, y'-shu - ot pa - nay w'e-lo - hay.
Trust in God for I shall yet thank him, the help of my face and my God.

Others include: *pazer* → *atnaḥ* → *silluq* (Ps. 4.3); *revia* → *atnaḥ* → *silluq* (e.g. Pss. 2.2; 2.12; 3.8); *revia* → *'oleh we-yored* → *silluq* (Ps. 42.5); *revia* → *revia-mugrash* → *silluq* (Ps. 99.5); and *revia* → *revia* → *silluq* (Ps. 117.2).

2.2.4. Quadripartite

Quadripartite structures are numerous. We have already seen *pazer* → *revia* → *atnaḥ* → *silluq* in 23.4 (Ex. 2). Other examples include: *pazer* → *'oleh we-yored* → *atnaḥ* → *silluq* (Ps. 132.11); *'oleh we-yored* → *revia* → *atnaḥ* → *silluq* (Ps. 1.3); *revia* → *'oleh we-yored* → *atnaḥ* → *silluq* (Ps. 1.1); *zinnor* → *'oleh we-yored* → *atnaḥ* → *silluq* (e.g. Ps. 132.12); *pazer* → *tifḥa* → *atnaḥ* → *silluq* (Ps. 98.1).

2.2.5. Qinquepartite

Although psalm-verses are not generally thought to exceed four stichs, there are cases where a five-stich division seems plausible. Ps. 127.1 (Ex. 8) unfolds itself in Solomonic magnificence as *'oleh we-yored* → *revia* → *atnah* → *revia-mugrash* → *silluq*.

Ex. 8. Psalm 127

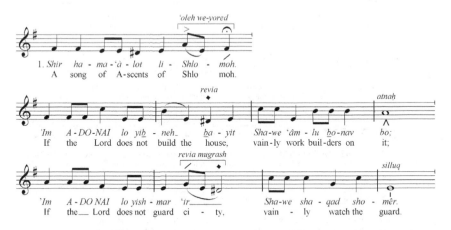

Of course, some might argue that this is really only three stichs: *'oleh we-yored* → *atnah* → *silluq*. But the conditional clauses surely merit a pause for emphasis, while *revia* and *revia mugrash* do mark cadence points, if of lesser weight than the others.

All in all then, the musical system embedded in the Masoretic cantillation was perfect for its task. Its distinguishing feature is fitness of music to text, both in word-painting and in a series of cadences that could be arranged with surprising variety.

2.3. Psalm 95

For Psalm 95, Haïk-Vantoura suggests not the minor scale, but a major scale with a minor sixth: E F♯ G♯ A B C D♯. Certainly, the major third seems more suited to this bold psalm than the minor, while the minor sixth (C) lends a piquant note to its appeals. However, partly to add zest to the D♯–F–E turn at the beginning of vv. 7 and 10, and partly for discovery, I am changing the F♯ to F natural. This gives the strong opening tetrachord of *Ahavah rabbah*. Yet since, in Haïk-Vantoura's system, *galgal* is the raised seventh (D♯), it becomes instead the fine old eastern scale known variously as the Byzantine or Persian or, among the Arabs, as *maqam* Hijaz Kar: E F G♯ A B C D♯.

Ex. 9. Psalm 95

Ex. 9. Psalm 95—*continued*

Those who have seen Haïk-Vantoura's *150 Psaumes* will notice differences between her transcriptions and mine. Some differences are textual. For instance, her frequent use of *tsinnor* follows Letteris, the text apparently recommended to her by Gérard Weil as best for cantillation. She was not to know how far Letteris departed from the more authoritative Aleppo Codex text, which she probably never saw.[7]

My rhythmic values also differ from Haïk-Vantoura's. This is partly superficial. Like other twentieth-century French composers, she used the quaver (eighth-note) for the basic pulse; I use the crotchet (quarter-note) for easier reading.

However, there are also more substantial differences of rhythmic notation. Haïk-Vantoura intentionally avoided any regular musical metre, insisting on 'the equality of time values for successive syllables'.[8] Thus her transcriptions are written without barlines and her recordings sound like a fluid ametrical Hebrew plainsong. My transcriptions, as in the psalm above, attempt to fit the poetic foot into bars. Temple rites involved processions, marches, and dances, accompanied by drums and sistrums, all of which will

---

[7] In the first half of the twentieth century, the Codex was kept in a sealed box and seen by few. It disappeared during riots at the Aleppo synagogue in December 1947, following the UN partition of Palestine. It reappeared in Israel in 1958, with some 40 per cent of the pages missing, and remained unseen until a photographic edition of the unrestored manuscript appeared in 1976. The situation now is quite different. The remaining pages of the restored Codex are at www.aleppocodex.com while the *Keter Yerushalayim* provides a printed reproduction of the entire text, the missing portions reconstructed from rabbinic responsa and the extensive notes of Moses Joshua Kimchi from the mid-nineteenth century.

[8] Haïk-Vantoura 1991: 368.

require some kind of regular metre as long as human beings have a regular number of legs.[9] I suspect that Haïk-Vantoura's insistence on ametricality was unduly influenced by her confessed admiration for Gregorian chant. I also suspect she may have been influenced by her native French, which happily places unaccented syllables on musical-poetic strong beats without the least discomfort.[10]

| *De*puis | plus de qua- | *tre* mille | ans | Nous le | promettaient | *les* prophètes.

| S'exhale | t'il rien | *de* sem- | blable | *au* milieu | *des* fleurs | *du* prin- | temps.

While this surprises strangers, the French do not notice it. In their syllable-timed language word-stress is unimportant. However, the Hebrew of the Psalms, as preserved in the Masoretic Text, is not syllable-timed like French. Its system of vowel reduction clearly proclaims it to be a stress-timed language. It would therefore have sought, like English, to align the natural stresses of the language with a poetic and musical pulse. Of course, Hebrew metre is subtle. There is no insistence on regular numbers of syllables between each stress, as in Greek and Latin poetry. The Hebrew poetic foot can contain four, three, two, or even just one syllable. Nonetheless, there was a poetic foot whose stresses reflected the natural stresses of the language.

The transcription above does not claim to be the only way that the words could have been sung in metre. Nor should its rhythmic values be woodenly followed. There would have been liberal use of *tempo rubato*, particularly in the cantoral cadenzas. It would also have been natural for the pulse to speed up at key points and slow down elsewhere, something found in eastern chant today. Nor is it the case that every psalm would have been rhythmically declaimed. Some, like Psalm 23, are hard to fit into a discernable musical-poetic pulse. Its pastoral tone recalls the *ranz des vaches* or the shepherd's pipe.

2.4. Psalm 122

Haïk-Vantoura sets Psalm 122 in the bright major mode, which suits well the Songs of Ascents, written for the Dedication of the Temple in Solomon's prosperous reign: E F♯ G♯ A B C♯ D♯

---

[9] Pss. 68.24–27; 150.4; M. Suk. 5.1; and my comments at Mitchell 2012: 355–78.
[10] Examples from French carols : *Il est né le divin enfant* and *Quelle est cette odeur agréable?*

Ex.10. Psalm 122

1. Shîr ha-ma'-a - lot   l' - Da - wid.
   Song   of As-cents.   Of Da - vid.

Sa - mah - ti b'-om - rim   lî   bêt   À - DO - NAI   né - lekh.
I was   glad when they said   to   me   'Let's go to the house of the Lord.'

2. O-m' - dot ha - yu   rag - le - nu   bi-sha-rayikh Ye - ru - sha - la - yim.
   Now.   stan-ding are our   feet   in your gates, Je - ru - sa - lem.

3. Ye - ru - sha - la - yim ha-b'-nu - yah k' - îr she - hu-b-rah lah yah - dav.
   Je - ru - sa - lem__ which is   built like a ci - ty   close-ly set as   one.

4. She-sham 'a - lu sh'va-tîm, shîv-tey Yah, é - dut l'-Yis-ro - el l'-ho-dot l' - shém A-DO-NAI.
   For there go   up the tribes, tribes of Yah, a   law for Is - ra - el, to   thank the Name of the Lord.

5. Kî sham-mah yash-bu khis-'ôt l' - mish - pat, kis - 'ot l' - bét Da - wid.
   For   there are set   up   the judg - ment thrones, the thrones of   Da - vid's house.

atnah   silluq

6. Sha-'a - lu sh'-lom Ye - ru-sha-layim, Yi-sh'-la yu o-ha-ba-yikh.
   Pray   for   the peace of Je - ru - sa - lem, May they pros-per, all who   love you.

atnah   silluq

7. Y' - hî sha-lôm b' - hé - lékh, shal - wah b'-arm-no-ta-yikh.
   And   there be peace in   your   walls, and sal - va - tion in your   pala - ces.

atnah   silluq

8. L' - ma-'an a - hai w'-ré - 'ai a-da-b'rah na sha-lom bakh.
   For   sake of my bro-thers and friends I will say 'Peace u-pon you!'

atnah   silluq

9. L' - ma-'an bét A-DO-NAI e - lo - hey - nu a-vaq'-shah tob lakh.
   For   sake of house of the Lord our God   I will seek your good.

A feature of this psalm is the change of speaker in the opening verses.

> *I* was glad when they said to *me*, 'Let us go to the house of the Lord!'
> *Our* feet are standing within your gates, O Jerusalem. (vv. 1–2).

Such changes indicate those points where the singing passed from the solo cantor to the Levite chorus. Avenary says, 'The various kinds of Jewish psalmody arose altogether from one formal principle: the confrontation of soloist and choir.'[11] And it is surely time that the Psalms' *parallelismus membrorum* was recognized not as a poetic or rhetorical device, but as essentially a matter of musical performance. It is the textual witness of how the sung text passed between cantor and chorus.

If we look at the Psalms with an eye to these exchanges, the first thing we notice is that the usual place for the semantic break is at the *atnah* pause. This is seen in vv. 4 to 7 of Psalm 122. This is the general pattern throughout the Psalms, leading to the conclusion that the *atnah* pause is the likeliest point of the cantor–chorus exchange. This is confirmed by other elements—refrains, response formulae, cantoral elicitations, changes of speaker—all of which routinely occur at the *atnah* cadence.[12]

However, there are exceptions, where the semantic break occurs not within the verse, but between a pair of verses instead. Verses 8 and 9 of our psalm offer a good example.

> [8] For the sake of my brothers and friends, I will say 'Peace within you!'
> [9] For the sake of the house of YHWH our God, I will seek your good.

Here, a cantor–chorus exchange at verse 8's *atnah* (here the comma) would not accord with any semantic break in the verse; it would rather interrupt the flow of thought. Instead, the semantic division is at the end of v. 8, while v. 9 repeats the structure of v. 8, but develops the thought. The two verses form a pair, bound by their rhyming ends, and should be treated together. In this case, then, it seems that the cantor–chorus exchange point was at the verse division rather than the *atnah* cadence. This allows us to see vv. 6 and 7, another rhyming couplet, in the same light and treat them accordingly.

Therefore, although the cantor-chorus exchange frequently occurs at *atnah*, it can happen elsewhere. And so we might plausibly divide vv. 1 and 2

---

[11] Avenary 1953: 1–13.

[12] Refrains: Pss. 115.9–11; 118.1–4, 8–9, 10–12, 15–16; 135.19–20; 136.1–26. Response formulae: 'Maker of heaven and earth' (Pss. 115.15; 121.2; 124.8; 134.3); 'from now until forever' (Pss. 115.18; 121.8; 125.2; 131.3); 'Let Israel now say' (Pss. 118.2–4; 124.1; 129.1); 'Peace on Israel' (Pss. 125.5; 128.6); 'YHWH bless you from Zion' (Pss. 128.5; 134.3); 'Hope, Israel, in YHWH' (Pss. 130.7; 131.3); 'His love endures for ever' (Pss. 118.1–4, 29; 136.1–26) 'Halelu-Yah' (Pss. 111–13, 115–17, 135, 136, 146–50). For change of speaker, see Ps. 91.9, where the first voice addresses YHWH before another addresses one, probably a king, who has made Elyon his dwelling.

in the same way, with the singular speaker of v. 1 giving way to the plural response at the beginning of v. 2.[13] Indeed, looking elsewhere, the complex responses of Psalm 24 often take place over several verses and suggest that a psalm could be divided between three voices: cantor, semi-chorus, and chorus, or cantor and two separate choruses.[14]

Finally, the cantillation reveals another marker: the cantoral melisma. In certain verses the cantillation becomes more complex (Pss. 23.4; 95.7, 10; 122.4). This surely indicates a more complex *melos*, which is just what we find when the *te'amim* are decoded. Such phrases look like a solo passage for the cantor before the choral response, which is confirmed by the fact that such melismas occur in the first part of a verse, before the *atnah* pause.

Weighing up all these markers allows intelligent decisions about who is singing what. All in all, the cantor–chorus exchange was surely as nuanced and multifarious as the cadence structures. An awareness of it will help us to better understand the deployment of musical forces in the performance of the Psalms.

3. Conclusion

This paper reflects on the musical implications of the *te'amim*, with reference to Haïk-Vantoura's system. It is fair to say that her work evokes strong responses. A prominent cantor assured me that her system is mistaken. An equally prominent archaeomusicologist cautioned me against becoming like Professor X, who toured the world singing a Sumerian laundry list. (Have we misunderstood the Masoretic Text all along?) Others again, especially those who met her, have a loyalty to her system that brooks not the least divergence from what she wrote. But her claims are too important either to dismiss or to be above scrutiny.

Of course, many will approach them with caution. Rightly so. To them I say, first, that much of what I have written here remains true whether we fully accept Haïk-Vantoura or not. It is clear that the traditional categorization of the *te'amim* as conjunctive and disjunctive would be better replaced with

---

[13] See similarly the singular–plural exchange at Ps. 118.21-2.

[14] The double questions of v. 3—dividing at *atnah* and repeating the thought in parallel—look as if they were taken by cantor and semi-chorus, with full chorus responding in v. 4. Likewise, 'Who is the King of glory?' (vv. 8a, 10a) requires a new speaker for the first response (vv. 8b, 10b), and yet another speaker, after the *atnah* cadence, for the second response (vv. 8c, 10c). In Nehemiah's time, the Levites sang with cantor and antiphonal chorus, section against section (Neh. 12.24, 40, 42) answering responsorially (Ezra 3.11). This was no Babylonian novelty, but was 'according to the hands of David' (Ezra 3.10), i.e. the cheironomy or 'hands of song' of the united monarchy period (1 Chron. 6.16 (ET 6.31)), which preserved not only the melodies, but the musical direction and deployment.

the musical categories of cadential and non-cadential. In fact, cadentiality was the essence of Temple music. It is clear that word-painting also played an important role. Clearly too, the rhythmic declamation of the Psalms and the cantor–chorus exchanges are things we have thought all too little about. Weighing up the *te'amim*, simply on their own merits, provides insights in these matters.

However, employing Haïk-Vantoura's system enables the Psalms to emerge in a new light altogether. With it, we find that the three Psalms above are quite different. Psalm 23 is a pastorale, without recurring theme or regular metre, free as the lark over Bethlehem fields. Psalm 95 is grander altogether. Solemn and austere, its great cantoral cadenzas are answered by the firm asseverations of the Levite chorus. Its more regular pulse might have provided a processional hymn for the approaching worshippers. Psalm 122 is a joyful song, sung by the Levites in the Temple courts, on the steps beneath the Nicanor Gate, closing in a perfectly regular musical quatrain. And elsewhere we meet hymns, anthems, chants, and roundelays. Some have recurring melodic material, others are a sequence of ever-varying rhapsodic lines. Some have regular metre, others do not. Some are evidently antiphonal, others look more like an instructional chant for one voice. Everything is there.

My own view is that Haïk-Vantoura's views regarding the Temple origins of the Masoretic *te'amim* stand up to scrutiny. If this is so, then the lost Temple song is ultimately recoverable. I also think that her deciphering system is a significant step towards this goal, not least in identifying the sublinear *te'amim* with the steps of the diatonic scale.

Bibliography

Avenary, Hanoch
    1953 'Formal Structure of Psalms and Canticles in Early Jewish and Christian Chant', *Musica Disciplina* 7: 1–13; repr. in Hanoch Avenary, *Encounters of East and West in Music: Selected Writings* (Tel Aviv: Faculty of Visual and Performing Arts, Dept. of Musicology, Tel-Aviv University, 1979): 105–11.
Gerson-Kiwi, Edith
    1980 'Cheironomy', in Stanley Sadie (ed.), *The New Grove Dictionary of Music and Musicians*, vol. 4 (London: Macmillan): 191–6.
Haïk-Vantoura, Suzanne
    1976 *La musique de la Bible révélée* (Paris: Robert Dumas).
    1978 *La musique de la Bible révélée* (Paris: Dessain et Tolra, 2nd rev. edn).
    1985 *Les 150 Psaumes dans leurs mélodies antiques* (Paris: Fondation Roi David).
    1991 *The Music of the Bible Revealed*, trans. D. Weber; ed. J. Wheeler (Berkeley, CA: Bibal Press).
Idelsohn, Abraham Zebi
    1948 *Jewish Music* (New York: Tudor).

Mitchell, David C.
  2012 'Resinging the Temple Psalmody', *JSOT* 36/3: 355–78.
Sachs, Curt
  1943 *The Rise of Music in the Ancient World East and West* (New York: Norton).
Sendrey, Alfred
  1969 *Music in Ancient Israel* (New York: Philosophical Library).

10

The Psalms in Judaism and Christianity: A Reception History Perspective

John F. A. Sawyer

When the *New English Bible* was published in 1970, all the headings of the Psalms were omitted. This was because, as G. R. Driver, Professor of Semitic Philology at the University of Oxford, and Joint Director of the project, explained in the preface, they contain musical instructions which are no longer intelligible, as well as 'historical notices' which are sometimes incorrect, and because they 'are almost certainly not original'. Some sixty verses of the canonical text were just thrown out, verses containing expressions only found there like אילת השחר 'hind of the dawn' (Ps. 22.1) and שיר המעלות 'the Songs of the Temple Steps' (Pss. 120–34), as well as the tradition that Psalm 51 is an integral part of the David and Bathsheba story. To many of us at the time it was inconceivable that a translation of the Bible, officially sponsored by the established churches, could do such a thing. It seemed like a soulless attack on biblical, Jewish, and Christian tradition, the logical *ne plus ultra* of the historical critical method, and we can only be grateful that the translators did not choose to do the same with the ending of the Book of Amos or, for that matter, Isaiah 40–66. In an early edition of the *Jerusalem Bible*, Psalm 122 v. 6 famously reads 'Pay for the peace of Jerusalem!' (London, 1966). There the omission of the 'r' was a typographical error, corrected in later printings. The omission of the Psalm-headings was deliberate, though fortunately it too was eventually corrected in the *Revised English Bible* (Oxford/Cambridge, 1989).

Admittedly the wholesale omission of parts of the canonical text as 'almost certainly not original' is an extreme example, but it illustrates how far we have moved since then. In those days it was almost universally assumed that the only goal of serious biblical scholarship was to get back as closely as possible to the original meaning of the text. This was partly due to Protestant suspicions of the Catholic tradition, which of course had always depended more on the Greek and Latin versions, especially the Vulgate, than the original Hebrew, but it was also reinforced by the flood of astonishing archaeological discoveries, including whole libraries of literature in Egyptian,

Sumerian, Assyrian, Babylonian, and Ugaritic, belonging to ancient Israel's neighbours. It looked as though the quest for the original meaning was within our grasp. The problem with that approach, however, was twofold, although it took about 200 years for this to be recognized. On the one hand, it implies that 'late' means inferior, while on the other it assumes that the text has only one meaning. Our commentaries used to be full of statements like 'this is a late interpolation': that was what was wrong with the psalm-headings. A late, that is, rabbinic interpretation is therefore unacceptable or at any rate irrelevant. Even the word 'post-exilic' had derogatory connotations for many, suggesting a decline from earlier, nobler forms of the biblical tradition. Luther's attacks on papist misinterpretations of Scripture were motivated by such presuppositions, as were Norman Snaith's derisive comments on Handel's *Messiah* as an interpretation of Job 19.25–6: that's not what the original Hebrew means.[1]

Today, mercifully, things have changed dramatically. Late no longer means inferior – the post-exilic period, now renamed the Second Temple Period, has become the focus of much of the most exciting research. Chronicles is as interesting a text to study as Samuel or Kings. Rabbinic Hebrew is as valuable as Akkadian or Ugaritic in biblical semantics, if not more so. The Septuagint is studied as a piece of Greek literature in its own right, not just as a means to an end. But what has really changed things as radically as the computer is the recent rush to incorporate even later interpretations into mainstream Biblical Studies. First subsumed under the title *Wirkungsgeschichte*[2] or *Rezeptionsästhetik*[3] or Reader Response Criticism[4] or simply the History of Interpretation,[5] reception history has now become a major element in its own right, as can be seen from recent SBL and SOTS programmes and university syllabuses throughout the world. Just over ten years ago Chris Rowland and I had the idea of starting a series of biblical commentaries which would include examples of how the text was interpreted in ancient and medieval Jewish and Christian tradition, in the Reformation, early modern, and modern periods, in literature, art, music, and film – as many media as space would allow. Fortunately Blackwell Publishing took it on and ten volumes of the Blackwell Bible Commentary series have now been published,[6] including the first of Sue Gillingham's two volumes *Psalms through the Centuries*.[7]

Oxford University Press have now published their own *Handbook of the Reception History of the Bible* (consultant editor: Chris Rowland)[8] and, in addition to my own *Concise Dictionary of the Bible and its Reception*,[9] there is the projected 30-volume *Encyclopedia of the Bible and its Reception* being

---

[1] Snaith 1994: 192.   [2] Gadamer 1975.   [3] Jauss 1982.
[4] Tompkins 1980.   [5] Rogerson 1992.
[6] www.bbibcomm.net (accessed 8 February 2012).
[7] Gillingham 2008.
[8] Lieb, Mason, and Roberts 2011.   [9] Sawyer 2009.

edited by H.-J. Klauck and others,[10] as well as two new journals, *Biblical Reception*, published by Sheffield Phoenix, and the online open-access *Relegere: Studies in Religion and Reception*, of which the first volume has now appeared.[11] There is an increasing number of undergraduate options available, such as seminars entitled 'Bible and the Arts' and 'David through the Centuries', as well as postgraduate courses like the MA in 'Reception of the Bible' at Bristol. Among many recent publications by biblical scholars working on this kind of material, I might mention Bernhard Lang's *Joseph in Egypt: A Cultural Icon from Grotius to Goethe*,[12] Martin O'Kane's magnificent *Biblical Art from Wales*,[13] and *After Ezekiel: Essays on the Reception of a Difficult Prophet* edited by Paul Joyce and Andrew Mein.[14] A very well-known and respected senior academic at Emory University Atlanta, Carol Newsom, said recently that all Biblical Studies students must be taught how to handle reception history: 'That's non-negotiable', she said, and added that she regrets not having had that opportunity as a student herself. Oxford leads the way with its Centre for the Reception History of the Bible; this pioneering conference on Jewish and Christian approaches to the Psalms is but another example.

What Reception History does, among many other things, is to encourage critical comparison between what the experts in Hebrew, textual criticism, and ancient history say about the text and what poets, painters, composers, and preachers have said, as well as feminists, liberation theologians, post-colonialists, and many other 'voices from the margin'. Such readers of the text ask different questions, fill in gaps in the narrative, and spot nuances and associations missed by modern commentators. Sometimes the ethical implications of a text can be better appreciated when its use or abuse can be observed in a variety of social and political contexts.[15] In discussing all this with colleagues over the years, I discovered that in fact most of them admit to quoting interpretations of the Bible by Artemisia Gentileschi or Milton or Byron or Benjamin Britten or Cecil B. DeMille or Martin Luther King or Madonna in their lectures and seminar discussions, but had always assumed that such material was not appropriate for scholarly essays and exam papers. Now it certainly is. Now it is not only appropriate, but rapidly becoming an essential part of Biblical Studies at all levels. I would like to illustrate this with some examples from the reception history of the Psalms.

First, the words 'Moab is my washpot', which appear twice in the Psalms (60.8; 108.9 AV), was used as the title of an autobiography published some years ago by the English television personality and comedian Stephen Fry.[16]

---

[10] Klauck 2007– .
[11] www.relegere.org/index.php/relegere/issue/current (accessed 8 February 2012).
[12] Lang 2009.   [13] O'Kane 2010.   [14] Joyce and Mein 2011.
[15] See Sawyer 1995: 153–68.   [16] Fry 1997.

He does not explain why he chose the title, but it's obvious to anyone who knows his views on the Church that it is a joke, intended to ridicule the language of the Bible and institutional religion in general. He was not the first to criticize the Bible. The anonymous writer of an eighteenth-century life of David, entitled *The History of the Man after God's Own Heart*, quoted with approval by Voltaire, wrote that narratives that would shock in profane history are read with reverence by readers of the Bible, and that even in his Psalms David breathes nothing but blood![17] And we have to admit that both he and Stephen Fry have a point. In his book *The Immoral Bible: Approaches to Biblical Ethics*,[18] Eryl Davies, of the University of Wales in Bangor, seeks to encourage readers of the Bible to reflect on ethically problematical passages, not least those which gloat over a defeated enemy like 'Moab is my washpot . . . upon Edom I cast my shoe; over Philistia I shout in triumph'.

As professional experts on the Bible, how are we to answer Stephen Fry's ridicule and Voltaire's moral outrage? One way is go beyond the standard commentaries to consider how real communities, Jewish and Christian, have interpreted such passages, and compare that with what feminist, post-colonial, or other ideological interpreters are saying today. To say that such rhetoric was normal in the ancient Near East doesn't make it any more acceptable. Nor is it acceptable to say that the Moabites and the Canaanites and the Hittites are not real people: they are just symbols of evil. It's one thing to use that kind of language to celebrate the defeat of Leviathan and other mythical forces of chaos and evil in the Psalms (e.g. Ps.74.13–14), but quite another to speak in this way of one's 'troublesome neighbours'.[19] Perhaps one day a panel of translators will decide to omit such passages, not because they are 'almost certainly not original', but because they are 'almost certainly immoral'. Like the last verse of Psalm 137, they are already omitted from many lectionaries.

My second example takes us from conflict to convergence. On the first page of a fifteenth century illuminated Jewish manuscript, probably from Ferrara in northern Italy (Plate 14), there is a picture of King David, surrounded by wild animals, playing his harp and apparently singing the words of Psalm 1: 'Happy are those who do not follow the advice of the wicked. . . They are like trees planted by streams of water, which yield their fruit in its season' (NRSV). The inclusive plurals of the NRSV are nicely represented in the background. The idyllic scene prompts comparison with classical images of Orpheus such as a second-century CE Roman mosaic on the floor of what is now one of the Science Buildings in Perugia University (Plate 15). There are obviously differences: King David is old and bearded, wearing a crown and fifteenth-century clothes, while Orpheus is young, unshaven, and not wearing anything at all. King David is seated on a couple of cushions and playing a

---

[17] Anon. 1820.   [18] Davies 2010.   [19] Briggs and Briggs 1907: 60.

small medieval-type harp, while Orpheus is sitting on a rock, playing a lyre. But what is most interesting is David's relationship to the animals who are unmistakably responding to his music, just as they are to Orpheus in the mosaic.

Now in the Hebrew text of the apocryphal Psalm 151 discovered in Cave 11 at Qumran, David says 'The trees praise my words and the flocks my deeds',[20] which comes very close to what is going on in these two images. Frank Moore Cross and others argued that the text does not mean that and rejected any possible Orphic influence, as did the Greek and the Syriac versions of the psalm where the words do not occur.[21] Of course the Ferrara manuscript does not establish the meaning of the 11QPsalms[a] scroll one way or the other, nor does it tell us anything about whether some variety of Judaism had been infiltrated by one of the mystery religions. What it does show is that some Jewish interpreters somewhere saw the connection, and their interpretation is reflected in this beautiful piece of Renaissance Jewish art. That is surely in itself a valuable glimpse into Jewish exegetical tradition.

Christian interpreters did something else with this image of King David, by putting a cross in his hand instead of a harp and substituting a flock of sheep for the wild animals, as in the famous fifth-century mosaic in the mausoleum of Galla Placidia in Ravenna. In such a context the figure is that of Christ, the Good Shepherd (Jn 10.11, 14), but the imagery is still David's and comes straight from the Psalms: 'The Lord is my shepherd . . . he makes me lie down in green pastures; he leads me beside still waters . . . (Ps. 23.2) . . . We are his people and the sheep of his pasture (Ps. 100.3) . . . Then he led out his people like sheep, and guided them in the wilderness like a flock . . . (Ps. 78.52) . . . Then we your people, the flock of your pasture, will give thanks to you forever . . . (Ps. 79.13)'.

But there is a very different side to the story of King David the musician. In a painting by the seventeenth-century Italian artist Francesco Barbieri, known as 'il Guercino', King David is shown playing the viol, bare-headed, his crown lying on a table beside him, and with a remorseful, soul-searching expression on his face (Plate 16). The scene is intended to reflect the state of mind David was in after he had taken the beautiful Bathsheba for himself, murdered her husband, been rebuked by his court prophet, and then watched their first child fall ill and die when he was only one week old (2 Sam. 11–12). The tradition that, at this low point in his life, David sang Psalm 51, the *Miserere*, one of the seven Penitential Psalms, goes back to v. 1 of the original Hebrew text: 'A Psalm of David when Nathan the prophet came to him after he had gone in to Bathsheba'. So this is a painting of David singing Psalm 51: 'Have mercy on me, O God . . . against you, you alone, have I sinned . . . purge me with hyssop . . . create in me a clean heart. . .do not cast me away from your

---

[20] Vermes 1987: 209.   [21] Cross 1978: 69–71.

presence ... ' These were the words in Guercino's mind as he painted his famous portrait of King David, which appears, by the way, on the front cover of a recently published collection of essays entitled *The Fate of King David: The Past and Present of a Biblical Icon*,[22] published in honour of David Gunn, a true pioneer of reception history who was already teaching an undergraduate course on 'King David through the Centuries' in Sheffield in the 1970s.

Another more recent interpreter of the story of David and Bathsheba had Psalm 51 very much in mind as well.[23] *Songs of Bathsheba* by the young Israeli composer Gil Shohat received a standing ovation when it was first performed in America in 2005, and was described by one critic as a 'vivid, moving, powerful, and (most important) memorable vehicle for conveying the message that melodic beauty and emotions like love, hatred, jealousy, and remorse are timeless'.[24] It is an oratorio for soprano, choir, and orchestra, in which Bathsheba, now the Queen Mother after David's death, gives her side of the story, while the choir sings a kind of reflective commentary. Bathsheba's words are an English translation of a text written by the Israeli poet Shin Shifra, while the choir sings verses from Psalm 51 in Hebrew. Bathsheba's words are unrelentingly bitter. At one point she quotes a verse from Psalm 51 herself: David always knew how to chant a psalm of lament, she says, to fix the blame on primaeval sin: 'I was born with iniquity and in sin my mother conceived me' (Ps. 51.5). It seems to me that this reading of Psalm 51, in dialogue with a modern feminist interpretation of the biblical story, while at the same time retaining something of its traditional liturgical function, really breaks new ground in the history of its reception.

My last example brings us back to the headings of the Psalms, and in particular to שירי המעלות ('Songs of Ascents') which is the heading of fifteen Psalms (Psalms 120–34). I have always been puzzled at the seeming reluctance on the part of scholars and other commentators to avoid the obvious translation of this phrase.[25] שיר ('song') as opposed to שירה and מזמור and other more specific or technical terms, is the ordinary everyday word for a song, and מעלה is an equally common everyday word for a 'step'. So the obvious translation of the title, in the context of Second Temple Period liturgical tradition, is 'Songs of the Temple Steps' of which, according to Ezek. 40.26, 31 and the Mishnah (Middot 2.5), there were fifteen. If the title 'Songs of the Temple Steps' is an appropriate title for this group of Psalms, then there is no need for any of the ingenious alternatives proposed, mostly, one must

---

[22] Linafelt, Camp, and Beal 2010.

[23] I am indebted to Siobhan Dowling at the University of Cork for telling me about it and giving me a copy of the libretto.

[24] *American Record Guide*, July/August 2005: see http://www.gilshohat.com/press1.htm (February 2011).

[25] Sawyer 1970: 32–3.

admit, by Christian scholars insensitive to the nuances of Second Temple Period and Rabbinic Hebrew.[26] מעלה in the sense of 'ascent' or 'pilgrimage' or 'return (to Jerusalem)' (Ezra 7.9) never occurs in the plural, and anyway, as Kimhi and others have frequently pointed out, several of the שירי המעלות are simply not 'Pilgrim Psalms', however we interpret them (Pss. 120, 124, 125, 130, 131). There is even less to be said for the suggestion that in this context מעלה means 'extolment'.[27]

So let us look at the 'Songs of the Temple Steps' (Psalms 120–34), and at how they have been used and interpreted, to see whether the title is appropriate. The fifteen psalms with this title are uniquely grouped together in the Psalter, immediately after Psalm 119, another unique psalm, incidentally, one hundred verses longer than any other psalm. They are all very short, being under nine verses in length in every case, except for Psalm 132 (eighteen verses); they comprise a wide variety of literary forms and, most significant, they are mostly extremely well known and popular in both Jewish and Christian tradition. They contain a disproportionate array of themes and phrases which in different languages have had a bewilderingly influential afterlife. One striking feature of this little collection, for example, is that the word 'peace'(Hebrew שלום) occurs seven times in no less than four of them, most notably in Psalm 122: 'Pray for the peace of Jerusalem' (122.6–8; cf. Pss. 120.6.7; 125.5; 128.6). Another is the recurring phrase 'maker of heaven and earth' (Pss. 121.2; 124.8; 134.3), discussed by Jonathan Magonet.[28] Every one of these psalms contains at least one memorable phrase that has become a familiar part of our biblical heritage, from NISI DOMINUS FRUSTRA (Ps. 127.1) on the coat of arms of the City of Edinburgh, to *De profundis* (Ps. 130.1; Vulgate 129.1) which has inspired poems by Tennyson ('Out of the deep, my child'; 1852) and Christina Rossetti (1881), to say nothing of Oscar Wilde's letter from Reading Gaol with the same title (1897), and has been set to music by numerous composers including Josquin des Pres (*c.*1450–1521), Liszt (1888–93), Parry (1891), Schoenberg (1950), and Arvo Pärt (1980).

All fifteen are recited on Sabbath afternoons, while one of them, Psalm 126, is sung as part of the ברכת המזון 'Grace after Meals'. The 'Fifteen' have a prominent place in Christian tradition as well, according the Rule of Benedict, for example, and are regularly highlighted in illuminated Psalters, as well as printed Breviaries and Books of Hours.[29] Four of Heinrich Schütz's *Psalms of David* (1619) are from the 'Fifteen' (Pss. 121, 122, 128, 130). Verses from Psalms 121 and 128 figure in Mendelssohn's oratorio *Elijah* (1846), and the last verse of Psalm 126 ('May those who sow in tears reap with shouts of joy') is put to beautifully effective use by Brahms in *German Requiem*

[26] Cf. Childs 1971: 137–50. [27] Dahood 1970: 195.
[28] Magonet 1994: 116–50. [29] Gillingham 2008: 103.

Plate 1. Ms. Parm. 1870 *(Cod. De Rossi 510)*, Palatina Library, Parma, Italy. Printed with permission from the facsimile of the Parma Psalter, at www.facsimile-editions.com.

Plate 2. Mosaic of Psalm 137 in the Chagall State Hall, Knesset. From Baal-Teshuva, *Chagall* (Cologne: Taschen, 1998): 240 (English version). Chagall®/ © ADAGP, Paris, and DACS, London, 2011.

ETINUIRTUTEMEIUSINMARI
RUBROQNMINAETERNU
MISERICORDIAEIUS
QUITRADUXITPOPULUM
SUUMINDESERTO QNM
INAETERNUMMISERI
CORDIAEIUS
QUIPERCUSSITREGESMAG
NOS QNMINAETERNUM
MISERICORDIAEIUS
ETOCCIDITREGESFORTES
QNMINAETERNUMMISE
RICORDIAEIUS

SEONREGEMAMORREO
RUM QNMINAETERNU
MISERICORDIAEIUS
ETOGREGEMBASAN QM
INAETERNUMISERICOR
DIAEIUS
ETIDEDITTERRAMEORUM
HEREDITATEM QNMINAE
INUMISERICORDIAEIUS
HEREDITATEMISRAHELSER
UOSUO QNMINAETERNU
MISERICORDIAEIUS
QUIAINHUMILITATENOSTRA

MEMORFUITNRI QNMIN
AETERNUMISERICORDIAEI
ETREDEMITNOSABINIMICIS
NOSTRIS QNMINAETER
NUMISERICORDIAEIUS
QUIDATESCAMOMNICAR
NI QNMINAETERNUM
MISERICORDIAEIUS
CONFITEMINIDOCAELI
QNMINAETERNUM
MISERICORDIAEIUS
CONFITEMINIDNODOMI
NORUQMINATNUMISIRI

PSALMUS

SUPERFLUMINA
BABYLONIS ILLICSEDI
MUSETFLEUIMUSCUMRE
CORDAREMURSION
INSALICIBUSINMEDIOEIUS
SUSPENDIMUSORGANA
NOSTRA
QUIAILLICINTERROGAUE

RUNTNOS QUICAPTIUOS
DUXERUNTNOSUERBA
CANTIONUM
ETQUIABDUXERUNTNOS
HYMNUM CANTATENO
BISDECANTICISSION
QUOMODOCANTABIMUS
CANTICUMDNIINTER

RAALIENA
SIOBLITUSFUEROTUIHIE
RUSALEM OBLIVIONIDE
IURDEXTERAMEA
ADHEREATLINGUAMEAFAU
CIBUSMEIS SINONMEMI
NEROTUI
SINONPROPOSUERO

Plate 3. Psalm 137, from the Utrecht University Library, Ms. 32, fol. 77r (with permission from the University Library).

Plate 4. Psalm 137 from Arthur Wragg, *The Psalms in Modern Life* (London: Selwyn and Blount, 1933; no page numbers).

Plate 5. Roger Wagner 'Canning Town', 1988. Collection Canary Wharf Ltd. © Roger Wagner (www.rogerwagner.co.uk), produced with the artist's permission.

Plate 6. Michael Jessing: Psalm 137. ©Michael Jessing (www.m-jessing.supanet.com).

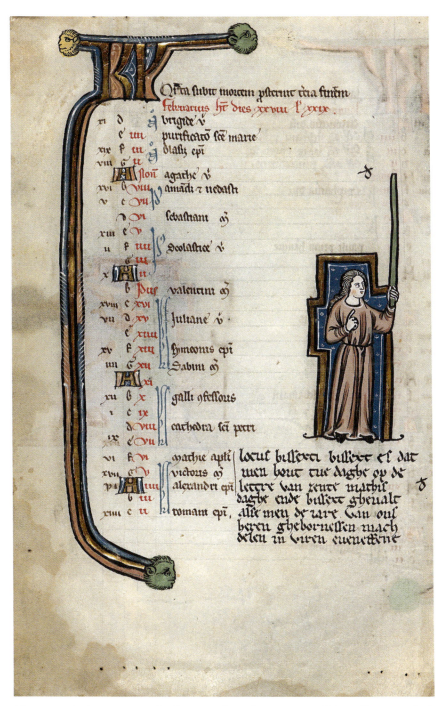

Plate 7. MS Liturg. 396. Calendar page for February. © Bodleian Library Oxford, University of Oxford.

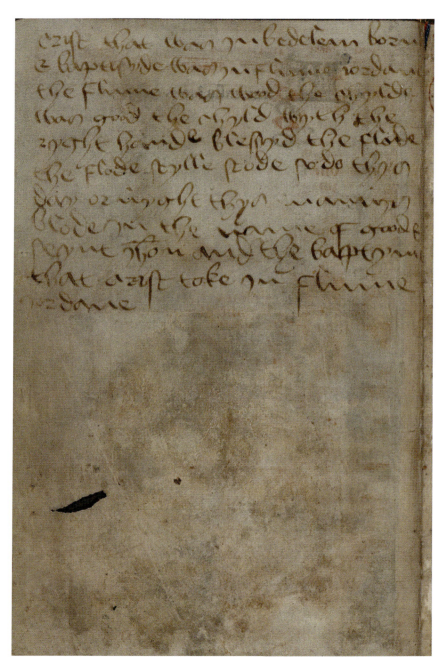

Plate 8. MS Lat. liturg. g. 1. An English poem with early sixteenth century additions, by hand. © Bodleian Library Oxford, University of Oxford.

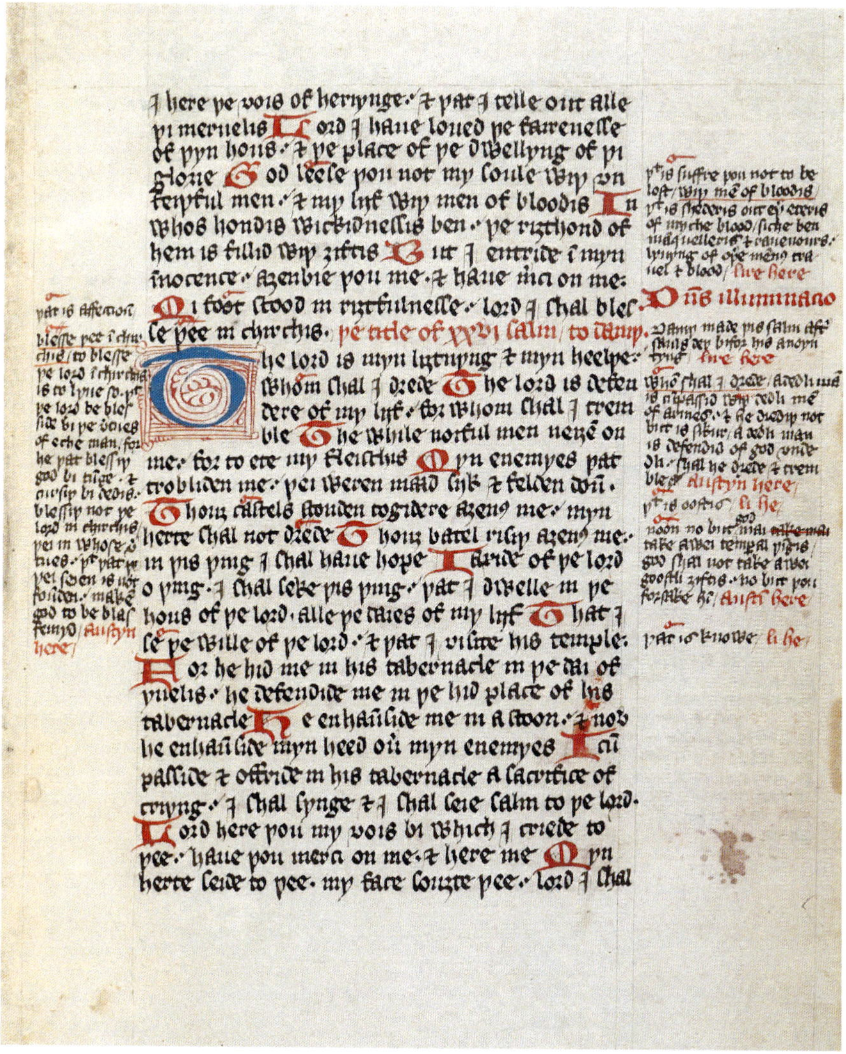

Plate 9. A Wycliffite Psalter with extensive Middle English Glosses. MS Bodl. 554.
© Bodleian Library Oxford, University of Oxford.

Plate 10. Marc Chagall, *White Crucifixion*, 1938. Oil on canvas. 154.3 × 139.7 cm. Gift of Alfred S. Alschuler. 1946.925. Art Institute of Chicago, Chicago. Photography © Art Institute of Chicago. http://www.artic.edu.aic.

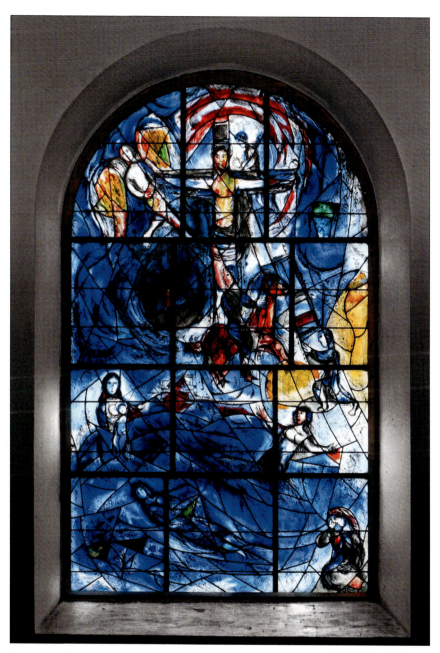

Plate 11. Marc Chagall, East Window, 1967, All Saints Church, Tudeley, Kent, UK.
Photography © Peter Tulloch ARPS DPAGB.

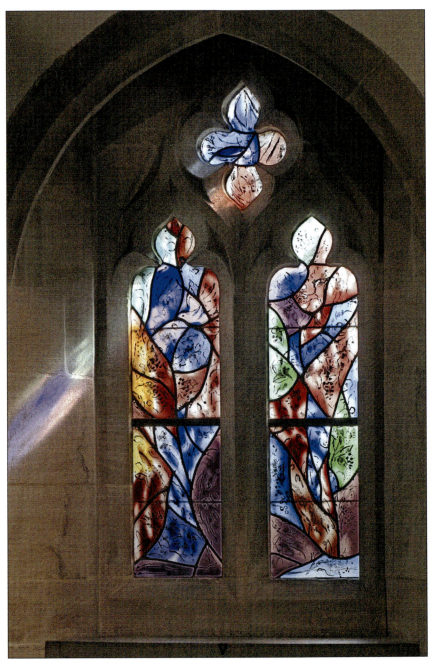

Plate 12. Marc Chagall, North Aisle Windows, 1978, All Saints Church, Tudeley, Kent, UK. Photography © Peter Tulloch ARPS DPAGB.

Plate 13. Marc Chagall, '. . . let everything that hath breath praise the Lord', 1978. North Choir Aisle, Chichester Cathedral, Chichester, UK. Source: Dean and Chapter of Chichester Cathedral. © ADAGP, Paris, and DACS, London.

Plate 14. *King David Playing his Harp to the Animals.* Rothschild MS 24, *c.*1470. By permission of Israel Museum, Jerusalem.

Plate 15. Roman mosaic. Second century CE. University of Perugia. Private photograph.

Plate 16. *King David Playing the Viol.* Guercino, 1617–18. Musée des Beaux Arts, Rouen. By permission of Scala Archives, London.

(1865–68).[30] Musical settings of two of them (Pss. 131, 133) provide the finale of Leonard Bernstein's *Chichester Psalms* (1965).

In the light of this very brief but I hope convincing look at what the fifteen שירי המעלות have in common, let us return to the question of what the title might mean. It refers to a clearly identifiable collection of fifteen short, popular psalms. It would make good sense to call them simply 'the Fifteen', by analogy with the '*shmonesreh*' or 'The Eighteen' (sc. Benedictions). But instead the rabbis (or their immediate Second Temple Period predecessors), with characteristic imagination and originality, called them after the fifteen semicircular steps leading up to the Temple from the Women's Court. There is a vivid description in the Talmud of a ritual in which a choir of Levites with musical instruments joyfully processes down the fifteen steps on the fifteenth day of Tishri, that is to say, on the first day of Succoth (Sukkah 51b). Whatever the origin of these rituals, and indeed whatever the original meaning of the title שירי המעלות may have been, it has always seemed to me that, in the context of the Psalter as we now have it, it is a mistake to look for a historical or technical meaning, as most scholars have done.[31] A far simpler and more obvious explanation is that it is an affectionate title for a group of special favourites among the Psalms, and should be translated as the 'Songs of the Temple Steps'.

However that may be, I want to end on a personal note with some comments on the fourteenth of the 'Fifteen', and a bit of nostalgia. Almost fifty years ago I attended Ulpan Etzion in Jerusalem to learn spoken Hebrew. Most of the class were '*olim chadashim*' or 'new immigrants': six young Moroccan women, an elderly couple from Brazil, a young man from Sierra Leone, a group of delightful young Bene Yisrael from Bombay, an American postgraduate, and the late Marcel Dubois, a French Dominican who later became the first non-Jewish Professor of Philosophy at the Hebrew University. It was a marvellous experience and part of it was the first verse of Psalm 133, which we sang like a kind of school song to various well-known popular tunes on bus trips and other outings. One version I came across recently on YouTube. It is sung by a group of women in Mendoza in northwest Argentina, and it seemed to me to be an excellent illustration of the global dimension of reception history and of how much listening to familiar words sung by new voices can add to our appreciation of the biblical text.[32] Here are ten Spanish women on the other side of the planet, a long way from the Temple in Jerusalem, singing Hebrew with a marked East European accent, and dancing an interpretation of Ps. 133.1 which could hardly be more convincing, their synchronized movements expressing unity and solidarity, the wide open

---

[30] Ibid: 223.   [31] E.g. Mowinckel 1962: 208; Weiser 1962: 141; Kraus 1960: 608.

[32] See www.youtube.com/watch?v=mA_HZ5bL9VA&feature=related (accessed 8 February 2011).

space they are in symbolizing freedom, and their solemn, cheerful voices exactly capturing the meaning of the Hebrew:

hinne ma tov u-ma na'im shevet achim gam yachad . . .

'What a wonderful thing it is when brothers and sisters get along together in harmony!' (my own free and inclusive translation).

Like my Ulpan class, conference delegates are an unusually mixed group, in this case living together for a few days in Worcester College, and representing a wide variety of academic disciplines, methodological approaches and presuppositions, not to mention diversity in age, nationality, and religious background. So, with the words of this famous psalm ringing in our ears, I wanted to express the hope that this conference, in such beautiful surroundings, will be an opportunity for us to look critically at our role in any conflicts between us, past and present, while at the same time celebrating occasions of convergence, areas of common ground—which I hope will be many. *Shalom u-be-hatzlacha!*[33]

Bibliography

Anon.
　1820　*History of the Man after God's Own Heart* (London: J. Carlile).
Briggs, Charles A. and Briggs, Emilie C.
　1906–7　*A Critical and Exegetical Commentary on the Book of Psalms* (Edinburgh: T. & T. Clark).
Buchthal, Hugo
　1974　'The Exaltation of David', *Journal of the Warburg and Courtauld Institutes* 37: 330–3.
Childs, Brevard S.
　1971　'Psalm Titles and Midrashic Exegesis', *Journal of Semitic Studies* 16: 137–50.
Cross, Frank M.
　1978　'David, Orpheus and Psalm 151: 3–4', *BASOR* 231: 69–71.
Dahood, Mitchell
　1970　*Psalms III: 101–150* (Anchor Bible; Garden City, NY: Doubleday).
Davies, Eryl
　2010　*The Immoral Bible: Approaches to Biblical Ethics* (London: T. & T. Clark).
Fry, Stephen
　1997　*Moab is my Washpot* (London: Soho Press).
Gadamer, Hans-Georg
　1975　*Truth and Method* (New York: Seabury).
Gillingham, Susan
　2008　*Psalms through the Centuries*, vol. 1 (Blackwell Bible Commentaries; Oxford: Wiley-Blackwell).

---

[33] '*Shalom and Good Luck!*' This last paragraph pertains to the conference delegates: but as this was the introductory paper, which captured the spirit of the conference, it has been included here.

Jauss, Hans Robert
    1982 *Towards an Aesthetic of Reception*, trans. T. Bahti (Minneapolis: University of Minnesota Press).
Jewish Study Bible
    2004 ed. Adele Berlin and Marc Zvi Brettler (Oxford: Oxford University Press).
Joyce, Paul and Mein, Andrew (eds.)
    2011 *After Ezekiel: Essays on the Reception of a Difficult Prophet* (London: T. & T. Clark).
Klauck, Hans-Josef
    2007– *Encyclopedia of the Bible and its Reception* (Berlin: de Gruyter).
Kraus, Hans-Joachim
    1960 *Psalmen* (BKAT, 15; 2 vols.; Neukirchen-Vluyn: Neukirchener Verlag).
Lang, Bernhard
    2009 *Joseph in Egypt: A Cultural Icon from Grotius to Goethe* (New Haven and London: Yale University Press).
Lieb, Michael, Mason, Emma, and Roberts, Jonathon (eds.)
    2011 *The Oxford Handbook of the Reception History of the Bible* (Oxford Handbooks in Religion and Theology; Oxford: Oxford University Press).
Linafelt, Tod, Camp, Claudia V., and Beal, Timothy K. (eds.)
    2010 *The Fate of King David: The Past and Present of a Biblical Icon* (London: T. & T. Clark).
Magonet, Jonathan
    1994 *A Rabbi Reads the Psalms* (London: SCM Press).
Mowinckel, Sigmund
    1962 *The Psalms in Israel's Worship*, vol. 2 (Oxford: Basil Blackwell 1962).
O'Kane, Martin
    2010 *Biblical Art from Wales* (Sheffield: Sheffield Phoenix Press).
Rogerson, John W.
    1992 'History of Interpretation', *Anchor Bible Dictionary*, vol. 3 (New York: Doubleday): 424–43.
Sawyer, John F. A.
    1970 'An Analysis of the Context and Meaning of the Psalm-headings', *Trans. Glasg. Univ. Orient. Soc.* 22: 26–38; reprinted in John F. A. Sawyer, *Sacred Languages and Sacred Texts: Studies in Biblical Language and Literature* (Sheffield: Sheffield Phoenix Press, 2011): 288–98.
    1995 'The Ethics of Comparative Interpretation', *Currents in Research: Biblical. Studies* 3: 153–68.
    2009 *Concise Dictionary of the Bible and its Reception* (Louisville, KY: Westminster John Knox).
Snaith, Norman H.
    1944 *The Distinctive Ideas of the Old Testament* (London: Epworth Press).
Tompkins, Jane P. (ed.)
    1980 *Reader-Response Criticism: From Formalism to Post-Structuralism* (Baltimore: Johns Hopkins University Press).
Vermes, Geza
    1987 *The Dead Sea Scrolls in English* (London: Penguin Books, 3rd edn).
Weiser, Artur
    1962 *The Psalms: A Commentary* (OTL; London: SPCK).

Part II

Reading the Psalter

11

The Psalter as Theodicy Writ Large

W. H. Bellinger, Jr.

1. Introduction

Elsewhere I have suggested an eclectic approach to the Psalms, an approach I labelled 'a hermeneutic of curiosity'.[1] In this paper, I reflect again upon the various approaches to the book of Psalms and what we can learn from them. Although I was educated as a form critic and biblical theologian and think that the form-critical approach still holds much promise for studies of the Psalms, contemporary interpreters carry out those studies in a different context from when I began to study the Psalms in the 1970s. Interpretation of the Hebrew Scriptures has been influenced by the broader field of literary studies. The application of this trend to Psalms interpretation has brought the poetic and theological dimensions of the Psalms to the primary attention of scholars, in addition to questions about origins. The work of Brevard Childs and other studies that attend to the Psalter as a whole became in the 1980s part of my research on approaches to the Psalms. While in sympathy with the concerns of those scholars, at the time I found their approach somewhat limited in its benefits. The work of the Book of Psalms Section of the Society of Biblical Literature over the last two decades as well as preparations for commentary writing on the Psalms, however, have brought a different perspective. I now think that reading the Psalter as a whole promises to add to the richly coloured tapestry of interpretative approaches available today. While I would still hold to an eclectic approach, the task in this contribution is to explore particular dimensions of it, including the shift from *Gattung* and *Sitz im Leben* (form and life-setting) to *Sitz im Buch* or *Sitz in der Literatur* (settings in literature) as well as theological issues raised by the Psalter as a whole. First, it is important to place my comments in the context of recent scholarship, and then come to the Hebrew Psalter.

---

[1] See Bellinger 1995.

2. History of Scholarship

2.1. Beginnings

Recent attention to the Psalter as a whole can be traced back to the work of Brevard Childs and his insistence upon a canonical approach to the Old Testament. In his *Introduction to the Old Testament as Scripture*, Childs' treatment of the Psalms concentrates on various emphases that characterize the final form of the Psalter in the Christian canon.[2] It is important to note that there were predecessors to Childs' work on the Psalms. Of particular import is Claus Westermann's study of the formation of the Book of Psalms, first published in 1962.[3] He suggests a collection framed by the wisdom Psalms 1 and 119 to which smaller collections were added, and he notes that the Psalter makes parallel moves from lament to praise and from individual to community.

The work that established the place of holistic readings of the Hebrew Psalter, however, is Gerald Wilson's Yale dissertation.[4] Wilson explores other ancient psalm collections and then looks to the 'seams' of the Psalter and its five books as a means of discovering the design of the whole. He understands the first three books (Psalms 1–89) to have a different editorial history from Books IV–V. Books I–III trace the history of the Davidic monarchy from its institution (Psalm 2) to its demise (Psalm 89). Books IV–V reassert the kingship of Yahweh as a basis for life in a post-exilic community without a Davidic king. One of the questions about Wilson's thesis has to do with his assertion of the failure of the Davidic kingdom suggested by Psalm 89. A number of interpreters have responded that he does not give sufficient account of the presence of Davidic elements in Books IV and V. David Mitchell, for example, has argued for an eschatological programme akin to that in Zechariah 9–14 as underlying the Psalter.[5] Wilson responds that 'no matter how unexpected it may seem, the role of David is *down-played* in the final form of the Hebrew Psalter'.[6] Wilson continues to maintain his position. Although there are many issues yet to resolve, his hypothesis for the editing of the Hebrew Psalter and its consequent shape has provided an important starting point for readings of the book of Psalms as a whole.

J. Clinton McCann, Jr. offers a variation on Wilson's interpretation of the design of the Psalter. He understands Psalm 2 in terms of the kingship of God. The emphasis is upon Yahweh as the true king rather than upon the anointed one, the Davidic king. Other royal psalms and enthronement psalms confirm that perspective and give the Psalter 'an eschatological orientation'.[7]

---

[2] Childs 1979: 513–14.   [3] Westermann 1981: 250–8.   [4] Wilson 1985.
[5] Mitchell 1997; Cole 2000.   [6] Wilson 2005: 401.   [7] McCann 1993a: 43–5.

That perspective offers hope in the hard reality of life in the aftermath of exile. McCann suggests that Psalms 1–2 set the interpretive agenda and provide an orientation for reading the book.[8] These introductory texts suggest that the Psalms are part of God's *torah* or instruction, and that the content is God's reign and the call to trust in that reign, which is present though opposed.

Other interpreters have followed in the wake of Wilson. James L. Mays has taken a similar view of the kingship of God as central to the final form of the Psalter; he has also emphasized the significance of *torah*.[9] Nancy deClaissé-Walford also reads the Psalter as a whole in terms of *torah* and God's kingship.[10] She especially attends to the beginning of the Psalter and the beginning of each of the five books of Psalms.

2.2. Other Readings

Walter Brueggemann has also emphasized *torah* in his holistic reading of the Psalter, though his approach is somewhat different.[11] He holds that Psalm 1 signals that all psalms should be read through the prism of *torah* obedience. In the course of the Psalter, obedience yields to communion in covenant with God and then to trust. The book ends in the full praise of God. The pivotal turning point is in Psalm 73 at the beginning of Book III where the preceding laments have raised questions about the exact moral calculus of Psalm 1, leading to a crisis that moves faith in a different direction. Jerome Creach finds refuge in Yahweh to be a central theme in the formation of the Psalter.[12] His recent volume presses the matter towards the place of the righteous in the reign of God.[13]

Very important in this account of readings of the book of Psalms as a whole are the several works of Frank-Lothar Hossfeld and Erich Zenger. Zenger's contributions on the latter part of the Psalter are particularly help-ful.[14] He notes the strong liturgical character of the fifth book of Psalms with connections to Zion and the Temple. At the same time, concrete references to the temple cult are absent. He thus characterizes Book V as 'post-cultic and meant to be recited/meditated upon as a "spiritual pilgrimage" to Zion which is the seat of the universal king Yahweh and of the God of Sinai who teaches his Torah from Zion.'[15] In the fifth book of Psalms, 'one is being called to praise the God who rescues *in the midst of affliction and suffering* . . . for this reason the point of view of the poor and needy is found right at the beginning

---

[8] McCann 1996: 664–5.   [9] Mays 1994a: especially 121–3, 129, 133–5.
[10] deClaissé-Walford 1997: 41–8, 55–6.
[11] Brueggemann 1991: 63–92.   [12] Creach 1996: 80
[13] Creach 2008.   [14] See e.g. Zenger 1997: 95–108; 2004: 173–90.
[15] Zenger 1998: 100.

of the fifth book (Ps. 107.41) and increases in intensity towards the end (see especially Pss. 140–143).'[16]

Two more works should be noted. First, Zenger refers to the important work of Matthias Millard, who helpfully suggests clusters of psalms that make up the five books.[17] Secondly, while most of the works I have cited look at the macrostructure of the Hebrew Psalter, David Howard works at the micro-level, noting linguistic and thematic connections between individual psalms.[18]

As is evident, even in this brief and selected sketch of works approaching the Hebrew Psalter as a piece of literature, there is a good bit of diversity. This approach to the Psalter is sometimes characterized as study of 'the shape and shaping of the Psalter'.[19] The works cited above fall along a continuum, from those concerned with the redaction or editing of the Masoretic Psalter (shaping) to those concerned with the final form of the book (shape). Some are more concerned with the composition of the Psalter and some more concerned with readers of the Hebrew Psalter in its final form, readers both ancient and more recent.[20] Shape and shaping are clearly related; I am more concerned in this paper with shape.

2.3. Convergences

While there is diversity and perhaps even conflict among these works, there are also at least two convergences. The first is that, in one way or another, all of these works take a literary approach. Particularly interesting is the approach of poetics, the systematic study of texts as literature, attending to artistic aspects and how they have impact upon readers. This approach depends upon a particular understanding of communication. Shlomith Rimmon-Kenan describes the reading process as a dynamic one in which readers make sense of texts. Signals in the text invite readers into the process.[21] Readers then transform the signals sent by texts.[22] Some would suggest that readers construct or create meaning.[23] It is in the receiving of the message that meaning comes to fruition. Edgar McKnight may be right that 'readers make sense',[24] but I suggest that the production of meaning comes some-where in the interaction between texts and readers. By readers I mean informed readers, careful readers of the Hebrew Psalter in antiquity and through the generations.[25] Texts provide clues for readers.

---

[16] Ibid. 101.   [17] Millard 1994.   [18] See e.g. Howard 1997.
[19] See McCann 1993b.
[20] For an insightful reflection on the reading strategies of this strain of Psalms scholarship, see Nasuti 2005: 311–39.
[21] Rimmon-Kenan 1983.   [22] Iser 1971: 3; 1974a: 107–34; 1974b: 275.
[23] Fish 1980: 327.   [24] McKnight 1985: 12, 133.   [25] Bellinger 1995: 89–107.

Critics from the broader field of literary studies often suggest that the sequencing of texts is one of the important clues in the production of meaning. Beginnings, for example, create important and often lasting impressions—the primacy effect—in the interpretation of texts. At times additional clues in the text lead the interpreter to change direction—the recency effect. The sequencing of texts provides clues for interpreters. That is true in individual texts, and the scholars who consider the Book of Psalms as a whole suggest that it is also true of the sequencing of poems together in a collection such as the Book of Psalms. The ordering of the psalms is an important interpretative clue for readers who attempt to make sense of the Psalter as a whole. That ordering can be viewed as part of a rhetorical strategy, understanding the rhetoric as the art of persuasion. By way of its literary art, its poetry, and its arrangement, the Psalter seeks to persuade its reader—of what?

That leads to the second convergence I see in the scholarly trajectory I have narrated. These works suggest that the issues the Hebrew Psalter confronts stem from the crisis of exile and its aftermath. That crisis brought with it concerns fraught with the questions surrounding theodicy, questions that, of course, are still pressing for contemporary readers. Theodicy issues loom in the studies I have surveyed. We have not often asked, however, the question of the persuasive impact of the Hebrew Psalter on a reading community. I want to turn to that question with these theodicy issues in mind.

Before proceeding, it is important to hear the cautions of Norman Whybray and Erhard Gerstenberger about reading the Psalter as a book.[26] It would be a mistake to conclude that interpreters will be able to fit all the parts of the Hebrew Psalter together neatly. There is a lot we do not know and, no doubt, a lot we will not know. Still, I am now convinced that there is an intentional shape to the Hebrew Psalter and that we add to our interpretative riches when we ask about the impact of that shape on reading communities. The question of when the Hebrew Psalter came to a close remains elusive, as does the initial interpretative community for this piece of literature. A number of interpreters suggest that the Psalter came to a close between the second century BCE and the first century CE. The issue relates to the interpretation of the Qumran materials, including the work of Peter Flint,[27] and to issues surrounding the production of the Greek Psalter. Dennis Tucker and Sue Gillingham suggest the earlier possibilities;[28] Gerald Wilson suggests the later.[29] Communities reading the Hebrew Psalter in that era would still be confronting theodicy issues going back to the exile. More recent communities

---

[26] Gerstenberger 1994: 3–13; Whybray 1996.
[27] See Flint 1997: 135–49; 1998: 453–72; 2007: 157–8.
[28] Gillingham 1996: 147–69; Tucker 2010: 723–31.
[29] Wilson 2000: 102–10.

who would have received and read the Psalter would continue to stand in that tradition.[30]

3. Theodicy

3.1. Kingship of Yahweh

The Hebrew Psalter moves in at least two directions in response to questions of evil, suffering, and chaos that characterize the aftermath of exile. First, underlying a number of the scholarly studies I have cited is the centrality of the affirmation of divine rule in Book IV. For example, Wilson understands the assertion as a response to the fall of the Davidic kingdom portrayed at the end of Book III, and McCann labels Psalms 93 and 95–9 as the theological heart of the Psalter.[31]

Book IV begins with a community lament, an appropriate introduction to a grouping of psalms that seems to reflect back on the crisis of exile for the faith community of ancient Israel. Psalms 90–2 continue that theme, set at the end of Book III and Psalm 89, with the fall of the Davidic kingdom.

> But now you have spurned and rejected him [David];
> you are full of wrath against your anointed.
> You have renounced the covenant with your servant;
> you have defiled his crown in the dust . . .
> and hurled his throne to the ground. (Ps. 89.38–9, 44)

In response to the crisis, this first cluster of psalms in Book IV articulates the theme of divine refuge. Psalms 93–100 press that theme to a central faith affirmation of the Psalter—the reign of Yahweh. Psalm 93 announces the theme and the following psalms articulate various dimensions of the theme. This hopeful affirmation of Yahweh's rule calls for a new song from the congregation, for hope and justice and faithfulness are possible in Yahweh's reign. Celebration of the reign of Yahweh is a hopeful response to the despair of exile and has implications for living just lives. Psalms 102–6 make up the final cluster of psalms in Book IV. These poems call the community to come to terms with this haunting crisis in the context of the affirmation of Yahweh's reign central to Book IV. These psalms describe Yahweh as compassionate creator and liberator of old who will continue to reign. The people

---

[30] The preceding paragraph uses two anachronistic terms—'book' and 'theodicy'. By 'book' I simply mean this Psalter that has a discernible beginning, middle, and end. While 'theodicy' is a more recent term, it is clear that the issues it encapsulates were real and present in the ancient world—issues of divine justice in the face of suffering and evil. There are, of course, various takes on theodicy in the Hebrew Scriptures and various definitions of the term with a variety of dimensions. For the moment, I leave the matter open.

[31] McCann 1996: 1053.

are called to come to terms with the woe of exile as those who can confess their failures and move forward as God's faithful community.

Book IV calls the community to go 'back to the future' by way of a return to a time before the Davidic monarchy, the time of Moses. The book begins with a psalm of Moses (Ps. 90). In that wilderness time, the community experienced King Yahweh's חֶסֶד, steadfast love. The hope is that the community can again, in the wilderness of exile after the defeat of the Davidic kingdom, hear the call to imagine once more Yahweh's reign and to live in that faith affirmation even in the overwhelming chaos of defeat and exile.[32]

The central affirmation in Book IV is the kingship of Yahweh. That affirmation of faith is central to the whole Psalter,[33] and Book IV places it squarely in the midst of the trauma of exile. Issues of theodicy or questions about God in the midst of suffering are thus central to Book IV, and this book begins to make it clear that these issues are at the heart of the whole Psalter. The faith community of ancient Israel pursues these issues of suffering as part of their reflection on faith and as part of their persistent dialogue with Yahweh; questions of theodicy must now also include the confession of faith that Yahweh reigns. This cluster of theological issues pervades the Hebrew Psalter, and especially Book IV, as it does our own contemporary conversations about faith in Judaism and Christianity.

Psalm 102 provides a good illustration. The psalm's first movement articulates an individual lament emphasizing human frailty (vv. 2–12; 1–11 NRSV). The second movement (vv. 13–23; 12–22 NRSV) begins with a contrast to the lasting quality of Yahweh's reign:[34]

> But you, Yahweh, sit enthroned forever
> and memory of you continues generation after generation.

The psalm then places this affirmation of divine kingship squarely in the community's experience of exile and articulates the hope that the everlasting king will restore Zion.

> You will arrive and have compassion on Zion,
> for it is time to be gracious to her;
> for the appointed time has come.
> For your servants hold her stones dear
> and her rubble they pity.
> Then nations will fear the name of Yahweh
> and all the kings of the earth your glory,
> for Yahweh will rebuild Zion
> and appear in glory
> and turn to the prayer of the forsaken
> and not despise their prayer. (vv. 13–17)

[32] See Klein 1978: 128–34; deClaissé-Walford 1997: esp. 105–18.
[33] See Mays 1994b; 1994a: 3–22; McCann 1996; Wilson 1985: 199–228.
[34] This and the following references are my own translation.

The poem's concluding movement (vv. 23–8) provides a reprise of the first two movements. The psalm seeks to integrate faith in the reign of Yahweh with the reality of exile and to put the faith affirmation in dialogue with the community's trouble and woe. The psalm affirms divine kingship even in the face of exile and asks God to bring that confession to reality. The language of the psalms in Book IV is not simply the language of reporting history and stating theological propositions. It is language that creates in the community's imagination an assurance and hope of living as part of the reign of Yahweh.

The end of Book IV:

> Save us, O Yahweh our God,
> and gather us from among the nations . . . (Ps. 106.47)

and the beginning of Book V in Ps. 107.1–3 where Yahweh has gathered in the redeemed 'from the lands' suggest that the Psalter's final book will also relate to the aftermath of exile. Zenger helpfully characterizes Book V in terms of 'spiritual pilgrimage' to Zion as the seat of Yahweh, the universal King, and the God who teaches *Torah*. In Book V the assertion of divine kingship is tied more closely to the community's suffering and affliction in the aftermath of exile. The hope is that the חֶסֶד of the divine king will become manifest even in the current distress; the opening psalm of Book V narrates memories of how that חֶסֶד has been experienced by the community. The book maintains the assertion of divine kingship in the face of trouble and woe—such as the community had experienced in exile—and calls the community to the faith journey of reading the Psalter as a means of realizing the divine way of life. The fivefold concluding doxology of the Psalter also emphasizes the reign of Yahweh. Furthermore, it is possible that the conclusion of Psalm 149 indicates the assignment of the tasks of the Davidic king to the community which, along with the praise of the divine king, execute the judgment decreed by King Yahweh.[35]

The assertion of divine kingship as an approach to theodicy questions is in line with a number of traditional approaches to such issues in Christian theology. McCann's view that the Psalter affirms God's reign as both present and opposed, along with his proposal of an eschatological dimension to the Psalter, provide helpful avenues for considering the approach. Another way of thinking about the matter emphasizes the liturgy reflected in the psalms celebrating the kingship of Yahweh in Book IV. Sigmund Mowinckel famously characterized cult as drama, as 'reality-generating drama' with real power to create.[36] The drama makes it possible for a community to imagine a life or a world, a social reality to inhabit. The words of David Clines from his work on the Pentateuch echo this approach to the poetry of the Psalter:

---

[35] McCann (1996: 1274) suggests this interpretation for the latter part of Psalm 149.
[36] Mowinckel 1961: II, 21.

To the degree that the hearer or reader of the story is imaginatively seized by the story, to that degree he or she 'enters' the world of the story. That means that the reader of the story, when powerfully affected by it, becomes a participant of its world. One learns, by familiarity with the story, one's way about its world, until it becomes one's own world too.[37]

The liturgy celebrating the kingship of Yahweh in Book IV creates the possibility for the reading community to imagine life in the reign of God and to live that life and encounter its reality.[38] The poems make possible a new way of looking at things. In that sense these texts can be very persuasive.

3.2. The Tradition of Protest

To summarize, one of the Psalter's approaches to questions of theodicy centres on the affirmation of divine kingship especially seen in Book IV. Another approach is also central to the Psalter. Book III, Psalms 73–89, has been central to proposals to account for the shape of the Hebrew Psalter. The groundbreaking proposal of Wilson suggests that after the introductory Psalm 1, the royal Psalm 2 initiates the Davidic kingdom.[39] That kingdom comes to an end at the end of Book III with the fall of the Davidic kingdom narrated in Psalm 89. Books IV and V reply to that crisis of the fall of Jerusalem and the ensuing exile. McCann suggests that the transition has already begun in Book III.[40] My study of Book III leads me to support McCann and suggests even more strongly that the crisis of exile is very much present in Psalms 73–89.

Book III begins with the Psalms of Asaph (Psalms 73–83). This collection begins with an individual lament anguishing over the prosperity of the wicked and then moves to a community lament. The loss of the community's centre in the Jerusalem temple colours much of this collection. While the temple has been destroyed in a defeat which was devastating for the community, the Asaphite Psalms insist on continuing to affirm the sovereignty of the creator and redeemer Yahweh. The community now awaits a demonstration of that sovereignty, and in the meantime remembers the history of the mighty acts of Yahweh on behalf of the faith community. Psalm 79 again narrates the brutal destruction of the treasured city of Jerusalem/Zion as this collection articulates movingly the difficult plight of this community of Yahweh's people:

---

[37] Clines 1978: 102.
[38] See more broadly Brueggemann (1988) and Bellinger (1995: 61, 21, 87, 110, 122) with reference to the work of Paul Ricoeur.
[39] Wilson 1985: 209. See also deClaissé-Walford 1997.
[40] McCann 1993a: 93–107.

> O God, the nations have come into your inheritance;
> they have defiled your holy temple;
> they have laid Jerusalem in ruins (v. 1)

Psalm 80 includes a prophetic call for the people to be faithful; at the same time this collection of psalms articulates in very honest ways the community's cries for justice.

Psalms 84–5 and 87–8 are Korahite psalms and continue the tone of lament and a yearning for the hope promised in the divine presence in Zion. Psalm 86 is an individual lament. The concluding psalms of Book III fervently express the needs of the person of faith and of the community to Yahweh. Psalm 88 is one of the darkest texts in all of Scripture, and the book ends with the demise of the Davidic kingdom. Book IV responds to this continuing crisis of exile.

The daunting crisis of exile colours all of Book III. Enemies as opponents of the community persist, but the emphasis in these psalms is the brutally honest dialogue of faith between Israel and Yahweh. Prayers detailing the anguish of the community and its righteous persons come to the fore in this book. The prayers are alarmingly honest; protest literature would be an appropriate label. Robert Cole notes the persistent presence of the questions 'Why?' and 'How long?' in these psalms.[41] From the beginning of Book III (Psalm 73), questions of theodicy have been central to the psalmists' agenda. Book III centres on those questions in light of the overpowering crisis of exile. Theodicy in this context is not a theoretical issue, however; it takes the shape of protest poems brought into the honest dialogue of faith. So while enemies are present, the focus is the dialogue between the faith community and Yahweh. These psalms thus instruct in prayer by example, and envision a worshipping community that persistently and honestly presses the raw issues of life in the relationship with the divine. The faith exemplified in Book III is true to a world with chaos flooding through the gate. It is the honest dialogue that persists in the crisis. The community of faith is called to continue to live with and claim these questions, all in the context of faith.

This tradition of lament continues in Book IV with Psalms 90, 94, 102, and 106 and intensifies in the laments of Book V with the imprecatory Psalms 109 and 137 as well as with Psalms 140–3. The overwhelming presence of lament in Books I and II anticipates the issues around exile and theodicy. Protest persists in the Hebrew Psalter.

I first came to the topic of this paper some time ago when I was reviewing James Crenshaw's volume *Defending God: Biblical Responses to the Problem of Evil*.[42] It is a helpful volume, but one of the things that struck me was how little it attended to this tradition of protest literature. In the theological world,

---

[41] Cole 2000: 231–5.   [42] Crenshaw 2005.

such an approach to theodicy resonates with Terrence Tilley's volume *The Evils of Theodicy* which bemoans traditional theological attempts to answer the questions of theodicy with theory that is not helpful to life and which can actually support structures that sustain evil.[43]

This approach centring on protest also resonates with an example from Jewish tradition. Renowned Holocaust survivor Elie Wiesel was present at the trial of God in Auschwitz. Robert McAfee Brown describes the story in the Introduction to Wiesel's play, *The Trial of God*:

> By the time he was fifteen, Elie Wiesel was in Auschwitz, a Nazi death camp. A teacher of Talmud befriended him by insisting that whenever they were together they would study Talmud—Talmud without pens or pencils, Talmud without paper, Talmud without books. It would be their act of religious defiance. One night the teacher took Wiesel back to his own barracks, and there, with the young boy as the only witness, three great Jewish scholars– masters of Talmud, Halakhah, and Jewish jurisprudence—put God on trial, creating, in that eerie place, 'a rabbinic court of law to indict the Almighty'. The trial lasted several nights. Witnesses were heard, evidence was gathered, conclusions were drawn, all of which issued finally in a unanimous verdict: the Lord God Almighty, Creator of Heaven and Earth, was found *guilty* of crimes against creation and humankind. And then, after what Wiesel describes as an 'infinity of silence', the Talmudic scholar looked at the sky and said 'It's time for evening prayers', and the members of the tribunal recited Maariv, the evening service.[44]

Wiesel recently spoke about the experience: 'I was there when God was put on trial . . . I was the only one there. It happened at night; there were just three people. At the end of the trial, they used the word *chayav*, rather than "guilt". It means "He owes us something". Then we went to pray.' The approach to theodicy is not a matter of an answer but a continuation of the tradition and practice of honest protest spoken to the divine. Such an approach is embodied in the Hebrew Psalter and has influenced generations of readers.

4. Conclusion

I entitled this paper 'The Psalter as Theodicy Writ Large'. I have come to view questions around theodicy as infused into the various parts of the Hebrew Psalter. In that sense the question is 'writ large'. While I find sequential reading of the Psalter to be helpful, I am coming to see the questions raised by the trouble and woe of exile and its aftermath as pervading all the parts of the Psalter. Those issues were pressing for the initial reading community; the

---

[43] Tilley 1991. See also Surin 1983: 225–47; Pinches 1989: 239–55; O'Connor 1988: 61–74.
[44] Wiesel 1979: vii.

issues continue to press succeeding generations of readers. The title also reflects the notion that the Hebrew Psalter is a remarkably multifaceted piece of literature. It has many dimensions and perspectives and no one approach will solve its riddles. I would still hold for an eclectic approach. I suggest that one of the multiple approaches that can enrich our interpretation is the literary approach of reading the Hebrew Psalter as a whole and attending to its sequences and how the Psalter as a piece of literature can have a persuasive impact on an interpretative community. Reading the Psalter as a whole leads to questions of theodicy. If not conflict, I have certainly found diversity in the Psalter and its interpretation but also convergences related to Christian and Jewish tradition.

Bibliography

Bellinger, Jr., William H.
  1995 *A Hermeneutic of Curiosity and Readings of Psalm 61* (SOTI, 1; Macon, GA: Mercer University Press).
Brueggemann, Walter
  1988 *Israel's Praise: Doxology against Idolatry and Ideology* (Philadelphia: Fortress Press).
  1991 'Bounded by Obedience and Praise: The Psalms as Canon', *JSOT* 50: 63–92.
Childs, Brevard S.
  1979 *Introduction to the Old Testament as Scripture* (Philadelphia: Fortress Press).
Clines, David J. A.
  1978 *The Theme of the Pentateuch* (Sheffield: JSOT Press).
Cole, Robert L.
  2000 *The Shape and Message of Book III (Psalms 73–89)* (JSOTSup, 307; Sheffield: Sheffield Academic Press).
Creach, Jerome F. D.
  1996 *Yahweh as Refuge and the Editing of the Hebrew Psalter* (JSOTSup, 217; Sheffield: Sheffield Academic Press).
  2008 *The Destiny of the Righteous in the Psalms* (St. Louis: Chalice).
Crenshaw, James L.
  2005 *Defending God: Biblical Responses to the Problem of Evil* (New York: Oxford University Press).
deClaissé-Walford, Nancy L.
  1997 *Reading from the Beginning: The Shaping of the Hebrew Psalter* (Macon, GA: Mercer University Press).
Fish, Stanley Eugene
  1980 *Is There a Text in This Class? Authority of Interpretive Communities* (Cambridge, MA: Harvard University Press, 1980).
Flint, Peter W.
  1997 *The Dead Sea Psalms Scrolls and the Book of Psalms* (STDJ, 17; Leiden: Brill).
  1998 'The Book of Psalms in the Light of the Dead Sea Scrolls', *VT* 48: 453–72.
  2007 '11QPs^b and the 11QPs^a-Psalter', in Joel S. Burnett, William H. Bellinger, Jr., and Dennis W. Tucker, Jr. (eds.), *Diachronic and Synchronic: Reading the*

Psalms in Real Time: Proceedings of the Baylor Symposium on the Book of Psalms (LHBOTS, 488; London: T. & T. Clark): 157–66.

Gerstenberger, Erhard S.
1994 'Der Psalter als Buch und als Sammlung', in Klaus Seybold and Erich Zenger (eds.), *Neue Wege der Psalmenforschung* (Herders Biblische Studien; Freiburg: Herder): 3–13.

Gillingham, Susan
1996 'Psalmody and Apocalyptic in the Hebrew Bible: Common Vision, Shared Experience', in John Barton and David J. Reimer (eds.), *After the Exile: Essays in Honour of Rex Mason* (Macon, GA: Mercer University Press): 147–69.

Howard, David M.
1997 *The Structure of Psalms 93–100: Their Place in Israelite History* (Winona Lake, IN: Eisenbrauns).

Iser, Wolfgang
1971 'Indeterminacy and the Reader's Response in Prose Fiction', in J. Hillis Miller (ed.), *Aspects of Narrative: Selected Papers from the English Institute* (New York: Columbia University Press): 1–45.
1974a *The Act of Reading: A Theory of Aesthetic Response* (Baltimore: Johns Hopkins University Press).
1974b *The Implied Reader: Patterns of Communication in Prose Fiction from Bunyan to Beckett* (Baltimore: Johns Hopkins University Press).

Klein, Ralph W.
1978 'Theology for Exiles: The Kingship of Yahweh', *Dialog* 17: 128–34.

McCann, J. Clinton, Jr.
1993a *A Theological Introduction to the Book of Psalms: The Psalms as Torah* (Nashville: Abingdon).
1993b (ed.) *The Shape and Shaping of the Psalter* (JSOTSup, 159; Sheffield: JSOT Press).
1996 'The Book of Psalms: Introduction, Commentary, and Reflections', in Leander E. Keck (ed.), *The New Interpreter's Bible: A Commentary in Twelve Volumes*, vol. 4 (Nashville: Abingdon): 641–1280.

McKnight, Edgar
1985 *The Bible and the Reader: An Introduction to Literary Criticism* (Philadelphia: Fortress Press).

Mays, James L.
1994a *The Lord Reigns: A Theological Handbook to the Psalms* (Louisville, KY: Westminster John Knox).
1994b *Psalms*, ed. Patrick D. Miller, Jr. (Interpretation: A Bible Commentary for Teaching and Preaching; Louisville, KY: Westminster John Knox).

Millard, Matthias
1994 *Die Komposition des Psalters. Ein formgeschichtlicher Ansatz* (FAT, 9; Tübingen: J. C. B. Mohr).

Mitchell, David C.
1997 *The Message of the Psalter: An Eschatological Programme in the Book of Psalms* (JSOTSup, 252; Sheffield: Sheffield Academic).

Mowinckel, Sigmund
1961 *Psalmenstudien, vol. 2: Das Thronbesteigungsfest Jahwäs und der Ursprung der Eschatologie* (repr., Amsterdam: Schippers).

Nasuti, Harry P.

2005 'The Interpretive Significance of Sequence and Selection in the Book of Psalms', in Peter W. Flint and Patrick D. Miller, Jr. (eds.), *The Book of Psalms: Composition and Reception* (SVT, 99; Formation and Interpretation of Old Testament Literature, 4; Leiden: E. J. Brill): 311–39.

O'Connor, David

1988 'In Defense of Theoretical Theodicy', *Modern Theology* 5: 61–74.

Pinches, Charles

1989 'Christian Pacifism and Theodicy: The Free Will Defense in the Thought of John H. Yoder,' *Modern Theology* 5: 239–55.

Rimmon-Kenan, Shlomith

1983 *Narrative Fiction: Contemporary Poetics* (London: Methuen).

Surin, Kenneth

1983 'Theodicy?' *HTR* 76: 225–47.

Tilley, Terrence W.

1991 *The Evils of Theodicy* (Washington: Georgetown University Press).

Tucker, Dennis, Jr.

2010 'Empires and Enemies in Book V of the Psalter', in Erich Zenger (ed.), *The Composition of the Book of Psalms* (Bibliotheca Ephemeridum Theologicarum Lovaniensium, 238; Leuven: Uitgeverij Peeters): 723–31.

Westermann, Claus

1981 *Praise and Lament in the Psalms,* trans. Keith R. Crim and Richard N. Soulen (Atlanta: John Knox Press).

Whybray, R. N.

1996 *Reading the Psalms as a Book* (JSOT Sup, 222; Sheffield: Sheffield Academic).

Wiesel, Elie

1979 *The Trial of God* (New York: Schocken).

Wilson, Gerald H.

1985 *The Editing of the Hebrew Psalter,* ed. J. J. M. Roberts (SBLDS, 76; Chico, CA: Scholars Press).

2000 'A First Century C. E. Date for the Closing of the Hebrew Psalter?' *JBQ* 28: 102–10.

2005 'King, Messiah, and the Reign of God: Revisiting the Royal Psalms and the Shape of the Psalter', in Peter W. Flint and Patrick D. Miller, Jr. (eds.), *The Book of Psalms: Composition and Reception* (SVT, 99; Formation and Interpretation of Old Testament Literature 4; Leiden: E. J. Brill): 391–406.

Zenger, Erich

1997 'Der jüdische Psalter—ein anti-imperiales Buch?' in Rainer R. Albertz (ed.), *Religion und Gesellschaft. Studien zu ihrer Wechselbeziehung in den Kulturen des Antiken Vorderen Orients* (Münster: Ugarit): 95–108.

1998 'The Composition and Theology of the Fifth Book of Psalms: Psalms 107–145', *JSOT* 80: 77–102.

2004 'Die Komposition der Wallfahrtpsalmen Ps 120–134: Zum Programm der Psalterexegese', in Martin Ebner and Bernhard B. Heininger (eds.), *Paradigmen auf dem Prüfstand: Exegese wider den Strich* (Münster: Aschendorff): 173–90.

12

The Psalter and Theodicy: Perspectives Related to a Rhetorical Approach

Dirk Human

1. Introduction

Theodicy as a *theolegoumenon* renders an existential theme for lively theological debate. By connecting this theme to the Psalter, which reflects almost all kinds of life situations and diverse faith experiences between Yahweh and his people, this life-related debate becomes particularly intense and dramatic. Even without treating 'theodicy' as the *Mitte* ('centre') of Old Testament Theology or of the theology/ies of the Psalter, the theme nonetheless encourages reflection about the multifaceted relationship between Yahweh and Israel, especially when this relationship is jeopardized by severe crises due to the behaviour of Israel, other people, or God.

Any portrayal of this theme is dependent upon the exegetical approach and hermeneutical stance of the exegete. The history of Old Testament scholarship illustrates a variety of reading strategies and hermeneutical approaches applied to our understanding of the Psalms. In his presentation Bellinger has made clear his own stance as a biblical theologian. His is an 'eclectic approach', which might be labelled as 'hermeneutic of curiosity'; it makes use of a 'literary-theological hermeneutic' and acknowledges the influence of the broader field of literary studies on the reading of the Psalms' poetry. This allows him to shift from an emphasis on the *Gattung* and *Sitz im Leben* to one on the *Sitz im Buch* (or *Sitz in der Literatur*) when analysing texts. The importance of the psalms as literature is hereby fully acknowledged.

2. Short History of Psalm Scholarship

Bellinger diligently outlines a short history of Psalm scholarship since the late 1980s. He notes how, in the last two decades, psalm studies have increasingly focused on reading the Psalms as a book or as a library with smaller clusters, groups, or collections. Attending to the Psalter as a whole, emphasizing the 'final form' of the book in the canon, and reading psalm groups holistically have all become familiar descriptions. Thus the seminal works of Claus Westermann, Brevard Childs, Gerald Wilson, Walter Brueggemann, F. L. Hossfeld, Erich Zenger, and Matthias Millard are all household names in psalm research and are frequently cited in Bellinger's paper, for these scholars have all contributed towards the ways in which we now read the Psalms as a whole or as a library/book with smaller groupings. Scholars such as David Mitchell, J. Clinton McCann, James L. Mays, Nancy deClaissé-Walford, Jerome Creach, and David Howard, amongst others, have contributed to the debate by offering refinements and a modified critique. Norman Whybray and Erhard Gerstenberger offer voices of caution about reading the Psalter as a book, and they and others have provided valid counter arguments in this discussion. So although other psalm specialists might have been added, these scholars are a representative selection of the main thrusts in psalm research today.

Bellinger's brief history of scholarship underscores the importance of the arrangement of the Hebrew Psalms. The shape and shaping of the Psalter involve the final form as well as the compositional and redactional processes of this book. In a complex process, which took place over a very long period, individual texts and 'smaller' collections were probably purposely designed in order to form larger collections and ultimately the Book of Psalms.[1] Although literary indications of groupings as well as linguistic and thematic connections between psalms and units are now 'a given' in psalm research, the theological intentionality of smaller groupings or indeed of the entire Psalter remains an issue of debate. It is not surprising that exegetes still differ on the extent, origin and date of many collections, and on by whom and to which communities these collections were directed. Bellinger has given us an explanation for this: the texts as literature have to be interpreted. The volume that appeared from the 2008 Leuven Psalm Congress provides clear evidence of these different possibilities.[2]

The five-part division of the Hebrew Psalter is undisputed. With Wilson and others, Bellinger accepts that Books I–III form a closer unit than Books IV–V. Books I–III (Pss. 1–89) suggest an editorial and redactional unity and reflect the history of the Davidic monarchy. After the rise (Ps. 2) and the demise (Ps. 89) of the earthly king, descriptions of the destruction of Jerusalem and the temple as well as God's abandonment of his promises to the king (Ps. 89) seem to leave Israel empty and vulnerable. What will happen to Israel after this crisis? Does she have any future?

---

[1] See Zenger 2008: 364–6.   [2] See Zenger 2010.

Books IV–V (Pss. 90–150) constitute the second part of the Psalter. Pss. 90–106 (Book IV) probably form the 'editorial centre' of the whole collection.[3] In this corpus, two groups of psalms seem to shape an intentionally ordered section which is bound by a particular theological concept or idea; namely, Yahweh as *refuge* (Pss. 90–2, 94), and Yahweh as *king* (Pss. 93, 95–9). Books IV–V provide a theological response to the agony over the destruction of Jerusalem.[4] In Psalm 89 the earthly king is overthrown. Who will reign now? The answer is: Yahweh is king. Not only is Yahweh described as the only reliably constant monarch, but this king-God is depicted as refuge and protector-ruler of Israel. The theological design of Books IV–V tends to compensate for the shattered hopes of Israel in her post-exilic crises. Wilson suggests that Pss. 93 and 95–9 hold the key to the theological meaning of the complete Psalter.[5] This viewpoint is convincing. These psalms form the theological heart of the Psalter. I will pursue both this notion and the programmatic key role that Psalm 93 plays in the Psalms later.

Despite the differences and diversity he identified among scholars' approaches and views, Bellinger formulates two convergences. The first is that *all scholars take a literary approach* where they read the psalms as literature and poetry. Meaning is created between texts and readers. Literary devices, the sequencing of texts, the ordering of the psalms, and the appearance of themes and motives at the seams of the collections all provide interpretative clues to help to determine the theological thrust and meaning of texts: this includes individual psalms as well as the Psalter as a whole. This type of interpretative exercise creates room for exegetes like Bellinger to identify and interpret the 'theodicy' theme, while the text remains as the point of departure.

The second convergence is the result of Bellinger's conviction that the issues confronted by the Hebrew Psalter *stem mainly from the crisis of the Babylonian exile and its aftermath*. This historical *Sitz im Leben* is the cradle where most theodicy questions start. Even when later Israelite generations were confronted by theodicy issues, these mirrored the dreadful circumstances of the time of the Babylonian exile.

3. Theodicy

The term 'theodicy' is used and applied in multi-disciplinary and multi-theological and religious contexts.[6] This anachronistic term was coined by Gottfried Leibniz in 1710. He argued that 'the evil in the world does not

---

[3] See Creach 1996: 99.   [4] Creach 1996: 98.
[5] See Wilson 1985: 216–17.   [6] See Weissler and Barton 2005: 224–39.

conflict with the goodness of God and that indeed, notwithstanding its many evils, the world is the best of all possible worlds.[7] This viewpoint was formulated in reaction to the sceptic Pierre Bayle, who denied 'the goodness and omnipotence of God on account of the many sufferings people experience in this earthly life'.[8] In imitation of Leibniz other scholars started calling their treatises on the problem of evil 'theodicies'. Since then the term has served as a vehicle for many nuances and different interpretations when the realities of evil and suffering are experienced: such miseries lead the sufferer into deep existential and religious debates in view of the belief in a good and omnipotent God.

Nuances of the theodicy debate are not restricted to a specific book or corpus of the Hebrew canon. Various aspects of this theme have a close relationship with Old Testament wisdom literature and its accompanying principle of retribution. Protest against this principle is captured in, for example, Job, Ecclesiastes, and Psalm 73. Pss. 37 and 49 also provide scope for contemplating this problem.

Fredrik Lindström (2003) considered two aspects of theodicy in the Psalms. The first concerns the role of Yahweh and how he engages with evil: is God doing anything to overcome evil or suffering? This leads to the second aspect: is suffering irrational or should evil remain irrational and mysterious? These important perspectives ensure that theodicy encapsulates the existential experience of the sufferer which is characterized by God's passivity, absence, hiddenness, and temporary inactivity – an experience of being abandoned by God.[9]

Bellinger's exposition of the Hebrew Psalms also considers two responses to the questions raised by theodicy – those of evil, suffering, and chaos, all characteristic of the Babylonian exile and its aftermath. He focuses, first, on the theological thrust of Books IV–V, and, secondly, on the role of the lament in the Psalter. On the one hand the Psalter (Books IV–V and the end of Book III) *affirms the reign of divine kingship* amidst all chaos of the exile and its after-effects; on the other, the *genre* of lament *encourages persistent protest* as a means of communion with and honest dialogue of faith in God.

Books IV and V clearly compensate for the shattered hopes caused by the Babylonian exile by focusing on God's reign over all powers of destruction and on the importance of righteous living in the present.[10] As a literary unit Book V offers a meditative pilgrimage through Israelite history where the afflicted servant of Yahweh travels from a position of agony and distress (as once experienced in exile) through to diligent instruction from the Sinai Torah, through to God's presence in Zion. At Zion Yahweh is actively present

---

[7] See Kempf 1912: 1.   [8] Ibid.   [9] See Doyle 2008: 389.
[10] See Gillingham 2008: 210.

as universal king, waiting to bless the god-fearing pilgrim who praises God as a wise servant in the company of the whole of creation.[11]

4. Three Complementary Examples

As a complement to Bellinger's perspectives on the important role of seam texts and Books IV–V in debate about theodicy in the Psalter, I would like to add three other eclectic examples: the programmatic Psalm 93 (Book IV); the Songs of Ascents (Pss. 120–34 in Book V); and Psalm 73 (Book III). Together these psalms illustrate how the reading community was persuaded to celebrate Yahweh's divine kingly presence in order to discover meaning amidst circumstances of affliction, iniquity, injustice, evil, and suffering.

An analysis of Psalm 93 demonstrates how the reader is persuaded to trust in the divine kingship of Yahweh despite the realities of evil or any other life-threatening power.[12] The realization of this kingship for the believing community is embedded in a life committed to the Torah and lived out in cultic activities which celebrate the presence of God.

The Songs of Ascents in Book V continue the theological trends delineated in Psalm 93. The spatial story of these Songs moves from distress and danger 'below' and ascends to the close presence of Yahweh on Zion to experience life, wholeness, peace, protection, and blessedness.[13]

Psalm 73, the 'Job' of the Psalter and the introduction to Book III, anticipates the theological concerns of Books IV–V about 'theodicy'. Despite the psalmist's anguish over the fate of the wicked and the inexplicable and mysterious nature of his own suffering, the psalm nonetheless affirms that the criterion for a wise and righteous life is not the absence of tribulations, suffering, and injustice, or the presence of prosperity and success, but a life that resides in close communion with Yahweh's presence.[14]

5. Conclusion

Bellinger has provided some considered and important insights on the relationship between the Psalter and theodicy and he has stimulated many reflections on this theme. Theological riddles and paradoxical themes in the Psalms cannot be unravelled by one single exegetical approach; however,

---

[11] Wilson (1985: 227–8) describes Book V as an answer to the plea of the exiles to be gathered from the diaspora. The answer is that deliverance and life thereafter is dependent upon an attitude of trust in Yahweh alone.

[12] See Human 2007: 147–69.   [13] See Human 2009: 63–87.

[14] See Potgieter 1994: 110.

Bellinger's holistic reading and literary approach offer some seminal perspectives. A few closing remarks might be pertinent at this final stage.

1. The phrase 'issues' or 'questions of theodicy' often occurred in Bellinger's presentation and I have quoted them here. Yet these 'issues' or 'questions' were not always clearly outlined: it was not always apparent what he had in mind. A working definition of the term 'theodicy' and its interpretative possibilities could be helpful in future discussions.

2. The lament as 'protest literature' indeed provides an excellent vehicle for stimulating *catharsis* for the psalmist, offering honest dialogue and reflection on faith in times of distress. Bellinger is further convinced that this genre's overwhelming presence in the first parts of the Psalter (Books I–II) prefigures the issues of the exile and questions of theodicy. This observation has not yet been properly substantiated and can appear to be over-generalized. Does this take into consideration all the *Sitze im Leben* of every one of the single psalms? In brief, are all the laments and suffering ultimately related to theodicy, and behind this, to the exile?

3. The relationship between the lament and the overwhelming hymnic character of the Psalter needs further investigation. As was seen with Psalm 93 and the Songs of Ascents, the relationship between the hymn and the theme of theodicy is an important one.

Bellinger is correct when he asserts that the Psalter provides no answer to the problem of theodicy. This is why psalm texts have developed in a number of different directions.[15] God is not justified in the Psalter either for his absence or for his silent participation in the lives of believers, and in this way the Psalter recognizes God's sovereignty. Yahweh's relation to all powers in creation is distinctly outlined as enthroned 'above the waters' (Ps. 93). His kingship surpasses all life-threatening powers – suffering and chaos included. This royal metaphor proclaims hope for both the present and the future. To participate in this kingship the rhetoric of the Psalter seeks to persuade the reader wisely to conduct a Torah-orientated life in *communion* with Yahweh and in his *presence*. Therefore the Psalter includes, *inter alia*, the paradoxes of hymn and lament, or prayer and imprecation: the convergence in this conflict is captured and brought together by the Psalter as a whole.

Bibliography

Brueggemann, Walter
    1984   *The Message of the Psalms: A Theological Commentary* (Augsburg Old Testament Series; Minneapolis: Augsburg Publishing House).

[15] Brueggemann (1984: 174) describes three such directions, initially explored by Claus Westermann. These are: a yearning for retaliation against an unjust enemy; assaults on Yahweh as the one who legitimizes theodicy; and a yearning for a return to a situation of 'orientation'.

Creach, Jerome F. D.
1996   *Yahweh as Refuge and the Editing of the Hebrew Psalter* (JSOTSup, 217; Sheffield: Sheffield Academic Press).

Doyle, Brian
2008   'Where is God when you Need Him Most? The Divine Metaphor of Absence and Presence as a Binding Element in the Composition of the Book of Psalms', in Erich Zenger (ed.), *The Composition of the Book of Psalms* (BETL, 238; Leuven: Uitgeverij Peeters): 377–90.

Gillingham, Susan
2008   'Studies of the Psalms: Retrospect and Prospect', *Expository Times* 119/5: 209–16.

Human, Dirk J.
2007   'Psalm 93: Yahweh Robed in Majesty and Mightier than the Great Waters', in D. J. Human (ed.), *Psalms and Mythology* (LHBOTS, 462; London and New York: T. & T. Clark): 147–69.
2009   'From Exile to Zion: Ethical Perspectives from the Twin Psalms 127 and 128', *Old Testament Essays* 22/1: 63–87.

Kempf, Constantine
1912   'Theodicy', in *The Catholic Encyclopaedia* 14 (New York: Robert Appleton): 1–3; http://www.newadvent.org/cathen/14569a.htm (accessed February 2012).

Lindström, Fredrik
2003   'Theodicy in the Psalms', in A. Laato and J. C. De Moor (eds.), *Theodicy in the World of the Bible* (Leiden: E. J. Brill).

Potgieter, J. Henk
1994   'Menswaardig of Godwaardig? Psalm 73', in C. J. A. Vos and J. Müller (eds.), *Menswaardig* (God, Mens, Wêreld; Johannesburg: Orion): 99–110.

Wilson, Gerald
1985   *The Editing of the Hebrew Psalter* (SBLDS, 76; Chico, CA: Scholars Press).

Wessler, Heinz and Barton, John
2005   'Theodizee', in H. D. Betz, D. S. Browning, B. Janowski, E., Jüngel (eds.), *Religion in Geschichte und Gegenwart* (HThR, vol. 8; Tübingen: Mohr Siebeck): 224–39.

Zenger, Erich
2008   'Das Buch der Psalmen', in Erich Zenger et al. (eds.), *Einleitung in das Alte Testament*, 7th edn (Stuttgart: W. Kohlhammer): 348–70.
2010   (ed.), *The Composition of the Book of Psalms* (Bibliotheca Ephemeridum Theologicarum Lovaniensium, 238; Leuven: Uitgeverij Peeters).

13

The Psalter as a Book

†*Klaus Seybold*

1. Introduction: The History of the Psalter as a Book

In the beginning there was the idea of a book. A written book was the best medium of conservation. It helped to preserve and keep alive texts that had been set aside because they had no further use: these texts would have been stored away in the archives of the temple, perhaps in something like a *genizah*. They might have comprised royal psalms from the time of the monarchy, or other cultic psalms from the first Temple, or hymns and liturgies of older festivals. But many would have been votive texts: originally these would have been prayers offered at the Temple as a testimony to answered prayer. They would consist of thanksgivings, so-called 'new songs', and various other recitals for the *todah* (thanksgiving service) after the experience of deliverance and salvation. After their use they would then have been left in the storerooms of the Temple priests. But was all this really *dead* material?

According to Hermann Gunkel we know that most of the psalmic material came from a particular time and place—a '*Sitz im Leben*', as he called it. Yet, as Gunkel also argued, many of these psalms would then have gone out of use. Those still preserved would have been a few creation hymns, other timeless wisdom texts, and maybe also some *Hallel* psalms and psalms of pilgrimage: many of these are texts in the second part of the Psalter (Pss. 90–150). But as for the first part of the Psalter (Pss. 1–89), almost all of the individual psalms, prayers and songs were distinctive texts of a particular individual at prayer and would never have been intended to be used by other people. They were composed for a purpose, but that purpose was for the use of that one original suppliant.

This was the last academic paper which Professor Seybold wrote. He submitted it in April 2011, and his untimely death on 31 May 2011 prevented him from revising the text more fully for its publication. It is a seminal paper, drawing together his various (and often original) views about the origins and development of the Psalter.

An obvious example is Psalm 40. The psalmist, having been rescued from deep distress, goes to the sanctuary to offer a thanksgiving and relate the story of his deliverance. He brings with him three texts: the story of his rescue, a new song of thanksgiving, and his prayer of lamentation. The story he tells is found in vv. 2–6: this is his new song, which is followed by vv. 6–12, his song of thanksgiving; his earlier lament, once written on a scroll, is in vv. 14–18 (identical to Psalm 70), and has been preserved as a sacred text because it serves as a testimony to God who had heard his prayer. The supplicant laid down all three texts as his votive offering: together these comprise Psalm 40.

It is probable that the notion of collecting such material for posterity arose around the fifth or fourth centuries BCE. We have no idea of the precise date, nor of the people who would have been interested in doing this. But it must have happened. Its beginning is as mysterious as the beginnings of other types of biblical literature in the Persian period. But what is clear is that the only way to preserve this material was to collect it as a written 'book'. At that time, of course, this was simply a *scroll* of texts, structured in its contents, furnished with titles and colophons, and 'published' as holy scripture (whatever that might have meant in those days) to be read and studied, copied and explained, translated and re-used. This first elusive scroll of the book of Psalms is the subject of this paper.

We need to bring together whatever available information we can glean of the earliest origins of this scroll. It is evident that there are at least seven descriptions of the forms of this book. Its oldest name in Hebrew is ספר התהלים, which it is called in the War Scroll from Qumran (first century BCE).[1]

2. The First Suggestion of a Book

The first edition of this 'book' influenced all those which followed it. Yet it is very difficult to determine its parameters, for the evidence is so sparse. However, the Septuagint translation of Ps. 72.20 does offer us some vital information: כלו תפלות דוד בן־ישי is read as 'The prayers ($o\dot{\iota}$ $\H{\upsilon}\mu\nu o\iota$) of David son of Jesse are ended.' Here we discover that there was once a collection of prayers of David: a collection of many prayers, joined together, combined as a unity, all on one scroll. One immediately thinks of the many psalms dedicated to David (לדוד) in the texts before Ps. 72.20, especially from Psalms 3–72 (although curiously Psalm 72 is a psalm of Solomon). This

---

[1] See 4Q491, Fragment 17 Z.4 (4QM^a) of the War Scroll, dated about the first century BCE, noted in Martinez and Tigchelaar (1997: 978–9).

leads us to ask what we are to make of the non-Davidic texts—for example, those of Korah (Pss. 42–9) and Asaph (Ps. 50)? After the completion of these 'prayers of David' it is evident that other Davidic texts were also included (for example, Pss. 86, 101–10, and 138–45). However, I suggest that the very first collection of the book of Psalms contained *the Davidic Psalms in Books One and Two* (Pss. 3–41; 51–72) with maybe some supplements with different (or no) headings. These texts would be known as prayers (תפלות), songs (שירם), or hymns (תהלים). Naturally, assuming an initial scroll of Davidic prayers creates many questions. But it might not look quite so improbable once we assess other factors.

So how did this collection of prayers of David come about? There is bound to be a certain degree of speculation. I suggest the following. The editors found old texts in the archives and were surprised and impressed; they thought they had found the songs of David, the great poet of the past and one of the greatest figures in the history of God and his people. So they selected many of these texts and edited them to fit with their own period. They marked all these texts with the stamp of לדוד—like the seals on jar handles with the stamp למלך—and, despite their diverse contents, they arranged them in a meaningful order, bound them together, and copied them repeatedly in Aramaic or Jewish letters on a scroll of some considerable size. So this was the genesis of the first book of Psalms—or so we think![2]

3. The Second Suggestion of a Book

We might well ask, where did all this take place? Perhaps at the Temple in Jerusalem; perhaps in one of the rooms nearby in the Temple area; maybe even in the scriptorium of the Temple library. Not much is known about a library in the Temple of Jerusalem. Only one apocryphal text of later times gives significant piece of evidence. This is in the second book of Maccabees and is part of a letter sent by the Jews of Jerusalem to Diaspora Jews in Egypt. The letter is believed to have come from Pharisaic circles in the first century BCE. There we read:

> The same things are reported in the records and in the memoirs of Nehemiah, and also that he founded a library and collected the books about the kings and prophets, and the writings of David, and letters of kings about votive offerings. In the same way Judas also collected all the books that had been lost on account of the war that had come upon us, and they are in our possession. (2 Macc. 2.13–15)

[2] Cf. Seybold 2010: 125–40.

The text reports the foundation of a library (βιβλιοθήκην) in Nehemiah's Jerusalem (the fifth to fourth centuries BCE) and refers to the books he collected there. And among other books 'writings of David' (τὰ τοῦ Δαυιδ βιβλία) are mentioned. Because the books of the kings are already referred to, these 'writings of David' are in all probability not the books of Samuel and Kings but the 'book(s) of psalms' which were preserved along with the writings (βιβλία) of the prophets in the rooms of this library.

Moreover the text records an event in the second century BCE, when Judas Maccabeus tried to collect 'all the books that had been lost on account of the war' and bring them back to the library. So they were now available, and they could even be lent out as far away as Egypt. Although this letter reflects the situation of the writer, the reference to a library at the Temple of Jerusalem is worth noting: so, by the Hellenistic period at least, there was certainly a 'book culture' when books were collected, preserved, and copied, and copies were then lent. And in Egypt there was a library and a 'house of writing' (a *Lebenshaus*, or 'house of life', as it was called in Egypt).[3] In this library a 'book of David' was found. And, as experts suggest, in another 'house of life', near the sanctuary at Jerusalem, there was also probably a room for 'holy scriptures', where the Torah (not mentioned in 2 Maccabees), the Prophets, and maybe also the book of the Psalms of David were to be found. This then provides us with evidence for the second stage of the history of the book of Psalms.

But let me propose another idea. If there was the opportunity to copy and borrow books, the book of Psalms could also have been borrowed for liturgical and musical performances: one such individual might have been the choirmaster (מנצח), who would have have used these texts for composing new songs, cantatas, or oratorios. He would have then registered these performances in those texts, and this explains in part how the multiple superscriptions over some psalms came into being.

Furthermore, this provided the opportunity to enlarge the book(s) with new psalmic material. New sets of songs and hymns would have been added: the psalms of Korah and Asaph; the psalms of God's Kingship; hymns; the Songs of Ascent; other groups of Davidic psalms; the *Hallel* songs; the gigantic poem of Psalm 119, and so on. They were added continuously and—most probably—in groups. The scrolls became longer and bigger; the number of copies increased. Yet in spite of all these additional copies there remained just one scroll which was regarded as normative, and to which all copies had to adjust themselves. This explains the conspicuous similarity of most of the manuscripts that were circulating during Qumranic times.

---

[3] Cf. Helck and Otto 1970: 206.

4. The Third Suggestion of a Book

The oldest 'Book of the Psalms' we know so far is the Psalms manuscript 4QPs[a] (4Q83).[4] The experts conclude that this manuscript was copied in an early semiformal hand dated to approximately the mid-second century BCE and is thus older than all other Psalms scrolls with the possible exception of 4QPs[x], which has been variously dated between 175 and 125 BCE (J. T. Milik) or the second half of the first century BCE (J. P. M. van der Ploeg). They note that, in view of the small script and the large columns, 4QPs[a] would originally have contained a complete Psalter. Fragments of nineteen psalms are extant, running from Psalm 5 (with many gaps) up to Psalm 69.[5] 'Since no identifiable text, however, is preserved after Psalm 69, no firm conclusion regarding the shape of this Psalter can be reached.'[6] Hartmut Stegemann calculated that the unpreserved rest of the scroll ran to sixty-one turns, equalling a length of 7.604 metres from Psalm 63 to the end of the scroll. Adding on the first half the scroll brings this to a size of more than 10 metres.[7] That would mean that it is the largest scroll found at Qumran; the Temple Scroll would have measured about 9 metres and the Isaiah Scroll (1QIs[a]) about 7.5 metres. The columns of 4QPs[a] are very big: about 23 cm high and 11 cm broad. If this calculation is correct, the layout of one column is nearly as large as one page of *Biblia Hebraica Stuttgartensia*.[8] In short, this scroll is the largest found in the cave libraries of Qumran—too long to be freely handled. One must suppose that it was regarded as a sample to be copied and divided into smaller parts. Given that it was written in about 150 BCE, in prose format, this suggests that it was not copied at Qumran but was imported from outside. It is worth supposing that the scroll was copied from the prototype of the Psalms Scroll: perhaps the official Book of Psalms at Jerusalem.

The fragments of this gigantic scroll present some crucial problems. The first concerns *the sequence of the texts*. The psalms from 5 to 69 on the whole are arranged as we know them from the Masoretic Text. But there are two exceptions. Psalm 31 is directly followed by Psalm 33 (as also in 4QPs[q]) and Psalm 38 is followed by Psalm 71, continuing on the same line, with virtually no interval, indicating that these were considered to be one psalm. The reason for these alterations may be scribal or redactional: it does not, in principle, disturb the order that may have already been fixed at the time of the 'Book of

---

[4] Ulrich et al. 2000: 7–22, especially plates I and II. See the review of this by Seybold (2002: 278–80).

[5] The fragments of nineteen psalms in 4QPs[a] are from Psalms 5; 6; 25; 31; 33; 34; 35; 36; 38; 71; 47; 53; 54; 56; 62; 63; 66; 67; 69.

[6] See Ulrich et al. 2000: 8.

[7] New measures and calculations of the scrolls are presented in Brütsch (2010: 117ff).

[8] The columns have lines of seventy-three (sometimes sixty) letters, much more than in the layout of the *BHS*, which usually has about fifty letters a line.

David' in the 'Nehemiah Library' or thereafter. This is also the case with the odd superscriptions which occur in 4QPsᵃ,[9] as well as the puzzling *Selah* integrated in the running text.[10]

A second problem concerns *Psalms 72–150*. The last psalm of the 4QPsᵃ scroll is Psalm 71. Psalms of Masoretic numbers 72–150 have not been found so far. So this raises the question as to whether this scroll contained only the first half of the Psalter (Pss. 3–72). Yet scholars believe it also contained the second half. So we might then ask: what was the order of this second half? Was it akin to the Masoretic Psalter or was it a Psalter with a really new order and new texts? Nobody knows. A Masoretic order following the Jerusalem text seems to be likely. Most of the other manuscripts—even the Masada fragments—follow in part the sequence of the Masoretic text, as has been shown by Peter Flint.[11]

A third problem is the *state of text*. The text of these fragments is close to the later Masoretic text, and in the main, only orthographic differences occur. The final kaph is regularly written with an *h*, as is the final long vowel *a* (for example in Ps. 69.6), in what has sometimes been termed the 'baroque style' of the Qumran writers.[12] However, the tetragrammaton is written in Jewish letters, not the Old Hebrew as with most of the manuscripts written at Qumran.[13] It seems that the manuscript was an imported one.[14]

A fourth problem concerns the *relationship of this scroll with the other thirty-nine Psalm scrolls found in the Judaean desert*. It may be that some scrolls have been copied from 4QPsᵃ; however, most of them are written later, in the first century BCE or the first century CE. The discussion is ongoing, as also the relationship of this composition with other Hasmonean psalms such as 4Q380/381.[15]

In conclusion, the 4QPsᵃ scroll—or rather, the fragments of the 4QPsᵃ scroll—are the first manifest evidence of the Psalter as a collection and in the shape of one single scroll beginning to be read as a 'book'.

5. The Fourth Suggestion of a Book

The 11QPsᵃ scroll is the best preserved of all Psalms scrolls of Qumran.[16] It contains twenty-nine continuous columns (with six columns of fragments).

---

[9] e.g. frag. 4,3 = Ps. 36.1; frag. 18,32 = Ps. 67.1; frag. 19,25 = Ps. 69.1.

[10] The *Selah* occurs in frag. 19,34 = Ps. 67.5.   [11] See n. 4 above.

[12] As to the 'baroque style', see Cross (1961: 174–7); also Tov (2000: 199–216, esp. 212).

[13] e.g. יהוה in frag. 4 I,9 (Ps. 33.8); 4 II,3 (Ps. 36.1); 9 II,5 (Ps. 71.1); 9 II,8 (Ps.71.5); 19,28 (Ps. 69.7); 19,32 (Ps. 69.14).

[14] 'The manuscript has been copied in a generally careful and meticulous manner although one correction may occur in Psalm 69.6': see Ulrich et al. 2000: 10. On the orthography, see ibid. 9, table 2.

[15] Cf. Schuller 1986.

[16] Cf. Flint 1997: 39–49 and Appendix 3, 254. See also Jain 2003: 529–39.

The last calculation suggests fifty-two columns for the whole scroll (with the handlesheet): this would be about 6.5 metres in length. Forty-nine texts are fragmentary, starting at Psalm 90, and the order is not identical to the Masoretic sequence. There are some ten additional apocryphal texts, several of them as yet unknown.[17] The scroll was probably written between 30 and 50 CE.[18] It is again in prose format—except for Psalm 119, which is in stichometric lines—and is written in the expanded 'plene' style of the Qumranic editors. Psalms 136 and 145 are longer than they are in the Masoretic tradition.

A key issue is a comparison of 11QPs[a] with the earlier 4QPs[a] scroll on the one hand and with later psalm manuscripts of the first century CE on the other. For example, was there a first part in the 11Q scroll, with texts from Psalms. 1, 2, and 3–89?[19] And if so, was this first part similar to the fragments of 4QPs[a]? Furthermore, is 11QPs[a], with its texts from Psalms 90–150, a continuation of the fragmentary 4Q scroll with texts only from Psalms 5–71, or might it be a competing alternative?

There are two possible answers to these questions. First, that the 4Q scroll was a copy of the official Jerusalem Psalter and was a first step towards the creation of the protomasoretic Psalter and the 11Q scroll. The new collection of texts thus might have been for the liturgical use of the Qumran Essenes. This is the older position and has been argued by scholars such as A. S. van der Woude, Patrick W. Skehan, Shemaryahu Talmon, and Moshe H. Goshen-Gottstein.[20]

A second answer was first proposed by James A. Sanders, editor of the 11Q Psalms scroll, later refined by Gerald H. Wilson, and most recently updated by Peter W. Flint. For example: 'many other Psalms scrolls represent at least three literary editions of the Book of Psalms: Edition I (Psalms 1/2–89), Edition IIa or the 11QPs[a]-Psalter (=Edition I plus the arrangement found in11QPs[a]), and Edition IIb or the MT-150 Psalter (Edition I plus Psalms 90–150).'[21]

This later theory has been discussed and criticized but to date still holds the order of the day. This is significant because Edition I and Edition IIb may well reflect the Jerusalem Psalter tradition.

The 11QPs[a] scroll has several other pertinent characteristics. Its layout is between twenty-five and twenty-six lines of between 13 and 17 cm: it is thus a handy size, like the Isaiah scroll. The tetragrammaton is again written in Old Hebrew. The psalm groups, such as the pilgrimage psalms (Psalms 120–34) and the *Hallel* in Psalms 135–6, are bound together. The ten apocryphal texts have been filled nearer the end, including the important colophon in prose

---

[17] Apocryphal texts are also found in 4QPs[f].
[18] These dates are proposed by Flint (1997: Appendix 2, 254).
[19] The order in 11QPs[a]: before 101 is 93; 76–78; 81; 86; 88; 89. The order in 11QPs[b]: is 77.18–21; 78.1. See Flint 1997: 253 and 260–2.
[20] See Flint 1997: 33. [21] See Flint 1997: 170–1.

style informing the reader how David composed 3,600 psalms out of a total of 4,050 compositions: 'All these he composed through prophecy which was given him before the Most High'. This text defines this collection as a 'book of David' and a prophetic book: it would appear that the aim of this new collection was to give it the character of a prophetic book in order to to add it to the canon of the prophetic writings.[22]

6. The Fifth Suggestion of a Book

In the second half of the first century CE there was a trend of writing psalms stichometrically. Here the lines are separated from each other and are mostly structured in two opposite parts. The development began with the sticho-graphical writing of single psalm texts: a good example is the acrostic form of Psalm 119, which is presented in this way in 11QPs[a] and in other Qumranic manuscripts such as 4QPs[g], 4QPs[h], and 5QPs containing fragments of this text.

The best example of stichometry is in the beautiful scroll 4QPs[b]. Inscribed in a late Herodian hand from the middle of the first century CE, it contains fragments ranging from Psalm 91 to Psalm 118 (Pss. 104–11 are absent) and the text is written in two opposite columns of cola, forming lines. One column has some seventeen lines and the height of a column is 14 cm. It is improbable that this relatively small scroll would have contained all 150 psalms.

Another scroll in stichometric format is MasPs[a]. Peter Flint writes:

This manuscript was discovered on 20 Nov. 1963 in locus 1039, the achaeological designation for the third wall casemate south of the synagogue at Masada. The palaeography indicates a date in the later Herodian period, more specifically the first half of the first century CE (Masada was conquered by the Romans in 74 CE). Most of Psalms 81–85 are extant in a stichometric arrangement, with few variants from the Masoretic Text.[23]

MasPs[a] is also unlikely to have contained a whole Psalter. But the case may be otherwise with the scroll 4QPs[c]. The surviving fragments preserve fifteen psalms ranging from Psalm 16 to Psalm 53. The experts concluded that the surviving pieces are parts of a very long and large scroll that originally contained all the texts of the Psalter.

---

[22] That the Qumran Essenes read the psalms and their Psalter as prophecies of their own time is shown by the *pesher* of Psalm 37 (4QpPs 37).
[23] See Flint 1997: 44.

> The original columns contained 33 lines . . . and were c. 26 cm high and up to 8.5 cm wide . . . The manuscript is inscribed in a late Herodian formal hand. Copied c. 50–68 CE it is roughly contemporaneous with 4QPs[b] (and) 11QPs[a] . . . The substantial amount of text preserved in 4QPs[c] shows few variants against other Judaean scrolls and MT; this manuscript may be regarded as a representative of the edition of the Psalter that is also preserved in the Masoretic Text . . . The format is generally stichometric, with two cola written to the line . . . 4QPs[c] is particularly interesting with respect to the arrangement of cola and the divisions between them.[24]

So a new form of the Psalter as a book was beginning to emerge. In the late first century it was discovered that the Psalms were of a poetic structure or, one should say, there were attempts to express the poetic structure of the Psalms. Attention was paid to the fact that most texts of the Psalter were composed of lines (or stichoi, verses) and the lines composed of cola (half stichoi), usually two cola. This was a poetic convention of most Semitic literatures: it was noticed centuries later and was named *parallelismus membrorum* by Robert Lowth. 'Parallelism' is now of course taken for granted as a common feature in the psalms.

Whence this new interest in the formal character of the Psalms? The stichographic Masada Scroll was found near the synagogue: it is likely or at least possible that this scroll was used in services. It is helpful for the reader of a text, if he or she knows the structure, to be able to articulate the meaning of the parallel structure of the lines.[25]

7. The Sixth Suggestion of a Book

The authors of the New Testament know a Book of Psalms. Twice the evangelist Luke speaks of it: 'For David himself says in the book of Psalms' ($\beta i\beta\lambda\omega$ $\psi\alpha\lambda\mu\hat{\omega}\nu$) . . .' (Lk. 20.42) and 'The text I (Peter) have in mind . . . is in the book of Psalms' (Acts 1.20). And in Lk. 24. 44 Luke places the Book of Psalms besides the Law of Moses and the Prophets. The references are probably from the Septuagint.[26] It must be supposed that beginning in the second century BCE there was also a Septuagint-Psalter in Greek, even though this Septuagint-Psalter is not available to us. We can only draw these conclusions from the Greek Codices Vaticanus and Sinaiticus of the fourth and fifth centuries CE as well from the New Testament. There are many

[24] See Ulrich et al. 2000: 50–1.
[25] As far as I can see, the strophic structure of the (longer) Psalm texts is not evident in these scrolls.
[26] See Gzella 2001: 19–47; also Cordes 2001: 49–60; Rüsen-Weinhold 2001: 61–87. See also Brucker 2006: 355–69 and 2005: 289–308. (I am grateful to Eberhard Bons of the Faculté de Théologie Catholique, Palais Universitaire Strasbourg, for these insights.)

quotations from the Book of Psalms in the New Testament, as we can see in the editions of Nestle's New Testament.[27] The situation is similar to that of the Qumran Library: the Psalms are esteemed as Holy Scripture and the Book of Psalms is regarded as a prophetic book.

The translation of the Psalms into Greek may be dated to the second century BCE. In the later editions of the codices there are traces of the use of the Greek translation in the Jewish service: these must have been added prior to Christian times. One example is the superscription noting a Jewish festival, namely the Consecration of the Temple (Ps. 29; MT Ps. 30); another, a reference to the Feast of Booths, or Sukkot (Ps. 28; MT Ps. 29); another, a reference to the anointing (of the High Priest: Ps. 26; MT Ps. 27). None of these is mentioned in the Hebrew texts. Other examples include the psalms for weekly use: Psalm 23 (MT Ps. 24) is for the first day of the week, Psalm 47 (MT Ps. 48) for the second day, Psalm 93 (MT Ps. 94) for the fourth, Psalm 92 (MT Ps. 93) for the sixth, and Psalm 91 (MT Ps. 92) for the sabbath, again none of which is mentioned in the Masoretic tradition. From all this it may be concluded that the received translation of the Greek Psalter was used as part of the translation of the normative Hebrew Temple Psalter. This may allude to Palestinian practices.

Traces of a Christian use of this Psalter are found in the use of the first verses of Psalm 13 (MT Ps. 14) in Rom. 3.10–18, as well as the superscription of Psalm 65 (MT Ps. 66) where we read ἀναστάσεως ('the [day of] resurrection').[28] But we cannot say much more about which copies of the Book of Psalms the New Testament writers used. The tradition of the Septuagint is very mysterious and complex.

8. The Seventh Suggestion of a Book

At the end of the process of development of the Hebrew Psalter through the use of manuscripts we come to the actual Masoretic Text—which we all know from the text of *Biblia Hebraica*. But the Psalter here is found as a biblical book in the list of Holy Scriptures. In the sample codices of Aleppo and St Petersburg (Leningrad) the Psalter is in its last phase of development. But I do not intend to consider the Psalter as a book within *Biblia Hebraica* because this is dealt with in commentaries. Let me instead close my paper with some remarks on some characteristic pecularities of the development of the Psalter as an ancient book.

[27] These give more than 400 quotations, 70 of which are introduced with formulas. See Evans 2005: 551–79.
[28] Cf. Rahlfs 1979: 72 ff.

9. Conclusions: The Pecularities of the Psalter as a Book

The development of the Psalter as a book is characterized by four factors:

1. as a collection of texts
2. by assimilation of the texts into psalms
3. by canonical intention
4. as a sample edition

9.1

Developed as a collection, the Psalter remains a collection. The internal relations, references, and connections of the texts we have found in the last few years are mostly of a redactional character. The successive addition of texts and groups of texts determines the book. There are a few orphans, more twins, even more families, groups, and series. It may be divided into five parts, or fewer. As a book it may have an opening in Psalm 1 or 2 or 3 and an end in Psalm 150 or Psalm 151, or even have David's compositions as a colophon. The Psalter of Moses and the Psalter of David form a kind of archive from the very beginning.

9.2

A collection in a book unifies and balances out the individual texts to a certain degree. The one-sheet scrolls of the individual psalms (מגלת־ספר of Ps. 40, for example) were copied into larger scrolls up to the dimensions of the Qumran scrolls 4QPs^a, 4QPs^c, and 11QPs^a —some extending as much as 10 metres in length—and these might be compared with other biblical books such as Isaiah or Genesis. Written on the same scroll in Aramaic or Jewish script by one individual hand in the contemporary manner of line and column division, perhaps also in stichographical lines, these texts were assimilated into each other. Close to each other are the shortest psalm, Psalm 117, and Psalm 119, the longest; both were placed between the Hallel Collection (Pss. 112–18) and the Psalms of Ascents (120–34).

9.3

The book of the Psalter has a distinctive propensity to become Holy Scripture: it reveals a canonical intention. Its development broadly follows two lines; each is possibly the result of the two centres which influenced the production of each edition of the book. One line is represented by the 4QPs^a tradtition;

this may be traced back to the Jerusalem Temple centre and its line of progression is to the Masoretic Text and so on to the Aleppo Codex of the tenth century. Its beginning is already fixed in the fourth or third century BCE, but any concrete evidence of its precise form and contents is missing and can only be reconstructed retrospectively from the Masoretic text. Generally speaking this line might be termed the 'Moses Psalter', for there are hints that this Psalter was composed with the intention to accommodate it to the Law of Moses. The division of the Psalter into five books may not be early but is still a clear sign that this book was intended as a copy of the Pentateuch.[29] Psalm 1, not evidenced in the Psalms scrolls of Qumran—only with Psalm 2 in the anthology 4QFlorilegium (4Q174)—reminds the reader of the way in which to use the Torah: 'Happy are those (whose) delight is in the law of the Lord, and on his law they meditate (Hebrew: murmur) day and night' (Ps. 1.1–2). This wise advice suggests that the whole Psalter is to be read as a wisdom text, in the same way. In effect this means that the Psalter (Pss. 1–150) is seen as an addition to the canon of the Torah. The aim was to canonize the whole collection.

It seems that canonization was also the aim of the so-called 'David Psalter' of the 11QPs tradition (Pss. 2–151). If we consider the conclusions of the earliest and latest Davidic texts—the last words of David (2 Sam. 23), the colophon of David's many works and 3,600 psalm texts, and the additional psalm (in the Septuagint, Ps. 151)—we see that in each case David is presented as a prophetic poet, anointed by Samuel. This seems to follow a different tradition from the Moses Psalter, probably emerging from a different centre, and seems to have undergone a different progression in the gradual canonization of the collection of David's songs and prayers. 'All these he composed through prophecy which was given him from before the Most High' (11QPs[a] Col. XXVII,11). Hence through this particular process of canonization the Psalter is connected more closely with the canon of the Prophets than with the canon of the Torah.

9.4

My last point is a hypothesis. I suggest that soon after the idea of a collection of prayers and hymns took shape and a single scroll with the selected texts emerged, perhaps in the third century BCE in the Temple library at Jerusalem, this scroll was known, read, and copied, achieved some importance, and was in the course of time given the status of a normative or standard scroll. The form of the text and the sequence of the psalms thus stabilized. I suggest that

---

[29] The five doxologies are only witnessed scantily in the Qumran scrolls: Ps. 89.53 is partially found in 4QPs[e] and 106.48 is possibly evident in 4QPs[d]. See Flint 1997: 127, 165.

the 4QPsᵃ scroll—and eventually also the 4QPsᶜ scroll—were copies of this Jerusalem standard manuscript. Most of the Qumran fragments of the manuscripts do not differ much from one another, and it is reasonable to assume that they were directly or indirectly dependent upon this fixed tradition, with the exception of the 11QPs scrolls and, obviously, the non-biblical psalm compositions. As far as we can see, this sample manuscript was a forerunner of the protomasoretic standard text. The development of new forms of stichometric editions and the attempt to produce an alternative Davidic Psalter, close to the normative Jerusalem Psalter, suggest that this process only came to an end in the late first century CE. Within this the Greek tradition added different numbering and also, later, influenced the medium of the codex form. From this the development of the Psalter as a book progressed until it, too, became part of the Masoretic manuscripts.

Bibliography

Brucker, Ralph
2005 'La Wirkungsgeschichte de la Septante des Psaumes dans le judaïsme ancien et dans le christianisme primitif', in Jan Joosten and Philippe Le Moigne (eds.), *L'apport de la Septante aux études sur l'Antiquité* (Actes du colloque de Strasbourg; Lectio Divina; Paris: Cerf): 289–308.
2006 'Observations on the *Wirkungsgeschichte* of the Septuagint Psalms', in Wolfgang Kraus and R. Glenn Wooden (eds.), *Septuagint Research: Issues and Challenges in the Study of the Greek Jewish Scripture* (Atlanta: Society of Biblical Literature): 355–69.

Brütsch, Matthias
2010 *Israels Psalmen in Qumran. Ein textarchäologischer Beitrag zur Entstehung des Psalters* (BWANT, 13 (193); Stuttgart: Verlag W. Kohlhammer).

Cordes, Ariane
2001 'Der Septuaginta-Psalter? Zur Geschichte des griechischen Psalmtextes und seiner Edition', in Zenger 2001: 49–60.

Cross, Frank Moore
1961 *The Ancient Library of Qumran and Modern Biblical Studies* (Garden City, NY: Anchor Books Doubleday).

Evans, Craig A.
2005 'Praise and Prophecy in the Psalter and in the New Testament', in Peter W. Flint and Patrick D. Miller, Jr. (eds.), *The Book of Psalms: Composition and Reception* (SVT, 99; Leiden: Brill): 551–79.

Flint, Peter W.
1997 *The Dead Sea Psalms Scrolls and the Book of Psalms* (STDJ, 17; Leiden: Brill).

Gzella, Holger
2001 'Die Wiege des griechischen David. Die Diskussion um die Entstehung des Septuaginta-Psalters in der neueren Forschung', in Zenger 2001: 19–47.

Helck, Wolfgang and Otto, Eberhard
1970 *Kleines Wörterbuch der Ägyptologie* (Wiesbaden: Harrassowitz).

Jain, Eva

2003 'Les manuscrits psalmiques de la Mer Morte', *Revue des Sciences Religieuses* 77: 529–39.

Martínez, Florentino García, and Tigchelaar, Eibert J. C.

1997 *The Dead Sea Scrolls*, vol. 2 (Leiden: Brill/Grand Rapids, MI: W. B. Eerdmans).

Rahlfs, Alfred

1979 *Septuaginta. Vetus Testamentum Graecum X, Psalmi cum Odis* (Göttingen: Vandenhoeck & Ruprecht).

Rüsen-Weinhold, Ulrich

2001 'Der Septuaginta-Psalter in seinen verschiedenen Textformen zur Zeit des Neuen Testaments', in Zenger 2001: 61–87.

Schuller, Eileen M.

1986 *Non-canonical Psalms from Qumran: A Pseudepigraphic Collection* (Harvard Semitic Studies, 28; Atlanta: Scholars Press).

Seybold, Klaus

2002 Review of *Discoveries in the Judaean Desert XVI, Dead Sea Discoveries* 9/2: 278–80.

2010 'Dimensionen und Intentionen der Davidisierung der Psalmen. Die Rolle Davids nach den Psalmenüberschriften und nach dem Septuagintapsalm 151', in Erich Zenger (ed.), *The Composition of the Book of Psalms*, Bibliotheca Ephemeridum Theologicarum Lovaniensium, 238, Leuven): 125–40 (also published in *Studien zu Sprache und Stil der Psalmen*, BZAW, 415, 2010, 309–30).

Tov, Emanuel

2000 'Further Evidence for the Existence of a Qumran Scribal School', in Lawrence H. Schiffman, Emanuel Tov, and James C. VanderKam (eds.), *The Dead Sea Scrolls: Fifty Years after their Discovery. Proceedings of the Jerusalem Congress 1997* (Jerusalem: Israel Exploration Society in cooperation with the Shrine of the Book): 199–216.

Ulrich, Eugene, Cross, Frank Moore, Fitzmeyer, Joseph A., Flint, Peter W., Metso, Sarianna, Murphy, Catherine M., Niccum, Curt, Skehan, Patrick W., Tov, Emanuel, and Barrera, Julio Trebolle (eds.)

2000 *Qumran Cave 4*, vol. 11. *Psalms to Chronicles* (DJD, 16; Oxford: Clarendon Press).

Zenger, Erich (ed.)

2001 *Der Septuaginta-Psalter. Sprachliche und theologische Aspekte* (Herders Theologische Studien, 32, Freiburg im Breisgau: Herder Verlag).

14

The Proto-MT Psalter, the King, and Psalms
1 and 2: A Response to Klaus Seybold

David M. Howard, Jr.

1. An Overview of Seybold's Paper

Professor Seybold's focus in this paper is, in his own words, the 'first imaginary scroll' of the book of Psalms.[1] By this he means the first complete Psalter, containing the 150 psalms of the later Masoretic Text (MT),[2] or the 151 psalms of the Septuagint. He attempts to reconstruct the process by which dozens of individual psalms—composed in many different places at different times by different authors—found their way into the single collection that we now call the 'Book of Psalms'.[3] He is not concerned in this paper to trace or suggest any *thematic* outlines to the Book of Psalms, and so his work here stands apart from much of the work done in the last twenty-five years that focuses on the contours and overarching themes in the Psalter. But it is of a piece with another prominent strand of recent work, which attempts to reconstruct the history of transmission of the Psalter. Both are valid approaches, and Seybold here makes a significant contribution to the latter.

Seybold marshals seven lines of evidence pointing to different stages of this book's formation:

1. *The first 'book' of psalms*: A Davidic collection consisting of Psalms 3–41 and 51–72, possibly collected from old texts in the archives.

2. *A 'library edition' of this book*: The book was collected at the Temple in Jerusalem, and was known as 'the works of David' (2 Macc. 2.13–15). We can thus speak cautiously of a 'Nehemian library' at Jerusalem, and a master, normative scroll of the Psalms, from which copies for reading were made, as well as for liturgical use.

---

[1] See pp. 168–70 above.

[2] Or 149 in the Leningrad Codex, due to Psalm 115 being conjoined with Psalm 114.

[3] See Flint (1997: 22–6) on different terms appropriate for referring to the collections of psalms in different periods and locales.

3. *The proto-MT 'book of Psalms' from Qumran: 4QPs^a*: The oldest *extant* 'book of Psalms' is the 4QPs^a scroll, dating to the mid-second century BCE, and containing fragments of nineteen psalms, from Psalm 5 to Psalm 71.[4] If this scroll contained all one hundred and fifty psalms, it would have measured more than ten metres in length, making it the longest at Qumran. This scroll—and the majority of later Qumran manuscripts—stands in the proto-MT tradition. Seybold sees it as a copy of the official Jerusalem Psalter.[5]

4. *The Cave 11 Psalms scroll*: The famous 11QPs^a scroll is the best pre-served of all Psalms scrolls at Qumran. It contains fragments of forty-nine (or fifty) texts, thirty-nine of which are known from the MT Psalter. All are from Books IV and V, with a different order and arrange-ment from the MT. The scroll dates to 30–50 CE.[6]

5. *Stichometric Psalms scrolls*: The poetic nature of the psalms was beginning to be represented in the written texts by the late first century CE.

6. *The Old Greek Psalter*: The New Testament authors (late first century CE) knew of a 'book of Psalms', most probably the Septuagint version (dating to the second century BCE). New Testament authors quoted more than one hundred psalm texts known from MT, but none of the non-MT psalms from Qumran.

7. *The MT Psalter*: The familiar MT Psalter developed, known from the Aleppo and Leningrad Codices (tenth and eleventh centuries CE).

In conclusion, Professor Seybold lists four factors characterizing the Psalter as a book:

1. The Psalter developed over time as a collection, and remains as such in the MT. There are redactional traces, but it remains a multi-faceted collection.

2. The collection of disparate psalms into a book 'unifies and balances out' the different texts such that Psalms 117 and 119, the shortest and longest psalms respectively, are given equal voice.[7]

3. This collection reveals a 'canonical intention' but this development took two different paths:
   (a) The 4QPs^a tradition as a proto-MT book at Jerusalem
   (b) The 11QPs^a tradition as an alternative preserved at Qumran.

---

[4] See Flint 1997: 33. *Pace* Seybold, who includes only Psalms 5–69 (p. 172), though he does mention Psalm 71 as included in 4QPs^a (p. 172, n. 5).

[5] See Seybold, p. 172.

[6] Flint 1997: 39–40

[7] See p. 178 above.

4. When a single scroll had taken shape in the Temple library at Jerusalem (in about the third century BCE), it functioned thereafter as a 'standard' scroll, a forerunner of the Septuagint, the majority of texts at Qumran, and the MT.

2. The Distinctive Contribution of Seybold's Paper

As I see it, Professor Seybold's primary contribution to the discussion is his focus on what presumably was the standard, official edition of the book of Psalms in Jerusalem, the forerunner to the Septuagint, the majority of Qumran texts, and, eventually, the MT. In so doing, Seybold restores this text to a central place in the discussion of the formation and transmission of the 'Book of Psalms' that we know today.

In recent decades, the tradition represented by the 11QPs[a] scroll has rightly received much attention, given that it presents the first hard data pointing to an alternative Psalms tradition. The debates as to whether the Qumran community considered it to be a liturgical manual or a genuine 'scriptural Psalter'[8] seems to have been settled in favour of the latter, due to the work of Gerald Wilson and Peter Flint, building on James Sanders' early work with this scroll, although some dissident voices continue to be raised.[9]

However, whether or not the Qumran community had its own canonical tradition(s) does not render the existence of a different canonical tradition in Jerusalem irrelevant. This is because the Jerusalem tradition stands as the forerunner of the Septuagint and the MT (to say nothing of the Qumran tradition represented by the 4QPs[a] scroll). So, in this respect, Seybold's work makes a distinctive contribution, calling us to (re)consider the history of transmission of this 'normative' tradition, and its role and function in the later traditions represented by Septuagint and MT.

And, at the very least, Seybold's work calls into question the hypothesis that the 'canonical' Psalter was not 'closed' until the late first century CE. Perhaps one strand at Qumran—one group of texts presented most clearly by 11QPs[a] – was not 'fixed' as 'canonical' until that time. But Seybold succeeds, in my estimation, in reminding us that there was a separate, 'normative' tradition, centred at Jerusalem, dating much earlier—as far back as the third century BCE, perhaps—which helps to explain the Septuagint and the MT, as well as other traditions at Qumran. As Sid Z. Leiman wrote many years ago:

> Precisely because of the sectarian nature of the Qumran community, scholars must bear in mind that the content and development of a sectarian canon

---

[8] Flint 1997: 204–17.
[9] See e.g. Mitchell 1997: 22–6; 2006: 543–5, esp. n. 81; Howard 1997: 26–7 esp. n. 6.

probably has little or no bearing on the content and development of other sectarian (or normative) canons.[10]

It is my hope that Seybold's work here will help to restore this normative Jerusalem tradition to future discussions.

3. The 'Moses Psalter', the King, and Psalms 1–2

In my remaining time, I would like to address an issue that Professor Seybold touches upon, if only tangentially, and that is the competing perspectives revealed by his use of the terms 'Moses Psalter' and 'David Psalter'.[11] By 'Moses Psalter' he means the normative Jerusalem Psalter, that is, the proto-MT book. It has come to be associated with 'Moses' because of several factors, among which are the placement of Psalm 1—a Torah psalm, reminding us of Moses as the great lawgiver—as well as the *midrash* on the Psalms linking the five books of songs that David gave to Israel with the five books of laws that Moses gave. The 'David Psalter' is represented by the 11QPs[a] scroll, with its lengthy prose insert about David's compositions.[12]

Gerald Wilson and others have argued for a wisdom 'framing' of the Psalter, one that emphasizes Yahweh as king and downplays the significance of the Davidic monarchy. The wisdom frame emphasizes Torah (Psalm 1), and thus Seybold's reference to a 'Moses Psalter'. Wilson speaks of the 'failure' of the Davidic Covenant, noting the prominent place of Psalm 89 at the end of Book III, a psalm that speaks of Yahweh rejecting the covenant, which is seen in the distant past. He also makes much of the placement, nature, and function of Psalm 1 as signalling a move away from a liturgical and royalist perspective to a wisdom and eschatological one. He sees a final wisdom frame consisting of Psalms 1, 73, 90, 107, and 145, that brackets –and thus offsets or negates the influence of—the strategically placed royal psalms (Psalms 2, 72, 89, 144).[13] He also notes the very different character of Books I–III (where royal 'framing' psalms are more prominent) in comparison with Books IV–V.

Wilson's perspective on the 'failure' of the Davidic Covenant has been challenged by many.[14] I find it interesting that in his final essays before his death he moved much closer to the position of his critics, allowing for the importance of Psalm 2 as a companion psalm of some sort to Psalm 1, for example, and thus allowing for a messianic understanding of the Psalter.[15]

---

[10] Leiman 1976: 34.   [11] See pp. 178–9 above.
[12] See my Appendix, p. 188 below.
[13] See Wilson 1993: 80–1.
[14] E.g. Mitchell 1997, 2006; Anderson 2000: 208–9; Howard 1997: 200–7.
[15] Most notably, Wilson 2005a, 2005b.

I would like to draw this together by highlighting one important aspect of the Psalter's understanding of the Davidic kingship. In a recent essay, Rolf Rendtorff identifies three main aspects of the picture of David in the Psalms:[16]

1. *As the 'messianic' king*: for example in Psalm 2 (where David is installed on Zion as משיחו – God's anointed one);

2. *As the exemplary righteous king*: for example in Psalm 1 in conjunction with Psalm 2 (so that the anointed king of Psalm 2 is the exemplar of the righteous man in Psalm 1);

3. *As the powerless fugitive*: for example in Psalm 3 (a lament by David when fleeing from Absalom his son).

What Rendtorff presents is a fleshed-out portrayal of the ideal Israelite king: one who is not primarily a warrior triumphing over his enemies—which was the dominant pattern elsewhere in the ancient Near East—but a righteous king who follows Torah (after the Deuteronomic ideal: Deut. 17.14–20), who often suffers at the hands of evildoers, and who leaves the battles to Yahweh—in other words, a profoundly counter-cultural picture.

I should like to highlight the work of just a few scholars who have emphasized this counter-cultural portrait of the Israelite king, and in the process have contributed—in my view—to a more accurate representation of the role of the king in the book of Psalms.

First, in his work *Kingship according to the Deuteronomistic History*, Gerald Gerbrandt demonstrates that the primary function of the God-fearing king was to lead Israel in keeping the covenant and to trust Yahweh for deliverance. Gerbrandt states that 'the correct question with which to confront the Deuteronomist ... is not whether he was anti-kingship or pro-kingship. Rather, we need to ask what *kind* of kingship he saw as ideal for Israel, or what *role* kingship was expected to play for Israel.'[17]

Secondly, in a discussion of the function of Psalms 1 and 2 as the introduction to the entire Psalter—*pace* Wilson and others who see only Psalm 1 as the introduction—Patrick Miller states the following:

> It almost seems as if we are once more before the Deuteronomistic theology of kingship. It may be that all of this in fact reflects a Deuteronomistic influence on the redaction of the Psalter. I do not know. If it does, then we are made even more aware of the centrality of that particular stream in biblical theology and its influence on the theology of kingship and the royal idea.[18]

Thirdly, in a brief essay entitled 'Wisdom and Royalist/Zion Traditions in the Psalter',[19] I emphasized many of the same points, including the significance of Psalms 1 and 2 as the joint introduction to the Psalter.[20] As such,

---

[16] See Rendtorff 2005. [17] Gerbrandt 1986: 41 (my emphasis).
[18] Miller 1994: 141; 1993. [19] Howard 1997: 200–7.
[20] See also Howard 1988, 1990, the latter a review of Gerbrandt 1986.

the twin themes of Yahweh as king (Psalm 2, where he is the divine king against whom the nations rage and who installs his own vice-regent on Mount Zion) and 'David' as Yahweh's anointed king come together in one psalm. Furthermore, the Davidic king is precisely the exemplar of the righteous man of Psalm 1, following the Deuteronomic ideal. The Psalter comes full circle at the end, with two psalms representing the Davidic king (Ps. 144) and the divine king (Ps. 145), echoing motifs introduced in Psalms 1 and 2.

Fourthly, in an essay on the many tight links between Psalms 1 and 2, Robert Cole argues persuasively that these two psalms 'both have as their central theme the identical royal and Joshua-like figure who is given absolute victory in battle,'[21] echoing the points that Miller and I have made. He has expanded these arguments in a more recent book.[22]

Fifthly, Jamie Grant demonstrates in great detail the influence that Deuteronomy's Law of the King had in shaping the final form of the Psalter, and devotes extensive attention to Psalms 1 and 2 as the Psalter's introduction, permeated with Deuteronomic themes.[23]

All of these works have the effect of countering Wilson's argument that the influence of any royal/Davidic theology in the Psalter ends after Psalm 89, giving way to a 'democratized' approach where wisdom and Torah reign supreme, and not any king, real or anticipated.

So, in conclusion: I suspect that Professor Seybold had no intent in his paper to engage in this debate with Wilson, but I thank him for opening the door to my doing so, and I thank him again for a stimulating paper.

APPENDIX

David's Compositions: 11QPs^a column xxvii, lines 2–11

And David, the son of Jesse, was wise, and a light like the light of the sun, and literate, and discerning and perfect in all his ways before God and men. And the Lord gave him a discerning and enlightened spirit. And he wrote 3,600 psalms; and songs to sing before the altar over the whole-burnt perpetual offering every day, for all the days of the year, 364; and for the offering of the Sabbaths, 52 songs; and for the offering of the New Moons and for all the Solemn Assemblies and for the Day of Atonement, 30 songs. And all the songs that he composed were 446, and songs for making music over the stricken, 4. And the total was 4,050. All these he composed through prophecy which was given him from before the Most High.[24]

---

[21] See Cole 2002: 75.   [22] Cole 2011.   [23] Grant 2004.
[24] Translation by Sanders (1967: 137) preserving the stichometric layout there.

Bibliography

Anderson, Bernhard W.
  2000 *Out of the Depths: The Psalms Speak for Us Today* (Philadelphia: Westminster John Knox).
Cole, Robert L.
  2002 'An Integrated Reading of Psalms 1 and 2', *JSOT* 98: 75–88.
  2012 *Psalms 1–2: A Gateway to the Psalter* (Hebrew Bible Monographs, 37; Sheffield: Sheffield Phoenix Press).
Flint, Peter W.
  1997 *The Dead Sea Psalms Scrolls and the Book of Psalms* (STDJ, 17; Leiden: Brill).
Gerbrandt, Gerald Eddie
  1986 *Kingship according to the Deuteronomistic History* (SBLDS, 87; Atlanta: Scholars Press).
Grant, Jamie A.
  2004 *The King as Exemplar: The Function of Deuteronomy's Kingship Law in the Shaping of the Book of Psalms* (SBL Academia Biblica, 17; Atlanta: Society of Biblical Literature).
Howard, David M., Jr.
  1988 'The Case for Kingship in the Old Testament Narrative Books and the Psalms', *Trinity Journal* 9: 19–35.
  1990 'The Case for Kingship in the Deuteronomy and the Former Prophets', *Westminster Theological Journal* 52: 101–15.
  1997 *The Structure of Psalms 93–100* (BJSUCSD, 5; Winona Lake, IN: Eisenbrauns).
Leiman, Sid Z.
  1976 *The Canonization of Hebrew Scripture: The Talmudic and Midrashic Evidence* (Transactions of the Connecticut Academy of Arts and Sciences, 47; Hamden: Archon).
Miller, Patrick D., Jr.
  1993 'The Beginning of the Psalter', in J. C. McCann, Jr. (ed.), *The Shape and Shaping of the Psalter* (JSOTSup, 159; Sheffield: JSOT): 83–92.
  1994 'Kingship, Torah Obedience, and Prayer: The Theology of Psalms 15–24', in K. Seybold and E. Zenger (eds.), *Neue Wege der Psalmenforschung. Für Walter Beyerlin* (Herders Biblische Studien, 1; Freiburg: Herder): 127–42.
Mitchell, David C.
  1997 *The Message of the Psalter: An Eschatological Programme in the Book of Psalms* (JSOTSup, 252; Sheffield: Sheffield Academic Press).
  2006 'Lord Remember David: G. H. Wilson and the Message of the Psalter', *VT* 56: 526–48.
Rendtorff, Rolf.
  2005 'The Psalms of David: David in the Psalms', in P. W. Flint and P. D. Miller, Jr. (eds.), *The Book of Psalms: Composition and Reception* (SVT, 99; Leiden: Brill): 53–64.
Sanders, J. A.
  1967 *The Dead Sea Psalms Scroll* (Ithaca, NY: Cornell University Press, 1967).

Wilson, Gerald H.

1985 *The Editing of the Hebrew Psalter* (SBLDS, 76; Chico, CA: Scholars Press).

1986 'The Use of Royal Psalms at the "Seams" of the Hebrew Psalter', *JSOT* 35: 85–94.

1993 'Shaping the Psalter: A Consideration of Editorial Linkage in the Book of Psalms', in J. C. McCann (ed.), *The Shape and Shaping of the Psalter* (JSOTSup, 159; Sheffield: Sheffield Academic Press): 72–82.

2005a 'King, Messiah, and the Reign of God: Revisiting the Royal Psalms and the Shape of the Psalter', in P. W. Flint and P. D. Miller, Jr. (eds.), *The Book of Psalms: Composition and Reception* (SVT, 99; Leiden: Brill): 391–406.

2005b 'The Structure of the Psalter,' in P. Johnston and D. Firth (eds.), *Interpreting the Psalms: Issues and Approaches* (Downers Grove, IL: InterVarsity): 229–46.

15

On Translating the Poetry of the Psalms

Nancy L. deClaissé-Walford

A question the readers of this essay might ask is 'What does the issue of translation have to do with the topic of the conference at which this paper was presented, and indeed which is the title of this book?' *Jewish and Christian Approaches to the Psalms: Conflict and Convergence* has, I believe, a sub-text, which is a study of the underlying hermeneutic and reception history of the book of Psalms—how the Psalter has been received, interpreted, and transmitted over the millennia. Current translations of the book provide insights into how the Psalter is received, interpreted, and transmitted today, and perhaps foreshadow how it will be received, interpreted, and transmitted in the future.

I begin with a disclaimer. I am not a bible translator by training or trade. But I have been translating the psalms for over twenty years in lecture and sermon preparations, in the classroom with students, and for various academic presentations. Each of these undertakings has been interesting, and, at the same time, rather ephemeral. The translations were not going to be preserved in print; they were for my own use, so I could 'play' with words and phrases and even, dare I say, theology. Between the years 2001 and 2010, however, I worked on two projects that required a more considered approach to translating. I will first briefly describe the projects and provide examples of the translation work from them and then comment on my experiences of translation work.

I shall start with what I consider the less conventional undertaking. In 2005, I was approached by David Capes, Professor of Christianity at Houston Baptist University in Houston, Texas, about working on a Bible translation project called 'The Voice'. This was the brainchild of Chris Seay, pastor of Ecclesia Church in Houston, a progressive Christian community recognized for exploring spiritual questions of culture and breaking new ground in art, music, and film. The website for 'The Voice' project describes the undertaking as:

> a fresh expression of the timeless narrative known as the Bible. Stories that were told to emerging generations of God's goodness by their grandparents and tribal

leaders were recorded and assembled to form the Christian Scriptures. Too often the passion, grit, humor, and beauty has been lost in the translation process. *The Voice* seeks to recapture what was lost.[1]

Seay, with the assistance of David Capes, assembled an eclectic group of songwriters, storytellers, poets, pastors, and biblical scholars, and organized their work in the following manner. The songwriters, storytellers, pastors, and poets (and, except for the pastors, most without formal theological training) were given the task of adapting the biblical texts (from English, primarily the New International Version) into literary forms that would appeal to the postmodern mindset, a mindset that is said to be more story-oriented than proposition-oriented. The artistic renderings were then passed along to biblical scholars like myself. We were to examine the adaptations for fidelity to our understandings of the intent of the texts in their biblical contexts. I worked on a number of the psalms. Two that I examined were Psalms 3 and 22. Psalm 3, a relatively unknown psalm, unless your vocation is the study of the psalms, was assigned to a screenplay writer from Texas named Jonathan Hal Reynolds. His rendering was as follows:

> [1]Almighty, my adversaries are countless!
>   They rise up like weeds in a garden
> —one moment they are not there;
>   the next moment, there are twenty to each flower.
> [2]Each weed howls tauntingly,
>   'God might as well be a fairy tale for you.
>   God will not give you help.'
> [3]But you, Gardener, weed them out.
>   You deepen my roots in rich soil and moisten my petals with the
>   honeyed dew of morning.
> [4]I lean toward you, the Great Sun, and bellow to the Heights.
>   You answer me from your Holy Place on high.
> [5]I lie my body down in deep slumber and then awake. I have all my energy,
> [6]no longer facing twenty weeds, but tens of thousands!
> [7]Awaken, Gardener, and come to my rescue. Break every weed-stalk in half
>   and pull each one out by its roots.
> [8]True liberation comes from God, the Gardener.
>   His blessings shower His people, His flowers.[2]

Reynolds' rendering was unique, artistic, and image-filled, but my role as biblical scholar was to determine whether, in my estimation, it conveyed the true sense of the heartfelt words of David in Psalm 3.3, words that in the *NRSV* read: 'O LORD, how many are my foes; many are rising against me—

---

[1] http://www.hearthevoice.com/about-the-translation (accessed February 2012).
[2] Reynolds' translation never appeared in printed form. I received it for review in the spring of 2006.

Rise up, O LORD! Deliver me, O my God! For you strike all my enemies on the cheek; you break the teeth of the wicked'. Can and/or should our adversaries be compared with weeds? Should God be described as the 'cosmic gardener'? And should the psalmist be the 'pristine plant' in the cosmic garden?[3]

After much critique and discussion, the final version of Psalm 3 in *The Voice of Psalms* was as follows:[4]

> [1]Eternal One, my adversaries are many, too many to count.
>   Now they have taken a stand against me!
> [2]Right to my face they say,
>   'God will not save you!'
> [pause]
> [3]But You, Eternal One, wrap around me like an *impenetrable* shield.
>   You give me glory and lift my eyes *up to the heavens*.
> [4]I lift my voice to You, Eternal One,
>   and You answer me from Your sacred heights.
> [pause]
> [5]I lay down *at night* and fall asleep.
>   I awake in the morning—*healthy, strong, vibrant*—because the
>   Eternal supports me.
> [6]No longer will I fear my tens of thousands of enemies
>   who have surrounded me!
> [7]Rise up, O Eternal One!
>   Rescue me, O God!
> For You have dealt my enemies a strong blow to the jaw!
>   You have shattered their teeth! *Do so again.*
> [8]Liberation truly comes from the Eternal.
>   Let Your blessings shower down upon Your people.
> [pause]

The final translation is much more in line with the Hebrew original and echoes strongly the more traditional English reception of the Hebrew text.[5] Here the 'cosmic gardener' has become 'the Eternal One'; the 'weeds' are 'adversaries'; and the psalmist is no longer the 'pristine plant'.

---

[3] Such a metaphoric image reminds this writer of the words of Barton 1996: 108–9. He writes, 'There is, as the old saying has it, "no such thing" as a weed: a weed is simply a flower in the wrong place. It is a matter of pure human convention which plants are to be regarded as "flowers" (and therefore desirable) and which as "weeds" (and therefore evil)'. He reminds us, though, that the determination of what is to be counted as flower and what as weed is not an individual one. 'One's intentions will be misunderstood if one insists on sending bunches of dandelions by Interflora; the neighbours will not be swayed by the argument that their roses are spoiling the appearance of a field of giant hog-weed'.

[4] As with most English translations, the words in italics are words that are not included in the Hebrew text, but are added in English to clarify the meaning of the Hebrew. The translation is from Friends of Ecclesia Bible Society 2009: 4.

[5] Versions which one might consult include the *King James Version* (*AV*) (1611), the *Revised Standard Version* (1952), the *New American Standard Bible* (1960), the *New International Version* (1978), and the *New Revised Standard Version* (1995).

The initial artistic translation by *The Voice* of a more familiar psalm in Christian circles, Psalm 22, was very different from the initial rendering of Psalm 3. Allison Smyth, a poet and writer from Missouri, translated its first eleven verses as follows:

> My God, my God, why have you turned your back on me? My suffering falls on
>   deaf ears.
> O my God, I cry in the day and You are silent and the night brings no relief.
> Still, You are holy, O You who permeates the praises of Israel.
> Our fathers trusted in You, they trusted and you kept them safe.
> They pleaded to You and they were spared; they trusted in You and You didn't
>   let them down.
> But I am a worm, not a man, an embarrassment, hated by all.
> Everyone thinks I'm a loser, they sneer and mock me saying,
> 'Rely on the Lord, let Him rescue him; Let Him save him because He is
>   fond of him.'
> But You are the One who granted me life; You infused me with trust as I
>   nursed at my mother's breast.
> I was thrust on You at birth; You've been my God from my mother's womb.
> Stay close to me because trouble is at my door and no one else will help me.

In this psalm, the poet maintains a good measure of the imagery and language of the psalm's traditional translation, in contrast with the original *Voice* rendering of Psalm 3. And, interestingly, for a postmodern translation, the translation includes two very glaring instances of gender-exclusive language (v. 4 'our fathers' and v. 6 'a man'). The final form of the first eleven verses of Psalm 22 appears in *The Voice of Psalms* in this way:

> ¹My God, my God, why have You turned Your back on me?
>   Your ears are deaf to my groans.
> ²O my God, I cry all day and You are silent;
>   my tears in the night bring no relief.
> ³Still, You are holy;
>   You make Your home on the praises of Israel.
> ⁴Our *mothers and* fathers trusted in You;
>   they trusted, and You rescued them.
> ⁵They cried out to You for help and were spared;
>   they trusted in You and were vindicated.
> ⁶But I am a worm and not a human being,
>   a disgrace and an object of scorn.
> ⁷Everyone who sees me laughs at me;
>   they whisper *to one another* I'm a loser; they sneer and mock me, saying,
> ⁸"He relies on the Eternal One; let the Eternal rescue
>   and keep him safe because He is happy with him."
> ⁹But You are the One who granted me life;
>   You endowed me with trust as I nursed at my mother's breast.
> ¹⁰I was dedicated to You at birth;

You've been my God from my mother's womb.
[11]Stay close to me–
    trouble is at my door;
    no one else can help me.[6]

A comparison of the two translations is an interesting study of innovation and convention. In verse 3, Smythe chose the somewhat abstract term 'permeate' to describe the indwelling presence of 'the Holy One' in Israel, which in Hebrew is the participial form of the verbal root יָשַׁב, 'sit down, dwell'. The final translation reads, 'You make Your home on the praises of Israel'. The final translation of v. 4 and 6 changed the gendered nouns 'fathers' and 'man' to 'mothers and fathers' and 'human being'. In addition, in v. 4, Smythe's translation of the verbal root פלט as 'kept safe' was corrected to 'rescued' to reflect the actual meaning of the Hebrew word; and in v. 6, her translation of בזה as 'hated' was corrected to 'an object of scorn'.

Interestingly, neither Smythe's translation nor the editors of *The Voice of Psalms* caught the beauty of the imagery of v. 9. The Hebrew says, literally, 'You brought me forth from the womb, making me secure upon the breasts of my mother'. Psalm 22 paints a moving picture of God as a midwife receiving the child from the womb and introducing it to the nurturing breasts of its mother. What an opportunity was missed in this postmodern translation![7]

As I worked through the artistic translations of the psalms in my consulting capacity, I noted with increasing frustration the translators' omission of the superscriptions of the psalms. I appealed to the editors of *The Voice* to include them in the translation, and, not surprisingly, they asked me to provide appropriate superscriptions. For Psalm 3, I offered the superscription: 'A song of the song singer: composed while fleeing from a betrayer'. For Psalm 22, I suggested: 'For the lead musician: a sunrise song. Composed by the song singer'. The final outcome was interesting.

In the final edition of *The Voice of Psalms*, the superscription of Psalm 3 is 'A song of David composed while fleeing from his son Absalom'.[8] The superscription of Psalm 22 is 'For the worship leader. A song of David to the tune "Deer of the Dawn"'.[9] Both superscriptions are strikingly close to the NIV rendering: Psalm 3 reads 'A psalm of David. When he fled from his son Absalom'; and Psalm 22, 'For the director of music. To the tune of "The Doe of the Morning". A psalm of David'.

How, then, do we understand the translation process and ultimate outcome of *The Voice* as a project? The website maintains that *The Voice* strives to be 'a fresh expression of the timeless narrative of the biblical text' with all of the

---

[6] Friends of Ecclesia Bible Society 2009: 32–3.
[7] See Trible 1978: 60–1; also deClaissé-Walford (forthcoming).
[8] *The Voice of Psalms*, 4.
[9] Ibid, 32.

'passion, grit, humor, and beauty; that has been lost in the translation process'.[10] In the end, however, I suggest that the project simply was unable to move very far beyond the traditional translations of the biblical text. The text's familiarity and the history of its transmission and reception were a formidable obstacle to any completely new rendering. Thus, the ideas of God as the 'cosmic gardener' (Ps. 3.3); of adversaries as 'weeds' (Ps. 3.1); of translating the Hebrew verb יִשְׂב as 'permeates' (Ps. 22.3); of picturing God as a midwife (Ps. 22.9); and of omitting David's name from the super-scriptions and simply referring to 'the song singer' were not possible in a translation project supported by a major Bible publisher.[11] The traditional translations and interpretations were simply too pervasive.

The second translation project in which I participated was markedly different from *The Voice*. In November 2001, at the Society of Biblical Literature Annual Meeting in Denver, Colorado, I met with Alan Myers and Robert Hubbard of Eerdmans Publishing to discuss my involvement in a team of three (along with Rolf Jacobson of Luther Seminary in Minneapolis, and Beth Tanner of New Brunswick Theological Seminary in New Jersey) in the production of the New International Commentary on the Old Testament volume on Psalms. The NICOT project required us to translate the psalms and then provide interpretative and theological reflections on each of them. The General Editor's Preface to the series describes its audience as 'scholars, pastors, and serious Bible students' who seek a rigorous examination of the text that respects the text's sacred character.[12] As we translated and provided a commentary for the psalms, a number of issues emerged: first, translating into English various Hebrew words; secondly, representing the deliberate repetition of Hebrew sounds, verbal roots, and words and phrases; thirdly, maintaining the word order of Hebrew poetry; and fourthly, using gender-neutral language, while maintaining the 'individual' quality of the individual laments and the individual hymns of thanksgiving. In this endeavour, I was not translating to produce a text for oral recitation, but rather one for the purpose of study. In a retrospective look at the four issues of translation outlined above, I offer the following reflections.

First, translating various Hebrew words into English was, to my surprise, the simplest of the translation issues. My two commentary colleagues and I met several times during the process of our work, and early discussions centred around translations of various Hebrew words. These included, among many others, חֶסֶד (*hesed*), יִרְא (*yara'*), אָדָם (*'adam*), נֶפֶשׁ (*nephesh*),

---

[10] See http://www.hearthevoice.com/about-the-translation (accessed 2 February 2012).

[11] *The Voice* is published and distributed by Thomas Nelson Publishers in Nashville, Tennessee.

[12] See http://www.logos.com/product/5185/the-new-international-commentary-on-the-old-and-new-testament (accessed 2 February 2012).

תורה (*torah*), and שלום (*shalom*). Out of these discussions, two questions emerged: (1) How should we translate these Hebrew words? And (2) should we always translate them in the same way? We might have involved ourselves in lengthy debate about semantic ranges and nuances of meaning, but the truth of the matter is that in the case of, say, *nephesh* and *shalom*, the concept is very much the same from psalm to psalm–one's *nephesh* is the essence of 'the all of who one is'. *Shalom* has to do with a complete sense of wholeness and well-being. And so, what English words render them best? I settled on 'inmost being' for *nephesh*, and 'well-being' for *shalom*. Thus, I translated Psalm 42.1 as:

> Just as a deer ever longs for running brooks of water,
>   thus my inmost being ever longs for you, O God.[13]

I rendered Ps 122.6–8 as:

> Ask well-being for Jerusalem.
>   May the ones who love you be at ease.
> May well-being be in your walls,
>   tranquillity in your towers.
> For the sake of my relatives and my companions
>   I will speak well-being within you.[14]

Yara' proved more problematic. Most often the word is translated as 'fear', but it has a wide range of meanings in Hebrew, depending upon the referent of the verb and the context in which it appears. My writing colleagues and I decided to render *yara'* as 'reverence' in reference to the relationship between worshipper and God, but as 'fear' in most other instances. I offered this translation of Ps 112.1:

> Hallelujah.
> Content is the one who reverences (*yara'*) the LORD,
> in the LORD's commandments greatly delighting.

However, I rendered this translation of Ps 112.7, in reference to the good person who shows favour and lends to others:

> From a malicious hearing that person is not afraid (*yara'*);
>   having a heart that is established in its inmost part in the LORD.

Hesed turned out to be perhaps the most difficult word to translate. After much discussion, we, the authors, decided to leave the word untranslated and to include an explanation for our decision in the introduction to the commentary. That explanation reads, tentatively:

---

[13] deClaissé-Walford, Jacobson, and LaNeal Tanner, *The Book of Psalms* (forthcoming).
[14] In Psalm 122, the threefold repetition of שלום (*shalom*) is not redundant, but rather is a poetic device that emphasizes the psalmist's heartfelt desire for the good of Jerusalem.

One peculiarity of our translation is that we have opted to transliterate, rather than translate, the Hebrew term *hesed*. The reason for this decision is that the wide arsenal of terms traditionally used to capture the term—mercy, loving kindness, steadfast love, faithfulness, covenantal love, and the like—simply cannot capture the theological depth of the term. . . . *Hesed* is a relational term, which describes both the internal character as well as the external actions that are required to maintain a life-sustaining relationship. Thus *hesed* is both who the Lord is and what the Lord does. The term also expresses God's will for who the chosen people shall be and what the people shall do both for each other and for the world.[15]

Thus my translation of Psalm 107 is:

> Give thanks to the LORD, for he is good;
>   For his *hesed* is for all time. . .
> Whoever is wise will hear these things,
>   And the *hesed* ones of the LORD will attend. (vv. 1, 43)

Secondly, representing the deliberate repetition of Hebrew sounds, verbal roots, and words and phrases was a far greater challenge than determining translation equivalents for individual words and phrases. I was particularly struck in my translation work by the repetition of sounds. That element of Hebrew poetry is, I think, the most difficult to transfer into English.

Psalm 145 is a classic example. Beginning at v. 14, the reader encounters a succession of participles. Because most of these participles are Qal Active, they lend what I call a round-mouthed phonemic quality to the verses that is pleasing and flowing. And when the Qal Active participle form joins with the round-mouthed vocalic quality of the word כֹּל (which occurs ten times in vv. 14–20) and other round-mouthed vowels, the verses glide along, moving the reader to the climax of the psalm, verse 20 (Hebrew 21):

14 סוֹמֵךְ יְהוָה לְכָל־הַנֹּפְלִים וְזוֹקֵף לְכָל־הַכְּפוּפִים:

15 עֵינֵי־כֹל אֵלֶיךָ יְשַׂבֵּרוּ וְאַתָּה נוֹתֵן־לָהֶם אֶת־אָכְלָם בְּעִתּוֹ:

16 פּוֹתֵחַ אֶת־יָדֶךָ וּמַשְׂבִּיעַ לְכָל־חַי רָצוֹן:

17 צַדִּיק יְהוָה בְּכָל־דְּרָכָיו וְחָסִיד בְּכָל־מַעֲשָׂיו:

18 קָרוֹב יְהוָה לְכָל־קֹרְאָיו לְכֹל אֲשֶׁר יִקְרָאֻהוּ בֶאֱמֶת:

19 רְצוֹן־יְרֵאָיו יַעֲשֶׂה וְאֶת־שַׁוְעָתָם יִשְׁמַע וְיוֹשִׁיעֵם:

20 שׁוֹמֵר יְהוָה אֶת־כָּל־אֹהֲבָיו וְאֵת כָּל־הָרְשָׁעִים יַשְׁמִיד:

The question was how to render these magnificently crafted verses in English, keeping in mind that I was producing a text for study. Here is what I finally settled on:

---

[15] deClaissé-Walford, Jacobson, and Tanner, *The Book of Psalms* (forthcoming).

14 ס   The LORD supports all who are falling
            and lifts up all who are bent down.
15 ע   The eyes of all look to you,
            and you give them their food in its time,
16 פ   opening your hand,
            and satisfying for every living thing its desire.
17 צ   Righteous is the LORD in all his ways
            and *hesed* in all his doings.
18 ק   Near is the LORD to all who cry out to him,
            to all who cry out to him in truth.
19 ר   The desire of the ones who reverence him he fulfills,
            and their cry for help he hears and helps them.
20 שׁ   The LORD watches over all who love him,
            but all the wicked he will destroy.

Repetition of verbal roots and words and phrases was an easier undertaking. And in the case of the Psalter, this was fairly easy to achieve. I offer Psalm 121 as an example. The verbal root שׁמר ('guard') occurs six times in the eight verses of this psalm, a deliberate repetition of the idea of watching and guarding. My translation for the commentary is as follows:

1   I lift up my eyes to the mountains;
        from where will come my help?
2   My help is from the LORD,
        the maker of heavens and earth.
3   He will not allow[16] to stumble your foot,
        the one who <u>guards</u> you will not slumber.
4   Behold, he will not slumber and he will not be asleep,
        the one who <u>guards</u> Israel.
5   The LORD is the one who <u>guards</u> you,
        the LORD is your shade, at your right hand.
6   By day the sun will not strike you,
        and the moon in the night.
7   The LORD will <u>guard</u> you from all malicious things,
        he will <u>guard</u> your inmost being.
8   The LORD will <u>guard</u> your going out and your coming in,
        from now and for all time.

Both the *NRSV* and *NIV* translate each instance of שׁמר in Psalm 121 as 'keep', while the *TaNaK* renders the verbal root as 'guard' throughout the psalm.[17]

In some places, though, the deliberate repetition of verbal roots and words is obscured in English translations. I am not offering here a particular critique of the *NRSV* or the *TaNaK*; I am simply citing them as the two translations

[16] The Hebrew form is ʾ*al* + imperfect, which is the usual form of the negative imperative.
[17] *TaNaK: The Holy Scripture* was first published by the Jewish Publication Society in 1985.

with which most of us are familiar. A good example of the stylistic repetition of a verbal root is הגה *hāgāh*, which is repeated, I think purposely, in Psalms 1 and 2. In Ps. 1.2, the happy/content person is described as one who 'meditates' (according to the *NRSV*) on the Torah. The *TaNaK* describes the person as one who 'studies' the Torah. The verbal root in verse 2 is הגה *hāgāh*. In Ps 2.1, the nations are described as 'plotting' in both the *NRSV* and *TaNaK*. Again, the verbal root is הגה *hāgāh*. The meaning of the verbal root is literally to 'to mutter'. The one who mutters over the Torah—in study or recitation—is content. The nations who mutter together—against the Lord and the Lord's anointed—will come to nothing. So, how would I translate Ps 1.2 and Ps 2.1? I did not work on Psalms 1 and 2 for the commentary, but perhaps something like this might be appropriate:

> Content is the one who does not . . .
>> but that one's delight is in the Torah of the LORD
>> and on the Torah that one *muses* day and night. (Ps. 1.1–2) [18]

> Why do the nations rage
>> and the peoples *muse* uselessly? (Ps.2.1)

Another example of deliberate repetition is found in Psalm 46. Verses 2, 5, and 6 contain the verbal root מוט, here translated as 'quake'.

> Therefore, we will not fear when the earth changes itself,
> and when mountains quake in the heart of the seas . . .
> God is in it (the city); it will not be quaked . . .
> The nations have sounded; kingdoms have quaked.

Verse 2 states that God will provide protection and stability even if the earth and the seas undergo quakes, because, as we learn in v. 5, the city of God will not quake. Kingdoms may quake, in v. 6, but the city of God will not. The *NRSV* renders מוט in these verses as 'shake', 'move', and 'totter' respectively. The *TaNaK*, however, renders the word consistently as 'topple'.

Another example is from Psalm 137. Verses 3 and 6 of this psalm both employ the verbal root שמחה 'rejoice'):

> Because there our captors asked us for words of a song,
>> our tormentors for rejoicing . . .
> May my tongue cleave to the roof of my mouth
>> if I do not remember you,
> if I do not raise up Jerusalem
>> as the highest of my rejoicing. (vv.3, 6)

The oath in v. 6 seems to be in direct response to the request of the captors in v. 3. That is, remembering Zion is to be the greatest point of rejoicing for the psalmists, far surpassing the joy—that is, the rejoicing—of song singing. It is

---

[18] I chose to translate the opening word of Psalm 1, *'ašrê*, as 'content' rather than 'happy' or 'blessed'.

evident that the composer of Psalm 137 deliberately repeated the word שׁמחה in the two verses in order to draw a poignant contrast.

In a course titled 'History of the Bible' I require my students to read portions of the Preface to the 1611 Authorized Version. In one place, it reads:

> An other thing we thinke good to admonish thee of (gentle Reader) that wee haue not tyed our selues to an vniformitie of phrasing, or to an identitie of words, as some peraduenture would wish that we had done, because, they obserue, that some learned men some where, haue beene as exact as they could that way. . . Thus to minse the matter, wee thought to sauour more of curiositie then wisedome, and that rather it would breed scorne in the Atheist, then bring profite to the godly Reader. For is the kingdome of God become words or syllables? Why should wee be in bondage to them if we may be free, vse one precisely when wee may vse another no lesse fit, as commodiously?[19]

I wholeheartedly agree with the sentiments of the translators of the Authorized Version, and I did not tie myself 'to an vniformitie of phrasing, or to an identitie of words' in my translation process. But I maintain that in particular instances, and perhaps more so in poetry than in prose, the deliberate repetition of words and phrases is a hermeneutical clue that we need to retain when at all possible.

The third issue with which I grappled was that of maintaining the word order of Hebrew poetry. A common poetic device in Hebrew poetry is the chiastic structure—in which a word or phrase is used to frame a bicolon of poetry, either at its beginning or its end, to signal some sort of significance for the word or phrase. I offer a few examples: Ps. 142.2 in Hebrew is:

$$\text{אֶשְׁפֹּךְ לְפָנָיו שִׂיחִי צָרָתִי לְפָנָיו אַגִּיד:}$$

I translate the verse as:

> I pour out before him my complaint;
> my oppression in his presence I make known.

The centrepiece of this verse is 'my complaint / my oppression', placed together as the B B′ portion of an A B B′ A′ chiastic structure, leading the reader to the main theme of this verse of Psalm 142. The *NRSV*, however, renders the verse as 'I pour out my complaint before him; I tell my troubles before him'. And the *TaNaK* offers, 'I pour out my complaint before Him; I lay my trouble before Him'. In both translations, the chiastic structure has been obscured in the interest of maintaining usual English word order.

Such a disregard for deliberate word order in Hebrew poetry permeates English translations of the Psalms. A few more examples: Ps. 108.7 is, in Hebrew:

---

[19] *The Holy Bible: Authorized Version, 1611*, 'The Translators to the Reader'.

אֱלֹהִים דִּבֶּר בְּקָדְשׁוֹ אֶעְלֹזָה אֲחַלְּקָה שְׁכֶם וְעֵמֶק סֻכּוֹת אֲמַדֵּד׃

The *NRSV* renders the verse as:

> God has promised in his sanctuary: 'With exultation I will divide up
> Shechem, and portion out the Vale of Succoth'.

The *TaNaK* renders the verse as:

> God promised in His sanctuary that I would exultingly divide up Shechem,
> and measure the Valley of Sukkoth.

I translate the verse as:

> God has spoken in his holiness
> 'I will triumph—I will divide Shechem,
>   and the valley of Succoth I will measure out.'

Disregarding the other obvious differences in the three translations, I will focus on the structure of the last two phrases of the verse, in which the geographic names Shechem and Succoth appear. The central focus of Ps.108.7 is, in my estimation, the geographical locations of Shechem and the valley of Succoth. Succoth was the first stopping point for the Israelites on the Exodus journey out of Egypt. Shechem, situated between Mount Ebal and Mount Gerazim, was the central site from which Joshua called on the Israelites to renew their covenant relationship with Yahweh, as recounted in Josh. 8.30–35. The two place names, then, call to mind the beginning and the end of the Israelites' wandering in the wilderness and are purposely placed at the centre of the structure of this verse.

The fourth and final issue in our translation work for the NICOT was that of using gender-neutral language while maintaining the 'personal' quality of the individual laments and the individual hymns of thanksgiving. Psalms contain either the words of an individual or the words of the community of faith, and distinguishing the individual from the corporate voice is, I maintain, important to the message, the theology, of the whole Psalter. Thus, Ps. 1.1 states, 'Content is the אִישׁ, the individual person, who does not follow the advice of the wicked … ' The *NRSV* translates the verse as "Happy (content) are those who do not … " (The *TaNaK*, however, maintains 'the man' and singular language.) The individual focus of the description (and by implication, admonition) in Psalm 1 is thus lost in the *NRSV*'s attempt to be gender-inclusive. I did not translate and comment on Psalm 1 for the NICOT, but I might suggest something like:

> Content is the one who does not …
>   but the Torah is that one's delight
>   and on the Torah muses day and night.
> One who does so will be like a tree planted …

In similar fashion, the first half of Ps. 107.43 states:

מִי־חָכָם וְיִשְׁמָר־אֵלֶּה

The *NRSV* translates the phrase as, 'Let those who are wise heed these things'. I translated the phrase as 'Whoever is wise will hear these things', in the hope of maintaining the individual sentiment of the admonition and of making it gender-inclusive (noting that the *TaNaK* renders the phrase as 'the wise man will . . .').

In one more example, Psalm 112, a psalm calling on humanity to respond in proper and faithful fashion to God's good care and provisions, states in v. 1, 'Content is the אִישׁ ('the man') who fears the Lord'. The *NRSV* renders the verse as 'Happy are those . . . ' The *TaNaK* has 'Happy is the man'. I chose to translate Ps. 112.1 as 'Content is the one . . . ' But that turned out to be the easy part of translating this psalm, because the singular 'he' language continues throughout the psalm. I finally rendered it in this way:

> Content is the one who reverences the LORD,
>   in the LORD's commandments greatly delighting.
> A mighty one in the land will be that one's descendant;
>   a generation of upright ones will be blessed.
> Riches and wealth are in that person's house,
>   and that one's righteousness endures for all time.

Summary and Concluding Remarks

A number of issues emerge when we attempt to translate the Psalms from Hebrew into English.

1. How do we determine, understand, and, then, most importantly, maintain fidelity to the 'original' intent of the Hebrew text? Is it justified, using twenty-first-century parlance, to liken enemies to 'weeds in our garden'? How much poetic licence should we grant to modern translators, keeping in mind that we do not know to what degree the ancient poets exercised such licence?

2. Do the psalmic superscriptions matter? Psalm 3 is a notable example. The artist/poet who first adapted Psalm 3 for *The Voice* equated the enemies of *David* to 'weeds in the garden'. Would an understanding of the 'story world' of the superscription of Psalm 3 have provided a different metaphoric image for that artist/poet?

3. The repetition of verbal roots and sounds is an important element of Hebrew poetry. Sometimes the repetition is easy to incorporate into English translations, as is the case of the verbal root שָׁמַר ('keep watch over') in Psalm 121. But in other psalms, such repetition is obscured in the English

translations, as is the case with the verbal root הגה ('mutter, muse') in Psalms 1 and 2, and the repetition of what I call 'round-mouthed' sounds in Psalm 145.

4. Word order in Hebrew poetry is often ignored and obscured in English translations: the beauty and significance of chiastic structures, especially, is ignored.

5. Finally, gender-neutral language is a major issue in Bible translation in general and in psalm translation in particular. In the interest of maintaining the individualistic language of certain psalms (an undertaking that I applaud), the *TaNaK* tends to maintain the male-oriented language of the Hebrew text. But the *NRSV*, in the interest of rendering gender-neutral language, makes plural the purposely individual language of many of the psalms.

Many of the issues addressed in this article apply equally to discussions of translating Hebrew prose; but I maintain that the issues are even more worthy of consideration when translating poetry. Would that we all could read and study the book of Psalms in Hebrew. But just as I must rely on English translators when I read great works of literature, so we who receive, interpret, and transmit the biblical text must strive to maintain the beautiful artistry of Hebrew poetry, thereby honouring the poets who composed these magnificent works. It is a daunting undertaking and one that affects both Jewish and Christian approaches to the Psalms.

Bibliography

Barton, John
  1996 *Reading the Old Testament: Method in Biblical Study, Revised and Enlarged* (Louisville, KY: Westminster John Knox Press).
deClaissé-Walford, Nancy L.
  (forthcoming) 'The Book of Psalms', in *The Women's Bible Commentary*, ed. Jacqueline Lapsley, Carol Newsom, and Sharon Ringe)
deClaissé-Walford, Nancy L., Jacobson, Rolf, and Tanner, Beth LaNeal (eds.)
  (forthcoming) *The Book of Psalms*, ed. Robert Hubbard (New International Commentary on the Old Testament Series; Grand Rapids, MI: Eerdmans).
Friends of Ecclesia Bible Society
  2009 *The Voice of Psalms* (Nashville: Thomas Nelson).
Trible, Phyllis
  1978 *God and the Rhetoric of Sexuality* (Philadelphia: Fortress Press).

Websites (accessed 2 February 2012)

http://www.hearthevoice.com/about-the-translation
http://www.logos.com/product/5185/the-new-international-commentary-on-the-old-and-new-testament

16

'Traduttore traditore', *Beowulf* and the Psalms: A Response to Nancy deClaissé-Walford

Philip S. Johnston

The well-known Italian aphorism 'Traduttore traditore' ('Translator, traitor') stands at the head of many a discussion of translation. As it happens, the English translation 'translator (is) traitor' captures both the sense and the alliteration of the original. But if both terms had been, say, infinitives, the literal English translation 'to translate (is) to betray' would have missed the alliteration. And a translation would then have been forced to betray either accuracy or alliteration. Such a possibility neatly captures the dilemma of translation, particularly regarding poetry.

Like Nancy deClaissé-Walford, I confess that I am not a professional Bible translator, though I do have a long-standing academic and confessional interest in the topic.[1] However, and more importantly in this context, all scholars of ancient literature have a lively interest in translation, and biblical scholars in particular interact regularly with translation issues in their research and teaching.

In her paper, deClaissé-Walford clearly presents, first, several key features of translation illustrated in two contrasting versions, and, secondly, several key principles of translation as they emerged in the second version, with a helpful concluding summary. This response will comment in turn on the two versions and the substantive issues.

The Voice is similar to many such projects over the last century, initially the work of individual translators like Moffatt and Goodspeed in the interwar years, then an increasing flood since the 1960s, particularly in evangelical Protestant circles. The best known, among many others, are probably Living Bible, Good News Bible, New Century Version,[2] Contemporary English

---

[1] I have taught courses on Bible translations over several decades, been a consultant for two modern versions (*NIRV*, *ESV*), and the leader of translation workshops in francophone Africa.

[2] Slight revision of the *International Children's Bible* (*ICB*), also published as *The Youth Bible*.

Version, and The Message.[3] So this particular version may be new in itself, but the impulse for 'fresh expression' is certainly not.

DeClaissé-Walford presents three interesting examples from *The Voice*, but in each case I would have liked to hear more of the editorial rationale. In Psalm 3 the modern poet sees enemies like garden weeds, 'twenty to each flower', their mockery of belief as 'a fairy tale', and God as the Gardener who should 'weed them out'. But the editors replaced these striking images with more traditional translation and the rather stiff imagery of God as an 'impenetrable shield'. Why? In Psalm 22 the poet uses contemporary language: 'deaf ears', 'let down', 'an embarrassment'. But most of this vivid language has been edited out and replaced by flat phrasing and more literary terms: 'ears are deaf', 'vindicated', 'a disgrace'.[4] Again, why? In the superscriptions deClaissé-Walford was imaginative but the editors prosaic—why? These changes hardly bear out the website's express wish for *The Voice* to recapture 'the . . . grit, humor, and beauty [which] has been lost'. It would have been helpful to know the editors' perspective on these examples.

Perhaps here, as is so often the case, a worthy project is swallowed up by non-academic but crucial commercial demands. Many publishers want to have their own version of the Bible, since popular versions sell well and generate dependable income. But in order to be popular a new version has to be accepted by a significant sector of the Bible-purchasing market.[5] So editors are tempted to play safe in order to win buyers—perhaps editors of *The Voice* considered their poets to be too imaginative for their imagined readers!

In strong contrast, the New International Commentary on the Old Testament (NICOT) has the great advantage of allowing commentators to justify their translation at length. Here we do not just have the occasional minimalist footnote—there are several paragraphs or even pages to discuss and defend a translation. And with the NICOT Psalms volumes there is the added dimension for deClaissé-Walford of dialoguing with co-authors in order to adopt a consensus. She has helpfully highlighted several central issues in her presentation, to which I would like to respond.

First, there is the question of the translation of key Hebrew words, with the related matter of resonances in repetition and echoing. Here the issue is less one of translation in each text and more that of uniformity across texts. Her proposed solutions for *nephesh* and *shalom* generally work very well. However, I wonder about the translation of *nephesh* in Ps. 124.4–5, where consistency would require 'a river poured over our inmost being' (v. 4). This

---

[3] Some of these have already appeared in revised editions, as have many more formal translations.

[4] One of the few vivid expressions retained is 'a loser'.

[5] The way versions are publicized illustrates many of the tensions faced by publishers. One advertisement which has appeared frequently in Christian magazines recently extols the *NASB* as both timeless and updated!

produces a clumsy mixed metaphor, which was hardly the psalmist's intent. The core issue is of course whether it is more important to translate each term uniformly or each phrase according to its overall meaning. This ongoing debate between formal and functional translation is easy to characterize (and perhaps to caricature), but often difficult to resolve in practice, especially in the context of a more formal commentary series. Nevertheless, in this particular instance, even the conservative and more formal ESV, which translates *nephesh* as 'soul' in Ps. 42.1, renders it simply as 'us' in Ps. 142.4–5.

It is a pity that deClaissé-Walford and her colleagues decided not to translate *hesed*. Admittedly languages sometimes do adopt foreign terms when there is no adequate equivalent in their own, as with 'angst' in English. But I remain unconvinced that this is necessary in Bible translation, especially if one allows different English renditions of Hebrew terms in different contexts. One consequence of leaving a term untranslated is that it conveys a sense of foreignness, of a gulf between the two cultures, undermining the purpose of translation. Another consequence is that the term then becomes static and frozen in meaning. Anglophone readers will need to find a definition of *hesed* which will give a range of its meaning. Then, since most are monolingual and have little awareness of the way language works, they will tend to assume that the full range of the semantic field of *hesed* is evoked at every mention. Where they would instinctively accept that the meaning of a common word like 'love' depends enormously on context, they will have a much less flexible attitude towards a foreign word, especially when reading texts they consider theologically significant.

Secondly, there is the repetition of sounds, illustrated by the round-mouthed vowels in Ps. 145.14–20. DeClaissé-Walford's paper highlights the many Hebrew 'o' vowels in the passage, but of course English cannot reproduce them consistently. It can mostly capture both the sound and the repetition of *kol* with the English 'all', though it loses it once in the dissimilar singular form 'every'. But the other round-mouthed vowels simply cannot be reproduced. Further, the contribution of participles to this phonemic quality is not even echoed (let alone reproduced), since the original has nine participles (including two nominal and one passive), whereas NICOT renders only two of these participially. So Ps. 145 illustrates well deClaissé-Walford's own conclusion that this element of Hebrew poetry is 'the most difficult to transfer into English'. As such, I would question whether it should even be attempted.[6]

Thirdly, there is the issue of maintaining word order. Strictly, of course, this is impossible, since every language has its distinct structure, as can easily be

---

[6] One exception might be the striking repetition of *šāmar* in Psalm 121. Here *TaNaK* has perhaps the best rendering, since 'guardian' captures the continuous aspect of the Hebrew participle, and 'will guard' echoes the finite forms of vv. 7–8.

illustrated by comparing many a sentence in English, French, and German. DeClaissé-Walford's examples show that she actually has a looser goal in mind, perhaps better termed 'reflecting the general syntactical structure, particularly chiasmus'. But unlike the previous issue of sound repetition, she clearly implies that this should be attempted, lamenting that 'a disregard for deliberate word order in Hebrew poetry permeates English translations of the Psalms'.[7] However, she is also aware that the common disregard of original word order in English translation is just as deliberate, since it occurs 'in the interest of maintaining usual English word order'.[8] The best-known examples of flouting usual English word order are the metrical psalms, treasured in many a Presbyterian congregation. But the peculiar word order in many metrical psalms only occasionally reflects Hebrew chiasm, and occurs more often for the sake of suitable rhythm or rhyme.[9]

At this point it may be instructive to note how translators of other ancient poetry handle similar issues. *Beowulf*, a poem composed in Anglo-Saxon some time in the seventh to tenth centuries, is now much studied and available in many translations.[10] Its poetic form has two controlling features, quite different to those of ancient Hebrew: (i) four stresses in each line, two each side of the caesura; and (ii) alliteration in lines, within half-line and across the caesura. For example:

> The fortunes of war / favoured Hrothgar
> And find friendship / in the father's embrace
> We heard of these princes' / heroic campaigns.[11]

Its language has another important feature, that of compound-making, or 'kennings', for example battle-torch, ring-giver, swamp-thing, house-guards, hall-defenders. Inevitably, both the poetic form and the language present challenges to translators.

The modern Irish poet Seamus Heaney recently produced a marvellously vivid and widely acclaimed rendering of *Beowulf*. It was awarded the 1999 Whitbread Prize, and for one reviewer 'released the poem from the syllabus back into literature'.[12] Heaney respects the Anglo-Saxon poetic and linguistic conventions as far as he can, but adds tellingly:

> In one area, my own labours have been less than thoroughgoing. I have not followed the strict metrical rules that bound the Anglo-Saxon *scop*. I have been guided by the fundamental pattern of four stresses to the line, but I allow myself several transgressions. For example, I don't always employ alliteration, and sometimes I alliterate only in one half of the line. When these breaches occur, it is

---

[7] See p. 200 above.   [8] Ibid.
[9] For instance in Ps. 121.1: 'I to the hills will lift mine eyes'.
[10] It has interesting parallels with *Gilgamesh*, but these cannot be explored here.
[11] Unconnected lines cited by Heaney 1999: xxviii–xxix.
[12] *Times Literary Supplement*; cited in Heaney 1999: inside front cover.

because I prefer to let the natural 'sound of sense' prevail over the demand of the convention: I have been reluctant to force an artificial shape or an unusual word choice just for the sake of correctness.[13]

In other words, Heaney translated this ancient poetry on the basis that form is certainly important, but should not override the need to make sense in modern English. This applies equally well to the translation of biblical poetry.

Fourthly, there is the minefield of gender neutrality. This is a prime illustration of difficulties associated with texts (unlike *Beowulf*) deemed to be 'sacred', that is, texts treasured by religious communities and still spiritually relevant to believers. In consequence, these texts are often required to be translated in currently acceptable language, including gender neutrality. DeClaissé-Walford tackles this issue bravely and directly. Yet her approach here, which might be happily endorsed in a version like *The Voice*, seems at variance with her previous points. There she chose to set aside modern forms of expression in order to convey the original pattern of the text. Here she chooses to set aside the original cultural expression of the text in order to conform to modern sensibilities. So in this as in the other issues addressed in her thoughtful paper, she shows that we will always bear out the aphorism 'Traduttore traditore'. In translation there is never a correct version.

However, I want to end on a more positive note. Derek Kidner's two-volume commentary on the Psalms is by today's standards fairly brief, unusually devotional, and rather dated, yet it still contains many astute insights pithily expressed. After surveying Hebrew poetry and summarizing Lowth's seminal analysis, Kidner concludes:

> A final point deserves emphasis, and this too was one of Lowth's observations. It is the striking fact that this type of poetry loses less than perhaps any other in the process of translation. In many literatures the appeal of a poem lies chiefly in verbal felicities and associations, or in metrical subtleties, which tend to fail of their effect even in a related language ... But the poetry of the Psalms has a broad simplicity of rhythm and imagery which survives transplanting into almost any soil. Above all, the fact that its parallelisms are those of sense rather than of sound allows it to reproduce its chief effects with very little loss of either force or beauty. It is well fitted by God's providence to invite 'all the earth' to 'sing the glory of his name'.[14]

Bibliography

Heaney, Seamus
  1999 *Beowulf* (London: Faber).
Kidner, Derek
  1973 *Psalms 1–72: An Introduction and Commentary on Books I and II of the Psalms* (Tyndale Old Testament Commentaries; London: Inter Varsity Press).

---

[13] Heaney 1999: xxviii.   [14] Kidner 1973: 4.

Part III

Past Contexts and Future Perspectives

17

Psalm 104 and Akhenaten's Hymn to the Sun

John Day

1. Introduction

For over a century, starting with the American Egyptologist James Henry Breasted in 1905,[1] scholars have been aware of a number of striking parallels between Psalm 104 and the fourteenth-century BCE 'heretic pharaoh' Akhenaten's great hymn to the Sun god Aten. This is inscribed in thirteen columns of hieroglyphics on the western wall of the tomb of Ay at Akhenaten's capital Akhetaten ('the horizon of Aten'),[2] now known as El-Amarna,[3] located in Middle Egypt half way between Thebes and Memphis on the east bank of the Nile.

This hymn is commonly known as the great hymn to the Sun (Aten) to distinguish it from the shorter hymn to Aten also known from El-Amarna,[4] and is generally regarded as the best testimony we have to Akhenaten's Aten cult. Akhenaten planned the move of his capital from Thebes to Akhetaten in the fourth year of his reign (c.1354–1337); in his sixth year he changed his name from Amenhotep IV to Akhenaten ('Beneficent for Aten [?]') in honour of his god; and he finally moved his capital to Akhetaten sometime between then and his eighth year. In his religious reform Akhenaten eliminated the worship of all other gods except Aten, a deity representing the sun disc and sunlight.[5] His campaign against the cult of Amun-Re, hitherto the chief god, was particularly virulent. However, the reaction against Akhenaten set in not long after his death, starting with Tutankhamun (c.1335–1326), who

---

[1] Breasted 1905: 371–6. Cf. later Breasted 1934: 368. Breasted (1894) had earlier analysed Akhenaten's hymns in his Berlin Latin dissertation, but he never mentions Psalm 104 there.

[2] See Davies 1908: VI: 18–19, 29–31, plates 27, 41; for a more up-to-date edition of the hieroglyphic text, cf. Sandman 1938: 93–6. For translations see Wilson 1969; Lichtheim 1976: II, 92–6; Tobin 1985: 234–7; Hornung 1995: 88–93, ET 1999: 79–83; Assmann 1997: 172–7; 1999: 217–23.

[3] Often called Tell El-Amarna, but this is not strictly correct.

[4] See Lichtheim 1976: II, 90–92; Assmann 1999: 214–17.

[5] On Akhenaten's cult see especially Hornung 1995, ET 1999; also Aldred 1988; Redford 1984, 1987, 1997.

changed his name from Tutankhaten in his second year, moved the capital away from Akhetaten to Memphis, and allowed the worship of other gods alongside Aten; but it was not complete till the time of Horemheb (c.1322–1295), the last pharaoh of the eighteenth dynasty, when many of Akhenaten's monuments were destroyed and his name was expunged from history. The reason the great hymn to Aten survived was that it was hidden away in a tomb.

Scholars debate whether monotheism or monolatry is the best term to use for Akhenaten's cult.[6] Either way, there are no good grounds for following Sigmund Freud, who, in his book *Moses and Monotheism*,[7] famously argued that Israelite monotheism was dependent on the cult of Akhenaten. First, Yahweh does not appear to have been a Sun god in origin. Secondly, such evidence as we have suggests that the historical Moses lived a century after Akhenaten. Thirdly, much of Freud's argument was fanciful, seeing connections, for example, between the name Aten and Hebrew Adon, 'lord', taking up an idea previously mooted by Weigall.[8] However, since Freud knew the work of Breasted and Weigall, it is surprising that he made no direct reference to Psalm 104, whose parallels with Akhenaten's hymn are so striking. However, I have spotted one previously overlooked sentence in Freud referring to a certain similarity between Akhenaten's hymn and the Psalms, without specifying which, and this presumably had Psalm 104 in mind.[9]

There is currently no consensus amongst scholars about how exactly we should explain the parallels between Psalm 104 and Akhenaten's hymn. Amongst the debated points are the following. Is the psalm in any way dependent on Akhenaten's hymn or not? If it is dependent, how could a Hebrew psalmist have had access to it when Akhenaten's 'monotheistic revolution' died out soon after his death? Was the dependence perhaps indirect, mediated through the Canaanites or Phoenicians, through later hymns to the Sun god Amun-Re, or is some other explanation possible? And if it is dependent, how much of Psalm 104 is dependent? These are the questions which I propose to discuss here.

---

[6] E.g., Akhenaten is seen as genuinely monotheistic by Hornung (1973: 240–6, ET 1982: 244–50) and Tobin (1985), but this is rejected by Bernhardt (1969: 198) and Williams (1971: 287–8).

[7] Freud 1939, ET 1939.

[8] Weigall 1923: 12, 32.

[9] Freud 1939: 38, ET 1939: 29. Freud writes, 'In the two hymns to Aton which have been preserved to us . . . he praises the sun as the creator and preserver of all living beings in and outside Egypt with a fervour such as recurs many centuries after only in the psalms in honour of the Jewish God, Jahve.' Even Assmann (1997: 191) overlooked this sentence in expressing his own surprise at Freud's failure to mention Psalm 104.

2. Parallels between Psalm 104.20–30 and Akhenaten's Hymn in Virtually Identical Order

In this essay it will be argued that Psalm 104 is indeed dependent on Akhenaten's hymn to the Sun but that this dependence is confined to Ps. 104.20–30. This is because the parallels here are especially impressive, all of them with one exception occurring in the same order, a point often overlooked, which seems too much to attribute to coincidence. The parallels are as follows.

2.1. First Parallel

Psalm 104.20–1

> You make darkness, and it is night,
> when all the animals of the forest come creeping out.
> The young lions roar for their prey,
> seeking their food from God.

Akhenaten, lines 27–37[10]

> When you set in the western horizon,
> The land is in darkness,
> in the manner of death.
> They sleep in a room, with heads wrapped up,
> Nor sees one eye the other.
> All their goods, which are under their heads might be stolen,
>   but they would not perceive (it).
> Every lion is come forth from his den;
> All creeping things, they sting.
> Darkness *is a shroud,*
> and the earth is in stillness,
> For he who made them rests in his horizon.

In this first parallel, which starts fairly near the beginning of Akhenaten's hymn, the point is made that with the setting of the sun (cf. Ps. 104.19b) the lions leave their dens. In addition, both passages speak of other creatures emerging, whether 'all the animals of the forest' (Psalm 104) or 'all creeping things' (Akhenaten), the word 'all' occurring in both instances.

---

[10] This and following quotations from Akhenaten's hymn are taken from Wilson 1969, with minor modifications of archaic language. For the line numbers I follow Assmann 1999: 217–22.

2.2. Second Parallel

Psalm 104.22–3

> When you cause the sun to rise,[11] they withdraw
> and lie down in their dens.
> People go out to their work
> and to their labour until the evening.

Akhenaten, lines 38–45

> At daybreak, when you arise on the horizon,
> When you shine as the Aten by day,
> You drive away the darkness and give your rays.
> The Two Lands are in festivity *every day*,
> Awake and standing upon (their) feet, for you have
>   raised them up.
> Washing their bodies, taking (their) clothing,
> Their arms are (raised) in praise at your appearance.
> All the world, they do their work.

In this second parallel both the psalm and Akhenaten make the identical point that when the sun rises people go out to do their work. The combination in quick succession of lions coming out at night in the first parallel and human beings going to work in the daytime in the second parallel is especially impressive.

2.3. Third Parallel

Psalm 104.24

> O Lord, how manifold are your works!
> In wisdom you have made them all;
> the earth is full of your creatures.

Akhenaten, lines 76–82

> How manifold it is, what you have made!
> They are hidden from the face (of man).
> O sole god, like whom there is no other!

---

[11] A strong case can be made that we should emend the verb תזרח from Qal 3rd person singular feminine ('the sun *rises*') to Hiphil 2nd person singular masculine ('you *cause* the sun *to rise*'). This not only provides a better contrast with v. 20, 'you make darkness', but is supported by the fact that in v. 19 the word שמש, 'sun', is masculine, whereas in v. 22 it is inconsistently feminine if we regard it as the subject of a Qal 3rd person singular feminine תזרח rather than the object of a Hiphil 2nd person singular תזרח. The resulting you-form address in this verse is then more in keeping both with vv. 20–30 as a whole and, significantly, with the parallel in Akhenaten's hymn to the Sun.

> You did create the world according to your desire, whilst you were alone:
> All men, cattle, and wild beasts,
> Whatever is on earth, going upon (its) feet,
> And what is on high, flying with its wings.

Here at the beginning of both passages there is a remarkable similarity in wording between the statements of wonder at what the deity has made. Both allude to the large number of things that the god has made. After this the psalm contents itself with a general statement, 'the earth is full of your creatures', whereas Akhenaten spells out in a bit more detail what these creatures are.

It is striking that this is the one instance out of all the six parallels where the psalm reference is out of sequence with Akhenaten's hymn. However, a number of scholars have previously noted that v. 24, with its general peroration of God's creation as a whole, seems somewhat premature in its current location in the psalm and would be more appropriate a little later, after the sea creatures of vv. 25–26 have been mentioned.[12] Significantly, Akhenaten does place the corresponding peroration a little later, subsequent to the reference to fish (and other creatures). So even this one deviation from the strict order in parallelism only serves to strengthen the case for dependence on Akhenaten's hymn.

2.4. Fourth Parallel

Psalm 104.25–6

> There is the sea, great and wide,
> creeping things innumerable are there,
> living things both great and small.
> There go the ships,
> and Leviathan whom you formed to play with.

Akhenaten, lines 53–8

> The ships are sailing north
> and south as well,
> For every way is open at your appearance.
> The fish in the river
> dart before your face;
> Your rays are in the midst of the great green sea.

One reason this is a particularly interesting parallel is because both texts make reference to ships, which at first sight might appear strange in a creation psalm. A number of scholars have felt obliged to emend אֳנִיּוֹת, 'ships' to

E.g. Berlin 2005: 81.

אימות, 'terrors' (e.g. Gunkel[13]) or to תנינים, 'dragons/sea monsters' (e.g. Weiser[14]) in order to provide what is deemed to be a better parallel to Leviathan. Grill, and more recently Loretz,[15] have also rejected 'ships' but without deciding which of these emendations should be accepted. However, the temptation to emend should certainly be resisted. First, אימות is not elsewhere used of Leviathan or the chaos waters, and תנינים is graphically quite remote from the MT's אניות. Secondly, the ancient Versions unanimously support reading 'ships'. Thirdly, as noted above, Akhenaten's hymn significantly has a reference to 'ships' at this very point. It is clear from the context that the reason that ships are mentioned in Akhenaten's hymn is that they are a sign of the human activity that occurs during the hours of daylight after the sun has risen. Because Psalm 104, in contrast, is not a Sun hymn, this original context has now been lost, thus making the mention of ships seem slightly out of place. There is no reason to follow Uehlinger and Köckert,[16] who think that ships are mentioned in Psalm 104 because they are Phoenician ships with prows in the shape of animals!

There is no consensus on whether we should read 'Leviathan whom you formed to play with',[17] or 'Leviathan whom you formed to play in it' (i.e. the sea).[18] Linguistically בו refers back more naturally to the noun 'Leviathan' rather than to the adverb 'there' (שם), let alone 'the sea', which is rather distant at the beginning of the previous verse, thus supporting the translation 'Leviathan whom you formed to play with'. This view also represents the oldest known interpretation, since already in the book of Job Yahweh taunts Job regarding Leviathan, 'Can you play with him as with a bird?' (Job 40.29, ET 41.5), implying that God does.[19] Similarly, the rabbis later believed that God played with Leviathan (*Abodah zarah* 3b; *Pirqe de Rabbi Eliezer* 9; *Midrash Jonah* 98; *Ḥasidim* 476), *Abodah zarah* 3b specifically singling out the last three hours of the day for this activity. These words represent the psalmist's version of Akhenaten's words, 'The fish in the river dart before your face'. Leviathan represents a more mythological, Canaanite expression than Akhenaten's 'fish', although Leviathan, like the fish, is thought really to exist, even if he is now in depotentiated form—'God's rubber duckey', as Levenson puts it.[20] Leviathan is here a sea creature frolicking with the deity,

---

[13] Cf. Gunkel 1895: 57 and n. 3, ET 2006: 36 and 305 n. 97; idem, 1925–6: 456.

[14] Cf. Weiser 1955: II, 455 and n. 1, 458, ET 1962: 665.

[15] Grill 1959; Loretz 1979: 111.   [16] Uehlinger 1990: 522–4; Köckert 2000: 270 n. 60.

[17] This is followed by Gunkel 1895: 57 and n. 4, ET 2006: 36 and 305–6 n. 98; Dahood, 1970: III, 32; Kraus 1978: II, 724; Terrien 2003: 708.

[18] This is followed by most modern Bible translations. Also Kirkpatrick 1906: 612; Allen 1983: 25; Seybold 1996: 26; similarly Goldingay 2008: 180, 192, though he is open to the other possibility.

[19] This grammatical understanding of בו in Ps. 104.26 further has the support of Septuagint, Vulgate and Peshitta, though they mistakenly take שחק to mean 'mock (at)' rather than 'play (with)'.

[20] Levenson 1988: 17, quoting a student.

just as the fish leap before Aten in Akhenaten's hymn. It will also be noted that Akhenaten and Psalm 104 similarly refer to 'the great green sea' and 'the sea great and wide' respectively, meaning the Mediterranean. However, whereas the fish as well as ships are in the Nile in Akhenaten's hymn, this distinctively Egyptian element has understandably been removed in the psalm, which appears to place both Leviathan and the ships in the sea.

2.5. Fifth Parallel

Psalm 104.27–8

> These all look to you
> to give them their food in due season;
> when you give to them, they gather it up;
> when you open your hand, they are filled with good things.

Akhenaten, lines 85–6

> You supply their necessities:
> Everyone has his food, and his time of life is reckoned.

Both passages refer to the deity's provision of food for all ('all', Ps. 104; 'everyone', Akhenaten). It should, however, be noted that whilst Akhenaten's hymn relates this specifically to humans, the positioning of the passage in the psalm means that it refers now to living creatures generally, human beings and beasts.

2.6. Sixth Parallel

Psalm 104.29–30

> When you hide your face, they are dismayed;
> when you take away their breath, they die.
> When you send forth your spirit, they are created;
> and you renew the face of the ground.

Akhenaten, lines 127–8

> When you have risen they live,
> When you set they die.

Here, in this final parallel, both passages depict the deity as the source of both the life and death of his creatures. However, whereas in Akhenaten's hymn the Sun is the source of life, in the psalm this is replaced by the divine spirit. Also the order of the statements about life and death is reversed in the psalm. Incidentally, the Akhenaten parallel coheres with the natural and generally accepted understanding of the MT of Ps. 104.29–30 as involving the creation and death of living creatures, not their death and resurrection, the latter supposition leading G. R. Driver[21] and the *NEB*[22] unnecessarily to emend the text so as to avoid the latter imputation and in the process avoiding any reference to death at all!

The above series of six parallels, all in the same order with one exception, strongly supports the dependence of Ps. 104.20–30 in some way on Akhenaten's hymn. All this seems too much to be due to mere coincidence. Moreover, as we have seen, the somewhat unexpected reference to 'ships' in v. 26 and the seemingly premature peroration of God's creation in v. 24 are both illumined when read against the background of the Egyptian hymn. It is also surely significant that the parallels start fairly near the beginning of Akhenaten's hymn and continue to near its end, suggesting that the psalmist had access to something resembling the entire hymn. Moreover, this conclusion is reinforced by the fact that these very same verses are in the you-form (see the Hebrew of vv. 20, 22,[23] 24, 26, 27, 28, 29, 30), unlike a fair amount of the rest of the psalm which is in the participle-form (vv. 2, 3, 4, 10, 13, 14 [+ 32[24]], to which should be added v. 5 [cf. Septuagint] and v. 19[25]). This difference between you-forms and participles is obscured in English Bible translations, which also tend to render Psalm 104's participles in the you-form. Incidentally, the participle-form in hymns is much more characteristic of Hebrew psalmody generally (cf. Psalms 33, 65, 103, 113, 136, 146, 147). It is therefore noteworthy that Akhenaten's hymn is in the you-form throughout. Thus, not only content but also form suggest that vv. 20–30 constitute a distinct unit.[26]

---

[21] Driver (1962; cf. *NEB*) translated, 'When Thou hidest Thy face, they are troubled; when Thou takest away their breath, they gasp; When Thou sendest forth Thy breath, they recover health, and Thou dost give fresh life to the whole earth'. This highly speculative rendering involves deleting 'and return to their dust' in v. 29 as a later gloss, translating גוע in the same verse as 'gasp' rather than 'die', and rendering ברא in v. 30 as 'recover health' rather than 'create'. Driver's error lay in supposing that v. 30 is referring to the identical creatures mentioned in v. 29, whereas it is more natural to suppose that they are simply other creatures of the same type.

[22] *REB* wisely reverts to the traditional rendering.

[23] See above, n. 11.

[24] The ending in Ps. 104.31–5 may possibly be a later addition, as Seybold (1984) argues.

[25] Verses 1, 7, 8 (end), and 9 are also in the you-form.

[26] In view of this unity, we must reject the theory of Spieckermann (1989: 41) and Köckert (2000: 270) that vv. 25–6 were the work of a later redactor. This is particularly strange in Spieckermann's case, since unlike Köckert he recognizes that the reference to 'ships' in v. 26 has its background in Akhenaten's hymn, alongside other passages in Psalm 104. It is surely simpler to envisage one author rather than two introducing the various Akhenaten parallels into Psalm 104, especially in view of their common ordering.

3. Dubious Parallels between Akhenaten's Hymn and Psalm 104

There are some other passages in Psalm 104 that certain scholars have connected with Akhenaten's hymn which should probably be rejected. None of them is particularly striking and none appears in verses using the 'you-form', which we have seen above is a feature of the parallels in vv. 20–30 and in Akhenaten's hymn itself. In view of space restrictions, I can consider only a few here.[27]

For example, near the beginning Ps. 104.2 speaks of Yahweh being wrapped in light, which might make one think of the sun, just as the hymn to Aten evokes the sunrise near the beginning (lines 15–19).[28] However, the early verses of the psalm in which this phrase occurs are depicting Yahweh as a storm god who conquered the watery powers of chaos at the time of creation and who subsequently brings the rain on which the earth's fertility depends. A reference to the lightning is thus more appropriate; cf. Hab. 3.4; Job 36.30; 37.11, which similarly speak of Yahweh's light אוֹר (the same word as in Ps. 104.2) in storm theophany contexts.

Again, take the following passage from Akhenaten, lines 97–99:

> For you have set a Nile in heaven, that it may descend for them,
> And make waves upon the mountains, like the great green sea,
> To water their fields in their towns.

This has sometimes[29] been compared with Ps. 104.6, 10:

> The deep covered it[30] like a garment;
> the waters stood above the mountains.
>
> You make springs gush forth in the valleys,
> they flow between the hills.

However, whereas from the context it is clear that v. 6 is speaking of God's control of the chaos waters at the time of creation,[31] Akhenaten is referring to Aten's provision of rain in the present for foreign lands (from 'a Nile in heaven'). The psalm is clearly dependent on Semitic *Chaoskampf* mythology here, something well attested elsewhere in the Old Testament (e.g. Pss.

---

[27] See the list in Auffret 1981: 280 n. 1.

[28] Levenson 1988: 62.

[29] Cf. Wilson 1969: 371 n. 13; Levenson 1988: 62.

[30] Reading כסתה for MT כסיתו with Aquila, Theodotion, Jerome, and Targum; cf. v. 9.

[31] Not Noah's flood, as argued by Barker 1986, which is contrary to the context. The flood was, nevertheless, from the Priestly writer's point of view a resurgence of the chaos waters over the earth. However, the fact that Ps. 104.9 speaks of the waters being controlled so as never to cover the earth again suggests Ps. 104's ignorance of a subsequent universal flood, and thus tells against Ps. 104 being a post-exilic composition dependent on Genesis.

74.12–14; 89.10–1, ET 9–10; Job 38.8–11),[32] not on Akhenaten. As for v. 10, in contrast to v. 6 this is speaking of the present, but it is referring to springs gushing up and flowing beneath the hills, not rain from heaven coming over the mountains. The two passages seem to be unrelated, in spite of superficial similarities.

Finally, take Akhenaten lines 46–52:

> All beasts are content with their pasturage;
> Trees and plants are flourishing.
> The birds which fly from their nests,
> Their wings are (stretched out) in praise to your *ka*.
> All beasts spring upon (their) feet.
> Whatever flies and alights,
> They live when you have risen (for) them.

This has sometimes[33] been compared with Ps. 104.11–14:

> Giving drink to every wild animal;
> the wild asses quench their thirst.
> by the streams the birds of the air have their habitation;
> they sing among the branches.
> From your lofty abode you water the mountains;
> the earth is satisfied with the fruit of your work.
> You cause the grass to grow for the cattle,
> and plants for people to use,
> to bring forth food from the earth.

However, quite apart from the very general nature of this parallel, it is abundantly clear that Akhenaten's hymn is praising the role of the sun with regard to nature, whereas the psalm is speaking of God's provision of rain. Following on the passage lauding God's control of the chaos waters (vv. 6–9), this passage is clearly continuing the theme of Yahweh as a storm god, and this is ultimately indebted to Canaanite ideas, not the Egyptian cult of the Sun god Aten.

4. How to Explain Psalm 104's Knowledge of Motifs in Akhenaten's Hymn?

How are we to explain Psalm 104's knowledge of motifs found in Akhenaten's hymn to the Sun? We may certainly dismiss the view of scholars such as Peet, Bernhardt, and Berlin[34] that the parallels do not indicate any connection at all

---

[32] Cf. Day 1985: 1–61.   [33] Cf. Wilson 1969: 370 n. 8.
[34] Peet 1931: 78; Bernhardt 1969; Berlin 2005: 75 n. 15.

with Akhenaten's hymn. For Peet the parallels are probably 'quite fortuitous', while for Bernhardt and Berlin they are explicable simply because both hymns have similar themes centring on creation, Berlin even claiming that this is the majority view nowadays. However, these scholars fail to take into account the full weight of evidence that I have presented above, including the common ordering of themes and the unusual reference to ships. The same objection applies to Uehlinger,[35] who proposes that the origin of Psalm 104 is to be sought entirely within Canaan. As already mentioned, his claim that the ships are referred to because of the animal prows of some Phoenician ships seems forced.

In recent years a number of scholars, including Köckert, Knigge, and Krüger,[36] have proposed that the psalm could have derived its 'Atenistic' parallels from later Egyptian solar hymns to the god Amun-Re.[37] However, when we come to examine the precise parallels with hymns to Amun-Re which have been proposed we find that they are singularly unimpressive: in not one of the countless Amun-Re hymns do we find a whole series of striking parallels together, let alone in the same order, such as we find between Akhenaten's hymn and Psalm 104. And not a single hymn to Amun-Re contains a reference to 'ships', such as we find in Akhenaten and Ps. 104.26. Having ploughed through vast numbers of hymns to Amun-Re in Assmann's valuable collection of Egyptian hymns,[38] I am forced to conclude that none of these hymns is particularly close to Ps. 104.20–30, and such parallels as exist are only of a very general character.

Rather than showing dependence on later Amun-Re hymns, it very much looks as if the author of Psalm 104 did indeed have access to Akhenaten's hymn to the Sun in some form. But how could this be? Barucq[39] thinks Psalm 104 might have drawn directly on the Egyptian of Akhenaten's hymn, but does not explain how this could have been possible. Could someone in the first millennium BCE have appropriated the hymn from the tomb of Ay itself? This is not an idea that anyone has hitherto proposed, but it should be noted that text 60 in the tomb of Petosiris, high priest of Thoth, from the late fourth century BCE, contains a few parallels to Akhenaten's hymn to the Sun from a thousand years earlier.[40] Since this tomb is at Tuna el-Gebel, on the very border of El-Amarna itself, one might speculate that the writer of this Petosiris tomb inscription had access to the nearby tomb of Ay. However, the possibility that someone at a later date, long after Akenaten's cult

[35] Uehlinger 1990.
[36] Köckert 2000: 272–4; Knigge 2000; Krüger 2010a; 2010b: 403–22.
[37] Köckert (2000: 274) relates this to the idea that Yahweh had been regarded as a Sun god; cf. Taylor 1993. However, the evidence for that is weak; see Day 1996; 2000: 151–63.
[38] Assmann 1999.
[39] Barucq 1962: 320–1.
[40] Lefebvre 1924: I, 36; 1923: II, 33–4; Couroyer 1950: 178; Barucq 1962: 318; Williams 1971: 286.

had disappeared, entered the tomb and laboriously copied out the whole text, after which it got translated into Hebrew or Aramaic so as to be excerpted in Psalm 104, does seem rather far-fetched, especially if a more likely scenario is available.

How then could Psalm 104 have had access to Akhenaten's hymn? The most likely explanation is that this took place indirectly, specifically that it was mediated to Israel via the Canaanites, as scholars such as Redford, Assmann, de Moor, and Reichmann have suggested,[41] or conceivably via the Phoenicians, as Nagel had earlier proposed.[42] In support it may be noted that it was only during the few brief years of Akhenaten and his immediate successors that the cult of Aten had prominence; after that it fell into oblivion. So it is only during that period that we can easily envisage the great hymn to Aten being passed on to the Levant. Moreover, Canaan was then part of the Egyptian empire and we know that relations between Egypt and Canaan were close. For example, Akhenaten apparently had two high officials of Canaanite or Syrian origin.[43] The first was the vizier, Aper-El (inherited from Amenhotep III), whose tomb at Saqqara reveals that one of his titles was 'first prophet of Aten'.[44] The second was Dudu (Tutu), Akhenaten's foreign minister and 'first servant' of the King in the Aten temple,[45] who was buried in El-Amarna. Moreover, the El-Amarna letters show that many rulers throughout Canaan and western Asia were in frequent contact with the Egyptian court. Interestingly, soon after Akhenaten came to power they recognized that it was no longer politic to mention Amun.[46] It thus appears that Akhenaten's devotion to Aten had become well known to Canaan's rulers. Moreover, one particular El-Amarna letter, 147.5–10 from King Abi-milku of Tyre, even seems to appropriate the language of Aten hymns when addressing the pharaoh:

> My lord is the Sun god, who rises over the lands day after day,
> as ordained by the Sun god,
> who gives life by his sweet breath
> and diminishes when he is hidden.[47]

---

[41] Redford 1992: 387; Assmann 1992: 166–8; de Moor 1997: 69; Reichmann 2009.

[42] Nagel 1950.   [43] Cf. Hornung 1983: 64.   [44] Cf. Zivie 1990: 157.

[45] Helck 1975; Hornung 1983: 64.   [46] See Golán 1992; de Moor 1997: 68.

[47] Cf. Albright 1937: 198. Note Ps. 104.29 (sixth parallel above), where Akhenaten's reference to the sun's setting has been transmogrified into an allusion to Yahweh's *hiding* his face (different verb). Grave (1982), however, on the basis of Egyptian parallels, has argued that *ina ṣapanišu*, which is generally agreed to contain a Canaanite gloss, means 'with his north wind' rather than 'when he is hidden' (lit. 'in his hiding'), and this has been followed by Moran (1987: 378, ET 1992: 233, 'and returns with his north wind'). However, 'north wind' is an extremely rare context meaning for *ṣpn*, attested only once, about a millennium later, in the biblical Hebrew of Song 4.16. We do not even know that *ṣpn* could mean 'north' in fourteenth-century Canaanite, let alone 'north wind'; it certainly does not have either meaning in Ugaritic, where it refers to Baal's sacred mountain (lit. 'look-out place'), from which location the meaning 'north' eventually arose.

Subsequently, lines 13–15 of the same letter also go on to apply Baalistic language to the pharaoh, 'Who utters his battle-cry in heaven like Baal, so that the land quakes with his cry', just as Psalm 104 attributes both Atenistic and Baalistic language to Yahweh. In conclusion, it is wholly credible that the great hymn to Aten could have become known in Canaan during the Amarna period.[48] Indeed, it is difficult to see how otherwise it could have been transmitted so as to influence the author of Psalm 104.

It is clear enough that Psalm 104 has some elements reflecting Canaanite mythology, such as the storm god and conflict with the waters motifs and the bringing of rain attested in vv. 1–18 (and the use of the name Leviathan in v. 26). Dion[49] has rightly argued that Psalm 104 constitutes an amalgamation of Canaanite storm god and Egyptian Sun god motifs to Yahweh—vv. 1–18 and 20–30 respectively.[50] However, this of itself does not require the Egyptian hymn to have been mediated through the Canaanites,[51] since these particular 'Canaanite' elements had already been assimilated by the Israelites themselves, as references to the conflict with the waters and to Leviathan in other parts of the Old Testament (including the Psalms) attest. Moreover, this psalm's amalgamation of features deriving from the storm god and the Sun god into one deity (Yahweh) clearly bespeaks a monotheizing outlook, surely the work of an Israelite. Rather, the arguments supporting Canaanite mediation of Akhenaten's hymn to the Israelites which should be deployed are those indicated in the previous paragraph.

5. Conclusions

Psalm 104 is indeed dependent on Akhenaten's hymn to the Sun, but this dependence is confined to vv. 20–30. Here the evidence is particularly impressive, since we have six parallels with Akhenaten's hymn (starting near the beginning of that hymn and concluding near its end) occurring in the identical order, with one exception. This point, which seems too much to attribute to coincidence, has frequently been overlooked in previous discussions. Even the one exception is illumined by Akhenaten's hymn, as is the

---

[48] Helck 1971: 577 speculates that this might have occurred through the mediation of Egyptian scribes in Canaan (whose existence is seemingly attested at Tyre by Abi-milku's letter) or alternatively through Egyptian singers there.

[49] Dion 1991.

[50] V. 19 is a bridge verse: it speaks of the sun (and moon), setting the scene for vv. 20–30, but is in participle-form like some preceding verses.

[51] *Pace* de Moor (1997: 69) who states 'since this psalm at the same time exhibits the typical local colour of Canaan, it is more than likely that the Israelites did not borrow this hymn directly from Egypt but used a Canaanite translation which formed an intermediary link.' De Moor's overall conclusion is justified but not for this particular reason.

unexpected reference to ships in Ps. 104.26, which has no other credible origin. Recent attempts to claim that the 'Atenistic' imagery was mediated to Psalm 104 through later Egyptian hymns to Amun-Re are unconvincing, since no truly impressive parallels have been found there, unlike in Akhenaten's hymn. Accordingly, the psalmist must somehow have had access to Akhenaten's hymn itself. Since Akhenaten's cult was suppressed soon after his death, it is most likely that his hymn became known in Canaan during the Amarna period itself, a time when relations between Egypt and Canaan were close. Eventually an Israelite author combined motifs from Akhenaten's Sun hymn with other motifs originating in the Canaanite storm god (vv. 1–18), thus producing the psalm we now have.

Bibliography

Albright, William F.
    1937 'The Egyptian Correspondence of Abimilki, Prince of Tyre', *JEA* 23: 190–203
Aldred, Cyril
    1988 *Akhenaten: King of Egypt. A New Study* (London: Thames & Hudson).
Allen, Leslie C
    1983 *Psalms 101–150* (WBC, 21; Waco, TX: Word Books).
Anderson, Arnold A.
    1972 *The Book of Psalms* (NCB; 2 vols; London: Oliphants [Marshall, Morgan & Scott]).
Assmann, Jan
    1992 'Akhanyati's Theology of Light and Time', *Proceedings of the Israel Academy of Sciences and Humanities* 7/4: 143–76.
    1997 *Moses the Egyptian: The Memory of Egypt in Western Monotheism* (Cambridge, MA: Harvard University Press).
    1999 *Ägyptische Hymnen und Gebete* (OBO; Göttingen: Vandenhoeck & Ruprecht, 2nd edn).
Auffret, Pierre
    1981 *Hymnes d'Égypte et d'Israël: Études de structures littéraires* (OBO, 34; Fribourg: Éditions Universitaires, and Göttingen: Vandenhoeck & Ruprecht).
Barker, David G.
    1986 'The Waters of the Earth: An Exegetical Study of Psalm 104:1–9', *Grace Theological Journal* 7/1: 57–80.
Barucq, André
    1962 *L'expression de la louange divine et de la prière dans la Bible et en Égypte* (Cairo: Institut français d'archéologie orientale).
Berlin, Adele
    2005 'The Wisdom of Creation in Psalm 104', in Ronald L. Troxel, Kelvin G. Friebel, and Dennis R. Magary (eds.), *Seeking Out the Wisdom of the Ancients: Essays Offered to Honor Michael V. Fox on the Occasion of his Sixty-Fifth Birthday* (Winona Lake, IN: Eisenbrauns): 71–83.
Bernhardt, Karl-Heinz
    1969 'Amenophis IV und Psalm 104', *MIO* 15: 193–205.

Breasted, James H.

1894 *De Hymnis in Solem sub Rege Amenophide IV Conceptis: Dissertatio Inauguralis Philologica* (Berlin, Friedrich-Wilhelms-Universität: B. Paul).

1905 *History of Israel* (New York: Charles Scribner's Sons, 1st edn).

1934 *The Dawn of Conscience* (New York: Charles Scribner's Sons).

Couroyer, Bernard

1950 'Idéal sapientiel en Egypte et en Israël', *RB* 57: 175–9.

Dahood, Mitchell J.

1966–70 *Psalms* (AB, 16, 17, 17A; 3 vols. Garden City, NY: Doubleday).

Davies, Norman de Garis

1903–08 *The Rock Tombs of El-Amarna* (6 vols; London: Egypt Exploration Society).

Day, John

1985 *God's Conflict with the Dragon and the Sea: Echoes of a Canaanite Myth in the Old Testament* (UCOP, 35; Cambridge: Cambridge University Press).

1996 Review of Taylor 1993, *PEQ* 128: 185–6.

2000 *Yahweh and the Gods and Goddesses of Canaan* (JSOTSup, 265; Sheffield: Sheffield Academic Press).

de Moor, Johannes C.

1997 *The Rise of Yahwism: The Roots of Israelite Monotheism* (BETL, 91; Leuven: Leuven University Press and Peeters, 2nd edn).

Dion, Paul E.

1991 'YHWH as Storm-God and Sun-God: The Double Legacy of Egypt and Canaan', *ZAW* 103: 43–71.

Driver, Godfrey R.

1962 'The Resurrection of Marine and Terrestrial Creatures', *JSS* 7: 112–20.

Freud, Sigmund

1939 *Der Mann Moses und die monotheistische Religion* (Amsterdam: Allert de Lange). ET *Moses and Monotheism*, trans. Katherine Jones (London: Hogarth Press and the Institute of Psycho-Analysis, 1939).

Golán, Josá M.

1992 'EA 164 and the God Amun', *JNES* 51: 287–91.

Goldingay, John

2008 *Psalms*, III: *Psalms 90–150* (Baker Commentary on the Old Testament; Grand Rapids, MI: Baker Academic).

Grave, Cecilia

1982 'Northwest Semitic ṣapānu, in a Break-up of an Egyptian Stereotype Phrase in *EA* 147', *Or* 51: 161–82.

Grill, Severin

1959 'Textkritische Notizen: 1. Ps. 104:26', *BZ* 3: 102.

Gunkel, Hermann

1895 *Schöpfung und Chaos in Urzeit und Endzeit* (Göttingen: Vandenhoeck & Ruprecht). ET *Creation and Chaos in the Primeval Era and the Eschaton*, trans. K. William Whitney, Jr (Grand Rapids, MI: W. B. Eerdmans, 2006).

1925–26 *Die Psalmen* (Göttinger Handkommentar zum Alten Testament, 2.2; Göttingen: Vandenhoeck & Ruprecht, 4th edn).

Helck, Wolfgang
1971 *Die Beziehungen Ägyptens zu Vorderasien im 3. und 2. Jahrtausend v. Chr.*
(Wiesbaden: Harrassowitz, 2nd edn).
1975 'Dudu', in Wolfgang Helck and Eberhard Otto (eds.), *Lexikon der Ägyptologie*
(Wiesbaden: Harrassowitz), I: 1151.
Hornung, Erik
1973 *Der Eine und die Vielen: ägyptische Gottesvorstellungen* (Darmstadt: Wissenschaftliche Buchgesellschaft, 2nd edn). ET *Conceptions of God in Ancient
Egypt*, trans. John Baines (Ithaca, NY: Cornell University Press, 1982).
1983 'Die Anfänge von Monotheismus und Trinität in Ägypten', in Karl Rahner
(ed.), *Der eine Gott und der dreieine Gott: das Gottesverständnis bei Christen,
Juden und Muslimen* (Munich: Schnell & Steiner): 48–66.
1995 *Ekhnaton: die Religion des Lichtes* (Zurich: Artemis & Winkler). ET
Akhenaten and the Religion of Light, trans. David Lorton (Ithaca, NY: Cornell
University Press, 1999).
Kirkpatrick, Alexander F.
1906 *The Book of Psalms* (Cambridge: Cambridge University Press).
Knigge, Carsten
2000 'Überlegungen zum Verhältnis von altägyptischen Hymnik und alttesta-
mentlicher Psalmendichtung: zum Versuch einer diachronischen und
interkulturellen Motivgeschichte', *Protokolle zur Bibel* 9: 93–122.
Köckert, Matthias
2000 'Literargeschichtliche und religionsgeschichtliche Beobachtungen zu Ps
104', in Reinhard G. Kratz, Thomas Krüger, and Konrad Schmid (eds.),
*Schriftauslegung in der Schrift: Festschrift für Odil Hannes Steck zu seinem 65.
Geburtstag* (BZAW, 300; Berlin: W. de Gruyter): 259–80.
Kraus, Hans-Joachim
1978 *Psalmen* (BKAT 15.1–2; 2 vols.; Neukirchen-Vluyn: Neukirchener Verlag). ET
Psalms 1–59, 60–150, trans. Hilton C. Oswald (2 vols; Minneapolis: Augsburg
Publishing House, 1988–9).
Krüger, Annette
2010a 'Psalm 104 und der große Amarnahymnus: eine neue Perspektive', in Erich
Zenger (ed), *The Composition of the Book of Psalms* (BETL, 238; Leuven:
Peeters): 609–21.
2010b *Das Lob des Schöpfers: Studien zu Sprache, Motivik und Theologie von Psalm
104* (WMANT, 124; Neukirchen-Vluyn: Neukirchener Verlag).
Lefebvre, Gustave
1923–4 *Le tombeau de Petosiris.* (3 vols; Cairo: Imprimerie de l'Institut français
d'archéologie orientale).
Levenson, Jon D.
1988 *Creation and the Persistence of Evil* (San Francisco: Harper & Row).
Lichtheim, Miriam
1976 *Ancient Egyptian Literature* (3 vols; Berkeley: University of California Press).
Loretz, Oswald
1979 *Die Psalmen. II. Beitrag der Ugarit-Texte zum Verständnis von Kolometrie
und Textologie der Psalmen 90–150* (AOAT, 207.2; Neukirchen-Vluyn:
Neukirchener Verlag).

Moran, William L.

1987 *Les lettres d'El-Amarna: correspondance diplomatique du pharaon* (Paris: Cerf). ET *The Amarna Letters* (Baltimore: Johns Hopkins University Press, 1992).

Nagel, Georges

1950 'À propos des rapports du Psaume 104 avec les textes égyptiens', in Walter Baumgartner, Otto Eissfeldt, Karl Elliger, and Leonhard Rost (eds.), *Festschrift Alfred Bertholet zum 80. Geburtstag* (Tübingen: J. C. B. Mohr [Paul Siebeck]): 395–403.

Peet, T. Eric

1931 *A Comparative Study of the Literatures of Egypt, Palestine, and Mesopotamia: Egypt's Contribution to the Literature of the Ancient World* (Schweich Lectures of the British Academy, 1929; London: Oxford University Press).

Redford, Donald B

1984 *Akhenaten: The Heretic King* (Princeton: Princeton University Press).

1987 'The Monotheism of the Heretic Pharaoh: Precursor of Mosaic Monotheism or Egyptian Anomaly?', *BARev* 13/3: 16–32.

1992 *Egypt, Canaan, and Israel in Ancient Times* (Princeton: Princeton University Press).

1997 'The Monotheism of Akhenaten', in Donald B. Redford, William G. Dever, P. Kyle McCarter, Jr., and John J. Collins, *Aspects of Monotheism: How God is One* (Washington, DC: Biblical Archaeology Society, 1997): 11–26.

Reichmann, Sirje

2009 'Psalm 104 und der *Große Sonnenhymnus des Echnaton*: Erwägungen zu ihrem literarischen Verhältnis', in Michael Pietsch and Friedhelm Hartenstein (eds.), *Israel zwischen den Mächten: Festschrift für Stephan Timm zum 65. Geburtstag* (AOAT, 364; Münster: Ugarit-Verlag): 257–88.

Sandman, Maj

1938 *Texts from the Time of Akhenaten* (Bibliotheca Aegyptiaca, 8; Brussels: Fondation égyptologique reine Elisabeth).

Seybold, Klaus

1984 'Psalm 104 im Spiegel seiner Unterschrift', *TZ* 40: 1–11. Reprinted in Seybold, *Studien zur Psalmenauslegung* (Stuttgart: W. Kohlhammer,): 161–72.

1996 *Die Psalmen* (HAT 1.15; Tübingen: J. C. B. Mohr [Paul Siebeck]).

Spieckermann, Hermann

1989 *Heilsgegenwart: eine Theologie der Psalmen* (FRLANT 148; Göttingen: Vandenhoeck & Ruprecht).

Taylor, J. Glen

1993 *Yahweh and the Sun: Biblical and Archaeological Evidence for Sun Worship in Ancient Israel* (JSOTSup, 111; Sheffield: JSOT Press).

Terrien, Samuel

2003 *The Psalms: Strophic Structure and Theological Commentary* (Grand Rapids, MI: W. B. Eerdmans).

Tobin, Vincent A.

1985 'Amarna and Biblical Religion', in Sarah Israelit-Groll (ed.), *Pharaonic Egypt, the Bible and Christianity* (Jerusalem: Magnes Press): 231–77.

Uehlinger, Christoph
1990 'Leviathan und die Schiffe in Ps 104,25–26', *Bib* 71: 499–526.
Weigall, Arthur
1923 *The Life and Times of Akhnaton, Pharaoh of Egypt* (London: Thornton Butterworth, rev. edn).
Weiser, Artur
1955 *Die Psalmen* (ATD, 14–15; Göttingen: Vandenhoeck & Ruprecht, 4th edn). ET *The Psalms: A Commentary* (OTL; London: SCM, 1962).
Williams, Ronald J.
1971 'Egypt and Israel', in John R. Harris (ed.), *The Legacy of Egypt* (Oxford: Clarendon Press, 2nd edn): 257–90.
Wilson, John A.
1969 'The Hymn to the Aton', in James B. Pritchard (ed.), *Ancient Near Eastern Texts Relating to the Old Testament* (Princeton: Princeton University Press, 3rd edn): 369–71.
Zivie, Alain
1990 *Découverte à Saqqarah: le vizir oublié* (Paris: Seuil).

18

The Psalms and Sumerian Hymns

Erhard Gerstenberger

1. Presuppositions and Preliminaries

Whoever wants to study the later ebb and flow of events or traditions is well advised also to study the early sources from which they come. So, although it is important to immerse ourselves in the rich and meaningful later reception history of the Psalms, it is also essential to consider the very early beginnings of psalm-like poetry in the ancient Near East, and from that vantage point to keep looking upstream where these traditions well up and flow on throughout biblical times and beyond. It is vital that we try to capture, as much as is possible, the spirituality and literary art of those most ancient singers of chants and hymns. Traditions are modified on their long passage through history, but to some extent they also carry with them the sedimentary materials of the territories and cultures through which they have once flowed.

Sacred songs of the eastern Mediterranean, including those of the Hebrew Scriptures, all share in a common heritage of poetry, and in the enactment of that poetry, for at least three thousand years before Christ.[1] Notwithstanding regional differences, the spiritual compositions from Egypt to the Hittite lands and from the Philistine coast to the Sumerian marshes all share the fundamental general beliefs and outlook characteristic of the inhabitants of the Fertile Crescent. They all concur that the world has meaning mainly on account of the heavenly abodes of the great gods above; and that the Netherworld, meanwhile, is a dreary place where defunct beings have their own sphere of dominion. They all accept that history has a beginning in bygone primordial times and starts afresh after a universal deluge; that humans are destined to be subservient collaborators with the deities above, although often humans seem more like autonomous executors of the divine will.

---

[1] The common cultural and religious foundations of biblical (Western) and ancient Near Eastern traditions have increased in recent decades: see e.g. Sasson 1995; Hallo 1996; Hallo 2003, with Hallo's general introduction in vol. I, xxiii–xviii.

The original forms and genres of spiritual poetry in the ancient Near East were most probably used in many different types of cultic or liturgical settings, whether tied to sanctuaries and distinctive temple structures or to particular sacred spaces, such as niches in private homes and other consecrated and holy places. In marked contrast to literary production in our day, texts written in antiquity did not serve to give pleasure to the individual: rather, they were public recitations. Ever since Hermann Gunkel and Sigmund Mowinckel[2] alerted the scholarly community to this fact, exegetes have been wrestling with the implications of their observations. It is an act of violation to tear any text away from its life-setting(s) and to fail to see its involvement in a living communication between different peoples. Texts receive their meaning not only from those who receive them, be they listeners or readers, but also from the exchanges, the interplay, and the paraphernalia of their being performed in ongoing communication.

The hymns of the ancient world constitute just one particular group of genres,[3] which, typically of ancient literature, are often juxtaposed with complaints, laments, and supplications. The *Sitz im Leben* of the hymns is usually a celebration of joyful events, such as bountiful harvests, victories in battle, and escapes from serious danger. The majority of hymnic texts which have come down to us reveal that they were used in large groups, accompanied by musical instruments and/or choirs, with expert singers and players leading the performance. Thus the primary importance of this genre was for larger organized societies, whilst the petitionary prayers would quite often belong to important but smaller groups.[4] The praise of the divine world expressed in these hymns seems not only to express thanks and rejoice over blessings received, but also acts to strengthen the benevolent divine powers. I shall focus on these aspects in Sumerian literature; these hymns are the oldest of mankind, preceding those of Babylon, Assyria, and, among others, those in the Hebrew tradition.

2. Sumerian Hymns

2.1. Definition and Availability

Over the past 150 years, after cuneiform tablets were first excavated and then investigated in the large museums, literally hundreds of editions and

---

[2] Gunkel and Begrich 1933 (ET Nogalski: 1998); Mowinckel 1962; Eisen and Gerstenberger 2010.

[3] See Burkert and Stolz 1991.

[4] See Gerstenberger 2009; Zgoll 2003.

translations of Sumerian literary texts have been published.[5] To facilitate my research and to communicate my references I propose to refer to the Oxford *Electronic Text Corpus of Sumerian Literature* (*ETCSL*) which is available on the internet.[6] This grand, but lamentably unfinished, collection of more than 400 texts was the result of the collaboration by a team of specialists, mainly under the direction of the late Dr Jeremy Black, until 2006. Looking for pertinent Sumerian hymnal compositions gives rise to the question: in this oldest literature of the world, which compositions actually qualify as *hymns*? Invariably, we are caught with our western, Christian understanding of 'hymnic praise': a poetic composition addressed to the one and only God, in sheer admiration and with integrity of purpose. Sumerian praise does not fit this pattern. Just taking the Sumerian shout *zà-mí* ('praised be N.N', corresponding more or less to Hebrew *'hallelujah'*) as a formal criterion,[7] and searching through *ETCSL*, the widespread use of the formula, which frequently appears at the very end of the affirmations of praise, is astonishing. This formula yields such a vast wealth of meaning and moods. So too, the objects of praise and the contents of the hymn are full of variety. Certainly there are poems which look familiar, whether in tone, style, agents, contents, or theological affirmations. Sometimes the unnamed singer of these praises elevates not only exemplary deities, but temple buildings, royal potentates, natural forces, and even agrarian tools. Many times the singer or speaker is mentioned by name; sometimes he or she will intone a hymn in unashamed self-laudation, be it addressed to a deity or to one of the deified kings of the Ur III period or later.

The contents as well as the style of these 'praise-songs' varies greatly, perhaps not surprising in view of the large time-span covered by the texts. The oldest examples date from about 2600 BCE, whilst the youngest Sumerian hymnic poem may have been written and used around 500 BCE. This means that during more than two millennia the Sumerian language, albeit no longer spoken in daily life since *c.*1900 BCE, was actively used in cult ceremonies throughout ancient Mesopotamia—much as Latin remained the sacred language of western Christianity. The laudatory contents offer a huge diversity, including epic tales, reports of voyages, admonitions, and counsels. Liturgical rubrics are present in about half of the poems.[8] Sumerian eulogies seem to reflect a constant fluctuation in their acknowledgement of powers, witnessing to the waxing and waning of authority throughout the known world.

---

[5] English collections include Jacobsen 1997; Foster 2005.
[6] The website is: http://*ETCSL*.orinst.ox.ac.uk
[7] Some 150 occurrences in *ETCSL* in about 84 different texts: see n. 16 below.
[8] For a survey of Mesopotamian hymnic compositions see Claus Wilcke 1976–80: 539–44.

2.2. Objects of Praise

In order to give some impression of the diversity of the objects and persons being praised, I shall offer a few examples, identifying them by the letters A to D.

A. The Keš temple hymn is one of the very oldest texts already extant in a fragment from the Abu Ṣalabikh finds of the pre-Sargonic era (*c*.2500 BCE). It lauds the archaic temple and mother Nintud as well as her son Ašgi, both venerated at Keš: the temple itself is visualized in a perfect personal way.

> House Keš, platform of the Land, important fierce bull! Growing as high as the hills, embracing the heavens, growing as high as E-kur, lifting its head among the mountains! Rooted in the Abzu, verdant like the mountains! Will anyone else bring forth something as great as Keš? Will any other mother ever give birth to someone as great as its hero Ašgi? Who has ever seen anyone as great as lady Nintud? . . . . House roaring like an ox, bellowing loudly like a breed-bull! House in whose interior is the power of the land, and behind which is the life of Sumer![9]

B. The hoe is also praised, even by way of direct address, as the founder of all human culture. No other tool, it seems, had such an impact on civilization:

> The hoe makes everything prosper, the hoe makes everything flourish. The hoe is good barley, the hoe is a hunting net. The hoe is brick moulds, the hoe has made people exist. It is the hoe that is the strength of young manhood . . . It builds the right kind of house, it cultivates the right kind of fields. It is you, hoe, that extend the good agricultural land![10]

C. The most pre-eminent universal gods are praised frequently, because the responsibility for the world rests on them, and they possess divine forces which can be contacted by humans. Noteworthy is the derivation of power from An, the primordial 'father':

> Lord of all divine powers, who establishes understanding, whose intentions are unfathomable, who knows everything! Enki, of broad wisdom, august ruler of the Anuna, wise one who casts spells, who provides words, who attends to decisions, who clarifies verdicts, who dispenses advice from dawn to dusk! Enki, lord of all true words, I will praise you! Your father, An the king, the lord who caused human seed to come forth and who placed all mankind on the earth, has laid upon you the guarding of the divine powers of heaven and earth, and has elevated you to be their prince.[11]

D. A younger hymn praises the exceptional goddess of Mesopotamia, Inana. The singer's voice is more clearly articulated than in example C:

---

[9] *ETCSL* 4.80.2, lines 14–20, 28–30; cf. Black et al. 2004: 326
[10] *ETCSL* 5.5.4, lines 94–7, 99–100, cf. Black et al. 2004: 314.
[11] *ETCSL* 2.5.6.2, lines 1–7, cf. Black et al. 2004: 270–1.

I shall greet her who descends from above, her who descends from above, I shall greet the Mistress who descends from above, I shall greet the great lady of heaven, Inana! I shall greet the holy torch who fills the heavens, the light, Inana, her who shines like daylight, the great lady of heaven, Inana! I shall greet the Mistress, the most awesome lady among the Anuna gods; the respected one who fills heaven and earth with her huge brilliance; the eldest daughter of Suen, Inana! For the young lady I shall sing a song about her grandeur, about her greatness, about her exalted dignity; about her becoming visible at evening; about her filling the heaven like a holy torch; about her stance in the heavens, as noticeable by all lands, from the south to the highlands, as that of Nanna or of Utu; about the greatness of the Mistress of heaven![12]

These four examples of Sumerian hymns illustrate the peculiarities of Mesopotamian spirituality, although several conceptualizations of the divine are analogous to those found in the Hebrew Bible. All of them consider the objects of their praise as central to the exercise of benign power, a power which was completely vital for the sustenance of life.

2.3. Forms, Themes, Motifs

We find a wide range of distinctive characteristics in Sumerian hymns, due to their linguistic, cultural, and historical peculiarities; however, we also find several overlaps and analogies with Hebrew psalms. A few examples must suffice.

First, the 'praised-ones' are either addressed directly (in the second person singular) or referred to in the third person (commending the object of their exaltation to their audience). There are several statements of their glorious achievements or their individual potentialities: 'You are great . . . mighty . . . radiant . . . frightening . . .' are typical examples used in the first type of address, whilst the attributions likewise occur in third-person discourse. Narrative and epic statements are used to recount the valour, wisdom, and generosity of the one being addressed: in particular it is their deeds which are the focus of the praise, such as creation, the defeat of chaos powers, the fertilization of the fields and herds, and their administration of artisanship, knowledge, and justice.[13] Statements of glory, authority, and power are articulated: these not only reveal the positive experiences of the worshippers but also their need to be persistent in asking for the continuation of a beneficial state of affairs. 'The hoe is barley, net, mould, life of the people' (as in example B) illustrates this well: implicit here is the hope for the ongoing realization of its positive effects. Similarly, Enki is praised for guaranteeing the

---

[12] *ETCSL* 2.5.3.1, lines 1–16, cf. Black et al. 2004: 263, cf. also the hymns of Išme-Dagan, Ludwig 1990.

[13] All these are evident in examples A–D.

spiritual backbone of the world order (as in example C). Inana, meanwhile, is praised for providing light and heavenly blessings (as in example D).

Secondly, the exuberance, music, and cultic movements of the performers and participants are often referred to; this is especially evident in particular expressions in the poetry as well as in the structure of the language. The mysteries of Sumerian poetry are not thoroughly known and so not yet properly comprehensible; nevertheless, the movement of the poetry evoking a powerful idealized glorification of the one addressed can be intuited through translation—for example in the imperatives, and in the 'wish-formula'. Metaphors and epithets not only suggest but also implement authority (for example, the references to the bull roaring in A). Hymns, by way of their forms, structures, and imagery, offer the worshipper an escape, an ascent heavenwards, away from the destruction and distress which are often nevertheless implicit in the words of jubilation.[14]

Thirdly, although the powers envisioned certainly include those which are both 'political' and 'material', they nevertheless presuppose that decision-making and benevolent rule is the property of divine beings or divine assemblies. The judgements of the deities do affect the ways of the world: they call into being or perhaps recognize a pre-existent state of affairs—what Sumerian theologians call *me, nam-tar, g̃ishur, esbar, inim* ('power'; 'fate; 'plan'; 'decision'; 'word'), and so on. In this way volatile and neutral forces seem to be working side by side, although the personalized deities are the only powers to be communicated with (as in example C.). These forms of divine authority need to strengthened by praise: 'I will recite your holy song! . . . I will enumerate your divine powers for you!'[15] Hence to 'recite' and 'declare' is a performative action which realizes that which is articulated.

Fourthly, the congruence and diversification in Mesopotamian tradition is illustrated well by one specific hymnic formula. We have already noted that the expression *zà-mí*, 'lauded be', usually followed by the name or pronoun of the praised subject, has roughly the same function of the Hebrew formula *hallelujah*. Does this imply there is an archaic hymnic element common to many cultures and religions? The expression is quite frequent in several hymnic texts.[16] 'Praise be to G.N.' at the end of a composition therefore declares the poem to be a powerful song and may well have been used in liturgies of praise. There is undoubtedly an archaic ring to this formula, and whenever it occurs in the body of a given text this impression is confirmed. *Zà-mí* belongs to the oldest Sumerian hymnic vocabulary. It denotes a powerful song of praise suited for special worship occasions, which may be found within the official level of state-cult or in wider community life.

---

[14] See Gunkel 1933 (ET 2008: 22–65). These formal aspects of hymnic poetry are also analysed by Wilcke (1974) and Black (1998).

[15] *ETCSL* 4.07.2, lines 63 and 65. See also Zgoll 1997.

[16] I counted 153 cases in *ETCSL* contained in 84 different texts.

Fifthly, praise in the Sumerian tradition is an emotional liturgical activity, reverberating the gratitude of a god-fearing people. By necessity praise presumes the involvement (or even sponsorship) of humans who readily acknowledge divine unpredictability yet at the same time a mutual responsibility. The believers' participation in the governance and sustenance of the world appears very clearly in these liturgies of praise. Such liturgies in fact strengthen and confirm the divine work and therefore must be used and re-used (particularly in temple services) without cessation. King Šulgi is particularly concerned to guarantee ongoing hymn-singing; this is also in order to keep alive his own semi-divine memory.[17]

The question of comparable common roots in ancient Near Eastern hymnology has been discussed many times but there is still the need for a good deal of further investigation, particularly from new perspectives. One example must suffice as *pars pro toto*. What are we to make of Israel's peculiar custom of praising Yahweh's extraordinary historical interventions in the struggle for survival in Egypt and Canaan, and what are we to make therefore of his apparent exclusiveness in relation to Israel? (For example, Exod. 15; Deut. 32; Judg. 5; also Psalms 46; 48; 76; 78; 81; 105; 132; 135; 136.) One answer might be that some of Israel's hymns celebrate the well-known saving feats of her God in order to guarantee the well-being and ongoing formation of the confessional Yahweh-community for which they were composed and in which they were used. Sumerian hymns, likewise, glorify the extra efforts of local and highest gods to save and protect and promote their own clients, be they governments of cities, states, or empires.[18] So it could be said that Yahweh, purportedly being the universal ruler over all humankind, behaves like a particular Mesopotamian deity.

2.4. Theologies

Generative praise presumes a concept of competing deities, rather than a purely monotheistic and all-powerful exclusivist Highest God.[19] What we find not only in ancient Mesopotamian hymnic literature but also in the Old Testament are different forms of monolatry. Sumerian hymns apparently direct their praises—in certain situations—to the highest ranking divine entities. On the level of state and empire there are apparently no eulogies to the lesser local and familial deities. (Similarly, prayer petitions from the lower levels of society are actually usually directed to these higher-ranking gods.)

---

[17] See *ETCSL* 2.4.2.05 lines 240–57; see also Klein 1981.

[18] Personal and familial hymns seem to be fairly unknown in the Sumerian tradition, and likewise in the Hebrew Scriptures: see Crüsemann 1969.

[19] This is to leave aside any inherent suspicion that pure monotheism is an illusion anyhow and never really can be practised.

Among the Sumerian great deities—those who form a ruling pantheon of a city or state—the dominant ones are addressed exclusively or at the very least as one among many, in concert with their colleagues. Interestingly, the *zà-mí* formula often calls the praised one 'father' (such as with Enki, Enlil, and Nanna), while female addressees are called 'holy' (for example, Ninisina, Inana, and Damgalnuna). Sometimes, several deities of the pantheon are mentioned, but the hymnic flow as a rule focuses on the leading figure in the group, so that the one prominent God can be lauded even by his colleagues in the pantheon. There is, consequently, a 'monolatristic' tendency in such hymnic praise.[20] For example, the Anuna-Gods pray to Enki after he has pronounced a lengthy self-laudation about his achievements, as in *ETCSL* 1.1.3, lines 61–80. This does not mean that the possible dominance of one deity in a given situation indicates absolute power. On the contrary. Many divine forces, whether they are conceived in personal or impersonal terms, participate in the moulding of history, and the share which praising communities have in the interplay of potencies is considerable.

A few Old Testament psalms fit into the same scheme. They consider Yahweh as the leading or presiding highest deity, for example in Psalms 58 and 82 (see also Gen. 1.26; Deut. 32.8–9; Job 1.6–12; 2.1–7; 1 Kgs. 22.19). The implication is that the idea of a divine council with the highest God presiding over an assembly is also present in the Old Testament. Furthermore, terms such as 'justice', 'peace', 'grace' do appear as fairly autonomous powers, especially in the Psalms (cf. Ps. 85.11–12 [NRSV vv. 10–11]; 45.5 [NRSV v. 4]; 89.15 [NRSV v. 14]; etc.). Furthermore, in Psalm 29 the 'sons of God' are called upon to 'deliver glory and strength' to the supreme deity.[21]

Only much later the lofty absolutely sovereign 'God of Heaven', akin to the Persian Ahura Mazda, is unrivalled. He is always active, expressing his power in an impersonal way; but he no longer really needs edification by human praises. This might explain why Neh. 9 and Ezra 9 are prayers of penitence; they begin with a hymnic section, but soon move instead to endless confessions of sin and deep contrition. Praise becomes blocked or submerged in the overwhelming feeling of sinfulness.

Of course, the concepts of God in Sumerian hymns and Hebrew psalms are nevertheless different. The most obvious examples are, first, that the Sumerian pantheon also consists of a number of deities, male and female, who are known by their names; secondly, that they possess a number of impersonal properties; and, thirdly, they freely interact according to human

---

[20] See *ETCSL* 1.1.3, lines 81–3; *ETCSL* 4.05.1, lines 100–8.

[21] NRSV translates Psalm 29: 'Ascribe to Yahweh, heavenly beings, ascribe to Yahweh glory and strength' (v. 1). The verb, in the imperative (הָבוּ from יהב) does not simply mean a theoretical act of recognition but rather an active effort in elevating the status of the lauded one: the inference is '(Bring here) Deliver power and strength!' The heavenly beings have to submit to the sovereign deity who is adored and they hand over authority to him.

patterns and they usually come out in favour of their worshippers. However, one could argue that these are all marginal examples, even though some parts of the Hebrew Scriptures adhere to very similar patterns. The break with the Mesopotamian concepts of God occurs only under Persian rule, when Yahweh is transformed into the unimaginable, all-encompassing God who provokes deep fear and apprehension, all of which choke free and hearty praise (cf. Psalms 90; 139).

3. Conclusions

This brief foray into ancient Sumerian hymnic literature makes clear, to my mind, that the biblical hymns belong to the wide stream of ancient Near Eastern praise tradition. Hebrew psalms must not be studied in isolation from the rest of cuneiform (and other) liturgical remnants of Mesopotamian cultures and religions. Patrick Miller and others have ably demonstrated how the songs and prayers of the Old Testament can be fruitfully understood when we see them in relation to the patterns of ancient Near Eastern singing and praying.[22] Of course, as has been pointed out, the differing modes of tradition, the specific life situations, and, above all, the varying social and religious organizations in Mesopotamia and those in homeless, stateless Israel have also to be taken into consideration.

The heart of the matter, it seems to me, is our theological predisposition to perceive and evaluate hymnic texts (and here I limit my statements to this genre) from a context outside the Bible. If we begin with assumptions about exclusivity and incomparability, and see all 'heathen' expressions of praise as separate and different in their hymnody, we postulate an abyss between the Old Testament and foreign texts. But this stance is impossible, at least in the case of hymnic materials, as Gerhard von Rad stated long ago: the psalm-genres belong to the category of a 'human response' to God's action, and therefore we cannot claim any qualitative otherness when we look at the answers to divine challenges in hymnic texts in other religious cultures. In my opinion there is neither logical nor theological justification for placing biblical human responses outside universal human history, although some Old Testament scholars still follow this line of reasoning.

The ancient hymnic tradition preceding Israel's coming into existence clearly shows a pronounced interaction between the highest gods and their adherents and protégés. Yet traces of this dynamic relationship can be found also in the Hebrew Psalter. In the most recent poetic compositions of the Hebrew Bible, however (if we can trust our dating predilections), we find

[22] See Miller 1994.

examples of much less overt and dynamic praise, but rather more devout and pious submission under the all-present, simply overwhelming power of the universal Lord. He really does not need any human elevation any more. For example, the so-called didactic psalms, which I consider products of the late Old Testament faith-community of the Persian Period, dispense more or less altogether with any empowering praise of God, and express instead feelings of fear, awe and devout submission.

To place the Old Testament hymns into the perspective of a much older hymnic tradition can also help us to evaluate the later reception history of the Psalms. The pre-biblical thought-world and motivation for praise will start to appear through the later Yahwistic over-layers, and the towering figure of Israel's God will begin to be seen within the context of a more ancient Near Eastern profile. We still need to consider and study a wide range of other problems—for example, the transmission history of all these sacred songs (such as the possible influence of scribal schools), and a more informed understanding of the '*Sitz im Leben*' of hymnody and its theological impact upon conceptualizing the Divine.[23] All these issues affect Psalm research to this very day, and are particularly pertinent for this publication with its title *Jewish and Christian Approaches to the Psalms*.

Bibliography

Black, Jeremy
   1998   *Reading Sumerian Poetry* (London: Athlone Press).
Black, Jeremy, Cunningham, Graham, Robson, Eleanor, and Zólyomi, Gábor
   2004   *The Literature of Ancient Sumer* (New York: Oxford University Press).
Burkert, Walter, and Stolz, Fritz (eds.)
   1991   *Hymnen der alten Welt im Kulturvergleich* (OBO, 131; Göttingen: Vandenhoeck).
Crüsemann, Frank
   1969   *Studien zur Formgeschichte von Hymnus und Danklied in Israel* (WMANT, 32; Neukirchen-Vluyn: Neukirchener Verlag).
Eisen, Ute E., and Gerstenberger, Erhard S. (eds.)
   2010   *Hermann Gunkel Revisited. Literatur- und religionsgeschichtliche Studien* (Exegese in unserer Zeit; Münster: LIT Verlag).
Foster, Benjamin R.
   2005   *Before the Muses: An Anthology of Akkadian Literature* (Bethesda, MD: CDL Press, 3rd edn).
Gerstenberger, Erhard S.
   1980   *Der bittende Mensch: Bittritual und Klagelied des Einzelnen im Alten Testament* (WMANT, 51; Neukirchen-Vluyn: Neukirchener Verlag; repr. 2009, Eugene, Oregon: Wipf and Stock).
   1988/2001   *Psalms* (FOTL, 14 and 15; 2 vols.; Grand Rapids, MI: Eerdmans).

---

[23] See Mowinckel 1962; Burkert and Stolz 1991.

Gunkel, Hermann, and Begrich, Joachim
   1933   *Einleitung in die Psalmen. Die Gattungen der religiösen Lyrik Israels* (Göttingen: Vandenhoeck); ET James D. Nogalski, *Introduction to Psalms: The Genres of the Religious Lyric of Israel* (Atlanta: Mercer University Press, 1998).
Hallo, William W.
   1996   *Origins: The Ancient Near Eastern Background of some Modern Western Institutions* (SHCANE, 6; Leiden: Brill).
Hallo, William W. (ed.)
   2003   *The Context of Scripture*, vol. 1. *Canonical Compositions from the Biblical World*; vol. 2. *Monumental Inscriptions from the Biblical World*; vol. 3 *Archival Documents from the Biblical World* (Leiden: Brill).
Klein, Jacob
   1981   *Three Šulgi Hymns: Sumerian Royal Hymns Glorifying King Šulgi of Ur.* (Ramat-Gan: Bar-Ilani University).
Ludwig, Marie-Christine
   1990   *Untersuchungen zu den Hymnen des Išme-Dagan von Isin* (SANTAG, 2; Wiesbaden: Harrassowitz).
Meißner, Bruno, Ebeling, Erich, et al. (eds.)
   1928–   *Reallexikon der Assyriologie und Vorderasiatischen Archäologie* (RlA; Berlin: Walter de Gruyter).
Miller, Patrick D.
   1994   *They Cried to the Lord: The Form and Theology of Biblical Prayer* (Minneapolis: Fortress Press).
Mowinckel, Sigmund
   1962   *The Psalms in Israel's Worship* (2 vols.; New York: Abingdon).
Sasson, Jack M. (ed.)
   1995   *Civilizations of the Ancient Near East* (CANE; 4 vols.; New York: Scribner; repr. Peabody, MA: Hendrickson Publishers, 2000).
Wilcke, Claus
   1974   'Formale Gesichtspunkte in der sumerischen Literatur', in Stephen J. Lieberman (ed.), *Sumerological Studies in Honor of Thorkild Jacobsen* (AS, 20; Chicago: University of Chicago Press): 205–316.
   1976–80   *Reallexikon der Assyriologie*, 5 (Berlin: de Gruyter).
Zgoll, Annette
   1997   *Der Rechtsfall der En-he-du-Ana im Lied nin me šara* (AOAT, 246; Münster: Ugarit Verlag).
   2003   *Die Kunst des Betens: Form und Funktion, Theologie und Psychagogik in babylonisch-assyrischen Handerhebungsgebeten zu Ištar* (AOAT, 308; Münster: Ugarit Verlag).

19

Problems and Prospects in Psalter Studies

Frank-Lothar Hossfeld and Till Magnus Steiner[1]

1. The Psalter as a Book

A basic problem when dealing with the Psalms is the fundamental question of which context one should consider for the exegesis of these texts. The *Sitz im Leben* and the *Sitz im Buch* (setting in life and setting in the book) are two types of contextualization, although not necessarily in conflict: they can in fact be mutually supportive in answering the difficult question posed by Hermann Gunkel: 'For what purpose was the Psalter combined?'[2] Indeed, classical psalm exegesis is complemented by more recent Psalter exegesis because each has to concede that the Psalter as a book is an entity consisting of 150 individual units.[3] The Psalter, as most other biblical books, developed gradually and needs to be read in a *lectio continua* as a composed book (as is the case with the scroll of Isaiah or the Book of the Twelve).[4]

The perspective of both 'Psalter exegesis' and 'Psalms exegesis' reflects, it seems, the inherent order in which the book should be read, as can be illustrated by the history of the book's title.[5] Already by the first century BCE the title ספר תהילים ('Book of Psalms': see 4QMᵃ) is documented in the Qumran scrolls. This title appears in the New Testament as βίβλος ψαλμῶν in Lk. 20.42; Acts 1.20 (see also Lk. 24.44) in what might be called the 'Davidization' of the book, pointing to David as poet, prophet, singer and

---

[1] The authors are most grateful to Prof. W. Dennis Tucker, Jr., for his vital help in translating this article into English.

[2] Gunkel and Begrich 1998: 339.

[3] 'It is apparent that with an exegesis of the Psalms a separate profile should reflect both the individual psalms as well as their inclusion in the immediate and wider context of the book. The dichotomy of either individual songs or a composite book is a false one, and is not justified by recourse to the text of the psalms' (translation of Zenger 1998: 35).

[4] See Leuenberger 2004: 8–40.

[5] F. Hartenstein correctly asks how in Psalter exegesis one can really ascertain ancient ways of reading, but he remains consistently open to this possibility: 'It [research] cannot reconstruct history, strictly speaking, but it can suggest reasons for assuming the existence of such ways of reading and can open up the possibility of such an approach' (translation of Hartenstein 2010: 232).

player of the harp. ספר seems primarily to indicate, in a technical sense, a scroll of psalms, in which a completed length of 150 psalms is fixed (the later introduction of Ps. 151 in the Septuagint illustrating this further). Codex A, with its superscription ψαλτήριον for the book of Psalms, understands it as the one (singular) work of David, an entity not so much referring to hymn tunes as to the words of the psalms. So in Codex A the term ψαλτήριον stands for a fixed unity of 150.[6] The development of the book's title from the emphasis in Hebrew on the *variety* of psalms in the term ספר תהילים to an emphasis on the *unity* of these 150 psalms in the use of ψαλτήριον indicates the importance of the unified order of the book of Psalms in its early reception history. St Jerome expressed this sentiment in the metaphor of the Psalter as *domus magna*—a great house.

2. The Building Technique: The Architectural Elements of the Psalter

The architecture of this 'great house', in its final form, is complex and cannot be restricted to viewing it in just one dimension: we encounter several different corridors and floors, and each offers infinite opportunities for the reception and delivery of different messages. A fundamental point, however, is that we need to recognize the basic features of the architecture: for example, the continuation of the end of one psalm into the beginning of the following psalm (e.g. Ps. 7.18 → Ps. 8.2,10 → Ps. 9.2–3; Ps. 148.14 → Ps. 149.1); a literal resumption, but with a change of meaning (e.g. Ps. 134.1–2 → Ps. 135.1–3); the creation of twin psalms, giving a mutual interpretation (e.g. Pss. 105 and 106; Pss. 111 and 112); 'cluster compositions', each with editorial concatenations (e.g. Pss. 3–7; Pss. 25–28); suggestions of groups of psalms through various compositional structures (e.g. Ps. 19 in Pss. 15–24; Ps. 29 in Pss. 25–34); indications of psalm groupings and collections, through the use of superscriptions (Davidic, Asaphite, Korahite, and Psalms of Ascent); indications of other groups, through the use of 'hallelujah' or 'hodu' formulas (Pss. 104–5; 111–13; 115–16; 146–50; also Pss. 105–7); and, finally, collections by theme or motif (for example the 'Yahweh as King' Psalms 93–100).[7] In many cases one psalm extends beyond itself into another—so that, in the house, different floors, corridors, and stairways appear, connecting to the different rooms in unexpected ways. The aim of 'Psalm and Psalter exegesis' must therefore be the exploration and investigation of the architecture and construction of this *domus magna*, always working with the assumption that the structure of the 150 psalms sustains the many messages of psalm groupings, collections, and the Psalter as a whole. This in turn has a reciprocal

---

[6] See Bader 1996: 9–10   [7] See Zenger 2010a: 31–43.

effect on our understanding of each psalm. The consequence is that 'Psalm exegesis' and 'Psalter exegesis' is an exploration and investigation not only of the theology but also of the *theologies* of the Psalter: this clearly entails an enquiry into more than just the theology of each psalm.

Since the doctoral dissertation of G. H. Wilson, published in 1985, it has become clear in many monographs and articles that a multitude of structural markers point the reader to an intentional theological macro-structure: 'The Psalter exhibits a complex literary structure that not only determines its shape but also provides the reader with interpretative clues for reading both the whole and its parts.'[8] The structure of the Psalter offers not only the possibility of reading the psalms as an entire collection of expressions of belief, but also the opportunity of taking seriously the literary character and intrinsic value of the structure of the smaller psalm groupings and collections within the Psalter as a whole. This acknowledgement of the structure (or structures) of the Psalter leads to an understanding of its purposeful development and from this to an appreciation of the theological message of the text itself.

Since the time of the church fathers a number of theological appraisals of the psalms have been written, but a theology dependent upon the synchronic final form and the diachronic growth is still nevertheless a *desideratum*.[9] It is interesting that Hermann Gunkel, for example, was not able to appreciate fully the theological dimension of the Psalter because his historical perspective limited his work to a phenomenological analysis of the 'lyrics' of ancient Israel. In the field of Old Testament studies—and ultimately affecting psalm studies—Gerhard von Rad played a seminal role in his rediscovery of the 'Theology of the Hebrew Bible': his work focused on two main literary deposits, one being the theology of the historical traditions, and the other, the theology of the prophetic traditions. The psalms are seen as a part of the historical traditions, in that they are a contextualized answer of the people of Israel to the actions of God:

> Not only did she [Israel] repeatedly take up her pen to recall these acts of Yahweh to her mind in historical documents, but she also addressed Yahweh in a wholly personal way. She offered praise to him, and asked him questions, and complained to him because of all her sufferings, for Yahweh had not chosen his people as a mere dumb object of his will in history, but for converse with him. This answer of Israel's, which we find for the most part from the Psalter, is theologically a subject in itself.[10]

[8] Wilson 1992: 129

[9] See Hossfeld 1999: 691. Discussions include different approaches for systematizing the theology of Psalms (see also Seybold 1997: 622) and different themes which run throughout the Psalter: for example, the dynamics from lament to praise, a royal-messianic reading, the theology of the poor, the temple theology and the role of wisdom in the psalms (see also Hartenstein and Janowski 2011: 492–4, 495–7).

[10] von Rad 1969 (6th edn): 366; ET 1962: 355.

Accordingly, the theology of the psalms starts as an anthropology of the psalms, showing, first, how salvation history was received by Israel and, secondly, how Israel understood herself before God. But the psalms are not the only response of Israel to God. The Psalms, Job, Proverbs, Wisdom, Sirach, and Ecclesiastes all witness to Israel's answer, and here the response is more obviously anthropological. It was von Rad's student, Hans-Joachim Kraus, who focused primarily on the book of Psalms in this way: his third volume, following his two-volume commentary, was entitled in the English translation *Theology of the Psalms*. Here he defined more precisely what was understood by the term *Antwort Israels* ('Israel's answer'). First, he argued that this is not the response of a dialogue partner, one who is on a par with God.[11] Secondly, as von Rad had also stressed, he recognized that a theology of the psalms can never be a pure historical 'science', but that the theologian must learn 'to interrogate each document, much more closely than has been done hitherto, as to its specific kerygmatic intention'.[12] In the same way, Kraus argued that the historical beliefs of the actual suppliants are not the object of a theology of the Psalms, but that they are testimonies, pointing us to what God is like—that is, they serve a kerygmatic purpose.[13] Thirdly, the psalms reflect a distinctive subject matter, given that they originate within the Temple of Jerusalem, the 'centre of the life of the Old Testament people of God'.[14] Kraus nevertheless recognizes a methodological problem inherent in this approach. He notes the tension between literary criticism and historical form-criticism on the one hand, but also 'an order of topics, which does violence to the subject matter' on the other.[15]

An ongoing concern for a genuine theology of the psalms, continuing and developing the studies of von Rad, is to be found in the canonical exegesis of the psalms in the work of Brevard Childs. This impulse is still a major influence in American pleas for a theology of the psalms (for example Patrick Miller, Clinton McCann, Walter Brueggeman, and, from Germany, Erhard Gerstenberger). In these discussions of the theology of the book of Psalms Hermann Spieckermann occupies a unique place: his post-doctoral thesis *Heilsgegenwart* ('Saving Presence') is a reconstruction of the original theology of the various psalms by way of reference to the Temple, using, however, a literary and redactional critique.[16]

To develop the theology of the Psalter based upon an understanding of its structure entails using the structure as an objective criterion which then controls the exegetical process. This, however, gives rise to the problem of the difficult relationship between diachronic and synchronic approaches. The

---

[11] See Kraus 1979 (2nd edn): 10; ET 1986: 12.
[12] See von Rad 1969 (6th edn): 118; ET 1962: 105–6.
[13] Kraus 1979 (2nd edn): 11; ET 1986: 13.
[14] Ibid. 10; ET: 12.   [15] Ibid. 13; ET: 14.   [16] See Spieckermann 1989.

Psalter does not have only one structure: it comprises many different structural levels, as we have seen already in the metaphor of the Psalter as a *domus magna.*

3. An Initial Walk through the Psalter

Whoever enters the Psalter through its main portal, Psalms 1–2, will find, when arriving at Ps. 3.1, a superscription referring to the subsequent psalm grouping, connecting Psalms 3–41 with the figure of David. Altogether there are five so-called Davidic Psalters in the whole Psalter (Psalms 3–41; 51–72; 101–3; 108–10; 138–45). Other psalms also assigned to David are, however, found outside these collections. Particularly notable is Psalm 86 (see also, however, Pss. 122.1; 124.1; 131.1; 133.1). Psalm 86 interrupts the second Korahite Psalter (Pss. 84–5; 87–8; 89), which is organized in a similar way to the first Korahite Psalter.[17] Not only does the superscription of Psalm 86 refer to David but also the frequent use of the self-designation עבד (vv. 2, 4, 16) connects this psalm especially with the final psalms in the groupings of the first two Davidic Psalters (Pss. 35–41 and 69–71).[18] Psalm 86 is a summary of the Davidic psalms, which, according to the colophon in Ps. 72.20 (כלו תפלות דוד בן־ישי), have already ended—assuming therefore a linear reading of the book of Psalms. This colophon is the only explicit 'meta-textual' structural marker, and more importantly, from an editorial perspective, as it is read it contradicts Psalm 86, with its superscription תפילה לדוד. Franz Delitzsch also addressed this point:

> No one taking a survey of the whole Psalter, with the many Psalms of David that follow beyond Ps. lxxii, could accidentally have placed this key-stone here. If, however, it is more ancient than the doxological division into five books, it is a significant indication in relation to the history of the rise of the collection.[19]

Christoph Rösel offers a convincing answer to this, comparing this superscription with Job 31.40, which serves as a delimitation of the speeches of Job in relation to the secondary speeches of Elihu, inserted by the redactor:

> The final note in each case was completed by the redactors who added the additional texts. Ps. 72.20 is therefore likely to be due to the one redactor who added the Psalms of Asaph. The author of Ps. 72.20 overlooked not only the preceding Psalms of David, but also the following Psalms of Asaph. The beginning of the Psalms of Korah in Psalm 84 belongs, however, to a later stage

---

[17] See Otto 1989: 1015.   [18] See Süssenbach 2005: 379.
[19] Delitzsch 1883 (4th edn): 520; ET 1877: 307

of redaction. This shows that the Elohistic redaction presupposes on the one hand the amalgamation of the David and Asaph psalms, and, on the other, it demonstrates that the redaction ends at Psalm 83.[20]

This explanation does not settle the question about the final relation between Pss. 72.20 and 86.1.[21] However, it does allow the exegete who is searching for the composition of the Psalter to account first for the *diachronic* process when assessing the different stages of growth of the Psalter.

4. A Second Walk through the Psalter

Again we enter the Psalter through its main entrance, Psalms 1–2, and starting with Psalm 3 we read the first Davidic Psalter, which forms the first book of Psalms in combination with Psalms 1 and 2. The doxology in Ps. 41.14, which closes the first book of the psalms, presages the uneven division of the Psalter into five books by other such doxologies (Pss. 1–2; 3–41; 42–72; 73–89; 90–106; 107–50).[22]

The doxologies hint at an overall hermeneutic of the Psalter: in the five different books the reader walks past 'historically prominent points in the history of Israel and as they merge together there then emerges the development of Israel's history in outline form'.[23] Reading the Psalter in a *lectio continua* from the Torah (Ps. 1) to the final praise (the *Hallel* in Pss. 146–50), the reader, or praying person, proceeds through the different stages of the history of Israel: first, the establishing of the Davidic kingship under David (Pss. 2; 3–41; 42–72); then onwards through the period of decline up to the catastrophe in 587 BCE (Pss. 73–89); then on again to the time of the exile (Psalms 90–106); and so, finally, arriving at the restoration period (Pss. 107–50), 'which returns in another form to what at one time had been the case with Psalms 3–72 and had been lost within Psalms 73–106'.[24]

Moving on from the colophon at Ps. 72.20, the doxologies are the only structural markers that appear throughout the Psalter. They divide the Psalter by their recurrence and structurally they offer a particular theology of history.

---

[20] Translation of Rösel 1999: 53. Rösel's thesis, that the colophon originally marked the end of the second Davidic Psalter, and that, because of the colophon, the first Davidic Psalter has been added in front of the second Davidic Psalter, prior to the creation of the Elohistic Psalter, is difficult to accept: see Hossfeld 2010: 200–13.

[21] This still does not answer the question why a later redactor did not erase the colophon. A hypothesis could be that, despite the tension Ps. 86.1 produces in a linear reading of the Psalter, the colophon was nevertheless preserved because it reflects a historic-theological perspective about the Davidic dynasty.

[22] It is striking that the first three books of the Psalter can be read royally/messianically on account of the royal psalms 41, 72, and 89, while the fourth and fifth books stress the theocentric perspective on the kingship of Yahweh.

[23] Translation of Kratz 1996: 21.   [24] Translation of Kratz 1996: 23.

However, this theology is not congruent with the fivefold division: the first and second books of the Psalter together 'describe' the reign of David in the unified kingdom of Israel, but the doxology in Ps. 41.34, which ends the first Davidic Psalter (dominated by individual laments), does not mark an important stage in the history of Israel, as the others do. Psalm 72 registers the universal kingship of the Davidic line and Solomon's inheritance of the kingdom; Psalm 89 registers the decline of this kingship and an uncertainty about the future of the covenant with David; Psalm 106 records a prayer of repentance from the exile, whilst Psalms 107–150 speak of the Restoration.[25] Perhaps it needs to be recognised that the doxologies do not appear to have been written down by only one redactor: the use of אלוהים as a proper name in addition to יהוה in Ps. 72.18–19 suggests that this doxology already existed before the Elohistic redaction, which involved Psalms 42–83 (cf. Pss. 66.20; 68.36).[26] Further diachronic evidence is the conformity of Pss. 41.14; 72.18–19; 89.53 with each other in their amen formula (or 'Amenbekräftigungsformel': אמן ואמן), while Ps. 106.48 has a different formulation.

Structurally it is clear that, after the end of the first and second books of the Psalter, a new psalm collection begins each time (Ps. 42—Korah; Ps. 73—Asaph); the fourth doxology, however, which marks the end of the fourth book of the Psalter, actually interrupts the 'hodu-triad' in Psalms 105–107. The doxologies nevertheless seem to stand in a diachronic relationship to one another: this can best be seen in the importance of Psalm 89 at the end of the third book of the Psalter, creating the main division of the Psalter.

Two important observations arise from this. First, Psalm 90 is the first time when a new superscription does not mark out a new collection of Davidic, Asaph, or Korahite psalms. Psalm 90 is the only psalm connected to Moses in its superscription.[27] The second concerns Psalm 89 itself. Often this psalm has been recognized as the main caesura in the Psalter, a turning point from lament to praise.[28] There is a considerable evidence to support this. After Psalm 89 the number of psalms without a superscription increases; there are no further psalms of the Asaphites or Korahites after Psalm 89; there are no

---

[25] *Contra* Kratz 1996: 1.

[26] Barbiero (2008: 87) writes about this colophon as follows: 'Clearly, v. 20 accommodates Psalm 72 within the second Davidic psaltery, Psalms 51–72. In a more immediate sense, however, it refers to Ps. 72 itself, identifying it as "prayers by David" for his son Solomon.' However, the application of the colophon cannot be limited only to Psalm 72. That is indicated by the specific Elohistic addition of the 'baruk/blessing formula' in the doxology which is different from Pss. 41.14 and 106.48, an addition which is very much in keeping with the intention of the Elohistic redaction.

[27] This superscription creates a reference to the Exodus and the Torah, extending back before the time of David. It is unclear how far the superscription of Psalm 90 reaches, and whether it covers Psalms 90–92 or even the whole fourth book of the Psalter (see, for example, the mentioning of Moses in Pss. 105 and 106).

[28] E.g. Hossfeld 2001.

melodic instructions after Psalm 89; the additional superscription למנצח
reoccurs after Psalm 89 only in Psalms 109; 139; 140; סלה as markers in the
psalms can be found after Psalm 89 only in Pss. 140.4, 6, 9; 143.6. After Psalm
89, free-standing psalms are found for the first time (Psalms 119 and 137);
and a new convention also appears whereby psalms are grouped by the use
of the '*hodu*-formula' in both super- and subscriptions (see Pss. 105.1; 106.1;
107.1; 118.1, 29; 136.1, 26). Furthermore, the fourth and fifth books of the
Psalter are characterized by their 'hallelujah-calls'—a feature which is absent
in the first three books of the Psalter (see Pss. 104–6; 111–13; 115–17; 135;
146–50).

These observations lead to the discovery that Psalms 1–89 is a relatively
closed corpus (sometimes called the Messianic Psalter, Psalms 2–89), while
Psalms 90–150 make up a more diverse collection. This result can be
explained through the process of what might be termed 'diachrony'.

5. One Last Short Stroll

If one is determined to follow the diachronic approach, even the easily
structured section of Psalms 1–89 reveals different structural levels (for
example, the double transmissions of Psalms 14 and 53; Pss. 40.14–18 and 70;
Pss. 57.8–12 + 60.7–14 found later in Psalm 108). A purely synchronic
approach cannot explain the structural composition of the Elohistic Psalter
(Pss. 42–83) for it needs to be read on several different structural levels: first,
as a part of the Messianic Psalter (Pss. 2–89); secondly, as a bridge between
the second and third books of the Psalter (Pss. 42–72 and 73–89); and thirdly,
as an enclosure to the second Davidic Psalter (Pss. 51–72).[29]

6. Synchronic and/or Diachronic?

These short walks through the Psalter should have made one point clear:
like a house, the Psalter needs to be understood as a three-dimensional construction. Such an edifice can certainly be outlined in a two-dimensional way,
but to be able to understand the building we need to venture to walk through
and explore the extent of its corridors and rooms. The Psalter has had a
complex growth, resulting in different structural layers which have produced

---

[29] This in turn raises the question about the origin in the book in its earliest beginnings
of diachronic growth. It is likely that the first Davidic Psalter marked the very beginning: see
Hossfeld 2010.

different macro-texts which create different opportunities for its reception.[30] To learn more about these different stages of construction is of fundamental importance: but this does not mean that working out how the Psalter arose also means that one has established its message.[31]

But not to pay attention to the diachronic process means that not only on the level of the psalm but also (and even more) on the level of the Psalter, the text would be without history—a timeless, autonomous, self-sufficient entity. The text would become disconnected from its origin in the historical and spiritual reality of the authors, redactors, and first recipients, whose dialogues were fundamental in forming the Psalter.[32]

As was seen when we took those short walks through the Psalter, a synchronic exploration of the structure of the Psalter leads necessarily into a diachronic exploration.[33] The diachronic and synchronic approaches are two parameters, which in a correlative way lead to the understanding of the growth of the final message(s) of the Psalter and of the final message itself. As Friedhelm Hartenstein convincingly argues:

> A methodological control will most likely work if it constantly combines the compositional reading of the Psalter with the question of its formation. The necessary interconnection of composition criticism and redaction criticism

---

[30] Not only the Psalter, and not only each individual psalm, but also the psalm groupings and the larger collections create different structural levels and are all 'texts' in their way they construct distinctive units.

[31] 'Even when the formation is reconstructed, the message of the final form is not resolved. Conversely, once the message is understood synchronically, the question of the formation of the Psalter is not a superfluous one' (translation of Steinberg 2006: 268).

[32] A disconnection of the text from the world of its origin 'may address the syntactical level. Nevertheless the deep structural semantic references to reality and the pragmatic function of the text cannot be delivered as if a timeless understanding might be possible; a synchronic analysis of the text simply opens up in historical context' (translation of Leuenberger 2004: 22 ff.). Even more, every single psalm is an expression by a specific person, at a specific time, at a specific place, expressed to God and a specific community of faith and written down. Those single voices were placed in order, placed in a 'narrative', and put in dialogue with one another. The Psalms are human answers in dialogue with God and a community of faith. They need to be taken seriously as speeches in and through time. The Psalter is the space in which those speeches have been brought into dialogue. Whoever seeks to understand this dialogue needs, first of all, to listen to the conversations, all of which are recognizable in the structure of the Psalter. To use another metaphor, the message of the Psalter is a symphony of different voices according to a special melody: and the reader, or the praying person, is directly drawn into this dialogue, this symphony. In short, the message of the Psalter is in its internal discourse.

[33] J. Steinberg criticized diachronic research into the structure and message of the Psalter as follows: 'Hossfeld and Zenger argue for the structure of the Psalter from small to large. But on the contrary, in order to understand the final form, the structure is better comprehended from the top down, beginning especially with the redaction and clear fivefold structure of the Psalter' (translation of Steinberg 2006: 268). Yet the fivefold division of the Psalter is just one of the many possible ways of reading the Psalter in its structural perspective: to make this one structural organization of the Psalter absolute means to silence and stifle everything else. Both the Psalter as a whole and the individual psalms require an exegesis that respects their character as a unit and as singular texts within this unit.

creates a conscious loop. The previous literary and tradition-historical knowledge acquired from psalm research can serve as a starting point and a counterbalance for the interpretation of the Psalter as well as of its collections of shorter texts.[34]

Because the text of the Psalter is a product of redactions and compositions, the diachronic perspective enlightens a synchronic understanding. But obviously caution and care are needed: the diachronic approach runs the risk of directing our understanding of the final form of the text based only on the diachronic hypotheses.[35] Literary criticism and redaction criticism must be used alongside a synchronic reading, using the latter reading as a safeguard to prevent the atomization of the text. This means that the structure of the Psalter must be emphasized and recognized, from both the top down and the bottom up. The diachronic approach remains necessary because it does not flatten out the text. To understand the composition/structure of the Psalter, which is the goal of Psalter exegesis, deductive and inductive perspectives must serve reciprocally as parameters.[36]

7. Prospects: A Case Study

A diachronic and synchronic Psalter exegesis necessarily starts with the exegesis of a single psalm as the fundamental unit of the Psalter; it then puts that psalm in the context of its psalm grouping, its collection, its book within the Psalter and finally in the Psalter as a whole. To reach the long-term goal of a theology of the Psalter—one that also presents the different theologies of the Psalter as found in its structure—it is necessary to disentangle the different threads, and these necessarily begin with an individual psalm. One of the threads which runs throughout the whole book of the Psalter (in addition to the dynamics from lament to praise, the 'Davidization' of the Psalter, and the theology of the poor) is the theme of 'Zion'. The following discussion serves as a working example of our search for a theology of the Psalter.

There are a number of psalms whose main theme is the theology of Zion as a city, mountain, or temple. Form-critically, Gunkel called these psalms 'Zion Songs', because, among other reasons, their focus was on Zion (Pss. 46; 48; 76; 84; 87; 122).[37] Criticisms of this proposed *Gattung* (or form) have been manifold. Against the older theory, that it is possible to reconstruct a pure

---

[34] Translation of Hartenstein 2010: 235.   [35] See Blum 2005: 11–40.

[36] Calling the diachronic method a 'critical parameter' also requires acknowledging the imperfections of its previous results: correcting the lessons learnt from diachronic study is essential: see Süssenbach 2005: 40; Körting 2006: 5, 145.

[37] See Gunkel and Begrich 1985 (4th edn): 80–2; ET 1998: 55–7.

original core theology of Zion out of the pre-exilic Psalms 46, 48, and 76,[38] Corinna Körting showed the plurality of concepts embracing the theme of Zion in the psalms.[39] The focus of her monograph is the exegesis of the individual psalm and the role Zion plays in it, and so she only partly addresses the comparative chronology related to the historical development of theological ideas in the psalms. The next step required is a diachronic analysis of her findings with a view to understanding the development and final structure of the Psalter. In the following discussion, Psalms 46 and 48 will be seen as a vital case study for this line of investigation, because in these two psalms is a representation of two different pre-exilic theologies of the 'City of God'.[40]

7.1. The Question of the Dates of Psalm 46 and Psalm 48

In her monograph Corinna Körting approaches the question of dating and chronology of the two psalms very carefully. She advocates a pre-exilic dating for Psalm 48, while she favours Psalm 46 as being dated after the exile.[41] She claims that Psalm 48 can be dated with relative certainty in the pre-exilic era for the following reasons: first, the royal appellation מלך רב which is derived from Akkadian and often found in relation to Sennacherib;[42] secondly, the reception and incorporation of the theology of the city of God in Lam. 2.15; 4.12;[43] thirdly, vv. 5–7, which should be read with its past tenses as a historical reminiscence of 701 BCE;[44] and fourthly, the presumption of statehood in vv. 13–14.[45]

In the case of Psalm 46 Körting assumes a post-exilic dating.[46] She argues

---

[38] E.g. Rohland 1956; Ollenburger 1987.

[39] Körting detached the question about Zion from the *Gattung* 'Zion Song' and investigated the theme 'Zion' throughout the Psalter. This new perspective led her to offer at least two critical conclusions: first, that the theme 'Zion' is 'a magnet of theological conceptions' and, secondly, it is the 'centre of progressive theological formation' (translation of Körting 2006: 221–5).

[40] On the relative chronology of these two psalms, Körting's doctoral supervisor, Hermann Spieckermann, has written: 'One can say that Psalm 48 concludes the reflection, which Psalm 46, with its line of thought, initiates' (translation of Spieckermann 1992: 23). Körting has followed his observations: 'The further development of the idea of the city of God, which bears the features of the Temple, shows in the shift of emphasis from the city of God to the praise of God that Psalm 46 is younger than Psalm 48' (translation of Körting 2006: 186). The difference between Spieckermann and Körting, especially in the question of dating, will be highlighted in the following section.

[41] See Körting 2006: 177–86.

[42] See Spieckermann 1992: 21; also Hartenstein 2011: 144.

[43] See Albrektson 1963: 224; also Berges 2002: 252 ff.

[44] For the historical dating of *Gottesschrecken* (terror of God) to Assyrian times in vv. 5–7 see Weippert 1997: 85ff.

[45] See Scharbert 1993: 304.

[46] Körting follows the argumentation of Hossfeld and Zenger (1993: 285) and understands v. 10 as a secondary element of the psalm.

this for the following reasons: 'The texts seek to combine the universality of the claims about the power of God among the peoples with the protection of the God of Jacob for his people . . . This awareness of a flaw [of Israel] in conjunction with the universal saving will of God is not possible until the post-exilic period'.[47] Verse 11 does not express a universal will of salvation for the entire world, but assigns to Yahweh the typical attributes of a Divine king (e.g. Pss. 92.3; 93.4; 99.2), emphasizing his fiefdom and world rule and superiority over the other nations.[48]

However, a pre-exilic date for Psalm 46 is also likely. This can be based on the following evidence. First, in extra-biblical literature, the centring of the world on the city of God, with its four rivers watering the earth, indicates, according to Hartenstein, one of the motifs of the rule of Sennacherib.[49]

Secondly, within the Hebrew Bible, the motif of chaos waters (vv. 3–4) is connected closely with pre-exilic literature such as Psalm 93. The motif of *Völkerkampf* (battle of the nations) in vv. 6–7 has an affinity with the pre-exilic description of the threat to Jerusalem in Isa. 17.12–14. Those two motifs, as well as the description of the voice of Yahweh as a theophanic instrument (v. 7), are all used in pre-exilic descriptions of theophanies (for example in Pss. 18.4–20; 29.1–10; and 68.8–32).[50]

Thirdly, in Ps. 46.7 the tense change (in cola A) into a historicizing perspective, describing the experience of the community threatened by the attack of enemy nations, seems to be referring to the events of 701 BCE.[51] The intention of this verse is to show the protection that is guaranteed for Jerusalem by God—a presumption that can be said and prayed after 587 BCE only with a 'nevertheless'. Verse 7 clearly has its origin in a way of thinking before the Babylonian exile.[52]

The specific arguments here—the inclusion of Assyrian propaganda and the theme of the deliverance of Jerusalem—suggest that both psalms point to the pre-exilic period.[53] That both psalms seem to be written in the same period may also be argued from their parallel forms, their use of lexemes, and their theological background. For example, numerous ancient lexemes can be found in both psalms: עיר אלוהים in Ps. 46.5 and Ps 48.2, 9; the mention of a holy (קדש) place/space in Pss. 46.5 and 48.3; יהוה צבאות in Pss. 46.8,

---

[47] Translation of Körting 2006: 186. See also Zapff 1998: 90–1.

[48] As with the secondary v. 10, a universal will of salvation may be argued.

[49] Translation from Hartenstein 2011: 143.

[50] So Hossfeld, 2011, who also argues that in Ps. 68.14 the motif of קול + נתן seems to be secondary.

[51] The lexeme המה connects this verse with Yahweh, and his *creatio continua* against the chaos in vv. 3–4, along the lines of a threat in the past which has come from the nations. While the threat is narrated in a historical perspective, the result of theophanic action of God is told in a continuous present form.

[52] See Hossfeld and Zenger 1993: 287.

[53] See Hartenstein 2011: 135–47.

12 and 48.9; God as מִשְׂגָּב in Pss. 46.8, 12 and Pss. 48.4, and as אֶרֶץ in Pss.
46.3, 7, 9, 10, 11 and 48.3, 11; and the destruction (שָׁבַר) of military equip-
ment in Pss. 46.10 and 48.8.[54] Moreover, as Erich Zenger has pointed out,
similar motifs occur in each psalm: for example, *Völkerkampf* (battle of the
nations) in Pss. 46.7a and 48.5; *Gottesschrecken* (terror of God) in Pss. 46.7b
and 48.6–7; the disarming of the nations in Pss. 46.10 and 48.8; Yahweh as
king of the nations and the whole world in Pss. 46.11b and 48.3; and the
acknowledgement of the greatness of God in Pss. 46.11 and 48.14.[55]

7.2. Similarities and Differences between Psalm 46 and Psalm 48

Both psalms combine a theology of the city of God with the protection of the
city by God: this is their main theme (Pss. 46.2, 6, 8, 12; 48.7, 12, 15). The
basic elements of this theology are the act of seeing (Pss. 46.9; 48.6, 9, 13f.)
the rescuing theophanic action of God (Pss. 46.7; 48.7) against the nations
(Pss. 46.7; 48.5–7). In contrast to Psalm 46, Psalm 48 describes the well-
fortified city (Ps. 48.13f.), but this is radically connected to the presence and
action of God (Ps. 48.15), as in Ps. 46.6. In both psalms the greatness of the
city cannot be seen separately from the greatness of God: this is made clear by
the close association of God with the city, whereby the use of מִשְׂגָּב serves as
a real metaphor for God (Ps. 46.8, 12; Ps. 48.4).[56]

The main differences can be found in the concept of God and the description of the city of God. Psalm 48 understands God as a secular, great universal
king (מֶלֶךְ רַב), who nevertheless reveals himself in the palaces and whose
power can be seen in the buildings of the city.[57] Hence the city of God is a
'*Realsymbol*' of God himself. Although Psalm 46 does not use explicit royal
attributes for God, v. 11 speaks about the majesty (רוּם) of God (cf. Ps. 99.2, 5,
9) to describe the heavenly Divine king. Furthermore in Psalm 46 the city is
still represented as a literal 'horizontal' part of the world, in that it represents
a paradisiacal counter-picture to the chaotic world:

> The conceptualized theology of Jerusalem in Ps. 46.2–8 is based on the symbol of
> a hub. In the middle (קֶרֶב) of the city of God, the holy habitation of the Most
> High (v. 5), Yahweh is present as the God who delivers Zion, while on the
> periphery, the natural and historical representations of chaos rage and clamour.
> (vv. 3f., 7), only to be suppressed by the sovereign God-king.[58]

In this worldview, the city of God is described in its paradisiacal quality
through its connection with the subdued primordial ocean (נָהָר—v. 5; cf.

---

[54] Pss. 46.10 and 48.8 seem to belong to the same secondary redaction.
[55] See Hossfeld and Zenger 1993: 284.   [56] *Contra* Körting 2006: 184.
[57] See Spieckermann 1992: 26.   [58] Translation of Janowski 2002: 45–6.

Gen. 2.10, 14). This points to the close connection of water with both creation and the temple (see also the bronze sea in the temple as in Ezek. 47).[59] Psalm 48 in contrast does not use metaphors of paradise to describe the city, but uses everyday metaphors such as the ordinary human sense of seeing. Zion is beautiful in elevation (v. 3a), the power of God can be seen in the buildings of the city (v. 13 f.); the use of the term קריאת especially stresses the city as the seat of God's royal power (v. 3). Because of those findings, Othmar Keel speaks about a 'spiritualization' which distinguishes Psalm 46 from Psalm 48.[60] However, the difference between the two psalms is at a more profound level, one which is particularly evident in the absence of the term 'Zion' in Psalm 46. Corinna Körting believes that this omission marks a shift in the theology 'from praise of the city of God to the praise of God', with a focus on God alone as protector, while the city in Psalm 48 is 'the only place where the divine protection is made manifest'.[61] However, against this, it is clear that Psalm 46, in its paradisiacal portrayal of Jerusalem (v. 5) and its assurance of its inviolability (v. 6), does not actually detach God from the city of God, as though the city were simply the place that manifested his power. Conversely Psalm 48 provides a vivid description of the city of God—yet not as an end in itself, but for the praise of God (v. 15).

It is indeed surprising that Psalm 46, as a classic 'Zion Song', does not name Zion. This observation guides the exegete to Psalm 68, which also deals with the theme 'Zion' without actually mentioning Zion. Special attention should be paid to the strophe in vv. 29–32, which clearly calls for a strict separation of the secular city of Jerusalem from the Holy Temple (v. 30). The temple is differentiated directly from the city through the use of the preposition על.[62] According to the priestly principle of the separation of the holy from the profane, the temple is separated clearly from Jerusalem (see also Ps. 122).[63] In Ezekiel, the temple is its main theme, but 'Zion' is not referred to (for example in the temple vision in Ezek. 40–8).[64] Psalm 48, by contrast, does not reveal such a strict separation, as is made clear by v. 4: the city itself carries

---

[59] See Keel 2007: 738.   [60] See Keel, ibid.   [61] Translation of Körting 2006: 185.

[62] 'The mention of Jerusalem serves to give substance to the prayer and orientate the one who prays. But even here the tangible nearness of God is withdrawn again with the preposition על. Unlike Zion, which is the connection between the earthly temple and the heavenly sanctuary, Jerusalem is presented as detached from that image. Kings can bring gifts to draw closer to God, but they cannot reach him. Without wishing to question the statement that the earthly and heavenly sanctuary are not separate from one another, a change of emphasis concerning the earthly site is made clear in what is said in v. 30. The throne of God is in the highest heavens, governing the world' (translation of Körting 2006: 152–3).

[63] Within the Psalms of Ascent (Pss. 120–34), the references to Zion are greater in this collection than in the rest of the Psalter. In fact, Psalm 122 is the only psalm which mentions Jerusalem without naming Zion. (In Pss. 125.1–2; 128.5; 135.21; 137.1, 3, 5–7 there is a tendency to create parallels between Zion and Jerusalem.)

[64] See Konkel 2001: 349–57.

the idea of being the place of the revelation of God and is called in this respect Zion. The city is in every way an accessible holy area because of its association with the holy mountain (Zion). Verse 2 uses the temple terminology הר קדשו (cf. Pss. 3.5; 43.3; 99.9)[65] and expands it by equating this with the Canaanite mountain of the gods, Zaphon, and identifying this motif with the whole city (קריאת).[66]

Psalm 46, on the other hand, describes the city of God as קדש משכני עליון, thus creating a temple orientation (see also Pss. 26.8; 43.3; 74.7; 84.2; 132.5,7).[67] As mentioned previously, the use of נהר leads the exegete into a temple context, so that in Psalm 46 two interpretations are possible: either the whole city is meant to be the temple, or the dwelling place of God in the centre of the city points to the essential place of the temple within that city. In contrast to Psalm 48, the city is neither visible nor corporeal; the only visible and tangible presence is the theophanic action of God. This distinction in fact accords with Körting's proposal that Zion as topos is 'a connection between the earthly temple and the heavenly place'.[68]

In Psalm 48 the worldly Jerusalem is a '*Realsymbol*' of the presence of God and in this respect, the earthly temple and heavenly palace are one. Psalm 46, like Psalms 68, 122, and Ezek. 40–8, points to the centre of the city as the holiest dwelling place of God. God is not only described as present in that city, but he is present in the innermost centre (בקרב). With its connection to temple terminology, the word משכן alludes to the temple as centre of the city. With its horizontal view of the world, Psalm 46 reflects a clearly priestly distinction between the chaos outside the city and the holy area of the city, which may be in itself distinguished into different areas of holiness. The absence of 'Zion' in Psalm 46, compared with the use of 'Zion' in Psalm 48, suggests that these two psalms offer two different and competing theologies of the city of God which were in circulation in the pre-exilic period. Psalm 46 is temple-orientated priestly theology; Psalm 48, in contrast, with its deliberate mention of Zion in which God is presented and portrayed as king of the world, focuses on a mediation between the heavenly sphere and the worldly sphere, pointing to the theology of the temple singers, who understood this mediation taking place between God, the priests, and the people.

---

[65] From the very beginning, Psalm 48 assigns the city of God as the place of the praise of God (see v. 2), making that one of the key functions of the temple.

[66] The redaction in vv. 10–12 brings the temple into the psalm. This results in a clear tension: God reveals himself (נודע) in the palaces (v. 4) and is present in them, while his people are assembled in the temple as a praying community (v. 10).

[67] See Janowski 2002: 46 n. 90. It is curious that instead of the typical plural with its feminine ending (cf. Pss. 43.3; 84.2), the plural with a masculine ending is found here (as in Ezek. 37.27 but in a profane use). If קדש should be read as a superlative, the word combination may be intended to emphasize that although on the one hand Jerusalem is among the holiest places of God, on the other hand it is just one, not the exclusive, dwelling place of God.

[68] Translation of Körting 2005: 153.

8. Future Prospects for the Theme of 'Zion' in the Structure of the Psalter

Psalms 46 and 48 are the first two psalms, in a *lectio continua* of the Psalter, which deal mainly with the theology of Zion, or the theology of the city of God.[69] In the previous section we noted the importance of a diachronic starting point when investigating the different pre-exilic theologies and different authorial intentions in the theological development of the topic 'Zion'. Thus far we have not read this topic theologically within the Psalter as a whole: the next step would be to assess contextually the integration of these two psalms within the further structural levels. The first level would be within the grouping Psalms 46–8; the second, as part of the Korahite Psalms (Pss 42–9 and 84–7); the third, in relation to the Asaphite Psalms (see especially Psalm 76) and to the Psalms of David (noting Ps. 68 and also Ps. 14.7); the fourth, as a part of the Elohistic Psalter; and then as belonging to the first three books of the Psalter. Particular attention would have to be given to Psalm 87 as an 'inner-biblical' interpretation of Psalms 46–8 in the Korahite appendix to the Elohistic Psalter. Similar consideration would have to be given to the more priestly influenced Psalms of Ascent (Pss. 120–34) as reinterpretations of the pre-exilic theologies of Zion after the exile. By comparing all these different theologies of Zion, it should be clear that Zion is not only a magnet for theological conceptions, but also a particular point of discourse for the different groups of authors, with all their different theologies, in different historical contexts, who each left their footprints on the structuring of the Psalter.

Bibliography

Albrektson, Bertil
   1963 *Studies in the Text and Theology of the Book of Lamentations: With a Critical Edition of the Peshitta Text* (Studia Theologica Lundensia, 21; Lund: Gleerup).
Bader, Günter
   1996 *Psalterium affectuum palaestra. Prolegomena zu einer Theologie des Psalters* (Hermeneutische Untersuchungen zur Theologie, 33; Tübingen: Mohr Siebeck).
Barbiero, G.
   2008 'The Risk of a Fragment Reading of the Psalms: Ps. 72 as a Case in Point' *ZAW* 120: 67–91.
Berges, Ulrich
   2002 *Klagelieder* (HThKAT; Freiburg: Herder).

---

[69] Before this only single verses mention Zion: for example, Pss. 2.6; 9.12, 15; 14.7; 20.3.

Blum, Erhard

2005 'Notwendigkeit und Grenzen historischer Exegese. Plädoyer für eine alttestamentliche Exegetik', in B. Janowski (ed.), *Theologie und Exegese des Alten Testaments/der Hebräischen Bibel* (SBS, 200; Stuttgart: Katholisches Bibelwerk): 11–40.

Delitzsch, Franz

1859–60 *Die Psalmen* (Giessen: Brunnen Verlag; 4th edn, Leipzig: Dörfling und Franke, 1883); ET F. Bolton, *Biblical Commentary on the Psalms*, vol. 2 (Edinburgh: T. & T. Clark, 1877).

Gunkel, Hermann, and Begrich, Joachim

1933 *Einleitung in die Psalmen: die Gattungen der religiösen Lyrik Israels* (GHAT; Göttingen: Vandenhoeck & Ruprecht; 4th edn, 1985); ET J. D. Nogalski, *Introduction to the Psalms: The Genres of the Religious Lyric of Israel* (Mercer Library of Biblical Studies; Macon, GA: Mercer University Press, 1998).

Hartenstein, Friedhelm

2010 '"Schaffe mir Recht, JHWH!" (Psalm 7,9). Zum theologischen und anthropologischen Profil der Teilkomposition Psalm 3–14', in E. Zenger (ed.), *The Composition of the Book of Psalms* (BEThL, 238; Leuven: Peeters): 229–58.

2011 '"Wehe, ein Tosen vieler Völker ..." (Jesaja 17,12). Beobachtungen zur Entstehung der Zionstradition vor dem Hintergrund des judäischassyrischen Kulturkontakts', in F. Hartenstein, *Das Archiv des verborgenen Gottes Studien zur Unheilsprophetie Jesajas und zur Zionstheologie der Psalmen in assyrischer Zeit* (BthS, 74; Neukirchen-Vluyn: Neukirchener): 127–74.

Hartenstein, Friedhelm, and Janowski, Bernd

2011 'Psalms/Psalter', in *RPP* 4th edn, vol. 10: 489–99.

Hossfeld, Frank-Lothar

1999 'Psalmen', in *LThK* 3rd edn, vol. 8: 689–93.

2001 'Von der Klage zum Lob—die Dynamik des Gebets in den Psalmen', *Biki* 56: 16–220.

2010 'Der elohistische Psalter Ps 42–83. Entstehung und Programm', in Zenger 2010b: 200–13.

2011 'Drei umstrittene Theophanien im ersten und zweiten Davidspsalter (Ps 18; 29; 68)', in E. Gaß and H. J. Stipp (eds.), *Ich werde meinen Bund mit euch niemals brechen!* (Ri 2,1) (Festschrift W. Groß; HBS, 62; Freiburg: Herder): 153–73.

Hossfeld, Frank-Lothar, and Zenger, Erich

1993 *Die Psalmen. Ps 1–50* (NEBAT 29; Würzburg: Echter).

Janowski, Bernd

2002 'Die heilige Wohnung des Höchsten. Kosmologische Implikationen der Jerusalemer Tempeltheologie', in O. Keel and E. Zenger (eds), *Gottesstadt und Gottesgarten. Zur Geschichte und Theologie des Jerusalemer Tempels* (QD, 191; Freiburg: Herder): 24–68.

Keel, Othmar

2007 *Die Geschichte Jerusalems und die Entstehung des Monotheismus* (2 vols.; Göttingen: Vandenhoeck & Ruprecht).

Konkel, Michael
2001 *Architektonik des Heiligen. Studien zur zweiten Tempelvision Ezechiels (Ez 40–48)* (BBB, 129; Berlin: Philo).
Körting, Corinna
2006 *Zion in den Psalmen* (FAT, 48; Tübingen: Mohr Siebeck).
Kratz, Reinhard G.
1996 'Die Tora Davids. Psalm 1 und die doxologische Fünfteilung des Psalters', *ZThK* 93: 1–34.
Kraus, Hans-Joachim
1979 *Theologie der Psalmen*, BKAT 15/3 (Neukirchen-Vluyn, Neukirchener Verlag; 2nd edn, 1989); ET K. Crim, *Theology of the Psalms* (Minneapolis: Augsburg Publishing House, 1986).
Leuenberger, Martin
2004 *Konzeptionen des Königtums Gottes im Psalter. Untersuchungen zur Komposition und Redaktion der theokratischen Bücher IV–V im Psalter* (AthANT, 83; Zurich: Theologischer Verlag Zürich).
Ollenburger, Ben C.
1987 *Zion, the City of the Great King: A Theological Symbol of the Jerusalem Cult* (JSOTSup, 41; Sheffield: JSOT Press).
Otto, Eckhart
1989 'צִיּוֹן', in *ThWAT* 6: 994–1028.
von Rad, Gerhard
1957 *Theologie des Alten Testaments I, Die Theologie der historischen Überlieferungen Israels* (Munich: Christian Kaiser Verlag; 6th edn, 1969); ET D. M. G. Stalker, *Old Testament Theology*, vol. 1 (London: SCM Press, 1962).
Rohland, Edzard
1956 'Die Bedeutung der Erwählungstradition Israels für die Eschatologie der alttestamentlichen Propheten' (unpublished doctoral thesis; Heidelberg).
Rösel, Christoph
1999 *Die messianische Redaktion des Psalters. Studien zur Entstehung und Theologie der Sammlung Psalm 2–89* (CTM, 19; Stuttgart: Calwer).
Scharbert, Josef
1993 'Das historische Umfeld von Ps 48', in F. V. Reiterer (ed.), *Ein Gott, eine Offenbarung. Beiträge zur biblischen Exegese, Theologie und Spiritualität* (Festschrift N. Füglister; Würzburg: Echter): 291–306.
Seybold, Klaus
1997 'Psalmen/Psalmenbuch', in *TRE* 27: 610–24.
Spieckermann, Hermann
1989 *Heilsgegenwart. Eine Theologie der Psalmen* (FRLANT, 148; Göttingen: Vandenhoeck & Ruprecht).
1992 'Stadtgott und Gottesstadt. Beobachtungen im Alten Orient und im Alten Testament', in *Biblica* 73: 1–31.
Steinberg, Julius
2006 *Die Ketuvim—ihr Aufbau und ihre Botschaft* (BBB, 152; Hamburg: Philo).
Süssenbach, Claudia
2005 *Der elohistische Psalter. Untersuchungen zu Komposition und Theologie von Ps 42–83* (FAT, 2/7; Tübingen: Mohr Siebeck).

Wilson, Gerald H.
  1992 'The Shape of the Book of Psalms', *Interpretation* 46, 129–42.
Zapff, Burkard M.
  1998 'Eine feste Burg ist unser Gott'—Beobachtungen zu Ps 46', in *BN* 94: 79–93.
Zenger, Erich
    1998 'Der Psalter als Buch. Beobachtungen zu seiner Entstehung, Komposition und Funktion', in E. Zenger (ed.), *Der Psalter in Judentum und Christentum* (HBS, 18; Freiburg: Herder): 1–57.
  2010a 'Psalmenexegese und Psalterexegese. Eine Forschungsskizze', in Zenger 2010b: 17–65.
  2010b (ed.) *The Composition of the Book of Psalms* (BEThL, 238; Leuven: Peeters).

20

Postscript

John Barton

St Ambrose in a well-known passage wrote:

> What is more pleasing than a psalm? David expresses it well: Praise the Lord, for
> a song of praise is good; let there be praise of our God with gladness and grace.
> Yes, a psalm is a blessing on the lips of the people, a hymn in praise of God, the
> assembly's homage, a general acclamation, a word that speaks for all, the voice of
> the Church, a confession of faith in song. It is the voice of complete assent, the
> joy of freedom, a cry of happiness, the echo of gladness. It soothes the temper,
> distracts from care, lightens the burden of sorrow. It is a source of security at
> night, a lesson in wisdom by day. It is a shield when we are afraid, a celebration of
> holiness, a vision of serenity, a promise of peace and harmony. It is like a lyre,
> evoking harmony from a blend of notes. Day begins to the music of a psalm, day
> closes to the echo of a psalm.[1]

The richness of the Psalms is such that I am surprised no one has organized
a *Theology of the Old Testament* around the Psalter. If we are looking for a
centre, a *Mitte*, for the Old Testament, then the book of Psalms provides what
we are looking for, since all the great theological themes of ancient Israelite
life and thought are somewhere to be found within it. It is a kind of Hebrew
Bible in miniature. Hence it is an ideal text to which to dedicate a whole
conference, and in the conference convened by Susan Gillingham, whose
papers are collected here, we had a wonderful array of speakers to plumb the
depths of this most evocative of Hebrew texts. Not least among them was
Sue herself, who worked tirelessly to put the conference together and to make
sure that it had a number of very special features, including an extraordinary
musical celebration showcasing both Jewish and Christian renderings of the
Psalms.[2] My hope is that the opportunity to read the papers, even if not to

---

[1] Ambrose 1962: CSEL 64:7, on Psalm 1.

[2] It proved impossible to include anything from that celebration other than the paper by
David Mitchell which also introduced the singing of Psalms 95, 122, and 150 to Hebrew cantilla-
tion. The Chaplain of Worcester College, Revd Dr Jonathan Arnold, compiled a memorable
feast of Jewish and Christian liturgical psalmody, including Psalm 67, set to music by Thomas
Tallis (Tallis's Canon); Psalm 121, composed especially for the occasion by Robert Saxton; and
Psalm 137, set to music and directed for the first time in public by Howard Goodall.

have shared in the experience of the conference, will stimulate scholars and students to ensure that Psalm-study moves forward, to become again a central part of the study of the Hebrew Bible. The papers bring out a number of significant themes, any of which could become a focal point for a reconceived study of the Psalms.

One is certainly the theme that was the stated concern of the conference: the *interrelation of Jewish and Christian use and study of the Psalter*. This is made most explicit in the exchange between Adele Berlin and Corinna Körting. Berlin introduces four medieval Jewish interpreters who concentrated on a *peshat* approach to the Hebrew text, and Körting responds by showing how this emphasis was often a reaction to Christian allegorical and, of course, messianic reading of the Psalms. Christians regarded Jewish readings as reductionist, an attempt to avoid the 'true' messianic meaning; Jews regarded Christian readings as what would now be called 'eisegesis', reading in messianic and Christological references where none were present. This is not the happiest period in Jewish and Christian interaction on the Psalms, but it is an important one, since it reflects the tone of much medieval interreligious dialogue, which was often hostile. On the other hand, at other times the Psalter has been a focus for Jews and Christians to come together. Aaron Rosen sees ecumenical potential in the stained-glass windows of Chagall, so many of which were for Christian churches, complementing the famous set for the Hadassah hospital in Jerusalem: Jews and Christians, he speculates, might learn together from Chagall's work, and might even be able to sing the Psalms together. 'If Jews and Christians can . . . attune themselves to the spaces and practices of the other's faith, perhaps it is possible, Chagall hints, for Jews and Christians not only to speak to one another but—just as importantly—to *sing* with one another.' Sue Gillingham's paper and Jonathan Magonet's response explore both similarity and difference in Christian and Jewish treatment of the Psalms, but look for potential common ground in a creative and eirenical way. Both scholars have extensive experience in the liturgical use of the Psalter, and this conduces to mutual understanding: praising God through the Psalms is not, after all, an enormously different experience in the two traditions. If we ask *what it is to sing a psalm* we may find that some tensions disappear.

A second theme is *the Psalter as a book*: a collection of individual psalms that is more than the sum of its parts. This has a historical dimension concerned with, as it were, both ends of the process: the original formation of Psalms within the ancient Near East (Erhard Gerstenberger, John Day), and the collection of the Psalms into a finished whole (Peter Flint, Geza Vermes, Klaus Seybold, David Howard, Frank-Lothar Hossfeld, and Till Magnus Steiner). The latter has, again, two aspects—the historical process of collection, and the interpretation of the collection as a book or 'work'. Both will continue to be of interest, but my strong impression is that it is the last that is the point of growth in biblical studies at the moment. How did Jews and Christians in the past read, not just individual psalms, but the Psalter; and how should Jews and Christians nowadays read this complex book? A sort of consensus seems to be emerging (not unlike the similar consensus about the 'Book of the Twelve') that the Psalter is not a random collection, but is planned to convey certain theological ideas. The seminal study, as a number of the writers here acknowledge, is Gerald Wilson's doctoral dissertation *The Editing of the Hebrew Psalter*.[3] It has of course always been known that certain clusters of psalms have thematic and stylistic links: Psalms 105 and 106, or 42 and 43. But since Wilson scholars have started to think that the Psalter as a whole, or at least each of the five 'books' it is said to be made up of, was carefully planned. This has set scholarship free to find all kinds of thematic unity in the book: one such is the theme of theodicy, highlighted here by Bill Bellinger, but there are many other possibilities. Along these lines the Psalms are ceasing to be of interest from a chiefly form-critical or 'cultic' perspective, and taking their place at the centre of Old Testament/Hebrew Bible theology. This may yet prove a fruitful way for Jewish and Christian scholars to come together in biblical study.

Thirdly, there is the question of how the Psalms should be 'received' in our own day and in the light of our own concerns. John Sawyer, arguably the pioneer of biblical reception history in Britain through his work on Isaiah, *The Fifth Gospel*,[4] argues here that we should abandon the quest for what the texts originally meant, and, through investigating what they have been taken to mean, come to an understanding of what they can mean for us today. And, as Nancy deClaissé-Walford and Philip Johnston show, that will very often be expressed through translation, which has the task of bridging the gap between *then* and *now*. Translators, like the illuminators wonderfully brought to life by Elizabeth Solopova, turn the ancient text into our contemporary, by transporting our concerns into the text. (A more homely example of this than 'customized' Psalters and Books of Hours, but working on exactly the same principle, would be the Family Bible of modern times, where a family's history and experience is somehow interwoven with the biblical text.) In the end scholarship, exegesis, interpretation, historical investigation of the text's reception, all coalesce in helping us to *appropriate* the Psalms in our own time. In thus making them our own, we are, paradoxically, doing something more akin to what their original authors and performers were doing than if we simply study them from afar. Psalm study has enormous theological, devotional, liturgical, and spiritual potential, and these essays, taken together, help to show us how this potential can be realized.

---

[3] Wilson 1985.   [4] Sawyer 1996.

Bibliography

Ambrose of Milan

> 1962   *Commentary on the Psalms* (Corpus Scriptorum Ecclesiasticorum Latinorum 64:7, New York and London: Johnson Reprint Corporation; ET of *S Ambrosis Opera Pars VI Explanatio Psalmorum XII*, ed. M. Petschenig (Vienna: F. Tempsky; Leipzig: G. Freytag, 1913. Available online at http://www.archive. org/details/corpusscriptorum64ambruoft (accessed March 2012).

Sawyer, John

> 1996   *The Fifth Gospel: Isaiah in the History of Christianity* (Cambridge: Cambridge University Press).

Wilson, Gerald

> 1985   *The Editing of the Hebrew Psalter*, ed. J. J. M. Roberts (SBLDS, 76; Chico, CA: Scholars Press).

Index of Names

Note: page numbers followed by *fn* refer to mentions in the footnotes.

Subject Index

Note: page numbers followed by *fn* refer to mentions in the footnotes.

Index of Psalms

Note: page numbers followed by *fn* refer to mentions in the footnotes.